Praise for Ken Lamberton's Writing

Wilderness and Razor Wire: A Naturalist's Observations from Prison

Winner of the 2002 John Burroughs Medal for Outstanding Nature Writing

"*Wilderness and Razor Wire* is what nature writing can be at its finest: a courageous and eloquent exploration of what nature can teach us about how to be human."
—Susan Tweit

"That one of the strongest new voices in American writing would emerge from behind prison walls is a bright surprise. *Wilderness and Razor Wire* is a shimmering manifesto of hope and the saving tonic of the wild wherever it can be found."
—Robert Michael Pyle

"Nothing is more grand and resilient than the human spirit, and this astonishing testament to the coexistence of beauty and brutality illuminates the presence of grace in tragedy."
—*Booklist* (starred review)

"This is a moving and troubling book that redefines 'sense of place' as a way of seeing and valuing where one is, rather than as coordinates on a green map. . . . A remarkable and significant work."
—Alison Hawthorne Deming

"Lamberton's measured and exemplary prose follows the interactions among the prisoners, their built environments, and the birds and plants they encounter there, tracing connections disturbing and consoling, ecological and metaphorical. [A] strange and compelling debut."
—*Publishers Weekly*

"Short, unbuffed essays that shuttle restlessly between natural history and prison life, and the unexpected moments of interpenetratic
—*Kirkus Reviews*

"The nature writing here may be some of the best to come our way in a generation. . . . Lamberton has written something entirely original: an edgy, ferocious, subtly complex collection of essays on the nature of freedom and the freedom of nature, whose true subject, and greatest accomplishment, may be its own narrative voice."
—*San Francisco Chronicle*

"[Lamberton] explodes the myth of nature as a place removed."
—*Gulf Coast* magazine

"Ken Lamberton not only finds the wilderness in the prison but makes us believe that it can be anywhere."
—*Stanford Review*

Beyond Desert Walls: Essays from Prison

"Lamberton is a skilled writer with a restless and discerning eye."
—*Booklist*

"The book is a thought-provoking account of one man's quest to look beyond his prison cell and find inner peace through nature."
—*E—The Environmental Magazine*

"Ken Lamberton writes with the precision of a scientist and the compassion of a man who has lost—and then regained—(almost) everything. *Beyond Desert Walls* is a book of heart-wrenching dualities: prison and the desert, candor and toughness, fanaticism and numbness, love and anger, loss and redemption. These narratives take the field of 'nature writing' in startling new directions."
—Scott Slovic

"Ken's book impressed me with its insistent drive to discover connections between his life and his work—his love of nature and his love of his family and how the two find common ground. Oftentimes nature offers intimate insights into his dilemmas, and other times renders stark questions that confront and challenge the author's humanity. . . . I sank right into his words from the very first page."
—Jimmy Santiago Baca

Time of Grace: Thoughts on Nature, Family, and the Politics of Crime and Punishment

"Biologist Ken Lamberton sees so keenly and writes so gracefully, it's nearly impossible to stop reading him. Its revelations, accusations, and deep humility jar us into rethinking multiple human messes we make, and to honor—or envy—his redemption."
—Alan Weisman

"This is a courageous, bittersweet book, a treatise on the nature of punishment and the sham of American justice. This testament will capture you, for its duration, until its breathtaking finale, when you will be fully released, transformed."
—Janisse Ray

". . . a probing exploration of nonhuman and human nature."
—*Orion*

"With lyrical grace, [Lamberton] chronicles his daily communion, blossoming into something of a nature mystic. . . . It is Lamberton's determination to evolve by maintaining some measure of self-expression that gives this book its vitalizing spirit."
—*Tucson Weekly*

Chiricahua Mountains: Bridging the Border of Wildness

"[T]wo desert aficionados pay fitting tribute to this unique mountain range that anchors the sunwashed southeast corner of the Grand Canyon state."
—*Bloomsbury Review*

Dry River: Stories of Life, Death, and Redemption on the Santa Cruz

"Time is, of course, a river. So as Ken Lamberton walks the two-hundred-mile length of the Santa Cruz River near Tucson, he travels also through the long histories of the people who sank their roots in the sandy washes. Lamberton is an amiable and well-informed guide, and the territory he covers is fascinating."
—Kathleen Dean Moore, author of *Wild Comfort*

"With scholarly expertise artfully enlivened by his five super-keen senses and much literary skill, Lamberton has produced a southwestern environmental classic."

—Harold Fromm, author of *The Nature of Being Human*

"Lamberton writes with scrupulous fairness, asking that readers accompany him patiently on his journey—waiting for years, if necessary—to witness the outcome of environmental repair efforts or his own striving for redemption."

—*High Country News*

"This is an elegant and important book from one of southern Arizona's most gifted writers."

—Bruce Dinges, *Southwest Books of the Year 2011*

CHASING ARIZONA

CHASING ARIZONA

One Man's Yearlong Obsession with the Grand Canyon State

KEN LAMBERTON

THE UNIVERSITY OF
ARIZONA PRESS

TUCSON

The University of Arizona Press
www.uapress.arizona.edu

Printed in the United States of America
20   19   18   17   16   15   6   5   4   3   2   1

ISBN-13: 978-0-8165-2892-9 (paper)

Cover designed by Leigh McDonald

Library of Congress Cataloging-in-Publication Data
Lamberton, Ken, 1958– author.
  Chasing Arizona : one man's yearlong obsession with the Grand Canyon state / Ken Lamberton.
      pages cm
  Includes bibliographical references and index.
  ISBN 978-0-8165-2892-9 (pbk. : alk. paper)
  1. Arizona—Description and travel. I. Title.
  F815.L36 2015
  917.9104—dc23
                              2014024124

♾ This paper meets the requirements of ANSI/NISO Z39.48-1992 (Permanence of Paper).

*For Richard Shelton:
an Arizona treasure, my
mentor, and my friend,*

*and for Lois Shelton, who
believes in words*

Contents

May: Two-tailed Swallowtail Butterfly

June: Apache Trout

July: Arizona Treefrog

August: Ridge-nosed Rattlesnake

September: Petrified Wood

CHASING ARIZONA

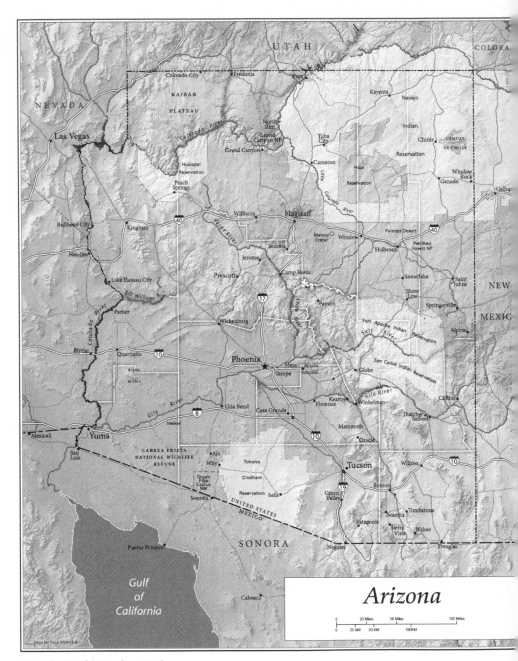

Maps by Paul Mirocha, 2014.

The Insanity of Bright Ideas

At the beginning of the year, I step onto the dirt track in front of my 1890s stone house and climb the old mule road in Bisbee's Mule Mountains. The road contours Escabrosa Ridge and Banning Creek. Where my route steepens and shrinks to not much more than a footpath, mountain mahogany and iron-hard branches of manzanita encroach. Silverleaf oaks reach out with pale, narrow fingers. A too-early two-tailed swallowtail drifts past my shoulder—Arizona's official butterfly. I take it as a sign.

The road remains after 140 years because the mule skinners needed a solid surface. All that raw copper destined for the smelters. Great freight wagons and their teams of mules hauled hundreds of tons of ingots, called "pigs," along this mountain road. In those years, if you had been standing on the front steps of my home, the sound and vibration would have shaken bones and shattered eardrums. The dust would have palled every green leaf not already fed to Bisbee's furnaces.

Where the mule road dumps me onto the pass, I come to the Old Divide Road, a two-lane strip of blacktop that once brought people over the mountain to Bisbee before the tunnel was built in 1958. These days the place is untraveled, except for a few local residents, dog-walkers, and rendezvousing couples. Below me, the oak-draped canyon drops away, twisting and spilling into the distant lavender peaks of the Whetstone and Mustang Mountains. The talcum grasslands of wine country shove up against the far-off Santa Rita range fifty miles away.

The earliest recorded name for this place is Puerta de las Mulas, Pass of the Mules. The name came long before the mule teams, before an army scout named Jack Dunn stooped to collect a few colored rocks while chasing Apaches here, before a middle-aged prospector named George Warren lost a footrace with a horse and his stake in what would become the Copper Queen, one of Arizona's richest copper mines. Locals call the place "the Divide" because of a hundred-year-old whitewashed marker shaped like an obelisk. It's a classic monument to a seventy-five-mile survey error. The actual Continental Divide splits New Mexico. Only Arizona would lay claim to a continental-sized geological feature that completely misses the state:

CONTINENTAL DIVIDE
ELEV 6030

ROAD CONSTRUCTED BY PRISON LABOR 1913–14
BOARD OF CONTROL
GEO. W. P. HUNT, GOVERNOR

Governor Hunt took office on the day Arizona became a state, February 14, 1912. The three-hundred-pound "Old Walrus" was a "fat bald liberal Democrat with several chins and a great, shaggy mustache," as Richard Shelton describes him in *Going Back to Bisbee*. Next month, on February 14, 2012, Arizona will celebrate one hundred years of statehood.

I've climbed to the Divide to consider a book about Arizona. In the middle of the night, I had a brainstorm—a perfect word for what happened to me because it means either a sudden bright idea or a violent, transient fit of insanity. My editor had wanted me to write a guidebook about fifty-two historical destinations in Arizona, one for every week of the year. I figured it would take years of research and travel. I procrastinated. I don't find guidebooks too inspiring. But then I had that brainstorm: Why not do it in *one* year? Why not make it a challenge to spend the entire year exploring the state's people, places, and treasures? And what better year than 2012, our centennial year? I could write about Arizona's natural environment, its people and its history, but also its "legendary" history, the history beyond the books that people will tell you when you ask them about the place where they live. I thought: *This won't be a guidebook. It will be an adventure story, a tale of Arizona. A road-warrior narrative.*

This was my idea, a goal: How much of Arizona could I see if I traveled every week for one year? Now, I need a plan. It will be an Arizona "Big Year" in the parlance of the bird watcher. But I won't simply be checking off places as if I were checking off one bird and moving on to the next. I've never been a drive-by tourist. My car won't become what writer and visionary Rebecca Solnit calls a "prosthetic machine" that alienates me from the world at eighty miles per hour. I want to *know* these destinations, to feel and taste them, to be emotionally and intellectually engaged with them. I want to experience a sense of place in *every* place.

This will be the challenge: How many places in Arizona can I *experience*? It means planning for the unplanned. It means being mindful when the ordinary happens with the miraculous. Along the way, I'll search for our twelve official state symbols. From saguaro blossoms to cactus wrens, bola ties to ringtails to ridge-nosed rattlesnakes, I'll look for these representations of how we as Arizonans define ourselves. Maybe in someplace like Tombstone I can track down our newest symbol: the Colt .45 Single Action Army revolver. I'll chase the four corners of Arizona, attempt every county, every reservation, every national monument and state park, from the smallest community to the largest city. I'll drive through the longest tunnels and across the highest suspension bridges, visit prehistoric sites and haunted hotels. And I'll talk to people.

This will be the *real* challenge. I'm shy about talking to people, more comfortable alone in the wilderness. Put me in the desert and I become the cholla, the spiny ocotillo, dropping leaf and bearing thorns. In the woods I will commune with manzanita leafgall aphids. But put me in a crowded room without a script and I am the wallflower—pretty but silent. One on one with a stranger? Expect long, awkward lapses in conversation. Put my wife Karen in the same room and she commands it, tossing around random facts and always entertaining with stories. She reads voraciously, a self-taught Evelyn Woodite. Put her within reach of words, any words—from abandoned magazines in a city recycling bin to instruction manuals for power tools at Sears—and she devours them like I eat chocolates. Her perfect recall allows her to talk about anything and keep her listeners riveted. Maybe I can work up one question. Let others do the talking. Even better, I'll bring Karen along.

Chasing Arizona will be a race against time and money. Karen, always the practical one, calculates that I won't see a profit for thirty-three years, *if* I sell twenty-six thousand books by then. "I've read your royalty statements," she says. "What statements?" I say, making her point. Then there are my friends who say I'm crazy, it can't be done, and then offer suggestions about where I "must go." I'm not sure I can find the time to write it, even if I can accomplish the research on a slimmer budget. And there are *always* the unforeseen interruptions in my life because I live my life on call. I can adjust my planned destinations along the way, throw in something like Rooster Cogburn's Ostrich Ranch if I have to make a run to Phoenix. Or stop in Benson on my way to Tucson. *Benson?* That will be a challenge. Mary Jo at Bobby Joe's Irish Pub says the best thing about living in nearby Mescal is that "It's not Benson." What if people say the best thing about Benson is shopping at Walmart? A billboard on I-10 actually advertises Benson as a tourist destination and lists Walmart as one of the places to visit. The world-renowned Kartchner Caverns didn't make the list.

In the end, I hope the book will show readers not just what makes Arizona the Grand Canyon *State* but what makes Arizona *grand*. If I make it that far, if I survive *Chasing Arizona*, I also hope it will give readers a kick out the door. The ancient Chinese philosopher Lao Tzu said the journey of a thousand miles begins with a single step. Which always reminds me of that poster of a bear standing in a river and catching a salmon mid-jump: "The journey of a thousand miles sometimes ends very, very badly." So be it, I say. The only thing worse than death is having a near-life experience.

So, where to start? I came up to the Divide with an idea. Now I have an outline, a way to go. Fifty-two weeks. Fifteen counties. Twelve symbols. Twenty-two tribes. Thirty state parks. Deserts, forests, and dry rivers. Moonscapes and graveyards. Try to be in the right place at the right time with the right people and see what happens. Make a plan, but set it in sand. Abandon the usual book structure. Keep to the chronology, of course—but not to the geography. I'll be the structure! A narrative voice the reader will (hopefully) follow wherever I go—the destination almost doesn't matter because he or she is willing, expecting, to experience the place with *me*. Fortunately, this twenty-thousand-mile joyride will have a map.

Finally, I'll bring along friends, daughters, wife, a personal psychologist. I'll pack a sleeping bag and fly rod. Eat peanut butter burritos. And always begin with a question: How far can I go to experience the place I live?

JANUARY

Turquoise

Haunted by the Blues

BISBEE

ELEVATION: 5,538 FEET | FOUNDED: 1880 | POPULATION: 5,996

I begin my yearlong adventure in the first week of January. Karen and I head for the southernmost mile-high city in the country—Bisbee. This isn't much of a trip. We live here. Ten minutes after passing through Bisbee's "Tunnel of Love," Arizona's longest mountain tunnel you can drive through (not counting our borderland drug tunnels), we pull up next to the boardinghouse built by Edith Oliver in 1908: the Oliver House.

We cross a narrow bridge, push through a rusted metal gate, and climb the steps—there are always stairs in Bisbee, always leading up. Karen says that going anywhere in Bisbee is uphill, always uphill. Flo, a large black Labrador mix, greets us from his couch on the porch by lifting his large black head, but only momentarily.

The door is locked. Karen knocks, but no one answers. We go around to the side door, through the kitchen to a sitting room, and find Patty, the owner and a longtime friend. She is playing bridge with the two Sues. I don't ask Patty who their fourth is—who the empty chair belongs to and the mystery of the dealt hand, thirteen cards facedown on the table.

This is my favorite place in Bisbee, and not just because it's haunted. What hotel in Arizona *isn't* haunted? Karen and I have been coming here for more than ten years, and occasionally we have the entire place to ourselves, all twelve rooms, upstairs and down. We always choose the Passion Flower Room, since it has its own private water closet and I don't have to wander down the hall in the middle of the night to find one of the shared bathrooms. You never know who you might encounter late at night in a dimly lit passageway in the Oliver House.

Like the last time: Karen and I were here alone. We never found the hotel managers in their office, so we checked ourselves in. We had gone to bed when Karen heard a noise in the hall. She got up and opened the door a crack. "Ken," she said. "You better come see this." When I looked toward the stairway, I saw light and shadow scaling the walls. Someone or something was coming up the stairs. A woman dressed in nineteenth-century clothing with dark curls and a hat and carrying a blue lantern rose out of the darkness and walked right past our door. Behind her followed a group of people, moving slowly and quietly in a long, unorganized file. No one noticed us.

"Are you real?" Karen asked, and several of them jumped and screamed.

It was the Bisbee ghost tour.

"At least twenty-six people have died in the Oliver House," said ghost host Renee Gardner, who has been leading ghost tours since she moved to Bisbee in 2007. "This is where a miner named Nat Anderson was murdered on February 22, 1920." Renee pointed to the head of the stairs and room 13. "The story is that Nat was having an affair with the wife of a man he owed money to. Apparently the man learned of the affair, since Nat was discovered at the top of the staircase with a bullet in his forehead. The murder was never solved. . . ."

I couldn't resist joining the group and followed Renee down the dark hall to the Grandma Room at the end, where we crowded inside and circled the bed. "This is where a three-year-old boy, sleeping here with his family, claimed a little old lady bopped him on the head," Renee said. "In the morning he woke with a giant black-and-blue mark on his forehead. Some people feel her presence right here." Renee waved her hand a few inches above the bed.

I placed my hand over the bedcovers. A tingling crossed my palm. "I feel it," I said.

"Me, too," replied the man next to me. "And I'm not even half drunk."

The Oliver House is one place in Bisbee where the walls have stories—a wall in one of the rooms, some say, has a blood stain that can't be painted out. These are stories about doors left open. Mysteries unsolved not because they can't be solved, but because they won't be. Doors sometimes bang in an unfelt wind. No wonder the front door is always locked.

We leave Patty and her guests to their card game and walk from the Oliver House past the Copper Queen Hotel, past Santiago's and the smell of molcajete with its five-hundred-degree lava-rock bowl and spicy, roiling volcanic contents. Beware: Warm beer soothes not the blistered tongue. Dinner can wait, however. We stroll up Brewery Gulch to St. Elmo, the state's oldest bar (*Since 1902*). I'm thinking about Dave's Electric Industrial Pale Ale, the local brew from Arizona's first microbrewery. IPAs have grown on me recently, and I'm always eager to try the local offerings.

The next morning, we walk over to the Bisbee Coffee Company to restock my Miner's Blend and enjoy a cup of The Blues. This one nods to the town's annual blues festival and is one of the many blends you can smell from the highway when Justin West roasts his select beans and their essence pours from the single stack on the roof. I order it large.

Rough-looking men in hats and coats and carrying pickaxes stare at me as I add a bit of low-fat to my coffee. All wear disapproving mustaches. Maybe it's my choice of scone—or the long look I gave the quiche. The miners pose for the camera—one of them is George Warren with his pick and shovel. "Only Arizona would put a drunken miner on our state seal," says a local man when he notices my interest in the photo. The life-size photos hang on the knotty-pine walls beneath mock-ups of typical Bisbee rooftops of rusting corrugated tin.

The "Police Beat" page of the *Bisbee Observer* is face up on my table. "This, if anything, will tell you about a town," Karen says: "Three brown-and-white cows were seen in the roadway near Hereford." "A squirrel was trapped in a cage near a resident's carport." "Continuously barking dogs in the 300 block of Brewery Gulch were reported." "Two residents reported trapped skunks that needed to be picked up and relocated." "A 1,000-pound concrete gargoyle was stolen from the 300 block of Washington Avenue." Only in Bisbee . . .

A group of bicyclists enters, each wearing a black-and-white Lycra shirt. More visitors—young couples with babies in snuggle sacks or puppies tucked into jackets, others primly dressed and recently showered—crowd the tables among locals sporting wild facial hair and uncombed locks spilling from wool stocking caps. One wears a shirt that explains everything: *6,000 Feet High and Miles from Reality*. The Coffee Company is where Bisbee intersects with the world. Its motto should read: "Caffeine is our common ground."

I've come to Bisbee with the idea that the right way to start off the first week of my yearlong obsession with Arizona is to locate one of its symbols, specifically, the state gemstone and Karen's favorite mineral: turquoise. Bisbee was born a copper town, but today it's really all about turquoise. There is even an annual turquoise hunt. Last October, rock hounds spent hours scouring something called the "Number 7 Stockpile" for what many say is the rarest and most valuable turquoise, the Bisbee Blue, a chocolate spider-web matrix set in a flawless Arizona sky. According to Doug Graeme, manager of the Queen Mine Tour, miners would scrounge nuggets of turquoise from the conglomerate rock discarded from the Lavender Pit. "You'll see the V-shape above the lake on the east side of the pit. It's a fossil canyon, as good as any place to start."

With the funky, soulful vocals of Bisbee's favorite musician, Dylan Charles, singing his hilarious "We wanna go skiin', on the Lavender Pit" song on the CD player ("Obama won't you please help us with this / let's make a lake out of the Lavender Pit"), I pull off the highway at the blue *Scenic View* sign. The open-pit mine isn't named for its beautiful color but for Harrison M. Lavender (1890–1952), who was vice president and general manager of Phelps Dodge Corporation during the mine's heyday. We smell sulfur rising off the tar-colored pool a thousand feet below us and carried to our faces by a stiff breeze. I look for a *No Skiing* sign.

From the east rim and the many eroded terraces circling the mine, my eyes shift westward to a building at the far end of the parking lot. Once the "Home of Bisbee Blue Turquoise Indian Jewelry," the place is no longer home to anything but red spider webs in a matrix of dust. "New cities keep on sprawling / Old towns falling too," the Calexico song goes, "Raining a river of color / And it's flowing Bisbee Blue." I've seen the river of color coming off the mountain opposite the Lavender Pit during a summer cloudburst. Gushing rivulets of chartreuse and rust and powder blue . . . Bisbee Blue.

Undaunted, we drive back to Old Bisbee and the Queen Mine Tour gift shop. There, we're confronted with tabletop agates and fossil ammonites the size of French horns ($599). Old wheelbarrows and ore cars brim with fists of rock ($0.99 each). A $500 "splash copper" sticks against the plank wall like a false-color image from a murder scene. An entire wall of glass-fronted display cases holds hundreds of minerals: azurite and cuprite, hematite, malachite in hues from deep cerulean to powder green, hyacinth to pistachio among medallions of native red copper. I scan the shelves, the colors, the labels: calcite, rhodochrosite, vanadinite, variscite, pyrite, chrysocolla (the stone for attracting love). Minerals with names like poetry. Then I see them: three chunks of turquoise from Bisbee's Lavender Pit.

I'm not impressed. They look more like yard rocks with a splash of house paint, expensive house paint at their prices: $75.99, $100.99, $175.99. I step inside the gift shop and ask the woman behind the counter, "So where is the famous Bisbee Blue?"

She moves behind me and opens a case of jewelry, turquoise and azurite in silver pendants, rings, bracelets, and earrings. A piece in the center catches my eye, a large necklace of silver chain with silver leaves and acorns enclosing an oval of turquoise the size of my palm. Chocolate veins sweep across the dark surface, while a single white blaze flickers from zenith to earth like a lightning strike.

"Too big for my taste," offers a woman standing next to me.

"And too rich for mine," I add, turning over the necklace and seeing the sticker: $1,499. "But is this the Bisbee Blue?"

"It's all we have," says the saleswoman. "You might try one of the jewelry stores on Main Street."

We stop first at Andrew Laws's Czar Jewelry. "We're looking for the Bisbee Blue turquoise," I say to Kiyomi, who's minding the store.

"We have these," she says, pointing to a case. A white label reads: *Natural Bisbee turquoise set in 14k gold.* "I don't know about 'Bisbee Blue.' You should talk to Andrew."

Andrew says he prefers "natural Bisbee turquoise" over Bisbee Blue. "They kind of borrowed the name, made it important. But their turquoise has plastic in it, pressurized, hardened resin to stabilize the softer mineral. Mine is all natural."

Karen looks over Andrew while I look over Andrew's rough-cut stones. There are a few good candidates, and I check off turquoise as my first state symbol for the year. Eleven more to go. Karen wants Andrew to resize her gold wedding band and set it with natural Bisbee turquoise. This month is our thirty-first wedding anniversary.

Outside on Main Street, a bumper sticker on a parked car reads: *Bisbee, Arizona: Like Mayberry on Acid.* I think: *Who does acid anymore? We're too old for acid.* Karen disagrees as well. She says Bisbee is more like a Norman Rockwell painting.

"Norman Rockwell on pot," I say.

"You mean medical marijuana."

Pancho Villa's Ride

DOUGLAS

ELEVATION: 4,006 FEET | FOUNDED: 1901 | POPULATION: 20,316

On Friday the thirteenth, Karen and I drive twenty-five miles southeast from Bisbee to Douglas to spend this night in the glamorous and historic Gadsden Hotel. An elegantly dressed couple celebrating their anniversary and smoking cigarettes greets us in the foyer. We cross the lobby among marble columns with gilded capitals, an Italian marble staircase, and a Tiffany stained-glass mural. Vaulted stained-glass skylights present a rich darkness to the high ceiling as the sun angles below the rim of the earth. At the front desk, a young man named Alex checks us into room 120.

"We just decided to come down to Douglas," I say, explaining our lack of reservations.

"Why would you do that?" he asks.

We laugh. "Well, you know," I say. "It's Friday the thirteenth. Haunted hotel . . ."

"Bisbee is full of haunted hotels."

"Yeah, it has five, but Arizona has twenty-nine documented, and I want to experience them all. The Gadsden is number two on my list."

I try to convince Alex to take us down to the basement in the hotel's ancient elevator, but Karen is already looking past me at the El Conquistador Dining Room. Instead, I ask him where I can find the best place to eat in Douglas.

Alex checks the time. "My grandma's," he says. I think he's inviting us home with him.

In ten minutes we're sitting in La Fiesta Café ("Aqui con Martha") at a table draped with red plastic. We eat chips and salsa. Norteño music plays from a radio in the kitchen. Dark-haired waitresses crisscross the red-and-white tiled floor like pieces on a checkers board. A newspaper article mounted to the wall says that La Fiesta Café won first place for

"Best Mexican Dish" at a food show commemorating the centennial of the Mexican Revolution. Is this still Arizona? Maybe I took a wrong turn somewhere in the dark. . . .

I decide to begin my quest for the perfect chimichanga, Arizona's proposed state food, with a green chile chimi, enchilada style. Karen orders ground beef tacos, asking if they're deep fried the way her father makes them, and a cheese crisp with fresh-roasted green chiles. When the appetizer comes, I taste mesquite-wood smoke. "Only in Mexico can you find tortillas as good as this," says Karen. She knows. She was raised on the translucent staple from across the border.

My chimichanga fills the plate. Twin ice-cream scoops of sour cream and guacamole mound the bulging tortilla set in lettuce and tomato. The chile is sinus expanding, the shredded beef dark and moist within its deep-fried shell.

"You're going to have to develop some kind of point system," Karen suggests.

"Like a zero-to-five scale?"

"But how will you choose from all the kinds of chimichangas? Green or red chile? Chicken or beef? Carne seca?"

"I'll stick with green chile, but I'm already biased. How can anything beat Pancho's?"

I tasted my first chimichanga at the Tucson restaurant when I was nine. Forty-five years ago and I remember it like I remember this morning. Carne seca. Rolled into a flour tortilla the size of a sombrero and covered with a jacket of melted cheese, lettuce, and guacamole. I had to eat it with farm implements.

Pancho's is long gone, but I've recently learned that Tucson's El Charro Café and Phoenix's Macayo's Mexican Kitchen are laying claim to inventing the "thingamajig," the G-rated translation of *chimichanga*. The word is probably an adaptation of a Mexican curse word, one you might hear coming out of a kitchen after someone knocks a heavy bean burro into boiling lard. Which is exactly what restaurant founder Monica Flin did at El Charro in the early 1950s, according to her great-niece, Carlotta Flores. Macayo's president, Sharisse Johnson, however, insists that her late father, Woody Johnson, created it in 1946 when he deep-fried unsold burros to serve the following day. Whatever the case, there's a campaign headed up by both restaurants to make the chimichanga the official Arizona state food. A great idea. I give it my vote for the official swearword as well.

We drive back to the Gadsden along 11th Street, past neat rows of Queen Anne cottages and redbrick churches. It's a picture of Douglas I haven't seen before, quiet and serene. A place where children still play in the streets at night.

Five years before Arizona became a state, the five-story Gadsden Hotel opened its doors to cattle barons and mining magnates, travelers and settlers, becoming a center of financial and social activity in the territory. Although destroyed by fire in 1927, a concrete and steel replica replaced the Douglas landmark within two years, and its 130 rooms have since seen such dignitaries and celebrities as Eleanor Roosevelt, Charles Lindbergh, and Lee Marvin, and even the less-dignified likes of Charlie Sheen, whose signed publicity photo remains on display.

And then there's Pancho Villa and his famous ride.

At the foot of the marble staircase, I read a posted story by Mackenzie Lee Reidy of Mrs. Cannon's class at Marion Donaldson Elementary School titled, "My Great-Great-Grandfather and Pancho Villa." His name was Will Maddux, and according to the story, in 1902 he rode his horse for thirty days and nights from Texas to the tent town of Douglas, where he went to work for the Phelps Dodge copper mine, helped build the Gadsden Hotel (twice), got married, and raised seven children. Mackenzie then writes that, "Will told the story to his children who told the story to their children, who told me the story of my great-great-grandfather and when he saw Pancho Villa at the Gadsden Hotel."

Apparently, Will Maddux also worked as a messenger for Western Union. One day, while Will was waiting in the hotel lobby to deliver a telegraph to a guest, Pancho Villa suddenly appeared, on horseback, "hooting and hollering" and shooting bullets into the ceiling. He then rode his horse up the staircase, chipping a piece of marble at the seventh step.

"I have never been so scared," Mackenzie writes, "as when I went to see the Gadsden Hotel and the stairs this past summer. I think I saw Pancho Villa's ghost."

I'm looking at the chipped marble at the seventh step when an apparition slips up behind me. I turn to face a man in his late seventies, slightly built with a full head of white hair.

"Please look around," he says, and then turns and slips away.

I encounter him again in the main foyer, where I'm studying a yellowed certificate framed inside a display case: a homesteading permit from North Dakota signed by "T. Roosevelt."

"Please look around," he says again, and then ducks through a doorway.

Karen learns that the hotel owner, Hartman Brekhus, and his wife, Doris, came to Douglas from North Dakota more than twenty years ago, that Hartman's grandparents are the homesteaders on the certificate. "The couple came here on a whim," she tells me, "and fell in love with the sunshine—they bought the hotel and never left. Now their son and daughter-in-law, Henry and Robin, run the place."

The apparition appears again, and I ask him his name.

"Hartman," he says. He's the owner.

We're standing outside the elevator, waiting for the operator to take us to another floor, any floor. The Otis elevator is one of the oldest manually operated elevators west of the Mississippi. But the elevator stands open and empty. Taking up Hartman's invitation to "please look around," I ask him about the basement.

"Oh, you may find more than you want down there," he says. "My daughter-in-law did."

Robin Brekhus is a square-jawed woman with straight blond hair. She's not the timid type. She shot the mountain lion that is mounted into a relaxed angle of repose on a table at the top of the staircase. But on Friday the thirteenth 1992, she got a real scare. Late that afternoon, the hotel power failed—lights, clocks, and the elevator. Taking the stairwell to the basement to search for candles, she began to sense something creepy. "I felt like someone was watching me," she later told people. "The hair on my arms stood up. The hair on my neck stood up."

She pointed her flashlight down the long hallway but saw nothing. Then, after locating the candles, she returned to the hall and shined her light in the other direction. There, at the far end, stood a man in a full-length duster and hat, faceless but staring at her.

Robin ran for the stairs.

"Tall man. Black pants. No head." is how Carmen Diaz, the hotel's elevator operator, who has been at her post for decades, described what she once saw in the basement. Some say the headless man is Pancho Villa, who was in fact a tall man, about 180 pounds, with a light complexion, and at one point very headless.

The story goes that, during his revolutionary days, Villa had buried a fortune in gold somewhere in the Sierra Madre and had the only map to its location tattooed on his head. When he was assassinated on July 20, 1923, the map went with him to the grave. That is, until about three years later, when grave robbers broke into his tomb at Parral, Chihuahua, and stole his head. To this day, conspiracy theories and myths abound, but no one knows—or at least no one is telling—where his head resides. This is where the Gadsden Hotel comes in. Some say that loyalists to Villa recovered his head and buried it under the ashes of the burned hotel to conceal the secret. When the hotel was rebuilt, the ghost of Pancho Villa began wandering its cavernous basement, searching for his head and the map to his treasure.

Karen and I have seen the basement before. In the fall of 1995, the first time we stayed at the Gadsden. We were part of Richard Shelton's "Going Back to Bisbee" trip, which he organized every year for his graduate class at the University of Arizona. I was one of his students.

Carmen Diaz, a short, wrinkled scarecrow of a woman, sat on her stool in the corner of the elevator as we climbed inside. "Will you take us down to the basement?" I asked, and although she seemed hesitant to do so, she pulled the handle to close the doors and the elevator began sliding between floors.

Earlier, I had tried to gain access to the basement by way of a stairwell, but the door was locked. This time, the elevator doors banged apart and a narrow hallway opened before us into a darkness that seemed to fall on us. The air smelled of mildew and nose-biting rust. My flashlight showed walls slick and black with dripping water. We were spelunkers, and Karen clung to my arm as we stepped along the wet floor, passing doorways opening into rooms that sucked the beam from my light. Everywhere stood jumbles of bent and twisted bedsteads.

At the end of the hallway, a noise like metal on stone startled us. A black shape darted across the floor. "It's a cat," Karen said, "and there's more than one."

Then a voice came from behind us. "You have to leave," it said. "You shouldn't be here."

Carmen had fetched the hotel manager.

Henry Brekhus, Hartman's son, escorted us back to the lobby, but he also entertained us with some of his own ghost stories. One involved a maintenance worker who had come to the basement for repairs. "He was on his back under one of the boilers," Henry said, "tools spread out around him, trying to tighten a pipe fitting. When he began groping for a larger pipe wrench, something slid it across the floor into his hand. He never returned to the basement again."

At 9:00 p.m., Karen and I walk the halls of each floor, hunting for spirits. No one appears to inhabit the upper floors. We take the unlit stairwell down to the third floor to a closed door. As Karen pushes the door, it groans on rusty hinges. "Oooh," I tell her. "Make it do that again!"

Eerie green lights guide us down the passageway to a green door marked 333, the most haunted room in the hotel. Guests staying here have reported noises and lights. One woman says a presence crawled into bed with her while she slept, an experience she found more relaxing than scary.

Back in the lobby, we retreat to the Saddle and Spur Tavern for drinks. Earlier we had met a woman who told us about her experience standing outside the Governor's Suite. "I felt a tingling up my arm," she explained, dragging a fingernail along her black sleeve from elbow to shoulder. "I think the ghost wanted to get past me." Now, she's sitting in one of the booths with three other people.

When she gets up to leave, I catch her eye and ask her name.

"Elvia," she says. "And this is my husband, Jeff."

I invite them to join us, and we pull out chairs and order more Copperhead Pale Ale. They're from Douglas. Jeff owns a tire shop and both have raised three children—two girls and a boy. We share photographs of our daughters, the blond trio. Elvia passes around a picture of their oldest, who has gorgeous dark hair like her mother.

"She's our '*güera*,'" Jeff says. "Our boy is our 'taco.'"

When the jukebox dips in volume, I ask what they like about living here.

"Douglas is a great place to raise kids," Elvia says without hesitation. Jeff agrees.

In the morning at the hotel's El Conquistador Dining Room, I order huevos rancheros and refried beans. I'm a bit frustrated. We have to postpone my planned side trip to the Slaughter Ranch east of Douglas. Our oldest daughter Jessica called yesterday. She and her fiancé have set a date, and today she wants us to come to Tucson to meet with the future in-laws, dressmakers, caterers, and DJs. "Bring your checkbook," she says.

It's only week two, and already I'm off my schedule. What was I thinking? Fifty-two destinations in fifty-two weeks! I'm questioning my original enthusiasm. How will I ever survive the year now that there's a marriage in the mix? (It's a bigger question than it sounds.) And knowing my daughter, her wedding won't be simple but a full-blown extravaganza. Probably two extravaganzas! Just like her sisters. Hopefully, unlike her sisters, she'll keep the ceremonies in the same state.

Karen digs into her French toast and hash browns. I sip coffee and look around the room. Maybe I can work the wedding into a destination—and take a post-wedding fly-fishing trip to Alpine for Apache trout. Wood carvings of helmeted conquistadors stare back at me in silence.

At checkout, Karen discovers that Douglas is home to Arizona's first official state song. "Is that right?" I ask the young woman at the front desk.

She hands me a booklet written by Cindy Hayostek, a Douglas historian and researcher. It says that "The Arizona March Song" is one of two official state songs (the other is Rex Allen Jr.'s 1981 "Arizona") and that it was written by two Douglas residents. Margaret Rowe Clifford wrote the words in 1915 and soon after solicited Maurice E. Blumenthal, a member of the town's "lively Jewish community," to compose the music. The song eventually fell on the ears of Governor George W. P. Hunt, who promised Margaret that he would spread the word. The Fourth State Legislature adopted the anthem on February 28, 1919.

"Generations of Douglas schoolchildren sang the state anthem," Karen reads from the booklet: "Come to this land of sunshine / To this land where life is young / Where the wide, wide world is waiting / The songs that will now be sung . . ."

"Jeez," I say. "'Land of sunshine where life is young'? I still think the U of A's fight song 'Bear Down, Arizona!' is the best state song."

Wanted Dead and Alive

TOMBSTONE

ELEVATION: 4,541 FEET | FOUNDED: 1879 | POPULATION: 1,562

I've heard that the pistol packers in Tombstone prefer guns more than women. This is because a gun won't leave you when you run out of ammo. But I don't believe it. I'm sure it applies to pistol packers everywhere.

At the Boothill Graveyard in the Town Too Tough to Die, I meet two friends from Tucson—Jerry Marzinsky and Bruce Baker. Bruce, a quiet, taciturn man, is an electrician, computer programmer, documentary filmmaker, and power-distribution wizard. "Bruce can take anything apart," Jerry says, "figure it out and, unlike most of us, put it back together again without leftover parts."

I met Jerry twenty years ago when he was a psychologist at the state prison, the same work he does today at the state hospital where he specializes in psychotic behavior. He's also a writer, currently publishing his ideas about the nature of psychosis. He has an unconventional theory about the "voices" psychotics sometimes hear—he believes the voices are real, that they're actual parasitic entities.

"The lunatics are in my hall." I hear the Pink Floyd tune every time I think of Jerry. "The paper holds their folded faces to the floor / And every day the paper boy brings more." I've told him that I hear voices, too, especially when I'm being extravagantly stupid, which is often. The voices always sound like my wife.

He says he helps people make the voices go away.

Today, Jerry has arranged a special treat for me: a private tour of the legendary town, courtesy of eighty-year-old actor and historian Art Weisberger and his longtime girlfriend Judy. Art, I've also learned, is a federal firearms dealer and just may own a Colt .45 Single Action Army revolver, Arizona's newest symbol and my next quest.

"I have something for you," Jerry says, as I step out of my car. He holds out a silver-cased bullet that's as long as the last two joints of his little finger and nearly as fat.

"Is this it?" I ask.

"Yep. Ammo for the Colt you're looking for."

We turn as Art and Judy pull up in a Toyota 4Runner. They're dressed for the part. Judy, in a black teardrop hat and blue Victorian bustle gown with black cape, carries a parasol in her gloved hand. Art wears a black vaquero hat, dark blue Abilene vest over a Laramie shirt, Silverton trousers, and black frontier boots with spurs. His twin gun belts hold a 28-gauge shot pistol and a Remington revolver. We've entered Tombstone's past, and I'm seriously underdressed.

"I want to show you something," Art says through a thick white handlebar mustache by way of introduction. He lifts a cover from the back of his SUV and pulls out a leather holster containing a Remington 1861 Navy revolver. "It's .36 caliber," he says, "using paper cartridges with black powder charges and lead balls." He demonstrates how the ratchet lever would ram the load into each of the six chambers of the cylinder.

"Look here." He turns the revolver over. Scratched into the brass trigger guard are the letters "Col F. W*m* CODY."

At the entrance to the Boothill Graveyard, a man behind the counter asks Art to check his guns. *Didn't they learn anything in this town?* I think, but Art obliges and hands over his gun belts. I'd read somewhere that the cemetery is a fake, a show for tourists. I ask Art about this, and he says that the graveyard is real and that there are actually two graveyards. "The cemetery was laid out in 1878 and used until about 1884. Afterward, the wooden markers rotted or, as with the Clanton gang, were stolen many years ago. Most of the grave markers are phony. No one knows who's buried where."

Art leads us past several unmarked stone mounds to the graves of Billy Clanton and Tom and Frank McLaury, the brothers who were buried together. Next to the graves, a marker reads: *Murdered on the Streets of Tombstone 1881.*

"Murdered?" I ask, surprised. "At the O.K. Corral?"

"Wyatt Earp was a pimp, a saloonkeeper, and a gambler," Art says.

"His only reason for being in Tombstone was chasing money." Art explains that after Ed Schieffelin made his silver strike in 1877 and Tombstone began its boom, the town was rich with miners loaded with cash. Wyatt Earp figured he could relieve them of some of that burden.

"To this moment," Art says, and I notice that he wears a silver star engraved with *Tombstone Vigilantes*, "there is a warrant out for the arrest of Wyatt Earp in Tombstone."

From Boothill, Art drives us over to the center of town and parks behind a building near Allen Street. He wears glasses with round lenses, the frames of which he says were made in 1879. "I try to be as authentic as possible."

On Allen Street, we stand next to signs that read *O.K. Corral Gunfight Site* and *Walk Where They Fell*. Tourists keep stopping to hear Art's stories and ask questions while Art patiently tries to dispel their movie-born myths. Across the street, two actors walk by with red sashes hanging from their belts. "See that?" Art says. "That's movie crap. The Cowboys would never have called attention to themselves like that." Earlier, Art had told us about the Hollywood-driven romantic lies of "the cowboy," and how even their hats took their rolled-up brim shapes to keep shadows from falling across the actor's face during filming. "If you worked with cattle or horses, you were either a herder or a drover. Despite what you think about John Wayne, *cowboy* was slang for *rustler*."

I'm starting to think that the Earps calling the Clanton and McLaury brothers "cowboys" were fighting words.

"It was originally called the 'Fremont Street gunfight,'" Art says, explaining that the shootout, which amounted to thirty shots in about thirty seconds, started in a narrow alley between the O.K. and Arizona Corrals and spilled onto Fremont Street. "The Tombstone Vigilantes perform the gunfight as it actually happened, and Bob Love, owner of the O.K. Corral, sued us, claiming that the gunfight took place at the O.K. Corral. The fight had nothing to do with it—it got the name from a description in Stuart Lake's book, which he later admitted was made-up. You want the most accurate account, read Tim Fattig's *Wyatt Earp*."

"Tombstone seems more interested in making money than in its history," I suggest, adding, "but isn't that what's been going on from the beginning? As you said, it's why Wyatt Earp came here in the first place."

"The O.K. Café is the best place to eat in town," Judy says, and so we head there for lunch. Outside, Johnny Cash's "The Ballad of Ira Hayes" blasts through a pair of speakers. A sign reads: *Cowboys Scrape Shit from Boots before Entering.* I wipe the Vibram soles of my Merrells and smile at something I remember Karen told me about Tombstone. Recently she attended a public meeting on a transportation issue when one of the "Wild West citizens," as she called him, stood up to complain that the government shouldn't be spending money on roads when the town couldn't even afford toilet paper. Apparently Tombstone had run out of supplies for its public restrooms. "You're kidding," I told her. "The Town Too Tough to Die can't live without toilet paper? I thought they still used corncobs."

Art recommends the half-pound one-hundred-percent Wyoming buffalo burger. "Order it medium rare because there's no fat," he adds, "with a pinch of salt."

Both Bruce and I take him up on his suggestion.

Art talks about his military career as we eat. He fought with the Marines in Korea, Guam, and the Philippines. Jerry adds how Art took out an entire North Korean patrol when he was a sniper. "I have four wounds from gunshots," Art continues, "some shrapnel, and one wound from a samurai sword."

I look over his six-foot-four frame and try to imagine the history carved into the man.

"I own the rifle that shot me, and the sword."

No one says anything for a moment—and then my eyes drop to Art's pocket watch, and the arrowhead fob dangling from his vest.

"I took the arrowhead out of the leg of the watch's previous owner," Art says.

It isn't necessary to ask him what happened to the previous owner. Art carries more than one souvenir of the dead.

After lunch, Art leads us down the boardwalks of Allen Street, pointing out historic places like Schieffelin Hall, "the oldest adobe building in the United States still in use," and the Campbell & Hatch Saloon and Billiard Parlor where Morgan Earp was murdered less than five months after the O.K. Corral shootout. "Big Nose Kate's Saloon," Art says, "was originally the Grand Hotel." The sixteen-bedroom luxury hotel, with carpeting and walnut furniture, chandeliers and oil paintings, opened in 1880 but burned in 1882. It was the place Ike Clanton and the McLaurys spent the night before the gunfight. When we step inside, we can go no farther. The place is packed. Large-screen TVs play the movie *Tombstone*. Dance-hall girls serve tables. George Strait sings "All my ex's live in Texas . . ."

At the corner of Allen and 5th, Art points toward the Crystal Palace and the Oriental Saloon. "This is where Virgil Earp was shot," he says, recounting the night in December 1881 when concealed gunmen ambushed the marshal, maiming him and putting an end to his Tombstone days.

Our last stop on Allen Street is the Bird Cage Theatre. Art says it opened after the gunfight and "was a combination saloon and whorehouse." It's the most authentic place in Tombstone. Just inside the parlor, Jerry and I count the bullet holes in a painting of Fatima Djemille, a belly dancer and the original "Little Egypt" (because she was overweight), who allegedly performed here. Fatima commissioned the oil painting and gave it to the theater, where it has hung on this spot since 1882.

"Wouldn't this have been a crazy place back in the day?" Jerry says. He should know. Jerry has seen crazy from day one. On his first day of work at Georgia's infamous lunatic asylum, the Central State Hospital, he nearly crashed his motorcycle when a man leaped from the bushes as Jerry pulled into the hospital parking lot. "He strode by as if oblivious," he told me, "wearing nothing but a pair of bright red tennis shoes, his johnson wagging from side to side like a blind man's cane." The naked man then ran off down an oak-lined street and disappeared into one of the cottages of the resident psychiatrists.

The Bird Cage sports 140 bullet holes. It was "the wildest, wickedest night spot between Basin Street and the Barbary Coast," according to a contemporary article in the *New York Times*. It closed in 1889, ending the world's longest continuously running poker game (eight years, five months, three days), after water began seeping into the mines and Tombstone went bust. Fortunately, the building was sealed, much of it intact.

"I used to play here as a kid in the 1940s," Art says. He gets us into the back rooms for free (after checking his guns), and we walk through the main gambling casino, dance hall, and stage with its fourteen overhanging, self-suspended red-velvet-draped "birdcages," the boxes in which the ladies entertained their guests. The original rosewood grand piano still sits in its spot in the orchestra pit, unmoved since 1881. The faro table used by Doc Holiday waits in a corner for the next card game. Old photos of Tombstone's historic citizens like Wyatt Earp and John Slaughter cover the walls of the stairwell, which Art leads us down to the basement poker room and wine cellar under the stage, his spurs clinking against the wooden steps.

"This is also where the girls lived," he says, and I peer into their tiny rooms and stare at their pictures on the walls, reading their names aloud: Dutch Annie, Jessie Jo, Annie Watson, Soap Suds Sal, Copperhead. . . . One photo, taken at Camillus Fly's Tombstone studio, is a nude, later retouched to look like she's wearing a sheer gauze peignoir. She's Josephine Marcus, "Sadie Jo." "The story goes," Art tells me, "that she gave this photo to Sheriff John Behan, rival of Wyatt Earp and her live-in lover. The photo was concealed until Behan's death in 1912." She looks directly at me, sultry and provocative.

Art drives us back to Boothill Cemetery by way of John Slaughter's house and a second cemetery "where the good people of Tombstone preferred to be buried." He has a casting call this afternoon, a chance for a role in his fiftieth movie.

"I have an 1890 .45-caliber Remington revolver if you'd like to see it," Art tells me before he drives off. He says it's similar to the Colt, but it's not the "Peacemaker" of Wyatt Earp fame. I agree to meet with him again, but I'm afraid Eliphalet Remington just won't do. The search must go on for Arizona's newest state symbol. It was Samuel Colt who made the gun with the ivory grips, the gun that won the West. The world's right arm. The icon that embodies Manifest Destiny. It was Sam Colt who made all yahoos equal.

Outnumbered by the Dead

DRAGOON, BUTTERFIELD STATION, AND THE AMERIND FOUNDATION

ELEVATION: 4,632 FEET | FOUNDED: 1858
POPULATION: 4 DEAD CONFEDERATES

In the last week of January, sixty miles north of Bisbee, I slip through the giant quartz monzonite boulders of Texas Canyon and arrive at the Dragoon Post Office to meet Jack Lasseter, Pat McGowan, Tom Leskiw, and Eric Meyer. Then, the five of us head across a rutted dirt road to a Confederate graveyard at the mouth of Jordan Canyon in the Dragoon Mountains.

"This is my favorite place in Arizona," Jack says. "No trinkets. No curio shops." Jack is an amateur historian and retired attorney. "All the security you see at the courthouse," he says, "is for people like me—divorce lawyers." Jack loves his retirement. These days he gives talks and leads tours to historic places like this one, Butterfield Station in what in 1858 was downtown Dragoon.

We follow Jack in his REI cap and blue sweatshirt over uneven, storm-gouged ground. Four high walls of stacked rocks rise among a black tangle of leafless mesquite trees. "In 1857, John Butterfield wins a contract with the U.S. government to haul the mail from St. Louis to San Francisco," Jack begins, staring up at the stone walls. "Twice a week it ran through southeast Arizona—from San Simon to Tucson. It only stopped at these stations for short breaks to change horses and for riders to eat or otherwise relieve themselves.

"Day and night," he goes on. "Picture yourself crammed into this stage—they put as many people on as they could to make money—and you're sitting cheek to jowl with someone who has not taken a bath for twenty-five days. It's why they needed rules like: 'Do not use hair oil' and 'Refrain from talking politics or religion.'"

Sounds just like our annual family vacation, I'm thinking.

"And he's probably drunk," he adds. "They say that aircraft can follow the Butterfield Trail by the reflection of all the broken whiskey flasks."

Maybe an Ed Abbey family vacation.

Inside the rock ruins of the Dragoon Springs station, Jack seats himself on the ground, takes out his copy of *Old West Adventures in Arizona* by Charles D. Lauer, and adjusts his glasses.

We circle around. Sit in the dirt.

"The night of September 8, 1858," Jack starts reading, "Lang stood the first watch. At midnight Silas posted Guadalupe Ramirez to take the second watch. St. John was asleep in the office. Cunningham was in the store room. Lang in the center room with the stock. Hughes and the two laborers were outside. An hour later St. John was aroused by an uneasy stirring of the stock. Then, wakened by the sound of blows and outcries, he leaped from his bedroll but was unable to grab his rifle from its scabbard attached to the saddle he was using for a pillow because he was set upon by the three Mexican laborers. . . ." Jack's voice rises among the stones as he relates the story of St. John's miraculous escape from death after he and his station crew had been ambushed from among their own ranks, how for four days the gravely wounded man drove off skulking coyotes, feasting ravens and buzzards, and packs of wolves "howling ghoulishly" until help arrived.

In the end, a surgeon dispatched from Fort Buchanan cleanly amputated St. John's severed left arm and "three weeks later he rode a horse to Tucson and was back on the job, a recovery so remarkable it was noted in medical journals." St. John, only twenty-three years old at the time, lived a long and useful life in Arizona and died at the age of eighty-four.

"And all that happened *right here*," Jack says, pointing to the ground. "I never get tired of this stuff."

Outside the ruins, we walk among four mounds of rough stones, the graves of the only Confederate soldiers killed in Arizona Territory during the Civil War. The soldiers were members of a foraging party out of Tucson, where Captain Sherod Hunter's Arizona Rangers were garrisoned. On May 5, 1862, three weeks after the Battle of Picacho Pass and nine days before Captain Hunter would order the evacuation of Tucson at the approach of Union troops, the party was herding cattle into a narrow box canyon nearby (probably Jordan Canyon) when a large band of Apaches led by the great Chiricahua chief Cochise attacked them. Most of the Confederates escaped, but they lost more than fifty horses and mules and these four soldiers.

Names mark only two of the graves. Chiseled into stone at one are the letters "S. FORD." The other depicts a cross with the name "RICARDO." The remaining graves are unknown, although Jack says one of them may belong to someone named John Donaldson. The Stars and Bars flies over each resting place. Below each flag, an iron cross shows a Confederate battle flag surrounded with a laurel wreath and the inscription: *The Southern Cross of Honor*. The graves are well tended.

Jack's history presentation was my request. I've dragged along Eric and Tom because, like me, they don't need an excuse to explore some untamed corner of the state. Jack and Pat McGowan had already planned to hike Jordan Canyon to check two remote wildlife cameras for my daughter, Jessica, the wildlife linkages program coordinator for Sky Island Alliance. The two are part of her team of volunteers who maintain cameras across southern Arizona, New Mexico, and Sonora, cameras that have recorded not just bears and mountain lions but also jaguars and, right here in Cochise County, the first evidence of a living ocelot in Arizona.

"Last month when we were up here," Jack says, "we kept seeing these footprints."

"They were small, and only a single set of them," Pat adds. "Right on the trail."

I imagine a lone hiker in this wild place, mountain lion country.

"We couldn't think of whose they might be," Jack says, "and then we decided they were your daughter Jessica's tracks." They both laugh.

Pat has worked in public transportation for forty-two years. He's the manager at Sun Van in Tucson and an Apache and Plains Indians history buff. He met Jessica at one of her weekend tracking workshops in northern Sonora. On one of his camera-checking excursions, he was so focused on watching the GPS coordinates on his Garmin that he nearly stepped on a rattlesnake. The snake struck and missed, and Pat has been hooked on tracking ever since.

I ask Pat about the Dragoon Mountains and the Apache warrior, Cochise. "I know you and Jack have hiked all over the range, looking for his burial site."

"We have!" he laughs. "He's here, somewhere, not buried but tucked inside some cleft of rock. But there's only one Anglo who ever knew the location."

"Tom Jeffords," Jack adds. "If you want to find Cochise, you go find Jeffords."

Pat says Jeffords was a U.S. Army scout and Indian agent in the 1860s and that his friendship with Cochise helped establish the short-lived Chiricahua Apache reservation in 1872 where today we have Cochise County. "I've seen Jeffords's grave in Evergreen Cemetery in Tucson," he says.

To which Jack adds, "The first time I went there I found a medicine bundle resting on his stone. Shows how important he was to the Apache, even today. They called him 'Taglito,' or Red Beard. After Cochise died, Jeffords and the Apaches entombed him up here in these mountains."

When we reach the cameras, Pat unlocks the case and replaces the batteries and compact flash drive. The group breaks out sandwiches. I munch an apple with slices of hard cheese and salami. At the second camera, Pat tells us about a recent mountain lion clip the camera recorded: the animal casually walked the rocky drainage in full daylight. "A day just like today," he adds, like this is something we might want to digest with our lunch.

I've never come face-to-face with a mountain lion . . . yet. I see their tracks and I get their photos—with cubs even—on my own remote camera near my home. I know they're watching me. I once came upon a pile of scat on the trail that wasn't there on my way *to* the camera. It's a trail I walk often while throwing fear and faith out before me. I tell my wife before each trip that if a mountain lion should decide to eat me, I'm okay with that. I'll take the less-traveled road of mammalian digestion over a slow hospital death any day.

On the way out of Dragoon, I see a sign for the Amerind Foundation, a 1930s ranch tucked into the boulder-strewn landscape that now houses one of the finest privately owned archaeological collections of Native American culture in the United States. I've never been here before. There's still some daylight, so I take the turnoff.

The dirt road takes me to the Texas Canyon Pioneer Cemetery, my second graveyard for the day and third this month. *This is going to be a year of graves*, I think. According to a sign, the place was part of the homestead of William and Ofelia Adams, who settled here in 1905. The young couple was the second of three waves of Adamses to come to the Little Dragoon Mountains from Coleman County, Texas, an influx of such magnitude that people began referring to the place as "Texas Canyon."

The cemetery is closed to newcomers. No reservations. You must be a Texas Canyon pioneer—a dead one, I'm guessing—to be planted here. I see that the Fultons have their own plot at the back of the cemetery. It's a name I recognize.

In 1937, six years after building his home here, William Shirley Fulton founded the Amerind Foundation. Born in Connecticut in 1880, Fulton made his first trip to Grand Canyon when he was twenty-six and instantly became fascinated with the Southwest. That first venture led to annual pilgrimages. Then, while operating a mine in the Verde Valley for his wife's father, Edward Hayden, Fulton stumbled upon an eight-hundred-year-old clay jar in a cave on Mingus Mountain. It would be the first artifact of a great Native American collection numbering in the tens of thousands. Fulton retired by the age of fifty and devoted the rest of his life to archaeology, moving to Texas Canyon with his wife and children to build a museum and laboratory.

As I enter the museum, I immediately notice the Josias Joesler influences in the scored, red-stained concrete floor and rough-hewn wood-beam ceiling. Two leather couches front a large fireplace. Glass display cases line the walls. Four large cases in the center of the room hold baskets from Chiricahua Apache country.

I scan the main gallery looking for clay jars. One eight-hundred-year-old clay jar. With my limited time, I want to see the thing that drove Fulton to shift both careers and landscapes, to build his home and museum in this remote place and spend his remaining thirty-four years expanding it. I want to see the object of his obsession.

I find it in the gallery that exhibits Fulton's notebooks and the foundation's local work on the San Pedro River (Presidio Santa Cruz de Terrenate) and Texas Canyon. The jar is smoky gray and smudged with charcoal; I could wrap both arms around it, which is what Fulton must have done that day he carried it home from its long interment in the Black Hills of central Arizona.

I decide I must come back. My Dragoon destination has become two points of interest. Maybe three. I should buy a GPS and set it for proximity alerts. I now count seven points of interest (POI) in Bisbee alone. Four in Tombstone. The Dragoon museum is a spacious, multiple-floor affair, and I have less than a half hour before it closes. A volunteer at the desk says I will need an entire day "at least." I promise to return.

Six weeks later, I'm back. During the interim, I've driven 2,700 miles, chased desert wildflowers at Picacho Peak, mesquite-fired tortillas at the Tumacácori mission, turquoise and petrified wood at the Flandrau Science Center and Planetarium, and ridge-nosed rattlesnakes at the Arizona-Sonora Desert Museum. Six new destinations and many more points of interest. But today, I'm looking for something specifically "Amerind."

The focus is necessary, since on my last visit, I discovered how overwhelming the place is. The foundation's primary interest covers "The Gran Chichimeca"—basically the entire Southwest, including Mexico north of the Tropic of Cancer. But the museum also displays artifacts from cultures extending from the Arctic Inuit to the Peruvian Nazca, spanning a time from the arrival of the first people on the continent to 1821, the date of Mexican independence. Now I'm looking for something Amerind and *local*.

My daughter Melissa has joined me. She's doing her own research while on spring break from Iowa State, where she's finishing her MFA in creative writing and environment. We circle around the ranch houses and stop in front the Fulton-Hayden Memorial Art Gallery and its pair of enormous hand-carved church doors from Michoacán, dating from 1665.

The stucco walls and clay tiles, open courtyards and arches typify the Spanish Colonial Revival style popular in southern Arizona during the early twentieth century. This was the vision of Tucson architect Merritt Starkweather, who's known for creating such desert icons as the Arizona Inn and for founding the Tucson Rodeo, La Fiesta de los Vaqueros. Starkweather designed the art museum around the dark, brooding Tarascan doors.

We climb the stairway to the gallery and meet Janie Swartz, a foundation volunteer who lives on a ranch at Dos Cabezas. Janie sends us on a self-guided tour of works of southwestern artists like Ross Stefan, who got his start displaying his oils in his father's Western-wear shop in Tucson, and John Coleman Burroughs, who began his career illustrating his father's Tarzan books. Others include Frederick Remington and Malvina Hoffman, casters of bronze, and Rudolph Carl Gorman, painter, sculptor, and lithographer, who was born at Canyon de Chelly, raised in a hogan, and became a code talker during World War II. The *New York Times* called him the Picasso of American Indian art. But I think his best work is his illustrated cookbook, *Nudes and Foods*.

An hour later, Janie finds us in the Pine Study, Fulton's work space. A Spanish vargueño stands in the corner. The seventeenth-century writing desk has walnut compartments inlaid with ivory and ebony crosses. The drawer pulls look like gold. We've been staring too long.

"I'm supposed to keep an eye out for anyone lingering too long," Janie explains. To distract us, she shows us an earthquake detector from China: an ivory elephant with a white marble resting on its back. "It vibrates with mining work miles away, and I've made it roll off by just walking across the room."

"You should place it on the writing desk," I suggest, "as an alarm system."

Next, we tour the museum, spending a couple of hours moving through its galleries, the stone bowls and hammer stones of the Texas Canyon people, the figurines and effigies (Melissa is drawn to the horned toad) of the mountain Tarahumara, the intricate geometry of the Apache basket weavers and the ceramic vessels of the Sobaipuri peoples. These are the locals, historically speaking. The Sobaipuri lived on the San Pedro River, where the Spanish failed to build their fortified Terrenate due to

Apache hostilities and left behind their horseshoes, lead shot, copper bowls, bronze crucifixes, and copper tankards—where would Anglos be without their tankards of hot chocolate!

Earlier, I had met with John Ware, the foundation's director for the past eleven years, who led me to the library, a beautiful two-story affair of beamed ceilings, leather chairs, and wrap-around bookshelves. The air was pungent with old leather bindings. It smelled like wisdom.

"This was originally a research institute," John said. "The museum was an afterthought."

John told me about Charles Di Peso, who spent thirty years as director of the foundation. Di Peso received the University of Arizona's first PhD in anthropology, studying under the legendary archaeologist Emil Haury. I knew about his work at Terrenate. I had seen his excavations. But I hadn't realized that the Spanish presidio was just one of two dozen Amerind projects he led. "Di Peso helped reconstruct the past stories of native peoples across the Southwest and northern Mexico," John said. "He is responsible for much of our understanding of our region's prehistoric cultural history."

If the Amerind Foundation does one thing, it shows us that there was no empty continent here before European arrival. From the twelve-thousand-year-old atlatls and Clovis points of the Paleo-Indians and the eight-thousand-year-old projectile points and grinding stones of the Archaic hunters and foragers, to the pottery and shell necklaces of the Hohokam and the cotton textiles of the Pueblo peoples, *we* are the newcomers. Our present layer of civilization is lint compared to the deep stratified bands of cultures beneath our feet.

"The dead will always outnumber the living," says Annie Dillard. Currently, she estimates about fourteen to one. "We live on dead people's heads." I should feel foolish every time I get excited about being alive. In this historical context, it's hard for me to believe that we are little more than wet bags of bacteria, unwitting escorts for germs. With respect to Samuel Colt, in this desert landscape, death is the great equalizer. Not far from here, the graves of four Confederate soldiers lie in the same mountains as the grave of Cochise. The honored graves of unknown soldiers and the unknown grave of an honored warrior. Practically side by side. Beyond this life, we all become soil and dust. We're only the next layer to be walked upon.

FEBRUARY

Cactus Wren

POINTS OF INTEREST TO DATE: 16 | TOTAL MILES: 329

Arizona's Civil War

PICACHO PEAK STATE PARK

ELEVATION: 2,000 FEET | FOUNDED: 1965 | POPULATION: 1 PARK RANGER

Beneath the dark, brooding thumb of Picacho Peak, I pull off I-10 and drive up to the visitor center. My first state park of the year and, so far, the farthest north I've traveled in Arizona. It's late afternoon in February. "Sunset is 6:00 p.m.," the ranger tells me as he takes my seven dollars. "The park's trails close at sundown."

A sign tells me that next month will be the annual Civil War reenactment of the Battle of Picacho Pass. I'm interested—my proximity alert sounds off. I know about the famous "westernmost battle of the Civil War," and I've read about the show. But I've never seen it. I point to the sign. "Where did the battle actually take place?" I ask.

The ranger raises his arm to the east, to a reddish stump of rock poking out of a flat desert now turning green. "Across the interstate, but there's no access. The evidence is long gone." Then his arm swings north toward a lone hill. "The battle will be there. Just follow the signs."

He hands me a brochure. "Today you might want to check out the Memorial Loop."

I drive the loop to an obelisk of mortared native rock. A plaque commemorates the soldiers of the 1st California Volunteer Cavalry killed at Picacho Pass on April 15, 1862:

LT. JAMES BARRETT, CO. A
PRIV. GEORGE JOHNSON, CO. A
PRIV. WILLIAM S. LEONARD, CO. A

An interpretive sign explains the battle as it unfolded. Arrows show troop movements and written descriptions overlay a modern photo of the valley before me. I study the display, comparing it with the landscape in the distance. I see how the Union plan of Captain William P. Calloway unfolded, how Lieutenant Barrett and his detachment of twelve men circled east of the Picacho Mountains while Lieutenant Ephraim Baldwin and his ten men circled west of Picacho Peak. Calloway and the remainder of the battalion would march straight up the valley, and the combined force of 276 men would surround the Confederate pickets, a guard of only ten men, forcing them to surrender. The plan should have worked. Except Barrett, against orders, rushed to engage the rebels.

Driving the loop road named for him, I wonder about the carelessness of the fallen lieutenant, whose grave, unmarked and undisturbed for a century and a half, lies near the dark line of railroad tracks that split the pass. If he wanted to make history, he certainly did. Without his rash actions, Arizona would have no claim to Civil War fame.

Hunter Trail, a two-mile route that winds and climbs 1,500 feet to the summit of the redundant "Big Peak Peak," tops out at an elevation of 3,374 feet. I don't have enough daylight to make the peak, but I'm hoping to reach the base of the cliff face and catch the sunset before rangers roll up the trails for the night.

A thin layer of green softens the rocky ground. Mexican gold poppies and lupines push up fat buds. I step along briskly, enjoying the cornflakes crunch under the Vibram soles of my Merrells. When I come to another sign, I have to laugh. *Trail beyond upper saddle is primitive, not recommended for children under 10.* The first time I hiked this volcanic prow was before the signs and pavement, before the rangers and fees. It was the spring of 1986, and Jessica wasn't even three years old. My daughter rode on my shoulders, wide-eyed at the desert floor shrinking into the hard, flat creosote distance as our trail lifted us into the sky. It was a glorious day.

Now, where the trail turns into a stair climb through yellow and orange lichen-splashed boulders, I meet a group of four people coming down from the peak. "Only two miles," I say.

"More like twelve," one of the young women responds in a strong British accent. She looks to be the age of my children, and just as slim and blond. Her face is sunburned—they're all sunburned, their pale complexions burnished red by the sun. "Where are you from?" I ask.

"The UK," the girl with the reddest face says. "Three of us, that is—we picked up this guy who's from Oregon." She indicates a man following up behind them.

It's their first time in Arizona, and they have just climbed Picacho Peak on a whim. I ask them what they like best about their visit.

"The weather!" the first girl says.

"And the sky diving!" the second girl adds.

Sky diving? They've been in Eloy all day, jumping out of perfectly good planes. Maybe their faces are more windburned than sunburned.

I gain the cliffs fifteen minutes before sundown. Somewhere a canyon wren trills: the essential sound of rock and grotto. I hang my legs off a boulder and watch as a thousand feet below, Picacho Peak sends a long shadow all the way to the Tortolita Mountains. Like two fingers of black lava creeping across an arc of the desert at the speed of shadow. Saguaros spike the hillsides, their uplifted crowns aglow even in the darkening penumbra of the peak.

Much more than what I see here lies beneath me, buried under thousands of feet of valley fill. Picacho Peak is only the eroded tip of a lava berg, an exposure of multiple lava flows that spread over the land during a time when the earth heaved up the Superstition and Chiricahua Mountains tens of millions of years ago.

Across the valley, the Picacho Mountains flare in brilliant relief as a lowering sun ignites the gneiss of the southern face. Unlike Picacho Peak, these are exposures of deep crust, part of the many tortured, concatenated shards of mountains—metamorphic core complexes—that stretch obliquely across southern Arizona from the Buckskins north of Quartzsite to the Huachucas and Chiricahuas near my home. I'm resting at the center of the West's Basin and Range Province, a region of crustal unzipping and landform warping and fracturing that created our desert sea of sky islands, one of the most grand and unique places on the planet.

I can't think of a better place I'd rather be than right here, right now. I decide I must return. Next month's reenactment will honor the one hundred fiftieth anniversary of the Battle of Picacho Pass, and after living here for four and a half decades, I should finally see it.

Six weeks later, I squeeze in a forty-mile run to Picacho Peak State Park between Tucson's fourth annual Festival of Books, where I just moderated a panel called "All Roads Lead to Arizona," and a Rogue Theatre music gig. I barely make it through the gates before they're locked. The reenactment begins in a half hour—good timing, considering I didn't know the schedule. I park and follow the crowd. Everyone speaks with a Southern accent. Women wearing spoon bonnets and camp dresses with pagoda sleeves and carrying parasols walk in pairs and threes between scores of white canvas army tents in neat lines. Men in gray uniforms sit on wooden crates in groups, playing cards beneath Confederate flags that catch and snap in a warm wind that smells of wood smoke. Somewhere I hear a harmonica. Someone whistles Dixie. I've stumbled into a rebel encampment outside Chickamauga!

Vendors and history buffs have set up displays among the tents. I buy some of Doc McGilly's Sasparilly. "Taste the Legend," the label says, "Since 1514." *Jeez*, I think. *The stuff goes back to when the Ottomans and Persians were battling between the north and south.* The drink is sweet, but not overly so, and only lightly carbonated—the taste of Southern belles and porch swings. I sip it at a booth arrayed with bone saws and scalpels and other pain-inducing steel instruments employed by surgeons during the Civil War.

At another booth, a man sells authentic Civil War weapons and gear—bowie knives (Arkansas toothpicks), cavalry sabers, Springfield rifles and Sharps carbines, haversacks, canteens, teapots, and coffeepots. He holds the latter, discussing coffee-brewing with bystanders. "Do you know how they separated the grounds from the coffee?" he asks.

When no one answers, I say: "With cold water—cowboy coffee."

"Yes, but it's not cowboy coffee unless you can float a horseshoe. Know how to tell strong cowboy coffee? You float the horseshoe, but the horse is still attached!" He laughs, a full face and belly laugh.

At the battlefield site, colorfully dressed spectators take seats across a boulder-strewn hillside as if this were an actual Civil War battle. In front, eight Union soldiers sit horseback. A ninth stands among a group of people discussing the famous battle. "Most of the soldiers were 150 pounds or less," the soldier says, "living on beans and bacon—bacon only if they were lucky! John Wayne at 250 pounds would've killed his horse."

His name is Bob Pinter. I ask him what role he'll be playing, other than holding the horses, and he says: "I think I'm one of the ones that gets killed."

As the battle begins, the riders—representing Lieutenant Barrett's detachment—move off. The Confederates appear. Eight men in gray march in a column, two-by-two, while an announcer at a loudspeaker gives us the history. He says something about rebel pickets guarding the Picacho Pass overland mail station. . . . The Confederate column has disappeared into a line of paloverde and bursage to my left, and now a burst of "yee-haws" on my right draws my attention to the mounted Union soldiers who've surprised three men hiding in the creosote. "You guys don't smell like cattle!" the lieutenant shouts.

Suddenly, a volley of musket fire thunders from the paloverde cover, and the Union soldiers drop from their horses. "Form a skirmish line!" Barrett yells, and as his men recover and begin firing and reloading their muzzle-loaders, he moves out in front. He empties his six-shot revolver into the trees and pluming blue smoke. More shots echo off the lava cliffs, and I begin to smell the sulfur of black powder. The Union troops advance, fire and smoke exploding from their muskets, but the men are too far behind Barrett. He goes down, spinning in his tracks and clutching his throat. Now the Confederates charge, screaming and firing as the cavalrymen retreat, leaving three dead before mounting their horses and charging away.

Rebel cheers rise among the smoke and dust. The crowd cheers. The Confederates have won. The South rises again. "Resurrection!" the announcer shouts. "The battle is over!" A skirmish that originally lasted perhaps ninety minutes is finished in fifteen.

Bob Pinter stumbles out from among the creosote, slapping dust from his blue uniform. "Little better aim, eh?" he says to one of the Union riders he passes. "Resurrection—thank God! We do it again tomorrow."

I take his picture where he stands among his fans, still talking history. "Most of what I say is true," he says to me as he turns to join the soldiers and they march away.

"I believe it," I say, smiling after him. "I always believe."

- - -

"History," says Thomas Sheridan, "lets Arizona stalk us through its past." I love that. I thought I was chasing this state, but perhaps Arizona is chasing *me*. This place of the Big Peak manifests history's complexities, from the geologic Basin and Range to the cultural American and Native American, even to the personal history of my own past. My young daughter's wonder—even the unmarked soldier's bones on which we tread—remind me that I can't possess anything. I can't chase anything. This wild landscape doesn't belong to us. We belong to it. And if we give it the chance, if we just stop clutching at it, it will show us something astounding.

A Taste of History

TUMACÁCORI MISSION
AND THE SANTA CRUZ CHILI & SPICE COMPANY

ELEVATION: 3,955 FEET | FOUNDED: 1691 | POPULATION: 569

In the second week of February, I drive 145 miles west to Tumacácori on the Santa Cruz River. Monstrous cottonwoods blush green. A gallery with potential. It's noon, and I have a couple of hours before my book presentation at the Tumacácori National Historical Park, so I pull into the Santa Cruz Chili & Spice Company, the oldest chile-processing operation in Arizona.

Parked cars hold license plates from Oregon and Texas. I step around antique farm implements and enter the gift shop and museum where a wall of nasal-clearing aroma stops me. The essence of chile soaks through my skin; I taste it on my tongue. A crowd of people fills the spice room. The walls hold hundreds of spices and chile-born concoctions in jars. I slip into the museum room where a table displays bowls of salsas to taste. I sample a rainbow of salsas while overhead a red-tailed hawk spreads its wings, beak agape, talons extended. The stuffed bird swings from wires among other similarly suspended relics: branding irons, rusted boot spurs, sprung coyote leg traps, horse bridles with reins as stiff and brittle as beef jerky.

Among old portraits and news clippings about Tom Mix, Ken Maynard, Esther Muir, two framed articles stand out: "Juliet Kibbey England Dies: Rancher, Historian, Businesswoman" and "Gene England, Rider, Flier, Dies." Gene and Judy England founded the spice company in 1943, a year after they were married. Judy was born in Sonora, Mexico, in a two-story fortress that stood on a fifty-thousand-acre ranch. She was the daughter of a prominent ranching family—her great-great-grandfather manufactured the famous McClellan saddle used by the U.S. cavalry.

Gene first came to Arizona in 1910 as a child. He learned wrangling and trick riding, performed movie stunts for Hollywood, and flew planes out of a Tucson airstrip that is now the rodeo grounds. When he came here to the Santa Cruz valley, he traded his airplane and a pair of pearl-handled pistols for a down payment on the Rock Corral Ranch in the Tumacácori Mountains. He'd recently met and fallen in love with Judy.

These days, the couple's daughter and son-in-law, Jean and Bill Neubauer, run the operation and ranch, processing two hundred thousand pounds of fresh chiles in a season. Karen and I shop here specifically for Chimayo chile powder for a vegetarian chili recipe, stocking up on the dried pods of chile negro, chile rojo, and poblano, essential for our slow-cooked barbacoa.

Chile is the archetypal southwestern flavor. If Arizona had a state question like New Mexico, it would be: Hot or mild? Eaten on a one-hundred-degree day, chiles are infinitely more refreshing than a tall glass of iced tea. Try it if you don't believe me. I prefer mine blistering. Karen likes them for flavor only. When we make a smoking skillet of fajitas, she'll pick out the beef while I'll fold the peppers and onions into a warm tortilla. We have a perfect marriage.

Santa Cruz Chili & Spice labels their chiles "mild," "medium," and "hot." This seems insufficient considering the thousands of varieties of peppers worldwide. There's certainly quite a bit of difference between a bell pepper and a "mild" jalapeño. In 1912, a chemist named Wilbur Scoville developed a way to measure the heat level. He used a panel of tasters who sipped ground peppers in a sugar solution in increasingly diluted concentrations until their mouths no longer felt the fire. A "Scoville Heat Unit" (SHU) is a number based on how much a pepper needs to be diluted to be burnless. For example, a pimento might rate one hundred SHUs while the Trinidad Moruga Scorpion, one of the fiercest peppers on the planet, can reach up to two million SHUs.

I've played with the idea of creating a pepper pain index based on Scoville but a bit more exponential, where each category raises the pain by a factor of ten: Category 0 (say bell pepper) to Category 6 (undiluted capsaicin). Capsaicin is the chemical in chiles that binds to nerve receptors and causes the burning sensation. Most peppers fall between Categories 1 and 5. A C5 (like the infamous ghost pepper) is one hundred thousand times as excruciating as a C1 (paprika).

I've discovered after tasting a few that numbers don't tell us anything about chile potency. Words are exponentially better. Especially as warning. Because if you make the brilliant mistake of eating a Moruga Scorpion, you will experience an incapacitating, on-your-knees-running-in-circles-leaking-from-every-orifice kind of pain. You will beg for your mommy's milk. You will think nothing of clearing your sinuses with an entire can of Cheez Whiz. Forced to choose, opt for a live scorpion.

"Nowhere are the mystery, pain, and pleasure more mixed than in those pungent peppers that Columbus took back from the Americas," writes Gary Nabhan in *Why Some Like It Hot*. He goes on to say that they can make human relationships . . . or break them. The difference, I suppose, may depend on the nature of the two—sweet and spicy or biting and blistering—relationships and peppers being so much alike.

With the smolder of some Category 3 salsas on my lips, I cross the street to Tumacácori National Historical Park to meet Vicki Wolfe, park ranger. She offers to take me on a tour of the mission grounds. "We have some archaeological work going on now," she tells me. "They're uncovering part of the mission garden wall."

Vicki introduces me to Jeremy Moss, the lead archaeologist on the project. He recently found some pottery he suspects is contemporary with the Franciscan mission expansion here. "The sherd is a Tonala Polychrome," Jeremy tells me, "which was made in Central Mexico from 1770 to 1820 and supports the date range for construction of the garden wall."

I know a bit about the Tumacácori mission, how the arrival of Father Eusebio Francisco Kino in 1691 at the brush ramadas of an O'odham village led to modest adobe and wood structures—a church and priest quarters—with orchards and gardens until the Jesuit expulsion in 1767. Then, about 1800, a blue-eyed Franciscan named Narciso Gutiérrez spent the next twenty years replacing the Jesuit church with a more ambitious design. A magnificent red-walled, white-domed house of God rose high out of the mesquite trees, a church rivaled only by the one at San Xavier forty miles to the north. It was never finished, but what remains today hints at the glory of the Franciscan church at San José de Tumacácori. If San Xavier is the soul of Arizona, the mission at Tumacácori contains its spirit.

Jeremy is pleasant, young—too young for archaeology, I think. His enthusiasm is infectious. I'm ready to join him, knee-deep in his excavations, but Vicki wants to show me the reconstruction of the historic Spanish-era orchard. "We are planting fruit trees from stocks introduced in the region by Jesuit missionaries in the seventeenth and early eighteenth centuries," she explains. "Apple, pomegranate, fig, quince, pear, and others, as identified by the Kino Heritage Fruit Trees Project, which is working to reestablish the original orchard." The trees are small, but I imagine twenty years from now walking along shaded paths beneath spreading branches of ripening fruit.

I smell mesquite smoke on our way back to the visitor center. Under a brush ramada, an O'odham couple prepares tortillas over an open fire. They offer us one, and I accept the warm package, wrapped around a spoonful of spicy chili and beans. "Perfect," I say with a full mouth. "I've already eaten too many," Vicki says. She's all smiles. A park ranger who loves her work. She started out as a camp fire girl in Escalante, Utah, and never looked back. She's worked for the Park Service for thirty years, in places like Death Valley, Arches, and Big Bend. Tumacácori is her latest adventure; she and her husband have lived here for three years.

"Where's the best place to eat?" I ask, my appetite stirred by the tortillas and beans.

"We like the Tumacácori Restaurant."

I tell her I'm on a quest for chimichangas. "The next state food," I say. "El Charro, the oldest Mexican restaurant in the country, claims to have invented it."

I cross the street again. "I'm searching for the best chimichanga in Arizona," I announce as I enter the Tumacácori Restaurant.

"I can help you with that," Robert Jr. says through the window to the kitchen. "The brisket is really good. I only use brisket."

While he prepares my order, we talk chimichanga history. I mention that botanist and chimi expert Tom Van Devender says Chinese workers probably brought "chivichangas" to Sonora in the early 1900s, and that he believes they have the same roots as egg rolls. "I remember my first chimichanga when I was a kid growing up in Tucson in the late 1960s and early '70s," I say. "It was huge, carne seca, and covered with melted cheese and guacamole."

"Tell me where—I know all the Mexican restaurants in Tucson."

"Pancho's, on Speedway, I think. There was a giant burning candle—like the world's largest. It was family-owned, but it's been gone for years."

"Oh, yeah, Pancho's on Grant Road," he corrects me. "I miss that place."

Maria brings salsa and chips, and asks what I'd like to drink. When I say Corona, her husband, Robert Sr., rises to his feet and slow-steps to fetch the beer from the cooler.

"How long have you two been together?" I ask the elder Robert.

"Married thirty years," he says.

"How many?" Maria interjects from the kitchen. "Fifty!"

The two have been running the Tumacácori Restaurant for half their married lives. Robert is ninety and still retains a full head of white hair. He was born in Mexico, where his dad worked on the railroad during the Depression. He met Maria in Nogales.

"Where my wife is from," Robert says, pointing to the photographs and paintings of Grecian seaports and ruins on the walls.

Ah, I think. *Maria is the goddess behind the amazing lemon-and-herb Athenian chicken!*

On the opposite wall hangs a framed flag, a red circle on a white field with handwritten Japanese characters in black. It's a World War II Hinomaru flag, the kind given to Japanese soldiers before deployment and signed by family and friends for good fortune.

"What about that one?" I point.

"I got that in the jungles of Burma when I was nineteen." He walks over to the wall and removes a framed certificate and carries it to me.

"World War II Honoree," I read aloud. "Robert Otto Ziegler." He's an army veteran.

"Not too many of us left," he says.

My chimichanga arrives, covered with crisp lettuce and tomato, Spanish rice and refried beans on the side. I cut into it with the edge of my fork. The brisket falls apart and spills out of the flaky tortilla along with fresh chopped green chiles. Steam rises and I inhale the tang of backyard summer cilantro. It is the best chimichanga since my childhood. History I can taste.

This is an inadequate statement. Karen is right; I need a more quantitative way to judge my chimichangas. If I can create a pain index for chiles, certainly I can make up something for chimichangas. A chimichanga pleasure index?

Let's see . . . a zero to five scale, with zero being a numb state of food consciousness. I think about all the chimis I've ever eaten and mentally lower my voice: *You are barely aware that you are chewing. The flat texture and tastelessness in your mouth may put you to sleep facedown in the refried beans.* Okay. . . . Category 1: Grease and ash with a hint of lard. To Category 5: Orgasmic. After one bite, people will ask if you want to be alone with your meal. I'll call it the Lamberton Chimichanga Index.

At the Foot of Black Mountain

TUCSON

ELEVATION: 2,389 FEET | FOUNDED: 1775 | POPULATION: 520,116

I could spend the entire year visiting places like Old Tucson Studios, Pima Air & Space Museum, Tucson Botanical Gardens, Arizona Inn, El Casino Ballroom, and Rogue Theatre and never leave the Old Pueblo. Or maybe start with the newly re-created eighteenth-century Presidio San Agustín del Tucson, the birthplace of the city, and work forward to the popular annual festival Tucson Meet Yourself. How do you deal with a destination as expansive and varied as Tucson?

Scroll down on the *Wikipedia* entry for Tucson to the "Arts and Culture" section and you'll see that the first listing is the Tucson Gem and Mineral Show. I'm would never say that this crazy, instant-tent-city, mega-rock-shopping-extravaganza is what primarily defines Tucson, but during the second week in February, it feels like all the world is focused on downtown, plugging up motels and restaurants, parking lots and streets. It is the biggest gem show in the United States. If Tucson had a voice this time of year, it wouldn't be the moaning of a Gambel's quail from some backyard seed block. It would be the murmur of the money-changers inside and around the Tucson Community Center.

Like many locals, we avoid the place. (Later, I learn that a uniformed officer guarded a glass case holding the state firearm: Wyatt Earp's 1872 Colt .45 Single Action Army revolver, and I'd missed it entirely.) I decide that my mission for the centennial weekend should center on Arizona's symbols. Now I have rocks on my mind, especially the state gemstone and fossil. And since the University of Arizona's Flandrau Science Center and Planetarium is featuring "The Minerals that Made the State," Karen and I head for campus.

At the entrance to Flandrau, displays of minerals by county crowd the room. A map depicts mines throughout the state: silver mines of Globe,

Superior, and Tombstone; copper mines of Morenci and Bisbee. An eight-foot monstrosity of shining native copper from Ajo rises from the floor. Copper, I learn, built towns and railroads and fortunes more than any other resource and "pushed Arizona to become the forty-eighth state, the last of the contiguous states." In an ancient wooden red-velvet-lined box, I stare at a chunk of history from Bisbee: the first copper smelted by George Warren in 1877. The metal is crude, misshapen. It hardly seems destined to become one of Arizona's five Cs of economic power.

We walk down a flight of stairs through a mural of Grand Canyon, descending in a few steps through two billion years of geologic history, and walk directly into two massive copper "pigs" (210 and 295 pounds, respectively) stamped "C * Q." They're from Bisbee's Copper Queen Mine. "Probably from 1904 or earlier," says Mark Candee, the assistant curator, who is on hand to answer questions about the 120-year-old UA Mineral Museum. "The weights must be close—I've tried to move them."

Mark invites us to look around at the more than two thousand specimens on display—Arizona's mining artifacts, minerals, and meteorites. Karen looks over nuggets of turquoise. I check out the collection of Arizona meteorites—my idea of a rock that represents our state. Most are iron chondrites, dark stones that look like doll eyes. They could be any metallic rock I might find in my backyard. "Samples of asteroids orbiting the sun," the card reads. A replica of the Carleton Meteorite stands in a corner. The chondrite was used as an anvil by a Tucson blacksmith named Ramón Pacheco, who found it in the mountains south of town and dragged it to his shop sometime around 1850. In 1862, fresh from his "victory" at the Battle of Picacho Pass, Colonel James Carleton "liberated" it and sent it to San Francisco as a memorial of his 1st California Volunteer Cavalry march into Arizona to free us of the rebel forces.

"It has the same fingerprint as the Tucson Ring," Mark says, referring to the large doughnut-shaped meteorite I passed upstairs, a replica of the original 1,400-pound meteorite now located at the Smithsonian Institution.

"I've heard both were discovered in Box Canyon and brought to Tucson but ended up at the Smithsonian. Why do we only have replicas? I propose we make the Tucson Ring Arizona's official state rock, rename the

Carleton for Pacheco, and demand their return!"

Mark laughs. He thinks I'm joking.

From the Flandrau, we walk across campus to Centennial Hall, arriving in time for a celebration called "Arizona 100: Through the Lens of Time." Karen and I find our seats in the balcony and look over the program, checking off the welcome by Tucson mayor Jonathan Rothschild; the poetry readings and historical notes; the UA dance ensemble, choirs, and orchestra; and there, in the center of the lineup, is Richard Shelton's name.

"Did you know he was going to be here?" Karen asks me.

"No. He said nothing to me."

"I hope someone got him dressed and drove him."

"He's probably still in his pajamas."

There's a long pause when he's due to present. The stage remains empty and I think, *He's not going to show.* . . . And then he appears. "Good afternoon," he begins. "It still is afternoon, isn't it? My name is Richard Shelton, and I am a has-been regents' professor of English and creative writing." He introduces his poem "Requiem for Sonora" by relating some of its publishing history and mentioning that it was produced as a ballet by a company in Phoenix. "I didn't think it was totally successful," he adds, "because the poem takes place in the dark. It was written during a period in the seventies and eighties when I wandered in the desert at night. During that time, I wrote a lot of nocturnal poems, and I was never attacked by an animal—a snake or anything like that—but I *was* attacked by dozens and dozens of plants. I found out that the plants in the Sonoran Desert . . . are territorial—and they protect their territory."

I'm immediately reminded of another story he told me recently, about how he took C. Day-Lewis, poet laureate of the United Kingdom and father of the actor Daniel Day-Lewis, on his first venture into the desert. "He reached out to touch a cholla cactus," Dick said, "and before I could stop him, it grabbed on to his hand. I tried to pull it off and both of us were stuck. Ever since then, I've had an attachment to C. Day-Lewis."

He pauses to slip on his glasses, then reads: "Requiem for Sonora. One. A small child of a wind / stumbles toward me down the arroyo / lost and carrying no light / tearing its sleeves / on thorns of the paloverde. . . ."

Afterward, Karen and I meet up with Dick and his wife Lois outside on the front steps. "Good to see you out of your pajamas," I tease. The two have had an important influence on the Tucson community since their arrival here in 1960. While Dick inspired young minds at the university with the beauty of language, Lois Shelton guided the nascent University of Arizona Poetry Center. Then, the center was only a modest cottage near campus, which Ruth Walgreen Stephan gave to the community with her collection of poetry books. The writer and philanthropist wanted to create a place to encourage people to "encounter poetry without intermediaries." Robert Frost read at its dedication on November 17, 1960.

Lois directed the Poetry Center for two decades, expanding on the original library (today, it houses one of the three largest poetry collections in the United States) and organizing a reading series with hundreds of writers, including poet laureates like William Stafford, Maxine Kumin, W. S. Merwin, and Lucille Clifton. Long after her efforts were done as director, you could still find her at the back of an audience, working her knitting and quietly listening. I once asked her if she also attended all her husband's presentations. "No," she said. "I've heard him read."

Lois proposed the home of the collection where it now resides: a beautiful architectural poem named for arts advocate, Helen S. Schaefer. But for me, it is Lois who will always be Tucson's Poetry Center.

In the evening, Karen and I drive to downtown Tucson for 2nd Saturday. People crowd the streets. The smell of roasted meats, kettle corn, and barbecue hangs in the air with the sound of rock 'n' roll. We check in with our much-loved Bisbee band, The Border Crossers, arriving just in time to hear Dylan Charles sing their Lavender Pit song.

Border crossers! Bisbee only *seems* to be across the line. Are you still a border crosser if only the border does the crossing? Some people have a long history at jumping rope with the current one. Just around the corner from here, stand the dark adobe walls of the place of Tucson's birth: Presidio San Agustín del Tucson. In 1775, the Irish mercenary Colonel Hugo O'Conor established the Spanish presidio here, on the east bank of the Santa Cruz River where it flowed in the shadow of *stjukshon*—the O'odham word for "at the foot of black" (mountain)—which we know today as Sentinel Peak or "A" Mountain. Thus, Tucson's birthday is August 20, 1775. But I would argue for an earlier date: September 27, 1698, the day Father Kino climbed Sentinel Peak and named the valley before him "San Cosmé del Stjukshon." Earlier today at the Centennial Hall celebration, Tohono O'odham poet Ofelia Zepeda spoke about this, trouncing both UA president Eugene G. Sander and Mayor Rothschild. Sander had boasted about the university being established in 1885; Rothschild then gloated about how Tucson was born more than a hundred years earlier. After she stepped to the podium, Ofelia began: "I couldn't help but overhear our first two dignitaries and their claims to history. . . ." The audience erupted with laughter and applause. "I don't think I need to say any more about that. As a language teacher," she continued, "I do want to tell you that Tucson is *stjukshon*. It is an O'odham word."

Tucson was founded long before the white guys got here with their astrolabes and compasses to draw lines on parchment. Now we have steel walls and stadium lights. In space, the astronauts tell us, no one can see the borders. Homeland Security is working to correct that.

Four weeks later, Karen and I return to the Old Pueblo for the Fourth Annual Tucson Festival of Books. The event, which draws book lovers to the University of Arizona campus the second weekend of every March, seems a fitting way to complete my Tucson destination. I've been involved with the festival since its inauguration when Richard Shelton and I read "poetry" to a crowd in the South Ballroom of the Student Union. Today, I'm moderating, "All Roads Lead to Arizona," with panelists Jim Kristofic, Alberto Ríos, and Richard Shelton.

By the time I round up the panelists at the Student Union and get them over to our venue, the classroom is packed—every seat filled—and the volunteer at the door says we'll have to choose another session.

"It's okay," I say. "Our seats are in the front."

As I introduce the three authors to the audience, Karen walks down to our table and sets a tub of capirotada in front of Tito. I had baked it for him last night. He pulls off the lid and digs right in. "First question, Alberto," I say into the microphone. "Your memoir, *Capirotada*, about growing up on the border in Nogales, takes its name from Mexican bread pudding. What is capirotada, and did you bring enough for everyone?"

I have three goals for the panel: to get the authors talking not so much about their *books* but about the *craft* of writing them, to make the authors' interactions lively and interesting, and to keep it funny. When I turn to Jim, who's the youngest, I say: "Your book, *Navajos Wear Nikes*, begins with a road trip your mom took from Pittsburgh to the Navajo reservation when you finished first grade. Your roads really *did* lead to Arizona. Tell us how you came to write about growing up as a white boy among the Navajo and what you learned by getting beat up every day."

Dick is easy, since we've had such a long history together: "Your memoir concerns a trip you take from Tucson to Bisbee," I say, "which I know only takes an hour and a half because I drive it twice a week. How did you manage to get 320 pages?—I know your wife Lois told you if you didn't hurry up and finish the book, you'd have to call it *Going Back to Benson!*"

On the Banks of the San Pedro

SAN PEDRO HOUSE AND MURRAY SPRINGS

ELEVATION: 4,080 FEET | FOUNDED: 1930 | POPULATION: 0

I drive thirteen miles west from Bisbee to the cottonwood-jammed San Pedro River, turning south after the bridge and following the dirt road to the San Pedro House. A sharp-shinned hawk perches in a Swiss Family Robinson–style cottonwood, eyeing a bright yellow cloud of lesser goldfinches feeding at a thistle sock. I enter the old farmhouse through the screened-in front porch and step across its creaking wood floors to meet Laura Mackin, the bookstore manager and one of the volunteers for the nonprofit Friends of the San Pedro River.

"Yes, the Fosters are still alive," she tells me when I ask about the people who originally lived here, in what they called the Wolf Place. "They have annual reunions." Laura takes me into one of the rooms and shows me several binders filled with photographs and news clippings.

One clipping dated 1954 says that one of the Foster children, Bailey (14), a Tombstone High School freshman, "is earning fame discovering skeletons of prehistoric monsters. . . ." The fossil was the third the boy had found in the area, what his sister Betty would later describe as "mastodons." One of the bones had spear points sticking out of it.

In her 2007 book, *The Five Fosters: Cowboys, Ranch Life, and Growing Up*, Betty Foster Escapule tells about a childhood at the "cow camp." There was no electricity, but there was swimming in stock tanks, shooting blackbirds and rabbits for dinner, learning beg-your-pardon cowboy manners along with the white-tablecloth etiquette of Emily Post. Her brother, she writes, "didn't stay on the road like the rest of us," and he was always finding half-buried pottery and arrowheads. Then one day he came home with a story of finding a large bone, larger than anything he'd ever seen. "It was the tusk of a mastodon lying in a shallow gully northwest of the house." *Northwest!* My proximity alert sounds. Today, the place is called Murray Springs. Arizona has a dozen mammoth kill sites, all in this area, but Murray Springs is one of the most significant ever found. Ten minutes from my home.

Sometime in the mid-1950s, the Fosters left the Wolf Place. In 1988, the homestead became part of the San Pedro Riparian National Conservation Area (SPRNCA) when Congress set aside forty miles of the river corridor between our border with Mexico and the town of St. David. From ancient mammoth hunters at Murray Springs and the first Spanish settlers at Terrenate to the late-coming ranchers and miners at Fairbank and Charleston, the river intersects long nodes of history. And among these nodes stretches habitat for an amazing array of wildlife, from black bears and beaver to more than 350 kinds of birds, more animal species, in fact, than the entire Yellowstone National Park.

These days, the San Pedro House/Wolf Place is a destination for thousands of bird watchers and other nature enthusiasts. Although the barns and corrals are long gone, the Friends of the San Pedro River have restored the old ranch house, and volunteers run it as a gift shop and bookstore. More than five miles of trails link visitors to the cottonwood gallery of the river with its ponds and oxbows and adjacent abandoned fields. On any given day, you can find volunteers leading walks for groups of short-pantsed, knock-kneed, binocular-clad bird lovers.

In March, I return to the San Pedro House with my daughter Melissa. We're on a mission—not to chase the most recent sighting of a green kingfisher or hairy-chested nutscratcher but to locate signs of Pleistocene megafauna. From the San Pedro House, we head northwest, unwinding the present landscape of obnoxious tarbush and whitethorn by thirteen thousand years.

During the Pleistocene Ice Age, a cooler, wetter climate encouraged vast tracts of grassland dotted with oak, juniper, and pine, its seeps and springs crowded with sycamore and ash. Here, mammoths stood knee-deep in boggy pools while giant ground sloths stripped leaves from trees not already left bare. Fanged cats and dire wolves competed for megafauna flesh, along with some new arrivals—two-legged hunters carrying obsidian-tipped spears.

Archaeologists call them Clovis people, named for a type of fluted spear point first discovered in the 1930s near Clovis, New Mexico. Since then, Clovis sites have been uncovered all over the Americas: North, Central, and South.

In 1966, two University of Arizona archaeologists, C. Vance Haynes and Peter Mehringer, were speculating about the possible existence of a Clovis site near Murray Springs, based on an earlier discovery of the nearby Lehner Mammoth-Kill Site. I wonder if they'd also heard reports by locals like Bailey Foster? In late March, on what Haynes describes as a "fine, sunny, spring day . . . studying alluvial deposits," the two were exploring upstream in an arroyo called Curry Draw when they noticed large animal bones sticking out of the sheer-sided gully. "To use an expression of the late John Lance," Haynes later writes, quoting his doctoral adviser, "the deposits were 'chucky jam full' of bones." What they found turned out to be astounding.

During their excavations from 1967 to 1971, the archaeologists uncovered four Columbian mammoths (a young adult, two full-grown cows, and a mature bull), eleven extinct species of bison, the bones of camels and horses, and the jaw of a dire wolf. And among these remains, something surprising. A kind of storybook in the dirt, the stratified layers like pages turning. Thousands of chert flakes, mostly concentrated in five small locations, told of human activity—knapping areas. And more: projectile points, chert cutting tools, quartzite and granite cobble hammers, obsidian nodules (blanks for making small tools?), and worked bone tools, including what Haynes calls a "mammoth bone shaft straightener"— something unheard of on this continent. It all spelled out a human drama right on this spot in the San Pedro Valley.

I imagine it was similar to a scene that could unfold presently on the African savanna. A severe dry season shrinks the rivers and streams, and the grasses turn to dust. A few mud holes remain, and the smell of them draws the large herbivores—not wildebeests and elephants but bison and camels and mammoths. And where the prey gathers, so do the predators. Giant cats and dire wolves circle the perimeter, waiting for an opportunity.

This is a situation the Clovis hunters would take advantage of.

The hunters were familiar with the place. Previously, they'd camped here for many days while curing the hides and meat from a small herd of bison they'd killed. Before that, there was an unlucky mammoth, a female that had succumbed to quicksand and wolves, an easy prize for the hunters. Now, however, they have been stalking a giant tusker, this one an old lone male recently outcast from the herd by a younger rival, another certain kill, if not as easy. . . .

Murray Springs tells one of the most extensive and detailed stories of hunting, butchering, tool making, and campfires of perhaps the first colonists of North America, the first humans to arrive in what is now Arizona: the mammoth hunters.

Melissa and I take the loop trail, stopping to read about life in the Pleistocene and discoveries made by Haynes and Mehringer, one of them the spear straightener. It looks like a bone magnifying lens, absent of glass and broken beneath the foot of a seven-ton mammoth.

Then we drop into the deeply eroded Curry Draw and trace the famous "black mat," a narrow seam that overlies the Clovis stratum. The layer splits the chocolate walls at eye level. This is where it happened not so long ago. "In the backwash of Fennario," Jerry Garcia's heartfelt vocals ring in my head, "the black and bloody mire / the Dire Wolf collects his dues, while the boys sing 'round the fire." The place evokes the Grateful Dead tune.

Melissa reaches out to touch the charcoal-colored layer, and I recall how she recently met Jerry Garcia's widow, filmmaker Deborah Koons Garcia. The two of them burned popcorn and set off the fire alarms during a screening of Deborah's latest film at Iowa State University, clearing the theater. But she's not thinking about that. I'm sure she's thinking: *How cool to see a mammoth tusk protruding from the ground! Mammoth! The state fossil of Nebraska!*

Iowa, where Melissa is living while studying for her master's degree, doesn't have a state fossil. They don't even have a state mineral, but if they did, it would probably be potash or saltpeter. Iowa has the shortest list of state symbols, which could be a reflection of its monoculture culture. Let's see—the cornflower (state flower), the golden cornfinch (bird), the gilded unicorn (mammal), and the longleaf cornstalk (tree).

Melissa suffers being away from the place of her birth. She often adds "Tucson native" to her publication bylines. She writes how she can't read the landscape, can't feel the bedrock beneath her feet. "For an hour's drive in any direction," she says in her essay, "Tracing the Creek Home," "this is the wildest country I could find—a patch of woodland thick with mosquitoes. I came looking for water. Heavy rains swept through central Iowa last week, and I've always ventured outside in the wake of storms to search for the signs of water's passage. But the heft and sway of Bluff Creek feels like an illusion. All gleam and glint, nothing to hold me here."

Now, deep in the water-ravaged Curry Draw, we plant our feet on ancient earth recently exposed. The words of our friend Alison Deming— it was Alison who first brought me to this place, to walk this very same drainage—come to mind: "In the desert, one finds the way by tracing the aftermath of water."

In grade school, Melissa drew her desert rivers with a brown crayon. "These arroyos," she says, "hunkered between mesquite trees and catclaw acacia, offered safe routes for jackrabbits and coyotes. . . . I called them rivers and never questioned the label. Centered within their borders, I knew I could always follow them home."

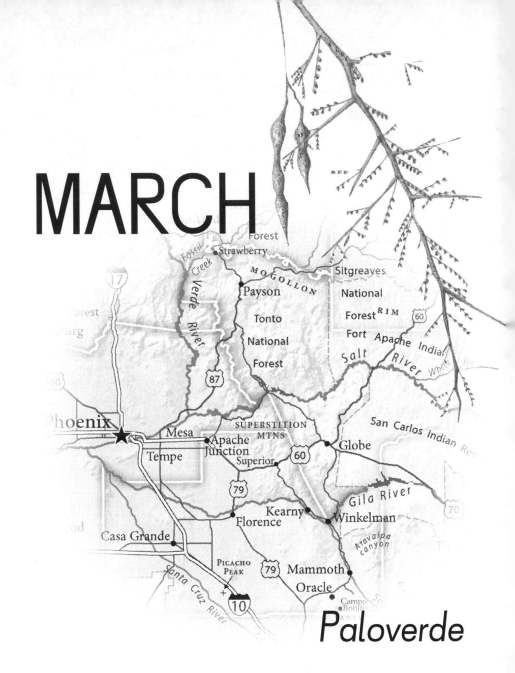

MARCH

Paloverde

POINTS OF INTEREST TO DATE: 27 | TOTAL MILES: 1,515

High Jinks in the High Desert

CAMPO BONITO AND HIGH JINKS

ELEVATION: 4,803 FEET | FOUNDED: 1879 | POPULATION: 2

Jerry Marzinsky and I drive north on Highway 77, heading for the town of Oracle with a pair of metal detectors in the trunk and gold nuggets on the brain. We push through the traffic clots of Oro Valley, then Catalina and Rancho Vistoso, some of the oldest and newest communities hugging the swelling undulations of the desert bajada under the western shins of the Santa Catalina Mountains. "My old stomping grounds," I tell Jerry. "I grew up here in the late sixties and early seventies, hiking the whole range from Pusch Ridge to Romero Canyon to the Cañada del Oro when all this was still ungated wild country. Back then, you might actually see *live* bighorn sheep in what is now La Reserve. Soon, we may again."

Jerry tells me that in the seventies he was working at Central State Hospital in Georgia. "Right out of college, it was an exciting time for me. Everywhere in the hospital's red-bricked psychiatric units were living, breathing examples of virtually every form of psychopathology known to man, and I would be free to explore them all. And not all of them were patients."

"Like the naked guy you almost ran over," I say, recalling his earlier story.

He mentions a psychiatrist who fancied himself a modern-day Sigmund Freud, complete with beard and pipe. "All the staff thought he was weird. But he became a laughingstock after a patient he was treating crept past three attendant stations to deliver a personal communiqué. One night, the patient broke into Sigmund's office, climbed up onto the desk, positioned himself square in the middle, and left a present—which he then sculpted into the perfect shape of a pipe."

Jerry says the patient escaped the hospital and was never seen again. But what he left behind was a masterpiece.

Past Oracle Junction is a sign for Biosphere 2, the tremendously expensive masterpiece in self-sustaining artificial habitats—the kind of closed ecosystem we might build to survive on Mars. Most people probably remember it as the "White Elephant in the Desert," a two-hundred-million-dollar glass jar of house plants overrun by ants.

Under its original design, Biosphere 2 was a complex integrated facility the size of two and a half football fields with five distinct biomes—a coral reef ocean and coastal fog desert, a mangrove wetland, a rainforest, and a grassland savannah—with living quarters and a farm, all connected and enclosed in an "airtight envelope," the largest of its kind ever created.

It was the brainchild of ecologist and engineer John P. Allen and financed primarily by Texas businessman and philanthropist Ed Bass. Their company, Space Biospheres Ventures, located the site here in the Sonoran Desert outside of the town of Oracle and began construction in 1986.

Five years later, and after months of tweaking the systems, the first mission crew of four men and four women entered Biosphere 2 and closed the airlock doors behind them. For the next two years, the eight "biospherians" were sealed inside. They planted, raised, harvested, and cooked their own food, and recycled their own waste, all while maintaining the structure and caring for the biomes. Energy in the form of sunlight and electricity went in. Information came out.

Later, a second mission began with a crew of seven but ended after six months when disputes within the management of Space Biospheres Ventures resulted in its dissolution.

As for the personality quirkiness of biospherians: Jerry would have a field day. There are only two ways that humans deal with personal relationships and the petri-dish people demonstrated both masterfully. They either wanted to escape from each other or they desired to hook up. The dark spaces and passages (and mattresses) inside the hollow rocks of the desert biome, a place I've crawled around in myself, served them well in both cases.

For a time, Columbia University took over management, refocused the science (like studying the effects of carbon dioxide on plants), and built classrooms and housing for visiting research students. After Columbia, when the property went up for sale, many thought B2 would be dismantled. But then the University of Arizona announced it would use the facility as a laboratory to study climate change. Last July the university took on full ownership.

For all its controversy, the price tag, and the craziness of the biospherians themselves, the original project led to real science and the publication of hundreds of articles in scientific journals. The agricultural system alone was the most productive in farming history, providing enough food for eight people to survive on for two years, despite their weight loss. It also had the best seal ever made. In one year, Biosphere 2 leaked only 10 percent of its oxygen. Compare that to the space shuttle, which leaks 2 percent a day.

"In our view, Biosphere 2 was a tremendous success," says Bill Dempster, director of engineering and designer of its "lungs." "Up until Biosphere 2, there had never been any biosphere in the known universe, except for Earth. All of a sudden everybody was very conversant with the idea of a biosphere, and now it's a common word." There's only one Biosphere 2, they say.

I remember its lungs. While Columbia University was managing B2 and its associated forty-acre campus as a teaching and research facility, plant biologist Dr. Jonathan Titus invited me to speak with his desert ecology students. My visits, which became regular during the Columbia years, always began with a guided tour. I'm still growing guava and succulents in my yard from seeds and pups I collected in B2. Mostly, though, I remember being overwhelmed: overwhelmed by the biology— by the million-gallon ocean with its own beach and tides. And the 3,800 species of plants, most of them in the rainforest, a dripping, moldering, dank-smelling tangle of vines and leaves. Its heat and humidity clung to the lining of my windpipe as we climbed to a perch above sixty-foot trees. And overwhelmed by the engineering—the plumbing alone took more than five miles of copper pipes, which coiled through the innards of the so-called Technosphere.

On my first visit, Jon Titus took me beneath one of the lungs, an echoing cavern of hot, shifting breath. They were the key systems of

Biosphere 2, he explained, keeping the giant greenhouse from blowing out its windows. Because the system was sealed, air pressure inside could become explosive as temperatures rose under the desert sun. At night, an implosion could occur as the air cooled—imagine a daily flexing and fluxing of the structure until the entire thing collapses. So the lungs were built inside a pair of huge airtight geodesic domes, allowing Biosphere 2 to breathe. Its four-ton synthetic rubber membranes attached to sixteen-ton aluminum disks rose and fell with the tides of air. "The membrane material came in on some big trucks," Jon Titus told me the first time he showed me the lungs. "It took like a week to unload and roll it out. Then they noticed a sign that said, *This side down.*"

Jerry and I take the turnoff to Oracle, formerly the camp of Albert Weldon, a Canadian prospector who came here in 1880 with his partners Jimmy Lee and Alex McKay to look for gold and silver. He named his first strike after the ship *The Oracle*, which had brought him safely around Cape Horn. We pass the First Baptist Church, formerly the famous Mountain View Hotel, where a hundred years ago the aging, wig-wearing William F. "Buffalo Bill" Cody would deposit his disapproving wife Lulu during visits to his worthless mines. Soon, on the old Mount Lemmon Road, the American Flag Ranch comes into view. It looks as long-ago abandoned as the church. Thirty years ago, I knew this as "Wheezie's Place"; the century-old house was once a post office serving the tent town of Campo Bonito and the dozens of gold claims between here and Apache Peak. Today, it is Arizona's oldest surviving territorial post office building.

I park the Kia Rio alongside Campo Bonito Road at a familiar drainage. I'm sure this is it. A place where history weighs on me like gravity, holding me to the landscape. Jerry and I slip on day packs and scramble up a hillside studded with stones as large and as treacherous as softballs. Catclaw mimosa shrubs tear at our clothes. At the top of the hill, the grave looks as I remember it, except the weathered cross fashioned from a shovel is gone.

"We called this Pima Joe's grave," I tell Jerry. "One of Cody's miners, killed by claim jumpers, or something like that. Camp stories. I remember coming here when I was twelve."

I pick up a fist of quartz and scratch the sign of a cross into a flat headstone, tracing a shallow depression carved there by countless others. But none recently. "The story goes that Pima Joe's soul will remain trapped in these hills until the stone is carved in two. I hope he doesn't mind the wait." I hand the quartz to Jerry who repeats my slow ritual, turning a pile of rocks into holy ground.

A half mile farther up the road, we hike the deeply rutted track above the Campo Bonito townsite into the oak-splotched hills under Apache Peak, stopping to poke around a bit where mine tunnels spill rocky debris onto the dry slopes. Jerry sweeps the tailings with his metal detector, which beeps for every nail, tin can, and rusted bolt. I could find the same junk without an expensive piece of machinery.

We scale the loose slopes to gain the saddle before dropping into the next canyon and the Southern Belle mine group. One hour and I'm winded. Seated among a jumble of rocks, I scan the distant San Pedro Valley and these corrugated hills. This was the same ridge Gillette Young crossed in 1880 while taking lunch to her husband working a mine under Apache Peak. Near here, the young Virginian wife of John Young rested on an outcrop. While catching her breath, she began picking at a vein of quartz with her hairpin when she noticed a dull yellow color. Gathering up a few pieces in her handkerchief, she carried them to her husband. It was the richest ore he'd ever seen. John Young named the claim—which would produce half a million dollars in gold—for his wife: Southern Belle.

Mine works like the nests of digger wasps dot the hillside. Some are deep holes, slipping into a bottomless darkness; others are rocky scree, spilling out the insides of the mountain. At the bottom of the canyon we find an old homestead, its vanished foundations now only flat terraces outlined by the glaucous blades of irises. Planted irises always point to a past life.

Broken pieces of china litter the ground, green on white. Jerry hands me fragments with a backstamp that says *J & G Meakin / Hanley, England* under a green crest. The china dates from 1890, and it immediately makes me think of Charley Brajevich and John Ivancovich, two prospectors who arrived here in 1879, found a six-and-one-third-ounce gold nugget, and built a three-room cabin in this canyon. I'm not sure if the two gave dinner parties with fancy china, but this certainly could be their home.

In the dry creek below Southern Belle, we search for gold. Recently dug holes mark the workings of other energetic seekers of riches. "We used to bring kids here with gold pans," I tell Jerry. "One boy found a nugget big enough to pay for a second week at camp."

Jerry's metal detector sounds off, and after a few minutes of shoveling, he lifts a dark, copper-brown bullet casing from the sand. "This is really old," he says. "A Sharps, I'll bet." He hands me a mashed casing the size of my little finger. "These .50 calibers used black powder and were first made by the Sharps Rifle Company in the 1870s. And get this. They made them specifically as a buffalo-hunting round—and they don't make them anymore."

"Could it be Cody's?" I ask, amazed.

"Who else? He carried a Sharps. . . ."

I turn it over in my hand, recalling the stories about William Cody and Campo Bonito, how unscrupulous mine promoters duped the aging circus star into squandering his fortune on the promise of worthless mines. He had a fascination with stories of Jesuit treasure and the Mine with the Iron Door. Around 1902, Cody started investing in the Campo Bonito mines. For a decade, activity at the mines seemed robust, but there wasn't much in the way of profits. It seems the miners were keeping busy extracting ore and salting it with high grade samples to inflate values. Cody was pouring money down his mine shafts.

When he first arrived at the Mountain View Hotel in the spring of 1911, Cody must have known something was amiss (especially if he listened to his wife). In the end, he owned more than two hundred worked-out properties. But it was as Cody-the-entertainer that he would be remembered. From High Jinks Ranch, his tent-frame cabin retreat built over his gold mine above Campo Bonito, he amused his friends by passing around a bottle and tossing coins to shoot out of the sky. On at least one occasion, he gave a performance that suited his long white wig and beard. On Christmas Day 1912, he arrived at Campo Bonito dressed as Santa Claus and carrying gifts for the miners' children, turning the day into a holiday festival with sporting events, food, and an evening dance at the camp's dining hall.

Late afternoon, Jerry and I climb back over the saddle and follow the road to Campo Bonito. Then, in a fencerow of manzanita, I hear the ratcheting of a cactus wren. "Our state bird!" I say, pointing to the large chocolate-spotted wren. "My second state symbol this year! I'm on a roll—only ten more to go!"

A few spindly fruit trees and some buried foundations are all that remain of the mining camp. The stone fireplace of the dining hall stands alone, crumbling into itself. History and gravity. I tell Jerry we should visit High Jinks, which I haven't seen since before Dean Prichard's death in 2007. "Dean had it put on the National Register of Historic Places," I say. "I don't know what's going on now, but he was making it a museum to Buffalo Bill."

When I knew him, Dean had been living at High Jinks for more than three decades, having raised five girls. At the time he was producing the national edition of the *Tombstone Epitaph* ("twenty years without missing a deadline"), teaching English composition, running a trail guide service, and riding in Tucson's rodeo parade dressed as Buffalo Bill.

We wrote back and forth about the rich cultural history of the area, about his work cutting a new trail past High Jinks, "a real beauty," connecting Oracle Ridge with the American Flag Ranch as part of the Arizona National Scenic Trail. "You can look down on Biosphere 2 in the distance," he wrote in 1994. "Some sight." Dean also said that Ed Abbey didn't actually live in Oracle ("as locals like to brag") but that he only used the Oracle Post Office as a mail drop to heighten intrigue. What I remember most about our conversations was the time I showed him an old map that said: "Spanish chests and jewels found in caves on Apache Peak by Sisto Castro in 1915."

"Could be," he said. "I once found an old Spanish sword while riding in these hills."

I park next to the rusted hull of a 1911 Case Touring Car, one I recognize from an old photo with William Cody in the passenger seat dressed as

Santa Claus. We're greeted by a blond woman wearing a T-shirt that says *Surly Wench* and Vibram hiking shoes sporting individual toes. Her name is Laurel Wilson, and she and her husband Dan Blanco own the place. "We bought it from Dean Prichard's estate," she says when I mention I knew him. "Two years ago, after hiking here from the American Flag Ranch."

Laurel and Dan had been dating for only six months, after meeting online. "No kidding!" she says. While working as a single mom and teacher, she saved money to open a martial arts retreat center in the town of Marana. Dan had come to the end of both a career and long-term relationship. Both were interested in living in the desert above five thousand feet. After learning that High Jinks was on the market, Dan asked Laurel to hike the Arizona Trail with him. He had a surprise in mind for her. "I topped the hill and saw this place in the distance," she says. "I got a palpable sense of fate coming into play."

They poked around, snuck in, perched themselves at the kitchen table, took in the scenery from the porch, "and got all dreamy." They talked about the amount of work to fix it up, the crazy wiring, ancient plumbing, and questionable water supply, the long dirt road to hospitals and schools and theaters, and the fact that they had no experience with this kind of restoration.

"Yet the magical feeling of the place persisted," Laurel explains. "We visited it again a few times, even camping on the roof one night."

While Dan negotiated the sale, he also proposed to Laurel. A couple of months later, the deal closed and Dan loaded up his backpack with tools, preparing to work on the place through the weekend. He never moved back home. A little later, Laurel did the same, quitting her job in Marana. The couple married one year after that first hike to High Jinks.

"The story since then," Laurel adds, "has been sweat equity, friendly ghosts of happy memories, organic food from our own garden, and wood-fired horse-trough hot tubs under the Milky Way. It's a dream come true."

When Dan joins us, Laurel leads us beneath the high wooden High Jinks sign and through a courtyard toward the house. In one of the stone walls, a bronze plaque in the shape of Arizona says: *Historic Site La Casa del High Jinks*.

Cody's tent-cabin retreat no longer exists. The stone structure was constructed after Cody's death by his foster son, Johnny Baker, with the help of Lewis Way, the husband of one of Cody's Wild West show equestrian jumpers. Lewis and the girl were married at Campo Bonito, and Cody gave the bride away. This High Jinks, with its plush living and dining rooms and its high penthouse, was both a home to the Bakers and Ways and a museum of Buffalo Bill's treasured mementos.

A stone fireplace dominates the sitting room with its dark wood beams and floor-to-ceiling bookshelves. But the relics I remember—those collected by Dean Prichard—are gone, except for a hand-painted stage prop from Cody's Wild West show.

We step through heavy double doors into daylight. Pine vigas protrude from the stone masonry above a terraced patio facing the San Pedro Valley. I twist my neck from a perfect lazuli sky to the jaundiced hills below. The view in every direction is spectacular.

"Yeah," Laurel says. "Amazing, isn't it? It's easy to lose track of time here. We even have a name for it. We call it 'Jinkselation.'"

"Dean wanted some of his ashes scattered here," Dan says when he notices me looking at a simple memorial garden in front of their home.

"But his nether regions," Laurel adds without explanation, "he asked to be scattered on Apache Peak."

That's so much like him, I think. *Leaving behind his jewels in this place.*

Roadside Snake Handlers

ARIZONA-SONORA DESERT MUSEUM

ELEVATION: 2,840 FEET | FOUNDED: 1952

POPULATION: 2,744 ANIMALS AND 500,000 VISITORS/YEAR

Gates Pass. The slow climb through the rock-strewn Tucson Mountains and its twisting blacktop cuts through the hues of wildflowers—gold poppy, blue lupine, bluer phacelia, and the neon pinks of penstemon. Here, for a moment at least, the desert shrugs off its austerity, softens its edges and thorns with leaf and petal.

On this sun-soaked spring day, week ten of the year, I'm headed for the Arizona-Sonora Desert Museum to meet with Stéphane Poulin, curator of herpetology, ichthyology, and invertebrate zoology, who has agreed to show me both the state amphibian and the state reptile. My plan is to learn something about these symbols of Arizona, photograph them, and check them off my list for the year. And what a better place to do this than at our world-famous zoo.

At the entry to the museum, two docents handle a live barn owl and a Harris's hawk, talking to visitors about the merits of the flesh-tearing raptors. When Stéphane arrives, he takes me to his office in the Glenn Charles Olsen Collections Facility. Wildlife art hangs from the walls, wonderfully detailed pencil and watercolor illustrations of salamanders, lizards, and snakes.

"Rachel Ivanyi's work," Stéphane says. "She's the wife of our director, Craig Ivanyi."

"Beautiful," I say. "I remember meeting Craig years ago when he had your job."

Stéphane tells me he first visited the Desert Museum while he was a university student in Montreal, during a desert ecology field trip to the Southwest. He met his wife on a subsequent trip, and after graduation, they both came to Tucson, where Stéphane worked construction for two years while volunteering at the museum.

"Sixteen years ago, I got a position in mammology and eventually in herpetology—reptiles were my focus. Sometimes you have to take a convoluted road to get somewhere."

"And now you work with ridge-nosed rattlesnakes?"

"When I first moved here, they were on my list to see. So, a lot of trips to the Santa Rita and Huachuca Mountains. I saw my first one in 1997. I was with a friend, it was a beautiful day, and I took countless pictures."

Stéphane knows about the snakes. The ridgenose is one of our three small mountain rattlesnakes, he tells me, the others being the twin-spotted and the banded rock rattlesnakes. He talks about their scorpion and lizard diet, and explains the kind of streamside habitat where I might locate one. "They're one of the few types of snakes that have to deal with cold. People see them out among patches of snow on a nice sunny rock."

He has a small group that he keeps for propagation, though the museum doesn't have a program to release the animals into the wild. "But because they are protected," he says, "they are managed through the Arizona Game and Fish Department. So when they get requests from other zoos or people throughout the country, we provide the animals under the guidance of Game and Fish. Right now we have three babies that were born last year, and they're already slated for placement, one or two going to ASU. It's not a big breed-and-release program, but at least it relieves the pressure from having them collected in the wild."

Currently, the museum isn't displaying ridge-nosed rattlesnakes. Since they require a colder environment, personnel are working on an exhibit dedicated to montane reptiles like the three rattlesnakes and maybe one or two nonvenomous snakes.

"What about the Arizona treefrog? Is it on display?"

"We only have one. With amphibians, the issue is that when you let them breed, you end up with several hundred."

I suddenly get an image of a human hand clawing from a frog's mouth in the 1972 nature-horror flick, *Frogs*. Egyptian plague, anyone?

Stéphane takes me to a room where dozens of plastic boxes are secured into a wall of shelves. I see my breath. It's a "hibernation room" for mammals, but the ridge-nosed rattlesnake is here because it likes the cold. He pulls keys and opens locks, sliding out a container and lifting its lid. "This is one of our females, a big one," he says. "They don't get much bigger than this."

The rattlesnake looks at me suspiciously through slitted pupils. "Don't tread on me," she says with her eyes, and I see now why she's our state symbol. Her red-mottled coils could fit comfortably on a china saucer. Stéphane uses a stainless-steel rod with a hook to lift the rattlesnake and place her on the floor. I get down on my knees with my camera. Her forked tongue licks the floor. She's the most gorgeous snake I've ever seen.

"Have you ever been bitten by a rattlesnake?" I ask, as he maneuvers the snake back into her box.

"No," he answers, lifting the lid on the three baby ridgenoses born at the museum. "The museum has rigorous training protocols."

Finally, Stéphane holds the bubble-eyed electric green Arizona treefrog, which climbs to the tips of his outstretched fingers. Cuteness anthropomorphized. He deftly catches the amphibian in his right hand each time it leaps, impatient with my fumbling efforts with the focus.

Later, I buy a ticket and head for the reptiles and invertebrate exhibits, originally the Small Animal Room and the place of my introduction to the Desert Museum. This is where I first came nose-to-glass with all the extraordinary biting and slithering and wart-studded denizens I live with. The darkened room with its walls of lighted, glass-fronted terrarium-dioramas holding toads, snakes, insects, and spiders hasn't changed much. A docent shows a large Sonoran mountain kingsnake to a circle of visitors, who stand in a place where I recall a childhood fascination with a giant motorized model of a sting-slinging scorpion.

First opened in 1952 as part of the Arizona-Sonora Desert Trailside Museum, this building and its creatures were little more than a roadside attraction, except that the museum focused on education and the proper treatment of its living collections. This was the vision of William H. Carr, who in 1944 left New York with "four suitcases and $400" and came to Arizona, where he found among its citizenry "a gross lack of knowledge" about the desert. A high-school dropout, the former nature counselor and eagle scout had a keen mind behind his vision. He surrounded himself with brilliant people, benefactors like the conservationist and *Nature Magazine* editor Arthur Pack (who built and, with his wife Phoebe, lived in Tucson's beautiful Ghost Ranch Lodge) and renowned local naturalists like Joseph Wood Krutch. Krutch's book, *The Desert Year*, first published the same year the museum was founded, remains a favorite classic of nature writing.

Carr's vision focused not only on interpretation of the local plants and animals but reached to embrace the entire region, Arizona *and* Sonora. And it included the ethnology of the native peoples, such as the basket-weaving, saguaro-fruit-harvesting Tohono O'odham, the museum's closest neighbors.

This Sonora connection, as it has from the very beginning, continues to this day, particularly with education and research programs and staff exchanges with universities in Mexico. Direct influences of the Arizona-Sonora Desert Museum, this year celebrating its sixtieth anniversary, have reached even as far as the guano-washed basaltic islands of the Sea of Cortez.

I remember the cage with George L. Mountainlion III (and IV) and the funding drive to get the animals out from behind the chain link and into more natural enclosures. One of the zoo's more innovative designs uses artificial rock, perfected right here in the early seventies by the then-director Merv Larson. The trails always led me to Cat Canyon with its ocelot and jaguarundi nooks. On our first visit together, Karen showed me what she had learned as a child—she yipped like a coyote and got the whole pack responding with their haunting ululations. We ran as the wolves began to howl. . . .

But for me, it was Hal Gras who defined the Desert Museum. His traveling Desert Ark held critters with names like Gregory Peccary and Julius Squeezer. I once plucked quills from his shirt after he hefted a porcupine to his shoulder, fed Quilly Mays a carrot, and admonished my Y-camp counselors and kids to "Leave them alone." Hal let me keep the quills as souvenirs. I grew up with his *Desert Trails* television program, which he hosted for thirty-two years on Channel 13. It was my church service on Sunday mornings, and today I can still hear its loony theme song in my head. My earliest response to living in the desert was to kill things. It was my first religion. Hal Gras taught me a better way to live, to believe.

From the reptiles and invertebrates house, I go against the suggested direction and take the path toward the pollination gardens, intending to check out the hummingbird and walk-in aviaries. Not far along the two miles of trails, I encounter a cactus wren patrolling the bursage and cholla for insects. I pause, amazed at my fortune. The bird is Arizona's first state symbol, chosen in 1931 along with the saguaro flower. Together with today's visit with Stéphane Poulin and the overhead paloverde trees (adopted in 1954), I count four symbols. Cactus wren, paloverde, rattlesnake, treefrog . . . not bad.

I look over the map the museum provided me. I'm sure I could find turquoise and petrified wood in the Earth Sciences Center, one of the greatest mineral collections in the world. I'll see a ringtail in "Life Underground," two-tailed swallowtails at "Butterflies," Apache trout at "Fishes and Amphibians." . . . If I return in May when the saguaro blooms and bump into a dude wearing a bola tie and packing a Colt (despite the warning sign, *No Weapons Allowed on Museum Property*), I could possibly get all twelve state symbols in one day at one place.

But this just won't do. Not only is it too easy, but where do I draw the line? Animals in cages but no taxidermy? Roadkill but no plastic models? Might as well count photographs.

I can accept the cactus wren. I found the state bird last week at Campo Bonito, and even here it's in its natural habitat. A butterfly could be as well, but not the treefrog or ridge-nosed rattlesnake. Those, along with the trout, the petrified wood, even the bola tie, I'll have to find where they live. Three weeks ago at the Flandrau, I located petrified wood and turquoise, but again, these were all on display. Out of reach. Out of touch. I'll accept the Bisbee Blue turquoise; at least I held it in my hand. That puts my count back to two symbols. Only two!

I will have to add to my list of destinations some side-excursions where I might see these symbols in more authentic settings: the Petrified Forest for the state fossil, maybe the Mogollon Rim or the White Mountains for the treefrog, the Huachuca Mountains for the ridgenose. The bola tie and Colt? Who knows? Wherever they are, I'll have to go there.

Natural habitat, yes. But also on destination—no counting ringtails living in my attic. No picking swallowtails out of the grill of my car. I'll also need photographic proof.

Now I've done it. Gone and moved the finish line.

Reshaping the Wild

FOSSIL CREEK

ELEVATION: 6,510 FEET AT HEADWATERS | DAMMED: 1908

In the second week of March, a spring break "Gathering of the Girls" launches me to my farthest destination yet. I pick up Jessica in Tucson, and we head north two hundred miles to the Mogollon Rim, a bench of rocks that stretches across the midsection of the state. We arrive in the town of Strawberry, the navel of Arizona, just after midnight at an A-frame cabin on Strawberry Hill. The others are asleep: Karen, who left Bisbee the day before with middle daughter Kasondra from Albuquerque, and Melissa from Iowa. No boys. Except me.

In the morning, a fire blazes in the wood stove while Karen prepares waffles. The sisters parade. Jessica wears a white bridal veil, a gift Melissa carried with her from Ames. Kasondra sings the wedding march. "Da da, da-da . . ."

"Oh, now you have something borrowed," Melissa says.

The girls have been making plans for Jessica's Big Day in July. It's obvious to me that the morning is a bust. I thought we were going fishing.

At noon the five of us dip tired feet into to the turquoise-clouded waters of Fossil Creek. I note that my daughters have my Roman toes as I check off one of the two streams in Arizona designated as a National Wild and Scenic River. The other is the Verde River, which comes later. From the piñon-and-juniper-smudged mesa, we followed four miles of ankle-twisting trail that dropped more than a thousand feet through layers of history, from the white solidified dunes of the Coconino, the baseplate of the Mogollon Rim, into the red sandstones and shales of Supai, with its lizard tracks from a time before the dinosaurs, to the gray limestone laid down as guck more than 350 million years ago when western America lay under a vast tropical sea.

Go out your door and walk any distance in Arizona and you'll leaf through the pages of an unfinished manuscript—God's work-in-progress for those that choose to read it that way. Touch the rocks and you'll stain your fingers with fresh ink.

Sky-blue western scrub-jays screech among the piñon pine, the dark branches tossed by wind. The breeze cools my sweat-soaked shirt and skin. Fossil Creek purrs over smooth rock, its water the color of stone.

"Travertine," Melissa says. She should know. She's been researching Fossil Creek for a book about water issues in the West, and we've made today's hike so she can see its historic dam, recently dismantled to allow the stream to reshape the wild. It is the first restoration project of this kind in the Southwest and one that marks a change in attitude about conservation of our rivers after a century of damming them. We're not here for the fishing.

In 1903, Iva Tutt realized that the dependable flow of Fossil Creek could be harnessed to supply electrical power to the swelling populace— about 5,500 people—of Phoenix. She contracted for water rights and, like Katharine Hepburn on horseback, led a team of engineers and surveyors into this rugged canyon country. Then she drew up plans and formed the Arizona Power Construction Company. A bold undertaking for any woman at that time, but even more so for one without any formal training.

Melissa says that Iva Tutt became something of a folk legend. Soon the company began constructing a power plant near Fossil Creek's confluence with the Verde River. Work camps sprang up along the forty miles of road where crews drove mule teams hauling concrete mixers on wagon beds. Tutt herself never shied from making the week-long journey during construction.

"Workers were paid two dollars a day," Melissa adds. "Within a year, they completed the dam and a seven-mile system of flumes, tunnels, and steel pipelines to divert Fossil Creek's water to the turbines of the new Childs Generating Plant." Childs, the first hydroelectric power plant in Arizona, operated until 2005 when Arizona Public Service shut it down, removed the dam and its flumes, and allowed a natural flow to return to Fossil Creek.

Soon, we hear the rush of water. A slip of creek rises to fill the canyon bottom, its flow charged by cascades emerging from the ground beneath our feet and spilling into the drainage though thickets of maidenhair fern and monkeyflower. A millennium of rain, soaking mesas and mountainsides and percolating down through the layers of sandstone and limestone and shale finds release in this place. As if all the Colorado Plateau were dissolving and funneling through rock and emptying itself here, and when the water runs out, northern Arizona will be gone.

The Great Flushing of Fossil Springs. Here, water is more than a rumor. More, even, than an invitation. It is a provocation. Melissa says the hot spring gushes enough water to fill an Olympic-size swimming pool

every thirty-four minutes at a year-round temperature of seventy-two degrees. *Hot spring? Maybe for the cold-blooded spikedace and razorback suckers.*

Downstream, the rampage of water jumps in amplitude where the creek tumbles over a travertine fall into a grotto of towel-draped boulders. A trailside sign reads: *Wilderness is a place where natural processes are the primary influences on land and human activity is limited to primitive recreation. It is a place where the imprint of humans is substantially unnoticed.* What I notice right off is the primitive recreation of all the bikini-clad sunbathers.

Melissa and I push past the university students communing with nature on spring break and follow a wide trail down canyon. We're way overdressed anyway. A mile later, we find the first flume—or what's left of the flume, a line of concrete footings spaced along the canyon slopes. Somehow, we've missed the dam.

"I'm starting to think that the waterfall we passed is what's left of the dam. . . ." I tell Melissa. "A human imprint substantially unnoticed?"

"The thought crossed my mind," she says. "That straight, clean edge . . . but it's only been a few years. It looked as if no one had ever touched it."

We hike back to the falls and clamber into the grotto beneath them, sunscreened by the leaves of cottonwood and sycamore. Green ribbons unfurl from the ochre wall of what we're sure is the base of the hundred-year-old masonry dam, stuccoed now behind travertine. Pulsing waves of mist form droplets on each hair of my arms and wet my face. The invitation calls me to dive in and explore the blue pools and caves. The water tastes warm, like schoolhouse chalk.

Melissa pulls from a small cataract a branch sleeved bone-white with rock. Then she lifts a rope of algae imbued with the same fine matrix of grit. The "fossils" of Fossil Creek. The intricate design of active geology—not grotesque but like a dusting of feathers on glass.

In her book, *Mythical River,* Melissa writes that mosses and algae are needed for the formation of travertine. "Permineralization," she calls it, when stone—in this case calcium carbonate from the surrounding limestone—seeps molecule by molecule into living cells. "Some scientists believe that all the earth's canyons and riverbeds, mountain peaks and flat desert floors can form without a single nudge from biology. Fossil Creek defies that. The mineral chinks and glues organic material together, filling in the voids," she says, my poet-geologist in her element. "As leaf matter and algae decay, mineral replaces it, taking on its shapes and patterns. Water smooths the stone, adding layer upon layer until the creek becomes a cascade of deep round pools and natural dams. Even the breath of microbes, invisibly lowering the water's pH, helps shape the body of the river. Life drives the creation of travertine. In turn, travertine cradles life, forming niches and pockets where teeming things gain a foothold and thrive."

We use dams to reshape the wild, but it isn't even a taming. Water is patient. The same water that courses through this desert canyon, runs in our veins, fills our cells. And while the desert passes on the gift, we hoard it behind dams, load reservoirs, erase history. Something borrowed indeed. On loan. At Fossil Creek we got it right. Communion is better than dominion.

When Melissa and I rejoin the girls, they peel oranges and hand us plump wedges one at a time. They complain about the length of our absence. They've eaten the rest of our lunch. On the hike out, my right heel begins throbbing. My "accelerator foot" I've been suffering from lately for all the miles I've driven this year. Most authors get writer's cramp. Then we encounter an official from the Strawberry Fire Department on a rescue mission for a man with a twisted ankle. He asks if we've seen him. His team is bringing in horses.

"There was someone about a mile back," Karen says. "But he didn't seem distressed."

"What about the sign at the trailhead?" I ask him, referring to a posted notice about the difficulty of the hike and the warning to hikers. "It says, 'No Rescue.'"

He says: "It should read, 'No *Free* Rescue.'"

In the evening, I take my vest and fly rod to the East Verde River where it curls beneath the highway above Payson and thread my way down through the willow and alder to its banks. I think about a woman we met earlier who's lived in Strawberry for twenty years. She called it "Small Town, USA," adding, "If you wait long enough, even the sidewalks will close."

I know what she means. I've been escaping the city and coming here my whole life.

Tomorrow, I'll drive the girls over to Kohl's Ranch and look for that deep pool along Tonto Creek where Melissa caught her first fish. That is, if the weather holds—we're getting reports of an escalating Pacific cold front on the way. If not, we'll hole up and make plans to wet some lines in the White Mountains this summer. Kasondra caught her first trout on the East Fork of the Black River. She out-fishes me every time.

Just before dark, I'm ready to quit and rejoin the girls at the cabin. Not even the mosquitoes are biting. But there's always one more cast . . . or two or three. Then, I notice a swirl on the surface near the opposite bank. I shoot my #16 Adams into its center and get my first strike. Fish on! I land a beautiful rainbow and stuff it into my vest. Breakfast for Karen.

We wake to knee-deep snow in the morning. Arizona weather: the first day, we lathered on sunscreen; now we don heavy coats, hats, and gloves. The cars look like twin white hills.

When a break in the weather comes, we dig out and make a run for it. The drive through Strawberry, Pine, and then Payson is excruciatingly slow behind a fortunate snowplow. The blizzard abates as we drop once again into the desert. Paloverde and cactus gleam in washed sunlight. "Look," Melissa says, "the saguaros have snow hats."

Queen of the Wood

MADERA CANYON

ELEVATION: 5,200 FEET | FOUNDED: 1857 | POPULATION: 8 FAMILIES

Where the narrow road begins climbing into the mouth of Madera Canyon, I shift into a lower gear. The Kia Rio slows with the rise in the landscape, entering a mesquite-clad bajada. Two million years of sediment spill from the insides of the Santa Rita Mountains onto the desert in a place that may be the best example of an alluvial fan on the planet.

I crank down the window and soon the tang of wood smoke and barbecue sauce fills the car. *I'm home*, I think. Harvard evolutionary psychologist Nancy Etcoff says our need to be in wilderness is hardwired into us and gives us a sense of well-being when it's met. She says that people seek out streams for beauty, low-canopy trees for shade and protection, and animals to prove the area is habitable. "Building windowless, nature-less, isolated offices full of cubicles ignores what people actually want," she adds. "We ignore our nature at our own peril."

Our nature is to be *in* nature.

My friends Lyn and JoAnne arrived at Madera Canyon a couple days ago for their semiannual stay at Madera Kubo #4. The two have been coming to the streamside cabin under the giant sycamores to escape the East Coast for eight years. I've joined them on many of their adventures in Arizona. Two years ago, we hiked Aravaipa Canyon among zone-tailed hawks and creek-swimming Gila monsters. Before that, we drove the Ruby loop from the wrinkled Tumacácori Highlands to Arivaca. Once we ventured into the Patagonia Mountains to the tiny border hamlet of Lochiel with Richard Shelton as our guide. He got us chased off private property.

"We decided, given the nuttiness of our work, that we needed a warm place for a break," Lyn says about how she discovered Madera Canyon. Being the travel planner, she started looking at Florida and the Everglades.

Then she researched southern Arizona and found Madera Kubo on a bird watcher's website. "We're not bird watchers, but I figured bird watchers would know pretty places to go." She phoned "Pecos," owner Richard Lansky's pet name for his wife, Cora, and asked about accommodations. Lyn's only requirement was that they had to have two sleeping spaces, as one of them had a serious snoring problem.

"Pecos burst out laughing and asked if I'd tried Breathe Right nasal strips," she tells me. "That settled it! But what put the candle on the cake was Richard Shelton. He said the two of you enjoyed hiking in Madera Canyon, and I knew we were sunk. It was Madera or nowhere."

Lyn and JoAnne chose Madera Kubo #4 for their first Arizona experience. Karen and our daughters and I have been coming to the same *kubo* (*kubo* is a Filipino word for *hut*) since Richard and Cora Lansky leased and remodeled the place for their bed and breakfast. They arrived here in 1974 with two small children. The couple had married six years earlier in the Philippines, where Richard was stationed as a radio operator in the navy. After his discharge, he joined the sheriff's departments in Long Beach, then Ajo, and finally Green Valley. "Then one day," Cora says in her strong Filipino accent, "he drove his patrol car up to Madera Canyon."

They decided it was the best place ever to raise kids.

For five years, the family lived in what Cora calls a "lease house." Then, after the U.S. Forest Service told owners to remove their cabins from Forest Service land—there were fifty-five leases in all—they bought a cabin on private land behind where the Kubo Gift Shop sits today.

"It wasn't much, but it had a screened-in porch and it was ours," Cora told me when I asked her about how she and her family came to be one of the eight families left in the canyon. "Then I realized something, and I had to ask Richard: 'Where are we going to sleep?'" Her husband had some ideas that involved very large timber.

I park next to the *kubo* under several scrawny apple trees planted by early settlers. Through the oaks, I see a bus-sized boulder, its face mottled with gray-green and yellow lichen and furred where clusters of hedgehog cacti rise from its seams and cracks as if potted there. The "Big Rock" is a landmark of history, marking the location of Bill Kirkland's 1857 sawmill camp—Arizona Territory's first lumber operation. It's also the place where 152 years ago nearly to the day, Larcena Pennington began her harrowing ordeal after Tonto Apaches kidnapped her and left her for dead in a snowbank fifteen miles away. She crawled through the desert for weeks before being rescued, and lived into her seventies as one of Tucson's pioneering citizens.

Madera Canyon has had several colorful characters over the years. There was Alcario Morales, a Yaqui Indian living at the mouth of the canyon. He gathered acorns, raised vegetables, and made cheeses by milking the local livestock to sell to the miners and lumbermen. He also milked the local agave, supplementing his income with proceeds from his homemade still. Then there was Ben Daniels, a thieving, back-shooting jailbird and professional hitman-turned-lawman, Rough Rider, Yuma Territorial Prison superintendent, U.S. marshal, and Pima County sheriff. He built a mining camp here. Camp Ben Daniels is now the Kent Spring Center. Supposedly he hunted bear in these mountains with Teddy Roosevelt. It was simpler to hide your shady past in the days before Google.

The smell of charcoal smoke leads me around the back of Kubo #4. Lyn and JoAnne are camped on the back porch, laptops aglow, and when they see me, I'm accosted with strange accents and warm hugs. We reminisce about previous visits with Dick Shelton and his wife Lois and our far-flung, whacky trips to obscure places in Arizona.

"Seen any ringtails?" I ask, noticing the bird feeders and bottles of hummingbird nectar—the state mammal's favorite targets to rob at night. I still need to see one.

"I got pictures!" Lyn says. "Honest to gawd! Hanging from the feeder!"

Later, I find Cora at her gift shop, and we relax into chairs on the porch. We talk about our children—she always asks about the girls' school, work, and marriages. We've had such adventures, from terrific canyon-scouring floods to bears climbing in the pyracantha bushes to our very first elegant trogon sighting. I ask about new bird arrivals and she mentions a blue-throated hummingbird. Cora learned birding on her own and recognizes by ear all of the species that visit her feeders. Birds are her second language.

People with binoculars and spotting scopes gather in front of the gift shop. A man wearing khaki shorts asks about the flame-colored tanager, one of his "target" species for his second trip to Madera Canyon. He's from Germany. "Mr. Flame," a rare migrant from Mexico, made his first appearance at Madera Kubo in 2003 and has returned for eight consecutive years. People from all over the world come to glimpse a bird only seen in the United States a few times.

Birders are an exuberant lot. They remind me of Elliott Coues. In 1865, the army surgeon wrote: "My enthusiasm runs so high that sometimes as I stand alone in the wilderness, thousands of miles from home and friends, hot, tired, breathless with pursuit, but holding in my hand and gloating over some new or rare bird, I feel a sort of charitable pity for the rest of the poor world, who are not ornithologists, and have not the chance of pursuing the science in Arizona." To this day, Richard Lansky, not one for crowds, regrets reporting the bird.

"Better than TV," I say, raising my binoculars as a new bird watcher catches my attention.

"Some people cannot live without TV and the telephone," Cora says. "And that's all what they'll do when they come here. You can do that in your own house, I tell them."

The whine of Richard's grinder pierces the canyon. He's working on his 1934 Chevy school bus, converting it to a travel home for a planned road trip. (Cora says to Alaska. Richard says Nova Scotia.) At sixty-five, he's looking forward, if not to retirement, then to a vacation. For thirty-two years, he's been constructing Madera Kubo. His two A-frames look like chalets transplanted from the Swiss Alps. A great barrel-chested man, he built them himself from materials from cabins whose owners had hired him to tear them down. He is a craftsman, a self-taught artist in wood. He built his home from scratch, harvesting, milling, and hauling huge pine timbers out of the Chiricahuas to hoist with cranes into place, the entire structure held together with dovetails and wooden dowels. Richard has never hammered a single nail into his beautiful two-story mountain cabin.

Cora sits on her porch wearing a black sweater and jeans as people come and go. "They'll hand me a debit card for a dollar-fifty candy bar!" she says, silver rings flashing on fingers with perfectly manicured nails. I smile, watching her in her handcrafted pinewood chair among her potted geraniums, the smell of jasmine in the air. Cora fits in these woods as much as the coati and ringtails, the streamside-chirping canyon treefrogs, as much as the flame-colored tanagers, elegant trogons, and magnificent hummingbirds. She is the queen of Madera Canyon.

I head home to Bisbee through Box Canyon, pulling off the winding dirt track near the saddle to catch a glorious sunset over the distant blue ridges of the Baboquivari Mountains. I scan the rugged canyon bottom before me as shadows pull darkness over its rocky grottos. Perfect ringtail country.

From past experiences with Kubo #4, I know that spending a night or two in Madera Canyon will give me the best opportunity to see the state mammal. I could return in the fall and search for the state butterfly as well. The Southwest's largest butterfly also prefers these mid-elevation riparian drainages, where it can drift among the chokecherry on tiger-striped wings.

In the morning, a two-tailed swallowtail comes to the yard and alights on half an orange I've stuck to the backyard fence for the newly arriving tanagers and orioles. I run for my camera and manage two pictures before it disappears into the oak and juniper. "Look," I tell Karen, who's reading a book and swinging under the elderberry tree in her hammock-chair. "The state butterfly! Right in the yard!"

"That was easy," she says, without looking up from the page.

"Not really. I've decided I should only count the state symbols I find on destination."

"This is a destination. It's Bisbee."

"But I've already done Bisbee."

"So? I think you should count it. It's the butterfly, and you've seen it."

"But . . ."

"You've seen it."

I'm afraid it will become an argument that will last the remainder of the year.

Lost Dutchman Hunters

SUPERSTITION MOUNTAIN MUSEUM

ELEVATION: 1,722 FEET | FOUNDED: 1979 | APACHE JUNCTION
POPULATION: 36,587

In the last week of March, I pick up my traveling compadre Jerry Marzinsky in Tucson and head north along the Pinal Pioneer Parkway to Apache Junction and the Superstition Mountain Museum.

"Hearing any voices lately?" I ask my tired joke.

Jerry's latest case is a former cocaine addict who's been following the advice of the voices in his head. Some time ago, while he was living in San Diego and low on cash, the voices said they could direct him to a marijuana field in Oregon. If he picked up some burlap bags and drove up there, they would show him where it was. "He followed them," Jerry says, "found the field up in the mountains, cut down enough to fill three sacks. Then they told him where to sell it. He bought all the liquor and drugs he could stand—hookers, too. Next the voices said they wanted to go fishing."

"You're kidding!"

"I'm serious. The voices told him where to throw the hook, how long to stay there, and when to move on. He was the only person on the Columbia River catching anything."

This is why I bring Jerry. He has entertainment value. He also shares the cost of gas.

The margins of the parkway bloom with thick cochineal and cobalt walls of penstemon and lupine. The sight of this stretch of road helps me to forget that gas is $3.76 a gallon, and I've already put more than four thousand miles on the Kia this year with forty weeks still to go. Many destinations fall in northern Arizona, hundreds of miles from Bisbee. Karen is going to confiscate my Chevron credit card. Four thousand, one hundred and ninety-five miles now.

With the giant black prow of the Superstition Mountains rising behind it, I pull into the museum and by twist of fate meet George E. Johnston, Dutchman hunter. He takes us out back to some benches in view of the mountains. A cactus wren calls.

George is ninety-two and owns the bag-of-gravel vocal chords to prove it. He is president emeritus of the Superstition Mountain Historical Society and is as much a fixture in these parts as the crusty, weather-beaten Dutchman himself was 140 years ago. I imagine I'm talking to Jacob Waltz in the flesh, just walked out of his gold mine in the Superstitions.

"A hundred and some have been killed in the mountains over the years," George begins. "It's no joke. When I first came out here in 1950, I took my two boys out there and we had shots fired over our heads. In those days you stayed on the trail. You start wandering off and messin' with a claim marker and you were writin' your own epitaph—and there're still people serious about that."

"I've met people still looking for the mine," I say, referring to the years in my twenties when I regularly blistered my feet on the trails in the wilderness area.

"There're a hundred and fifty people who say they found it . . . until you say 'show me.' They're not going to show you anything. They're a bunch of nuts. But most of those nuts are dead. Now we're in third- and fourth-generation nuts."

I think of Bob Corbin, Arizona's attorney general during the eighties, who came to the state from Indiana after reading about the legend and is probably out in the mountains with his metal detector this weekend. He is another Dutchman hunter—the name for the men and women who venture into the Superstitions and leave behind their own enigmatic stories. People like Adolph Ruth, who disappeared in 1931 and whose dismembered skeleton was found a mile from his bullet-ridden skull.

George tells us about some of the others, fathers and sons who've spent their lives in the mountains looking for the mine. R. J. Holmes stood by as the Dutchman expelled his last wordless breath. Holmes raised his child, "Brownie," with tales of lost gold, stories that would haunt him during his own forty-year quest. Brownie's partner, Clay Worst, a serious researcher and writer who owns what's left of the Mammoth mine, still searches for the Dutchman today.

"These guys meet once a year, up in the mountains, these old Dutch hunters and their relatives. They sit in the dark around a big fire, all with their stories to tell."

"Do you meet with them?" Jerry asks.

"I go up there, have a couple of beers. I got a few stories of my own."

Jerry's mouth hangs open. I can't tell if he's picking up his therapist pipe or putting on his prospector's cap. He presses George for his most "outlandish story," so George begins telling us about Bob Ward, a Dutchman hunter he describes as a skinny David Carradine. "Bob shot two people," he says, "one man in a claim dispute and another over a woman. Both were legitimate shoots in Arizona in those days," he adds, laughing.

"Bob had emphysema so bad that doctors told him he had three months to live, and they proved right. He said before he died, he wanted Clay Worst and me to come in there and he would show us all he's found out looking for the Lost Dutchman for forty years."

Clay wasn't too sure about the idea, believing Bob to be a lunatic. George and Clay argued for weeks about whether or not they should take weapons. The issue was the extra weight. George told him you have to be out of your head to carry ten or eleven pounds—a pistol and ammunition—rather than carry water.

But Bob Ward did own some curious relics of interest to both of them, particularly two stone Spanish crosses with mysterious engravings that supposedly gave clues to the mine. So with a reluctant but well-armed Clay Worst on board, the three of them and a hired wrangler set out on horseback into the Superstitions in the late spring of 1990.

It was supposed to take three days. It ended up taking six. They didn't get started until May. By then, the temperatures were peaking above one hundred degrees and most of the streams had already shrunk to rock-strewn arroyos with little water for the horses. The ride turned into a hike when the wrangler departed with the stock, leaving the trio to trudge along narrow box canyons, following Bob's directions. Then, about three days in, George came down with dysentery. Montezuma's revenge. A perfect irony considering he was looking for Spanish gold.

"We were camped at a place called Whiskey Springs," George says. "In the middle of the night, I'd tip-toe down to the creek and splash the canyon walls on both sides. I had no extra clothes. I'd have to wash my shorts out, wash everything. Of course, I did it right. I did it on the downstream side away from camp where we would drink. I put up with that for another three days. I thought I was going to die. Never again do I want to be in the Superstitions with every orifice clenched."

We laugh, and Jerry asks: "Was it worth it?"

"No," George says. "It was bull. I'll tell you an example. We're in this slot canyon, the three of us walking abreast just fitting in, and all you see is a slip of sky. Bob says, 'Look up there on those walls. You see them three crosses?'

"'No . . . ' we say.

"'Don't you see them?'

"I said, 'I see some iron oxide coming down some horizontal cracks. If I use my imagination . . . '

"'That's them!' Bob says.

"'Yeah, then how'd they get up there?'"

George tells us that Bob tried to explain that the Jesuits had made ladders. George wasn't buying it and Clay was looking at him with his eyes rolling back in his head, although later Clay admitted that Bob Ward had shown him things he'd never seen before.

"You see what you want to see," George says. "Some of these guys read a book and they go out there, and three days later, they're pulling their bodies out. And it's still going on."

George takes us into the museum to see the original Peralta Stones. Popular accounts say Travis Tumlinson, a police officer from Oregon, discovered them in 1949 after pulling his car off Route 60 near the Queen Creek Bridge to get a better look at the Superstition Mountains. What he found, half-buried in the ground, was a twenty-five-pound rectangular slab of smooth sandstone with engravings on both sides—the so-called Horse and Priest Map. A year later, he returned and uncovered two more stones, the Trail Map and the Heart Map, along with a hand-sized stone like a Valentine candy heart that fits precisely into a carved-out recess.

The four stones have become known as the Peralta Stones because of the names *Pedro* and *Miguel* carved into them, names associated with the historic Peralta mining family of Sonora, Mexico. Many believe the Peraltas created the maps and that they lead to their mines, including the Lost Dutchman.

"This trail that you see going up here like this," George says, pointing to the Trail Map and tracing his finger along a line to the Heart Map, "those dots continue, and this little circle is the top of what's called Coffee Flat Mountain. That's where we were going on our expedition. We were following this trail with Bob Ward. We got up there and we looked high and low for a day, but we couldn't find a thing."

"What do you think?" I ask. "Real or hoax?"

"I don't know. There's a guy on our board who says he knows exactly where the map leads. He believes it's authentic. You guys look around. Maybe you'll find the answer."

Behind us, sixteen framed "Treasure Maps to the Lost Dutchman Gold Mine" hang on a wall, including the "Waltzer Drawing" and those from R. J. Holmes and Julia Thomas, witnesses of Waltz's death.

Another wall displays twenty depictions of Jacob Waltz, although a sign says there are no known authentic pictures of him. In James Swanson and Tom Kollenborn's book, *Superstition Mountain: A Ride Through Time*, one witness describes him as having a face "parched dry from the desert sun and as hard as leather," his beard "almost snow-white and somewhat stained by tobacco below his chin." The many drawings of him fit the bill, nearly all showing him wearing an unruly large-brimmed hat. The quintessential Arizona prospector.

I remember his story from childhood. The Dutchman and his fabulous gold. When I lived near the Superstitions in my youth, I hiked alone in places with names like Reavis Ranch, Peralta Canyon, and Weaver's Needle. On cold, moonless nights, with great horned owls calling from the saguaros on the perimeter of my dry camp, the very rocks would speak the legend.

Jacob Waltz was born sometime around 1810 in Germany (then Prussia) and came to the United States in the early 1840s, working his way across the country from gold field to gold field until growing rumors of rich strikes and vast wealth brought him to California. It was in Los Angeles that Waltz became a naturalized citizen. He soon arrived in Arizona Territory and filed several mining claims in the Bradshaw Mountains near Prescott. Apparently, his stakes played out, for in 1868, Waltz had a 160-acre homestead on the Salt River where downtown Phoenix sits today.

"He never lived big," George Johnston had told us earlier. "He lived in a little adobe house, and when he needed money, he'd take his burro into the mountains and come out with a little poke or two of gold. Everybody knew he was getting gold, and people would follow him in there. He was the only one who ever came out."

There seems to be as many theories about where Jacob Waltz got his gold as there are Dutchman hunters. Four of them, however, stand out, and they span from the most realistic to the most romantic. The first theory says that Waltz stumbled upon a gold-bearing vein of quartz in what today is the Goldfield Mining District, just west of the Superstitions and the only gold mine in the region. Goldfield would be the site of several rich claims like the Black Queen and Mammoth, both filed shortly after Waltz's death. The second theory claims that Waltz, between Prescott and the Salt River, had lived in Wickenburg and worked the Vulture Mine, which became the most productive gold mine in Arizona history. The third is nefarious: that Waltz and a partner named Jacob Wiser (or Weiser) jumped the claim of two Mexicans of the famous Peralta family, murdered them, stole their gold, and hid it in the mountains near Weaver's Needle, one of the oldest landmarks in the Southwest carrying an Anglo name.

But it's the fourth theory that is a favorite among the hunters and the one that George Johnston believes. It maintains that Waltz located a hidden Jesuit treasure, the gold of which the Spanish missionaries had mined, processed, and cached in the Superstitions before their expulsion from the region in 1767. This explains the inordinate richness of his mineral specimens. "You look at the Dutchman's gold, which I have," says George, "and you can hardly see the quartz in it. It's all gold."

Theories abound, but what's certain is that Jacob Waltz had quantities of gold. On October 25, 1891, he died of pneumonia, taking with him his secret and leaving behind perhaps the greatest legend of a lost mine ever told, one that drives people mad to this day. "If success can be measured by what a man leaves for posterity," writes Swanson and Kollenborn (neither of whom actually believe in the Lost Dutchman mine), "Jacob Waltz was one of the most successful men in history." I don't know about any Lost Dutchman, but I've stumbled upon a gold mine in the Superstitions, and it's called George Johnston.

I read over a long list of clues (nineteen) that Jacob Waltz gave about the location of his mine. Number 2: "If you pass three red hills, you have gone too far." Damn. In a glass case, I see an authentic Colt Single Action Army revolver. Then I find a stuffed Apache trout and ringtail (labeled "Miner's Cat"). My first state fish and mammal for the year—too bad they don't count.

Adjacent to the museum, at what remains of the Apacheland movie studio, a monstrous wood-beamed twenty-stamp ore crusher rises into the sky. State-of-the-art technology for processing gold in the 1800s. The terrific noise must have carried all the way to Los Angeles. Two wooden grave markers read: *Her Cold as Usual. Him Stiff at Last.*

Before heading for home, we stop for dinner at the Mining Camp Restaurant and Dutchman's Hide Out. We walk past the restaurant, which serves reservation-only all-you-can-eat family-style meals with live entertainment. The washtub and jaw-harp bluegrass sounds of the Amazing McNasty Brothers pour from the doorway. We take seats in a booth beneath an eight-foot shoulder-strap, gas-powered two-man chainsaw. *Run the chain slowly when oiling*, a label on it reads. I think: *In case the steak needs cutting?* Brushed copper–topped tables sit on a plank floor. Lanterns swing from wagon wheels among twisting ceiling fans. Punched-tin figures of miners hang from pinewood walls.

When our server, Jan, arrives, I order the Gold Strike burger (medium) with the local brew, a Four Peaks Kilt Lifter, and when the food comes, I can hardly get my mouth around the ten-ounce mesquite-seared beef topped with fried onion, green chiles, and pepper jack.

"Perfect!" I tell Jerry, who sips ice tea while sizing up a Mammoth chicken sandwich.

When Jan brings the bill, I ask her about the "historic" part of the place.

"It was built in 1961 where the miners camped," she says. "The restaurant was modeled after the old cook shanties. The ponderosa pine was hauled down from Payson."

I explain that Jerry and I have been looking into the local mining history, that we just came from the Superstition Mountain Museum and Apacheland.

"I just got married in the Elvis Chapel!" she says, pushing her straight black hair away from her face and smiling. "It was wonderful! I wore a Western dress with a cowboy hat. I figured this time around, I had to do it the cowboy way."

We ride south along the Apache Trail, Superstition Mountain at my shoulder, flaming red in the late afternoon sun. I feel its pull. Of all Arizona's low desert ranges I've explored over the years, this looming volcanic prominence holds me like no other. Maybe it's the mystery of the place, or its fantastic story that borders on legend, on myth.

I want to pull over and take a walk. Trade weapons for water (I have neither). Get lost for a few days. People will always disappear here. But I wonder if the reason is less a lust for gold than the lure of the Superstitions themselves. There are many ways to lose a life in these mountains.

APRIL

Saguaro Blossom

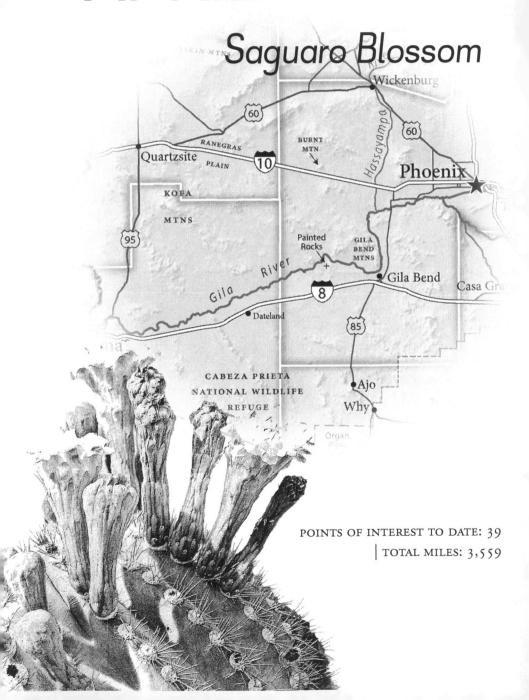

POINTS OF INTEREST TO DATE: 39
| TOTAL MILES: 3,559

A Living Ghost Town's Garden Spot

SUPERIOR AND THE BOYCE THOMPSON ARBORETUM

ELEVATION: 2,446 FEET | FOUNDED: 1929 | POPULATION: 3,091

A week later, I once again drive the Pinal Pioneer Parkway north toward Florence Junction. Along the blacktop, the cadmium eruptions of desert marigold compete with the cobalt and viridian of lupine, the colors broken by the speeding Kia as if the scene were a painting from the palette of Claude Monet.

Gas is now $3.87 a gallon, but I don't care. I still have the Chevron card.

Just beyond Milepost 115, I cross over Tom Mix Wash and pull off the road at a covered picnic table where a pillar of mortared stones holds the iron figure of a head-bowed, saddled-but-riderless horse named Tony. A bronze plaque reads:

> Jan. 6, 1880–Oct. 12, 1940
> In Memory of
> Tom Mix
> whose spirit left his body on this spot.
> And whose characterization and portrayals
> in life served to better fix memories of
> the Old West in the minds of living men.

The elaborate *descanso* of Tom Mix. Where many roadside deaths get a simple wooden cross, the cowboy actor with the white ten-gallon hat rates a ten-foot sculpture. On that warm Saturday in October, the sixty-year-old silent film star was on his way to visit a friend in Florence, coming off a long night of drinking and playing poker at the Santa Rita Hotel in Tucson. With his shiny aluminum suitcase tossed into the backseat—and loaded with winnings amounting to 1,085 silver dollars, some stories say—he sped north along Highway 79 in his bright-yellow 1937 Cord Supercharged Phaeton convertible with tooled leather stone guards on the rear fenders and a Smith & Wesson revolver tucked into its holster under the dash.

The road before him opened up once he left town and he floored the gas pedal, another tooled leather affair, custom fitted to his cowboy boot. South of Florence, he missed a sign that warned of a washed-out road under repair. A construction crew watched in astonishment as he stood up on the brake, swerved twice, crashed through the barriers, sailed into the arroyo, and flipped the Cord. The workers rushed to the scene but found the actor already the color of toast, his suitcase having slammed into the back of his head, breaking his neck.

I look up at the sad figure of Tony the Wonder Horse. Tom Mix was Hollywood royalty, a true entertainer. Richard Jensen in *The Amazing Tom Mix* says Mix claimed he was "the best showman on earth, even better than Buffalo Bill Cody." His last show on earth was his best ever.

Gila woodpeckers call from the tops of fat saguaros, drawing me into the desert beyond the monument. Thick-leaved creosote bushes flower yellow. Cholla cacti hang chains of green fruit. Magenta blossoms crown clusters of hedgehog cacti at my feet. A breeze brushes the stems of new grasses and carries a single raven across a cloudless sky.

A particularly robust paloverde tree with swollen buds the size of capers holds a birdcage of mistletoe, the semiparasitic plant laden with sand-ruby berries, food for the black-robed, window-winged phainopepla. Our only bird of the silky-flycatcher clan. I look for male mistletoe in flower, breathing deeply, my upper lip lifting in flehmen curl. The fragrance of desert mistletoe has only one equal—that of creosote following a monsoon thunderstorm. Bioluminescence, the cool blue light of fireflies, may be the first language. But the smell of these desert plants speaks to you with something deeper than words. You can call yourself a true desert native when either scent, no matter where you are, draws you home.

I check off the state tree from my list, symbol number three for the year after the turquoise and the cactus wren. I'm feeling a bit of pressure since these state symbols are the easiest. It's already April. I have nine more to go. But perhaps I'll see the state butterfly on this trip. Surely the Boyce Thompson Arboretum holds a two-tailed swallowtail? At least this is my plan. There will be other botanical gardens this year, but the Boyce Thompson is Arizona's first and largest. The world's plants live there, and butterflies like plants.

Paloverde bloom popcorn-yellow at roadside as I approach Gonzales Pass on U.S. 60, the lesser-known twin to the famous Route 66. Commissioned in 1926, the highway originally ran coast to coast, Los Angeles to Virginia Beach. Today, particularly outside California and western Arizona, much of U.S. 60 remains unchanged—probably more so than the 66. All it needs is a catchy song. "Get your kicks on nifty Route 60?"

Three miles west of Superior, the green oasis of the Arboretum lies tucked into Picketpost Mountain. I park and walk to the gift shop to purchase a copy of Hermann Hagedorn's *The Magnate: William Boyce Thompson and His Time, 1869–1930.* The clerk mentions he lives in Superior when I say I'm from Bisbee. When I ask my question, he says, "If you like mountain biking, Superior's the best. I like the dilapidated feel of the place, a mining town without tourist shops." I guess he wouldn't care for Bisbee, a dilapidated town *of tourist shops.*

Outside, an impressive ten-foot Sonoran rock fig grips the boulder in its pot with an enormous hand. I head for the gardens along a pathway walled by blooming succulents: orange tufts, magenta plumes, lavender asters, some spiking and others spraying and spilling. Fragrance and sound fill the air: The nose-wrinkling cat-urine pungence of gum-tree resin, the whirr of hummingbird wings, a cardinal's slurred whistles, the clenched-teeth cheedling of a Bell's vireo.

Among the many apricot-hued sleepy orange and sulphur butterflies, I locate one swallowtail, the beautifully iridescent (and bitter-tasting) blue-black pipevine swallowtail—not my target species, but anything so unruled by gravity is a pleasure to encounter. The butterflies are named for their host plant, a tropical trailing vine with mouse-ear flowers, only one species of which occurs in the Sonoran Desert. The vines the caterpillars feed on contain poisonous alkaloids and storing them in their bodies works against hungry butterfly eaters. Which all seems very risky to me.

The butterfly is relying on a lizard or bird's previous bad experience with munching a family member. Suppose you're the first one in line?

I move on through the gardens: the Hummingbird and Butterfly, the Heritage Rose, the Children's Horticultural, the Desert Legume—I'm expecting a garden named for Eden. Here are boojum trees (ho! ho!), magma ridges, and aboriginal seeps. Among the Australian eucalyptus and the Chihuahuan graythorn, the South American golden torch cereus and the African euphorbias, photographers and bird watchers mingle with dog-walkers and tree huggers. A northern saw-whet owl may spend the day with a Mexican spotted owl like a Michigander visiting with a friend from Sonora. The place is an intersection of people and wildlife and walking paths, a literal crossroads with signs. I hear the languages of the planet: Spanish and Insect, German and Birdsong, and others I don't recognize—speaking the natures of the world.

I follow the trail around Ayer Lake with its desert pupfish and leopard frogs. A great blue heron, its crooked neck spring-loaded, stands on its watery shadow, blatantly feeding on the protected animals. Deep into the Upland Sonora Natural Area a sign warns: *Rattlesnakes Only Beyond This Point*. I hear the rush of falling water. A high cataract roils through the upturned paddles of a prickly pear cactus and spills into a deep grotto. The drainage draws my eyes to a canyon clotted with impossibly green cottonwoods. Two hundred feet above them, a twenty-six-room estate called Picket Post House perches on the edge of a cliff. Its surrounding walls of native stone appear as organic to the place as if sprouting from the landscape itself.

This is the work of Doby Tom, a mason from Yugoslavia who raised these walls by hand for William Boyce Thompson. Thompson was born on May 13, 1869, in Alder Gulch, Montana, first child of Anne Boyce of Missouri and William Thompson, a Canadian contractor and builder. According to poet and writer Hermann Hagedorn (who was also the friend and biographer of Teddy Roosevelt), young William was an imaginative boy and more sensitive than his peers. He started his first mineral collection at four years old. Before he turned ten, he learned he could make money by melting the solder from tin cans and panning the lead from the ashes as if he were separating gold from river gravel. A solid bar of lead brought him fifty cents.

By seventeen, the creative dreamer was also a go-getter and gambler. Over the next twenty years, he tried school, twice, finding some interest as an engineering student at Columbia University's School of Mines before quitting and returning to Montana to explore several mining ventures. He got married and settled in Helena, then moved to New York City to try his luck with mining stocks on Wall Street, then came back to Montana, this time Butte, where his silver mine soon pinched out. Money went out, little came in.

Then, an acquaintance brought Thompson news of a promising copper mine in Clifton, Arizona. Soon, he made his first trip to the Southwest, and with "something beguiling in his personality, his evident integrity, and the charm of his shy, boyish smile," he extracted from the owners an option on a quarter-million-dollar mine for five hundred dollars cash and a promise. The Shannon Mine was a success, and by the age of forty, Thompson had made his first million.

"I get my thrill in taking something that looks hopeless and making a success of it," Thompson was fond of saying. Enter Superior. From 1870 to 1890, silver had been king in this valley, producing the richest silver mine in Arizona history and building a town of two thousand people called Pinal City, named after the Arizona county with its pine-clad mountains. But by the end of the century, even the queen of the silver mines had finished, and Pinal City with its churches and breweries (always in pairs) became a ghost town almost overnight.

Ten years later, a team of Thompson's engineers came upon the four-hundred-foot-deep abandoned shaft of the Silver Queen. Tests showed no ore in sight, but the geology looked promising—if not for silver then for other minerals. Thompson didn't even option the mine; he bought it outright. "You wired me that the geological conditions were excellent for finding a mine," he told his engineers. "Go to it now and find it." He christened it the Magma.

What they found was copper. Vein after vein of rich ore, thousands of feet beneath the original silver cap. From that one deep, hot mine, its many shafts tunneling through layers of geothermic crust, grew the town of Superior, its 3.6-million-dollar smelter ("the finest smelter in the world"), the longest steam-powered locomotive carrier in the United

States, and the first air-conditioned mine in North America. Today it is a National Historic Engineering Landmark.

Years later, Thompson the mining magnate would climb the mountain wall known as Apache Leap to look down on his Magma copper mine and the "single street lost in gray twilight" that was becoming the thriving town of Superior. From that vantage point, he first laid eyes on the cliffs above Queen Creek and the place where he would raise the clay-tiled roofs of his "Castle on the Hill." Thompson spent the remainder of his years before his death in 1930 enjoying his Picket Post House and building his arboretum as a museum "to help instill in humanity an appreciation of plants." In 1976, his vision became Arizona's eighteenth state park.

The trail runs me into Queen Creek, its quiet water coursing among shade-gathering cottonwoods, the ground quilted with their leaves. The trees release duff that drifts among clouds of insects in the screened sunlight and gives a Disney quality to the air. A gulf fritillary glides by on wings like twin flakes of rust, no doubt searching for passion among the vines. At the Clevenger House, a stone structure that once belonged to a family of homesteaders, I run into a photographer who thinks he's just seen some ringtails. Proximity alert!

"They're in the trees just past the herb garden," he says.

Ringtails are nocturnal, but finding them out in daylight isn't unheard of. I hurry to the place he'd indicated, scanning the walnut and hackberry trees for movement. Then, high along a cliff where a tall velvet ash brushes up against the face, I see something leaping among the branches. A pair of rock squirrels. Nuts. They're close, in the sense that they're mammals. But the rodents aren't any more related to ringtails than the primate photographer himself.

From U.S. 60 near Superior, the ragged cliff face of Apache Leap rises in the east like a crenellated battlement. Legends say the place recalls a band of warriors who jumped to their deaths rather than surrender to cavalry soldiers. The tears of their families turned into the black glassy obsidian stones found all over the area. Thompson's smelter stack pokes the sky above grades of black refuse that terrace the olive hillsides. Five thousand feet beneath me, radiating from eight shafts, stretches a web-work of tunnels on thirty-six levels—the Magma Mine that the magnate founded on a $130,000 gamble. It became Arizona's deepest mine and one of its greatest copper troves, the kind of mineral wealth that drove the territory to statehood.

The mines have ceased production for some decades. Superior, having begun as a camp of ramshackle buildings and huts, has returned to one. The streets are deserted, except for a few ATVs. Many of the businesses look closed, vacant. Superior *is* a living ghost town.

On Main Street, a quad races by. "It's the best thing about Superior," says a teen standing outside a boarded-up Sprouse-Reitz Company across from the abandoned MacPherson's Magma Hotel. "Makes the time go real fast." The Rolling Rock Gallery/Copper Triangle looks open, based on the quads parked in front. The place is an art gallery connected to a store selling mining supplies—saw blades, core bags, sample boxes, field notebooks, and such.

"Freeport-McMoRan," says dark-eyed Toni Sanchez when I ask her who buys the stuff. "But we do sell a few gold pans to other people." I recognize the name from the mining conglomerate—the world's largest copper company—operating in Bisbee. Toni was raised in Superior and loves the town and its people. "It's so quiet," she tells me.

Aren't ghost towns usually? I think, then ask: "Is it all mining?"

"No, history and folklore, too." She invites me to look around the gallery with its wall hangings of paintings and photographs of local artists. I'm drawn to a sculpture in the center of the room, an iron grave marker of arching railroad spikes and barbed wire enclosing a metal rose and Colt revolver by artist Larry Jochai. "He made it for Mattie Blaylock," Toni says.

Kathy Long, who also has lived in Superior all her life, explains that Mattie had come to live in nearby Pinal City after her relationship with Wyatt Earp ended in Tombstone. She and Wyatt had visited the town earlier, and after Wyatt left her for Josephine Marcus, she returned and took up prostitution again. But in the mid-1880s, the silver boom had played out and the town was already dying. Potential clients had moved on. On July 3, 1888, at the age of forty, she swallowed a lethal dose of laudanum. She is buried in a small cemetery among anemic prickly pear and paloverde where Pinal City once stood.

"The grave marker was removed to the gallery because it isn't historic," says Kathy, adding that the artist had created it to replace a stolen headstone. "Mattie's remains were kidnapped recently," she says. "But they were returned and reburied. Some kids had dug up her grave and took the coffee can with her ashes in it."

"Kids around here are working too hard," I say. "I remember when all you had to do was drive down any road named Miracle Mile to find a girlfriend."

Superior: the town that rose from the rocky scree because of one man's gamble when Pinal City was "dust and ghosts." The sheer wall of Apache Leap turns to cayenne in the falling sun. The high rampart from which William Boyce Thompson first scanned the valley with half the state spread out before him "in the radiance and other-world magic of an Arizona dusk" and found a home he called Picket Post. A century later, the state he loved and to which he gave his life still tends his garden.

An Arizona Treasure

RICHARD SHELTON

ELEVATION: 5 FEET, 10 INCHES | FOUNDED: 1933

I drive along I-10 west toward Phoenix and Tempe with Richard Shelton in the passenger seat. We're headed for Arizona State University to give a talk to students and faculty about prison writing workshops. Last February, I spoke at the English department's Prison English Conference, and the organizer asked if I could get Richard involved.

So here we are, in the second week in April, me and the state treasure. This is not a chimichanga; I'm not proposing a new Arizona symbol. Dick Shelton is an *actual* Arizona treasure. I was present in 2006 when he received the University of Arizona's Henry and Phyllis Koffler Prize for outstanding accomplishment in teaching and, with his wife Lois, the Arizona Humanities Council's inaugural Arizona Literary Treasure Award. Governor Janet Napolitano proclaimed April 22, 2006, "Richard Shelton Day" to recognize his accomplishments as an author and poet, a regents' professor, a prison volunteer, and a mentor of writers (like me).

As I pass the Rooster Cogburn Ostrich Ranch, Dick asks if I've ever stopped in to feed the giant birds, "which would just as soon take off a hand as look at you," he adds.

"No," I say, with an image popping in my head of a recent photo I saw on the Internet of a camel swallowing the entire head of a small child. The caption read: "Your child is being eaten by a camel. Do you: a) save your child or b) take a photo?"

"Stick to feeding the lorikeets," he says, pointing to a yellow sign. "I had a cat that hatched a whole brood of chickens after a rooster killed the hen. I can still remember my grandmother with that rooster tucked under her arm, marching over to the next farm to trade it out for another rooster."

I can tell that Dick has been working on his new book about his childhood in Idaho, a funny, poignant memoir full of stories "of a family and how a family got that way." Stories like when his mother, Hazel, "wearing her fanciest dress and a little round hat like a cow pie with a veil that reached just to the tip of her audaciously turned-up nose, opened her handbag (which matched her shoes and gloves), pulled out a Colt .45, and began firing in the general direction of my father. . . ." Or how his father first met his future mother-in-law, "the embodiment of respectability and quiet, conservative fashion," after stepping from beneath a freight train where he'd been riding for the last hundred miles. Leave it to Dick Shelton to teach us about the American family. He's titled it, *Nobody Rich or Famous*, but my wife and I call it *Getting Out of Boise*.

Near Picacho Peak we look for wildflowers. The winter annual—gold poppy and lupine—bloom is past, but desert marigolds still border both sides of the interstate.

I know what's coming.

"Do you know what the state flower of Arizona is?" Dick asks.

"No . . ." I say—I do, but I've heard this before, so I play along. "What is the state flower of Arizona?"

"The California poppy!"

We laugh as if it's the first time I've heard his joke. And then we're on a roll.

"I understand the state fish is the sand trout," I say. "What about the state fossil?"

"I don't know . . ." he says.

"John McCain? As in rare, precious, and beautiful? What about the state nut? State bird? No waving fingers at passing cars."

"Rosy-breasted pushover?" he says. "Extramarital lark?"

And suddenly I'm thinking about the Engleman dingleberry game he describes in his book, *Going Back to Bisbee*, in which he takes visitors on desert treks and makes up the names of the birds they see, getting more and more preposterous as he goes along.

The game could work as well with the Arizona state symbols. Perhaps as a slide-show presentation. "Arizona has twelve official state symbols, and several proposed ones," I would tell an audience of winter visitors, say at a bookstore or church in Green Valley. "In 1931, Arizona adopted our first state symbol from one of our most majestic and symbolic succulents,"

I say, throwing up a photograph of a squat, gray spineless cactus with a single white bloom. "The peyote bachelor button." As Dick says, if I can get away with that, the sky's the limit. The next slide I produce I identify as the state tree, adopted in 1954. It's a picture of a bonsaied paloverde. "There were budget cuts that year," I explain, and then I watch their faces to see how well I'm doing. I can see some indecision, a dialogue going on inside someone's head.

Is he pulling my leg? He lives here. I guess he would know. . . .

Then the clever visitor might ask a probing question, a question that would be appropriate whether I'm kidding or not, something like, "Just how bad were those budget cuts?"

I reply in an off-hand way, but with complete seriousness. "Oh, they were pretty bad. The legislature wanted to adopt the two-tailed swallowtail as the state butterfly that year but was afraid people would think it too extravagant. Even the one-tailed swallowtail was too much."

The visitor looks satisfied. Score 2 for the offensive team. Then I throw up a couple pictures of real state symbols as sucker's bait, maybe the Arizona treefrog as the official amphibian and the ridge-nosed rattlesnake as the reptile, both so unheard of they're believable. When asked about the new state firearm, I show a slide of the boomerang-like Hopi throwing stick. Anybody can see that it's a formidable weapon, especially for native Arizonans in their fight against rabbits. So far so good. Move up to the next level.

I look out over the audience for someone wearing a bola tie and point it out. Then I ask if anyone knows what Arizona's official neckwear is, and as people make suggestions, I flip to my next picture—a hangman's noose.

The game will be over right there. But if it isn't, I'm prepared to go on to all my proposed state symbols, like a food that certainly occupies its own food group and just might be illegal north of the Gila River—the Sonoran hot dog.

"I once watched a border patrol agent eat a Sonoran hot dog," I tell Dick as we cross the Gila River. "He checked it for its papers first."

We have lunch at the Fulton Center across from the main campus. Dick talks about how in 1885 ASU was first called the Tempe Normal School ("subnormal" for those lacking a high-school diploma) and later the Arizona State Teachers College. "It was the Arizona State College before I began teaching at the university, and there was an uproar about the Great Name Change." His comment reminds me of his joke about why he stopped taking sabbaticals at the UA: "Every time I came back, they had moved the university!"

After lunch, we head for Professor Joe Lockard's classroom. Over the years that I've known him, Joe has always been modest about his accomplishments, preferring to give credit to the students and faculty who take his ideas and make them a reality. The Prison English Project is his effort to bring literature to diverse groups, some as far afield as China.

The Prison English Project includes two internship programs, one called Pen Project whereby undergraduate students critique the poetry and prose of prisoners in New Mexico. The other involves graduate students who teach classes in Shakespeare, American literature, and creative writing to men at the Florence State Prison. ASU is one of the few schools to do this, and students and teachers who participate in the program call it life changing.

Dick has taught writing as a volunteer in Arizona's prisons for forty years. Today, we discuss our roles working with the writing of incarcerated men, focusing on a prison writing journal we publish with grants from the Lannan Foundation called *Walking Rain Review*. We each choose a few selections of poetry, then he reads his introduction for issue 6 called "Hard-Ass and the Innocents." It deals with his work with the prison workshops and the accomplishments of the men who participate in them.

It is one of my favorite pieces of his. In it, he talks about the realities of writing as compared to the realities of prison. He reminds himself that when he is tempted to be kind rather than critical, he knows it is a disservice to the men who've learned since childhood that to be tough means to survive. They will survive his criticism.

"I am not a psychologist or a therapist," he reads. "I am not running a support group or a treatment program. . . . The only thing I know how to do, the only thing my entire life's experience equips me to do, is to help people improve their writing skills. This much I can do." Dick's voice is rising now, and he pulls his legs beneath him to prepare to stand, his white tiara of hair shining in the fluorescent lights. "I can cut with a sword through those 'undisciplined squads of emotion.' . . . I can drive them, almost with a whip, to improve their work to the level at which it can be published, and then I can drive them shamelessly toward publication, something I would not do with my students at the university. . . ." When he finishes, the room is dead silent. I see many wide eyes, and I'm thinking, *Okay! Here we go.*

Dick turns to me and asks me to remove the brick from my backpack. "You need to get out some paper and something to write with," he tells the class.

The Brick Exercise. John Buri, a prisoner in one of his workshops, first introduced the lesson many years ago, and Dick has used it since. Now, he asks the class to describe the brick with as many words as possible, words that he writes on the whiteboard behind us: *red, rectangular, heavy, rough.* . . . They all go on the board. When it is filled, and fewer descriptions are forthcoming, he asks everyone to write a poem about the brick.

"It can be any kind of poem you like," he says, pointing to the whiteboard. "But you can't use any of these words. Start writing."

He moves among the students, and I watch him, smiling to my-self. He's in his element. Retired from the university since 2005 but still teaching in the prisons, he's a tireless pedagogue, drawing blood from his would-be protégés. Not that long ago, I sat in one of those seats while he stood, looking over my shoulder at some nervous attempt of mine with

language, pointing to me, asking me to read aloud what I had written. I watch him, seeing the waves of nervousness roll over the young and innocent as he raises a finger in their direction, and I envy them.

Karen's favorite Richard Shelton poem is called "The Hole." He read it at her graduation ceremony for her master's degree. The poem is about an excavation in his yard that "moves with great care and precision between the stars." In his book, *The Other Side of the Story*, "The Hole" precedes my favorite poem, "The Stones." I think about this poem every time I drive up his driveway with its long wall of stones set in place without mortar (and usually falling down in places). He wrote "The Stones" as he attempted to lay up this wall. Just as he wrote "The Hole" while digging up the ground for his "trap for goldfish" that now waters his gray herd of javelina.

"I love to go out on summer nights and watch the stones grow," he begins, insisting that younger stones move about more than what their elders consider is good for them, that old stones prefer to remain comfortably where they are, getting fat as a matter of distinction. Whenever I read the poem, I imagine him standing in the desert of his yard, talking to the young stones of his wall as he piles them on top of the old, fat ones, working through the heat of the evening as the sun retreats and the moon rises large and silver above the distant Rincon Mountains.

The moon, he writes at the end of the poem, is always spoken of in whispers by the elder stones. "Feel how it pulls at us," one says, "urging us to follow." Another says, "It is a stone gone mad." Dick placed thousands of stones carefully atop one another, forming a high wall that contours the long curve of the dirt drive to his house. How many late night hours did that take? He always refuses my offer to help with repairs, insisting that he alone can properly set stone upon stone. I can see him now, walking the undisciplined squad of his wall in the moonlight, his arms raised like the semaphore saguaros surrounding him. He admonishes the young stones to remain with their elders, unconcerned about his neighbors closing their blinds to the lunatic poet. Richard Shelton, godfather to my children, treasure of Arizona, teacher of stones.

The Last Camp of Hi Jolly

QUARTZSITE

ELEVATION: 879 FEET | FOUNDED: 1989 | POPULATION: 3,665
PLUS 1.5 MILLION SNOWBIRDS

Quartzsite calls itself the Rock Capital of the World. But what it really is, at least in the winter months, is the World's Largest Swap Meet. In ninety-degree heat, I make it through Gila Bend and the Tonopah Desert, past Burnt Mountain and the equally Burnt Well and into the basalt-cobbled, creosote-weary Ranegras Plain without air conditioning. Gas is $3.74 and the Kia is getting thirty-nine miles per gallon. I don't mind trading sweat for extra miles.

I scored my first saguaro flower in Gila Blend, figuring I would, given the west-to-east-trending wave of blossoms now moving across Arizona. In Tucson, the crowns of the giant cacti had just started showing nipple action. Near Casa Grande, buds were standing erect. By the time I reached the town of "Five Old Crabs," we had full bloom. State symbol number four!

At Quartzsite, I pull into the Chevron station ($3.95/gallon!) to fill up and get my bearings. Misty, a pleasant girl with a wry smile beneath her dark hair and glasses, tells me the Grubstake has the best food in town. When I ask about Quartzsite, she says she "loves the small-town feel, except in winter when all the people arrive."

"The reason I came in April and not February," I say. "A million and a half geezers sprawled all over the desert in their RVs, stuffed into their quads while plugging up the streets, turning Quartzsite into the world's largest parking lot. If you want to know what the Apocalypse will look like, try Quartzsite on Groundhog Day."

"It's not too bad, actually, the crowds, if you know when to go out to avoid them."

Like midnight, I think. *When they're all tucked into their sleeper sofas.* "I'm looking for the Red Ghost," I tell her, finally, just blurting it out.

"Oh . . . Hi Jolly's tomb. Take the dirt road across from all the trucks." Misty draws me a map with her hands on the countertop.

First, I take Misty's suggestion for lunch, but the Grubstake Social Club and Waterin' Hole looks deserted. My habit of eating lunch late in the day means I'm usually alone. I walk through a front door with the sign that reads *Not an Entrance.* A guy appears from the back wearing a blue T-shirt that says *Made in England.* He pours me a beer and tells me his name is Darren. He has a British accent. I should have ordered the Guinness.

"Can I sit anywhere?" I ask, as he hands me the glass.

"Preferably on your bum!" he says. "You weren't expecting that!"

I find a seat at a small plank table in the center of the room. More planks form the walls and corrugated tin dresses the front of the bar. A pool table crowds one corner near a jukebox. Overhead, scores of license plates from states across the country are nailed to the ceiling among hundreds of dollar bills, many inked over with names and places like "Whitney from Alabama."

"It's a paper trail," Darren says, handing me a menu and seeing my interest in the ceiling. "Like when cowboys would leave dollar bills tacked to the ceiling of the bars they visited after taking their cows to market, knowing that when they returned broke, they could still buy a drink."

"I'm sure I see one with my name on it," I say.

"You know what 'one for the road' means? An English factoid for you—one more drink before taking the long walk to the executioner. The irony—how it stays with the meaning!"

Darren, I soon learn, is full of stories, and I struggle to write them down as he tells them through his gap-toothed smile. At his suggestion, I order his signature dish, the fish and chips. While he disappears into the kitchen to prepare it (this afternoon, the Grubstake manager is also my barman and chef, my host and server), I catch up on my notes.

He's from Manchester, England (a Mancunian!), and he came to Quartzsite eight years ago for the weather. "The first winter I was here, I was barbecuing on my front porch on Christmas Day. Christmas Day!—unheard of in England!"

The food comes out fast. Two huge cod filets, breaded and fried, lie atop a pile of fried potatoes and mound of slaw. "The food was good here when I came. I made it better." He watches me take a bite.

"So light—I can taste the fish."

"The breading should only be a vehicle for the fish," he says, as if it were a mantra.

While I eat, Darren leans against the bar and talks. He knows the history of the area, the people who've lived and died here.

"Have you ever heard about the Red Ghost?" I ask.

He laughs. "People say they see it, usually after drinking all night. They see Hi Jolly's pink elephant, too. But I met an old Indian in Blythe who swears he'd seen it. He told me he'd never come to Quartzsite because the ground is cursed. 'Never let your bare soles touch the ground there or you'll never leave,' he said. 'If you do, you're destined to always return.' And what do we have? Millions of winter visitors who come every year and they don't know why!"

"Beneath every desert is a parking lot," I say.

"Keep your shoes and socks on!" he warns me. "They're crazy. They keep coming in here and taking my quart buckets to dry pan for gold!"

Darren is on a roll. I'm an audience of one, but he's primed for prime time.

"Another example: This guy comes down from Canada—an Englishman. We become best of friends. He's been asking all over town about the rock shows. He's driven all the way down here for the rock shows. 'I heard Quartzsite has the greatest rock shows on earth,' he says. 'Who do you have for the bands?' He's so disappointed. No bands, no music, just dumb rocks. Someone sends him to the Grubstake for consolation. Guinness draft and fish and chips!"

Not a bad consolation, I think. *Darren's fish and chips should be our official seafood.*

After lunch, I follow Misty's countertop instructions to the Hi Jolly Pioneer Cemetery. Seven layers of mortared native stone rise above all other markers, narrowing into a ten-foot pyramid with a copper cutout of a dromedary at its apex, silhouetted against a chrysocolla sky. The Great Pyramid of Quartzsite.

The Kia's engine ticks. A raven crosses overhead, calling with dry rocks in its throat. It's bloody hot. Through squinted eyes, I stare at a bronze plaque. Words welded onto its stained surface, read: "The Last Camp of Hi Jolly. Born somewhere in Syria about 1828. Died at Quartzsite December 16, 1902. Came to this country February 10, 1856. Camel driver—packer scout—over thirty years a faithful aid to the U.S. Government. Arizona Highway Department 1935."

A dark metal cylinder with a cap and the date 1935 protrudes from the stone below the plaque—the "time capsule" that legend says contains the ashes of the Arab and Topsy, the last camel of his original herd, his favorite companion that died in a Los Angeles zoo.

In his book, *Arab/American*, my friend Gary Nabhan says that Hi Jolly "appears to be the first Moslem from the Middle East to arrive on the North American continent" and that he "came in the company of camels." He was half Syrian and half Greek, a man with many names: Filippou Teodora, Philip Tedro, Felipe Teatro(w), and Hadji Ali among them. Hi Jolly is a corruption of the latter, probably stemming from his thick-lipped crew of immigrants and soldiers who helped him drive the first camels seen on this continent since the Pleistocene.

Hi Jolly's caravan passed through Arizona Territory in the fall of 1857 in what would be the U.S. Army's great Camel Corps experiment in the American desert. It must have been quite a sight: a short olive-skinned man with sharp black eyes, dressed—as I imagine him, like Lawrence of Arabia—in a white cotton thawb, with the traditional kaffiyeh and agal wrapped around his dark head, and speaking an unknown language to unheard-of creatures. Seventy camels (or maybe a hundred), some laden with six to eight hundred pounds of cargo, together with their attendant drovers, soldiers, horses, mules, and sheep, traveled overland from Texas by way of Big Bend and the Rio Grande to Albuquerque, then across the Painted Desert to Grand Canyon, and south to the Colorado River near Fort Mohave. When they arrived at their destination at Fort Tejon after crossing California's Mojave Desert, Lieutenant Edward Beale was convinced. "The harder the test they are put to," he praised the camels, "the more fully they seem to justify all that can be said of them."

But the army regulars were not as impressed as Beale. Horsemen, it seems, prefer animals less temperamental, less smelly, and not so prone to spitting. Warriors ride great steeds, not clown-faced monsters. Perhaps they hadn't heard the stories of how Hi Jolly on his camel ran down a band of attacking Indians with his scimitar raised and robes flapping, shouting the Bohemian rhapsodic *Bismillah!* and scattering the natives out of fear alone. In the end, however, it was the country's move toward civil war that finished the experiment, the animals eventually being sold at auction (and subsequently turning feral in many cases).

Hi Jolly would stay on, at first scouting for the army and later setting up a freight business using his camels to haul supplies between Yuma and Tucson. In Tucson, he met and married a Sonoran woman named Gertrudis Serna, and the couple had two daughters. He tried settling down, setting his camels to wander and taking up saddle-making, then digging for silver or gold in the Patagonia Mountains. But soon the old Arab was back to camel whispering, this time at Tyson's Well, where he entertained the locals with his stories of fighting with Geronimo.

The last people to see Hi Jolly alive said he told them he'd be out in the desert looking for his camels. Years later, some cowboys in a bar in Quartzsite would tell a story about hunting for stray cows after a terrific dust storm and coming across a body half buried in the sand, the lifeless man with his arms still wrapped around the neck of a dead camel. According to Gary Nabhan, Hi Jolly died "somewhere along an old desert road between Wickenburg, Arizona, and the Colorado River," leaving behind only three silver coins, a pack of tobacco, and his line shack at Tyson's Well. And maybe his ghost, too, its robes flying as he rides a seven-foot-high dromedary named Topsy. Who says the dead live only in the past?

As the old Randy Sparks ballad goes: "Old timers out in Arizona tell you that it's true / You can see Hi Jolly's ghost a-trav'lin' still / When that desert moon is bright / He comes ridin' through the night / Leadin' four-and-twenty camels 'cross the hill."

History is a strange soil. Usually it grows stories like wheat or cotton in straight rows for easy weeding. But sometimes it nurtures the thick, woody tubers of legend that swell underfoot and can never be wholly rooted out. I can't think about Hi Jolly without connecting him to the tales of the infamous Red Ghost, the beast that terrorized the territory during the time the Arab drover was chasing his feral camels across Arizona. The story begins in 1883 at a ranch on a tributary of the Gila River called Eagle Creek. One morning, a woman heard her friend's terrible screams shortly after she headed off to the spring to fetch water. She saw a giant reddish and misshapen animal race by with the devil himself strapped to its back. Fearing for her life, she barricaded herself inside the cabin and waited for her husband and his partner to return. They discovered the woman at the spring, trampled to death, the earth surrounding her body churned up with weird cloven hoofprints. Tangles of red hair clung to nearby shrubs.

A few days later, a huge unrecognizable creature ransacked the camp of some prospectors and disappeared into the night. Again, daylight showed cloven tracks and strands of red hair. Stories spread of a wild beast ridden by a demon bent on rampaging and killing. People called it the Red Ghost. A rancher named Cyrus Hamblin said he'd seen it on the Salt River and claimed it was a camel with a skeleton strapped to it back, but no one believed him. Then, another group of prospectors spotted the animal near the Verde River and managed to get shots off. They noticed something fall from its back as it bolted away and soon located a grinning human skull, stretched with a parchment of skin and hair.

Over the next year, the Red Ghost tore through a camp of teamsters, upsetting freight wagons and scattering the frightened men. Then it took down a horse and the cowboy who attempted to rope it. Always they saw the fleshless rider. Always they found cloven tracks and red hair. The legend of the Red Ghost grew over the next decade until a rancher dropped the animal with one shot while it browsed on vegetables in his garden. He found scars all across the camel's back, evidence, he said, of the flesh-tearing straps that had once held the body of a man.

Some believe the Red Ghost was a lost camel with some hapless soldier who perished while tied to its saddle, the aftermath of some cruel joke.

That would be the story part of the legend. But to this day some still see the Red Ghost and its headless rider, drifting over Arizona's blown plains of sand and creosote. Who could argue it, when legends grow to myth?

On my way out of town, I stop at Tyson's Well, the second-to-the-last camp of Hi Jolly, the place he spent his last years chasing camels. His corrals and stone cabin are long gone. Next to Dorothy & Toto's Ice Cream Shoppe lies the spot where Charley Tyson built his adobe stage stop in 1866, a station with "no grass but good water" that took advantage of miners and the military hauling equipment and supplies from the river port at Ehrenberg to points east. Jacob Waltz probably came this way. The old Dutchman would have puzzled over the strange-toed tracks along his road to the Bradshaw Mountains.

The Tyson's Well Stage Station Museum still has a dirt floor in one of the rooms "for authenticity," a ceiling of saguaro ribs (more authenticity), and the original fireplace, still in use during Quartzsite's (most unauthentic) winters. Three wooden grave markers lean against an adobe wall, one of them with a barely legible, "William Tate 1875–1945." A pair of camel statues, an adult and young one, honors the drover, no doubt.

The walls that remain of the station and its sleeping rooms measure exactly the dimensions of my living room. I try to imagine the mix of livestock with people. A sign says that one traveler thought the accommodations were "crude."

In her memoir, *Vanished Arizona*, Martha Summerhayes writes about traveling from Fort Whipple to Ehrenburg with her husband for his new army detail. The couple passed through this stage station, but Martha opted to sleep in her tent, noting in her journal: "for of all places on the earth, a poorly kept ranch in Arizona is the most melancholy and uninviting. It reeks of everything unclean, morally and physically."

I sniff the air but detect nothing offensive, no affront to my virtuous sensibilities, such as they are, no raw slap to my sinuses. Only the partially imagined stink of camel. Like the rush of a thousand spoken curses.

Five Old Crabs at the Crossroads

GILA BEND, PAINTED ROCK, AND THE OATMAN MASSACRE

ELEVATION: 735 FEET | FOUNDED: 1872 | POPULATION: 1,980

The most promising metropolis on the Gila River in 1864 consisted of "three chimneys and a coyote," according to the Irish travel writer J. Ross Browne. Today, Gila Bend has surpassed all expectations. Karen and I drive past the famously outdated welcome sign—*1,700 Friendly People and Five Old Crabs*—and pull into the Space Age Lodge. The woman behind the desk says most or all of the Old Crabs are dead. My proximity alert goes off.

"We have only two left—rooms, I mean," dark-haired Silvia says.

"We'll take one," Karen says. It's 8:00 p.m., and we've been on the road most of the day. We're looking forward to the whirlpool hot tub and pool.

Silvia introduces us to Mario, who does everything—cooking, maintenance, prep work for the rooms. Both are from Orlando, Florida, and only moved here a month ago. "We're here for the peace and quiet," she says, "and we love meeting people from all over the world."

"So you haven't felt the heat yet?" I ask.

"Tomorrow it will be 111 degrees," Mario says. "Welcome to Gila Bend in April!"

I explain to Mario and Silvia that I'm working on a book and that Karen and I are planning on seeing Painted Rock and the Oatman Massacre site. "One hundred and eleven degrees. Probably the hottest day this year, and we have to experience it in Gila Bend—hiking!"

Mario suggests I check out a book called *Gila Bend* by Vincent Murray. "We're on page 114, a little paragraph. Maybe you can write more about us, and include Silvia and me!"

"Yes," Silvia adds. "And you must send me your book, or I'll never know about it."

"Done." I say. "I'll even come to Gila Bend and give you a signed copy."

After checking in, Karen and I walk over to the restaurant for dinner. In the gift shop, I find a copy of the book Mario mentioned. The caption below the photograph of a flying saucer lodged among a dozen tall palms reads: "One of the most iconic places in Gila Bend," adding that the hotel once had a "Sputnik-style" satellite fixed to the roof. The replica of Sputnik was replaced with a more "futuristic" model of a spaceship—a twenty-eight-foot-diameter craft out of *Forbidden Planet*—during renovations in 1996. The original design for the lodge came from owner Al Stovall, a manganese supplier for the government during World War II and later owner of a copper mine and plastics factory. Stovall built the place in the early 1960s during the thrust of the NASA space program—he was a friend of Dwight D. Eisenhower—and many of its spacey features came from his own inspiration. Today, the new owners, Duke and Carole Fox, carry on Stovall's dream of a Roswell hotel in the Arizona desert.

In the restaurant, a Jos Villabrille mural of the starship USS *Enterprise* (Constitution class) sails out of its blue frame, casting a shadow across the wall, planets hanging behind it. Beneath the ship's primary hull, light beams from the sensor array illuminate the words "Outer Limits" where "NCC-1701-A" should be. Framed photographs and paintings decorate the place, what remains of Al Stovall's collection. Many are signed. Several

by Alan Bean. Above our booth is a framed painting of Mercury Seven, depicting a liftoff with the faces of the astronauts in the clouds. From the first American in space to Gene Roddenberry's fictional *Star Trek*, the place is a crossroads to the universe.

In the morning, we meet Charlotte at the front desk. She says she grew up in Gila Bend. Her grandfather was born in Ajo, just forty miles to the south, and moved here after marrying her grandmother from the O'odham tribe. "He worked for Stout's Hotel and Gila Bend Waterworks—you can still see the water tower once used by Union Pacific."

"What do you know about the Five Old Crabs?" I ask, thinking about a new chase.

"They're actual people—I don't remember their names. . . . One was a little guy. Kept getting in car accidents . . ." Charlotte solicits some help from another women passing through the lobby, and together they start coming up with names: "Ann Peterson, Bryon Nelson, Bill Henry . . . no, he died two years ago."

"So there are only four now?"

"No. People vote. There's a contest every year to decide who will be the next crab."

I wonder if there's a waiting list for Crabdom in Gila Bend.

Gila Bend was once known as the "Fan Belt Capital of the World" because travelers who stopped here needed one. It might as well have been called the "Exploding Radiator Capital of the World." Today, the Chamber of Commerce prefers "Crossroads of the Southwest."

We head west for a crossroads more ancient. A slash of blacktop through a black-rock desert of blooming saguaro and paloverde leads us to the Painted Rock Petroglyph Site, an outcrop of jumbled boulders like a freeway pileup. At number two on my list of prehistoric places, this is the largest of forty recorded petroglyph sites in the area. Spanning maybe two thousand years, the dark rocks hold about eight hundred images, from concentric circle and spiral glyphs of the Hohokam to horse-and-rider depictions to various names and symbols etched by travelers with Juan Batista de Anza, the Mormon Battalion, Butterfield Stage, and even General George Patton. A Kokopelli site if I ever saw one.

The stillness magnifies the heat and the buzzing of sweat-thirsty flies. A chuckwalla poses on a rock. A desert iguana scurries beneath a creosote bush, pausing in pencil-thin shade to lift one foot after another from the furnace of rubble and gaze upward with one half-lidded eye. Lizards crouching on rocks, considering lizards pecked into rocks.

Desert voyagers have left messages on this ancient blackboard for others to follow. But as far as I can tell, they might as well be attempted and forgotten physics equations for turning stone into bread or squeezing water from rock. I've seen similar indecipherable symbols under freeway overpasses. We circle the stacked rocks. Some of the weather-rounded boulders show signs across their whole face. Others hold markings on just a forehead or cheek. Or on a chin like the tattoos of Olive Oatman.

If Arizona had an official state graffiti, it should be petroglyphs. They represent an attempt to carry history forward, one way a culture—or one person—might outlast the forgetfulness of time: "I once met a man here, riding on the back of a horse . . . it was hot enough to make us spin dizzy circles . . . we shared a lizard for lunch . . ."

From the Painted Rock petroglyphs, our directions to the site of the Oatman Massacre are a bit iffy. Karen questions what I found online. Landmarks are verified but not the distances. I should cross the Gila River in six miles, then turn right then left through a ranch gate. "The residents do not mind, but their dogs do." Later, there are irrigated fields, a slightly hilly area, and another set of fields. Then more hills and more fields. Finally, I'm supposed to take a small road "through some bushes" and park.

Now we walk. Or slog. The cotton field has flooded its furrows and water spills into the road. Mud rises to our knees, hot, slick muck, and no way to avoid it. A hundred yards and we find the grave site. A tarnished bronze plaque on a granite headstone reads:

IN MEMORY OF
THE OATMAN FAMILY
SIX MEMBERS OF THIS
PIONEER FAMILY
MASSACRED BY INDIANS IN
MARCH 1851

Gila Bend, the hub of a wheel with spokes extending outward. For the Oatmans, this is where the wheel came off. Sometimes a crossroads becomes a cross hairs. Sometimes in the vastness of wilderness, you meet eternity.

We push through a ditch clotted with mesquite and saltbush and then climb above the floodplain along a road that the Mormon Battalion cut into a volcanic bluff more than 160 years ago. A cast-iron pavement of rock, stabbed with a few bulimic saguaro, slides north. Sunlight slams against the ground and rises up with a raised fist. Our steps sound like breaking glass. A pile of rock and a simple metal sign say this is the place of the Oatman Massacre.

They were dissident Mormons, followers of James Brewster headed for California. Roys and Mary Ann Oatman and their seven children had just spent a wet night on a sandbar in the Gila River and most of the day unloading their wagon to get it and the travel-weary stock to the top of this ridge. They were resting here, taking a meal of beans and bread, when a band of Yavapais approached looking for food and tobacco. Roys invited them to sit down. "Suddenly," writes J. Ross Browne, "with a terrific yell, they jumped in the air and dashed with uplifted clubs upon the doomed family." Fourteen-year-old Lorenzo fell to the ground with the first blows. Roys fell next, along with Mary Ann, a baby in her arms. The Yavapais stripped the seven bodies of valuables and ransacked the wagon. Two girls—Mary Ann (8) and Olive (13)—were taken captive and later sold to a group of Mojave Indians living on the Colorado River.

Lorenzo Oatman survived and spent the next years searching for his two sisters. Five years later, he was reunited with Olive—Mary Ann had died of starvation—and Olive's story became a national sensation. Her photograph, taken about that time, still captivates people with her vacant eyes and her chin lined with tattoos.

After the killings, the explorer, politician, and "Father of Arizona" Charles D. Poston gathered up the bones of the family, which others had placed under a cairn on the bluff, and reburied them in the present location near the river. Taking a board from his wagon, he carved "The Oatman Family 1851" with his penknife to mark the grave. J. Ross Browne visited the site thirteen years later and made some drawings of a "small enclosure near the road, with a board and inscription." Except for the mesquite and saltbush, the scene looks the same today.

Near the grave, a single phainopepla calls from a mesquite tree. I wonder about the number of *unmarked* graves that lie beneath my feet. How many buried civilizations—Hohokam, Patayan, Yuman, O'odham— dot this landscape? I breathe in fiery air, tasting of basalt and dust, and wipe the sweat from my eyes. The place reminds me that the world is a graveyard. That we eat the bones of those who have come before us. That we are all being fed into the earth one layer at a time.

In the late afternoon, Karen and I return to Gila Bend. We try the Texaco station, Charlotte's suggestion this morning for tracking down the Five Old Crabs. We get blank looks. Next door, at Bill Henry's Auto Parts, we meet Ralph "Chico" Ruiz, who's lived in Gila Bend since 1962. His dad worked for the railroad. "We lived in the coach cars," he tells us through his million-dollar smile. "Yeah! And we moved with the gangs."

Chico hands me an article with a picture of himself as a child at the counter of the shop. "Been working here since 1979. Bill Henry was a good boss." The article says Bill came to Gila Bend from Oklahoma in 1954 and took a job pumping gas. After many years of saving his money, he bought the gas station, and eventually added a radiator shop and service center.

"He was Crab Number Three," Chico says. "Yeah, and Clyde Kreeger is number four. But you should talk to Tom Lee over at Ironwood Towing."

Tom is a member of the town council, but he only wants to talk about dairy farming: "About five o'clock that brown cloud comes in—best shit you ever smelled." Tom introduces us to Tim, a lifelong Gila Bender. "The original five were Elks members," Tim says, "and Bill Elms was the first. The old fart worked the railroad. You should check with Steve at the Shell station."

By now I'm confused. Too many old crustaceans talking about too many old crabs at too many gas stations. I thought there were five, but I'm off my count, and I still haven't figured out who, if anyone, is replacing the dead crabs. I've heard that students at Gila Bend High insist the five crabs refer to the school administration. I've also heard that any one of the five crabs is just as likely to run you out of town as off their property.

The Shell station is out of town.

MAY

Two-tailed Swallowtail Butterfly

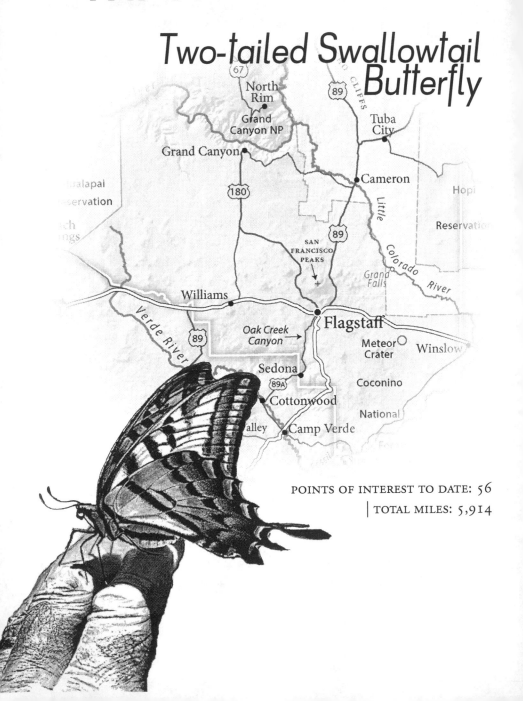

POINTS OF INTEREST TO DATE: 56
| TOTAL MILES: 5,914

Fallen from the Sky

BOX CANYON

ELEVATION: 4,744 FEET | FOUNDED: MIOCENE EPOCH,
15 TO 8 MILLION YEARS AGO | POPULATION: 1

Seventy miles west of Bisbee, deep in a canyon in the Santa Rita Mountains, I lean against the hood of the Kia at 9:00 p.m. and bathe in moonlight. Poorwills call from the oak trees, asking their two-note questions: *Who's there? Who's there? Who's there?*

"Just me," I say, loud enough to startle myself. "Here for the night."

It's early May, and the first meteor shower of the year peaks tonight—the Eta Aquarids. The moon, however, is a problem. And it's not just any moon, but a "supermoon," the closest moon of the year. (Later this month, this moon in its new phase will slip across the sun forming an annular eclipse, and I plan on watching it with legs dangling into Grand Canyon.) But I figure it will set near 3:30 a.m. and give me an hour or so of blackness splitting needles of light. Excuse enough to spend a night alone in the desert. Tonight, darkness is my destination. I've arrived.

Hercules rises. Next will be Aquila. Then finally Aquarius in the east. The constellation is the radiant for the shower, the point in the sky where the meteors seem to originate as the earth passes through the ice-and-dust-strewn orbital trail of Halley's Comet.

It was a night like this, twenty-six years ago, camping in the desert west of the Tucson Mountains, that I saw the fuzz ball of Halley's when it made its last, somewhat disappointing appearance. I've seen much better comets, each spewing their own dust plumes, which, if the heavens align perfectly, create their own meteor spectacles. By far the best meteor shower I've witnessed was the Leonid on November 18–19, 2002. It was a rare, once-every-hundred-years show with thousands of meteors flaring each hour. Screaming into our atmosphere at forty-four miles per second. A meteor storm of raining light. I watched it stiff-necked from a lawn chair at the end of my Tucson driveway with my friend Steve Gladish. They say nature abhors a vacuum. On that night, the vacuum of space was filled with sprays of cosmic embers, a revelation reflected in the astonished looks of our upturned faces.

Comets give us meteors to shower in, while asteroids shed chunks of space to weigh in our palms. Originally, comets and asteroids carried the oceans to our world and maybe even the seeds of life to populate it. Now, they are 4.5-billion-year-old leftovers of the solar system. I find a strange comfort in knowing that even when God puts something together, there are leftover parts, a few remaining nuts and bolts rolling around in the drop cloth of space-time.

Somewhere near here, one of his extra washers came to earth. I first saw a replica of it after the Flandrau Science Center and Planetarium opened in 1975. The peculiar dark torus—the Tucson Ring meteorite—stood on its base against the wall of one room, weighed down with its history. John Bartlett, the U.S. boundary commissioner and one of the earliest to make a record of the meteorite, writes in 1852 that a Tucson blacksmith was using the 4-foot-diameter, 1,400-pound space rock for an anvil. "It was found about twenty miles distant towards Tubac, and about eight miles from the road, where we were told were many larger masses." It's Bartlett's mention of additional "larger masses" that has intrigued meteorite hunters for decades.

One story says Jesuit missionaries discovered the meteorite in these mountains at a place called Puerto de los Muchachos. Another relates how Juan Bautista de Anza was so taken with the iron ring that he brought it to the presidio at Tucson with intentions of shipping it to Spain. Whatever its origin, a few years after Bartlett made his examination and sketch, a U.S. Army doctor named B. J. D. Irwin found it half buried in a Tucson side street, claimed possession, and sent it off to the Smithsonian Institution where it remains today.

In the late 1970s, the then-director of the Flandrau, Richard Willey, became interested in finding Puerto de los Muchachos, hoping to locate other meteorites. The problem was that no map located the pass. Crisscrossing the Santa Cruz valley with a copy of the 1849 title for the La Canoa Mexican land grant, Willey eventually recognized that La Canoa's present northwest corner was more than three miles off and that Mount Fagan in the northern extension of the Santa Ritas was the mountain peak of the Pass of the Children. The place where the Tucson Ring most likely crashed to earth is today known as Box Canyon. Right here. Fallen from the sky.

By one estimate, the chances of being hit by a meteorite are one person every seven thousand years. Tell that to that monk in Milan in 1650. Or the English shepherd and his five sheep in 1725. Then there's the case of Mrs. Hewlett Hodges of Sylacauga, Alabama. On November 30, 1954, a ten-pound meteorite tore through her roof, smashed her radio, and slammed into her hip while she slept, before it finally spun to a stop on her living room floor. She survived, and I remember in grade school being fascinated by photographs of her gruesomely bruised abdomen.

In his book, *The Fallen Sky: An Intimate History of Shooting Stars*, Christopher Cokinos estimates that one million meteorites in the two-pound class strike the planet each year, and objects weighing as much as the one that woke Mrs. Hodges from her slumber fall to earth five times a day. Larger events become increasingly rare, however. The Tunguska impact in 1908 flattened whole forests and roasted reindeer on the hoof.

What we should worry about are the so-called planet killers, asteroids of a sufficient size—like three miles in diameter—that have earth-crossing orbits. If you want to scare yourself, take a look at the "potentially hazardous asteroids" that Lincoln Near-Earth Asteroid Research (LINEAR) has documented. There are 1,384 known and you can click on any one to see a 3-D diagram of its current orbit. Wind it forward into the future, if you dare.

On April 28, 2000, LINEAR discovered my daughter Melissa's asteroid, Minor Planet 15624 Lamberton, which was named in her honor as a finalist in the 2001 Discovery Channel Young Scientist Challenge. It, too, is a planet killer, but so far remains safely tucked into the rumble-tumble belt of leftover planet-makings between Mars and Jupiter in its 3.66-year orbit.

This night, I couldn't see Melissa's asteroid even if I had a telescope of sufficient power. It crosses the sky during daylight hours. In five months, however, her asteroid will be overhead at midnight in an orbit bringing it closest to earth—but no closer, barring any unforeseen nudges.

In these mast-laden woods, I slip into my sleeping bag and become a soft taco for a bear. Haunting squeaks leap from one oak after another: elf owls, recently arrived from Mexico to celebrate Cinco de Mayo. I'm surrounded by night-bird voices, sipping the fruit of the blue agave from Zacatecas, gift of a friend from the Mexican hamlet. Galileo Galilei may have preferred wine with his stargazing, but I'm commemorating the holiday with tequila, which settles into my joints as my mind drifts toward blackness.

At 3:30 a.m., I wake to moonset in the center of the Astronomical Capital of the World, home of the Dark Sky people. Vain Cassiopeia swings in her starry chair in the northeast. Cygnus spreads its wings and flies down the Milky Way, which blooms with stars as thick as clouds as the sky turns to ink. I lie against a cold pillow with cold cheeks and watery eyes.

Night in the desert is absolute. Nothing else exists in the world. No cities with their night-wash of light. No headlights or beacons. It's a darkness without end, and I lie alone at the far side of it. Darkness but not emptiness.

The first meteorite splashes from Aquarius to Aquila and bright Altair, leaving a blue track in its wake that brightens and fades. "Whoa!" I shout into the silent black oaks with involuntary vocal cords. Then another streaks across the curve of my eyes, which dart from horizon to zenith and back. And another . . . firefall! An hour later, the sky blues in the east. I rise and start my coffee. The western kingbirds sound wake-up anyway, their chirps like smoke detectors on low battery.

On my way home, I stop in Sonoita at the Dos Cabezas WineWorks, which I made a note of yesterday (proximity alert!) on my way to Box Canyon. I fell in love with local wines after Karen and I moved to Cochise County, and my favorite is this winery's 2006 El Norte.

I know nothing about wine. I can't pronounce most of them. The most expensive wine I ever tasted came from a friend—a fifty-four-dollar bottle of Cloudy Bay Chardonnay. But I know what I like, and the Dos

Cabezas El Norte has a wonderful, rich spiced-fruit flavor for a red wine. It had also scored an eighty-eight on *Wine Spectator* magazine's one-hundred-point scale. No Arizona wine has scored in the nineties—yet! I suspect, however, that this year's grapes will get us there. Arizona wine is on the rise.

I walk into the tasting room with some unease. I've never done this before. But the blond woman who greets me answers my questions with a smile, laughing easily. No pressure. No intimidation. Her name is Kelly Bostock, and she and her husband, Todd, have owned Dos Cabezas since 2006 when the couple bought the eighty-acre vineyard near Willcox and moved the winery to Sonoita where the family had another vineyard in nearby Elgin.

"Elgin is still undiscovered," she says. "And we wanted a chance to be part of something from the ground up. Our production is out back. Would you like to try a tasting?"

I hesitate. She hands me a printed sheet with a listing of eight wines and sets a glass in front of me. "This is our newest release, a 2011 Meskeoli from our Cimarron vineyard." She pours the chilled white wine into the glass. "It's a blend of white grapes that we describe as vibrant and nervy. Some say it smells like wet rocks, lime zest, and sassafras, and once in the mouth, the flavor reminds me of Mexican limes. . . ."

I pull the glass to my lips. It is the best wine I've ever tasted. I still can't pronounce the names: Viognier, Pinot, Mourvèdre, Meskeoli, but my shyness eases. Then it comes to me. I'm comfortable in nature because I understand the language. I can read the words. Language is the key. With a bit of effort, I can be comfortable with anything. Conversation, people, even wine.

Galileo called wine "sunlight, held together by water." (Not bad for a guy born three hundred years before anyone worked out the equation for photosynthesis.) I drive away from the winery with a bottle of 2009 El Norte tucked into the passenger seat. Lest this book become "Chasing Southern Arizona," in two weeks, I head north to Flagstaff (Arizona's first International Dark Sky City) and Grand Canyon. I'll pass through the Verde Valley, another region getting attention for its wines. I'll make a list of vineyards to explore—breweries too—and add my latest discovery of a premier rum distillery. Then there's the Willcox Wine Country Fall Festival. This means chasing Arizona wine and beer and spirits—because I'll certainly need something to wash down all the greasy chimichangas. Tell that to my Baptist-raised wife!

Time to practice my wine descriptions. Let's see, a blend of white grapes both vibrant and nervy, with a heady nose that envisions dry rocks, ephedra, and cactus nopalitos, and an unctuous, persistent textural quality in the mouth that keeps it occupied with a tart green chile fruit Velcro clinging to the palate . . . nice. I hear *Wine Spectator* is looking for contributors!

Digging Graves

PATAGONIA

ELEVATION: 4,050 FEET | FOUNDED: 1898 | POPULATION: 913

In the second week in May, I join Jerry Marzinsky at Gathering Grounds, a coffeehouse in Patagonia run by Heather and her sister Audrey, both natives to the area. Brandon, a young man with dark curls and Audrey's husband, waits on us. "If I had to say one thing about Patagonia," he tells me, "it would be the friendliness."

Jerry has his "Black Toads" essay with him and so we look it over as we sip rich Guatemalan coffee. A patient he's treating is hearing voices and seeing toadlike shadows coming out of her doctor's mouth as he speaks. "Lacey," as he calls her, is addicted to methamphetamine, a drug he says opens channels to the voices. He says the problem can't be solved with additional drugs, antipsychotic or not, which only treat the symptoms. Jerry has found a way to make the voices go silent, a way to empower the patient with a remedy that uses only prayer and meditation. But it hasn't been easy. He once had a patient, speaking for the voice in his head, threaten: "You have no right to interfere with our way of life!"

"If the professionals knew what I was doing," he says, "I'd lose all credibility."

"You're making enemies with parasitic entities," I say. "Credibility is the least of your problems." Jerry is just the kind of person I want with me whenever I visit old haunted ruins, crumbling prisons, and, in the case of today's adventure, a hundred-year-old graveyard—yes, *another* graveyard. Number seven this year. The last time I poked around the Harshaw Cemetery, there were human bones rising out of the rocky soil as if the ground were speaking.

We drive east out of town along Harshaw Road into the Patagonia Mountains. The air is warm with dust and the pungence of unscrolling sycamore leaves. Gould's turkeys cross the road, unconcerned about private property. I've seen a plethora of *Keep Out* signs: "This property is protected by nine dogs, one .357, and one sheriff (if needed)." The Patagonias are home to some of the oldest mining communities in Arizona, places with names like Mowry, Duquesne, Washington Camp, and Harshaw that sprang up around silver and lead mines with workings dating back to Spanish times. The last mines closed in the 1960s, but the people living here—probably not Spaniards—still value their privacy, even more than life itself . . . your life, that is.

A Coronado National Forest sign indicating *Harshaw Townsite* stands in front of a few melting adobe walls. Vacant eye sockets of window frames stare through the trees. Plaster peels from walls like dead white skin. It's all that remains of a town of two thousand people. There are more people in the graveyard at Harshaw than living around it.

The town is named for David Tecumseh Harshaw, a rancher who found more profit in what lies beneath the ground than what grazes over it. In 1877, he stumbled on an outcrop of silver ore while tending his cattle. Word spread about the strike as one to rival Tombstone, and within a few years, hotels and dancehalls, stores, blacksmith shops, stables, and seven saloons—always saloons—lined both sides of the three-quarter-mile road.

Then it all ended . . . until it began again—and again. Twice, maybe three times, as the price of silver fluctuated or the mines played out or wildfires swept through the mountains. Harshaw saw its last spurt of activity during the 1940s and '50s, when the American Smelting and Refining Company (ASARCO) worked the Flux and Trench Mines. Then, in 1953, the town became part of the Coronado National Forest. A decade later, a few score residents still lived among the buckled buildings and abandoned cars. Since they owned no titles, the Forest Service considered them squatters. But federal relocation efforts failed. For some reason, people didn't trust the government. Today, a few holdouts remain among the oak-dappled hills, fingers locked around the stocks of their rifles.

A desert grassland whiptail lizard greets us at the entrance to the graveyard with tilted head and flicked tongue. "Scariest animal on the planet," I tell Jerry.

"Why? Is it poisonous?"

"No. Worse," I say. "The lizards are female. They reproduce without sex, laying eggs that hatch into little clones. She doesn't need a mate. In fact, there are no males in the species."

"That *is* scary," Jerry says.

Someone has trimmed back the dry grasses from around the white-plastered grave vaults and jumbled rock piles. There are fresh plastic flowers. The mesquite trees look pruned. Angel Soto's bronze marker shines like new. We walk among the

well-tended dead. The Harshaw Cemetery is mostly the family plot of Angel and Josefa Soto, a pioneer couple who settled here in the 1880s. Their descendants care for the fifty marked graves and still have retreats at the Soto family home, one of the few remaining houses in Harshaw.

Jerry finds the oldest grave: Freddie Lee Sorrells was five when he died in 1885. He would rest nineteen years alone on this hillside before Angel Soto joined him, and then many others. I stand over the grave of Pablo Lopez Acevedo, formerly a driller for the Flux Mine. He was thirty when he died of "internal injuries and multiple contusions over his entire body, owing to an accidental dynamite explosion." The life of a miner wasn't only hard on the children. "These are the voices I want to hear from," I tell Jerry.

Recently, several Canadian mining companies have laid claims in the Patagonia Mountains. One of them, Wildcat Silver Corporation, has its eyes on the Hermosa properties and the 3,200 acres of national forest surrounding them, woodlands that harbor a species of oak that grows nowhere else in the United States. But the company says the area holds 315 million ounces of silver. Relying on vast quantities of mined groundwater, the open-pit operation would become the largest silver mine in the country.

Dr. Elizabeth A. Bernays, a retired entomologist and regents' professor at the University of Arizona now living in the town of Patagonia, writes eloquently about what she calls the "Other Patagonia." "I'm struck by the biological diversity here," she says in *Natural History* magazine (and

I can hear her Aussie accent in the words), "sky islands, washes, desert flats, and grasslands that attract wildlife of all kinds . . . more than 300 species of birds, including violet-crowned hummingbirds and black-bellied whistling ducks." In her article, she says most creatures come to the area because of the creeks, and she expresses concern about the scarcity of water. The proposed mines weigh heavy on her.

The irony of open-pit mines among the graveyards of miners. In some places—Iowa cornland, Mississippi cotton country—graveyards are all that remain to remind us of what was once vast tangled prairie or old-growth longleaf pine forest. The cemeteries are genetic seed banks of the dead. If open-pit mines come to the Patagonia Mountains, if our economic drive for copper continues to outweigh our need for conservation, we'll at least have graveyards like Harshaw to recall *what* we've lost among the whom.

Two and half months later, at the end of July, I return to Patagonia and take the beaten road to Liz Bernays's beautiful straw-bale home. Liz has invited me to stay at her guesthouse and join her on an early morning trip into the Patagonia Mountains to band hummingbirds with Susan Wethington at her off-grid place on Harshaw Creek. But I have butterflies on my mind.

"Are you seeing any two-tailed swallowtails in your garden, Liz?" I had asked her recently, trying to hide the desperation in my voice.

"Yes, but not recently," she said. "But Susan has a flower garden too."

Dr. Susan Wethington is a former IBM engineer who fell in love with hummingbirds while volunteering at the Arizona-Sonora Desert Museum. She is one of the three founding scientists of the Hummingbird Monitoring Network, a grassroots conservation organization that she runs out of her home. The nonprofit has thirty stations from Mexico City to British Columbia and relies on 1,500 volunteers. Citizen science for the love of hummingbirds—all to improve their lives. By trapping and banding what she calls "little flying laboratories," Susan gathers habitat and climate information along the hummingbirds' migratory path from Alaska to Mexico. The information tells her how well they are adapting to any changes. "Hummingbirds bring joy to all who watch them," she says. "There is something very right about a world that created hummingbirds."

I walk in the rain to Liz's back door, stepping over wet stones embedded with fanciful iron figures created by "Metal Joe," a local artist. Since my last visit to Patagonia in May with Jerry, the monsoon thunderstorms have begun. I was fortunate enough to catch the first sky-splitting detonations and downpour in the Santa Catalina Mountains with Karen and two fire spotters named Dave and Gus the dog. It's been a wild eight weeks: seeing the fiery ring of a solar eclipse at Grand Canyon, watching a once-in-lifetime passage of Venus across the disk of the sun at Kitt Peak, hearing wolves in the White Mountains, handing off my oldest daughter in marriage. I've just spent the last few days in the Huachuca Mountains searching for the ridge-nosed rattlesnake with a friend and a couple of Texas herpetologists we met who are also looking for the state reptile. Tomorrow afternoon I'll see if Tony and Arianna have had any luck.

We rise at 4:00 a.m. the next morning and Liz prepares eggs for breakfast, which she has just collected from her chickens. Then we drive in the predawn light to Susan's and Lee Rogers's solar-powered Rastra home, which the couple built together. Lee is waiting for us at the hummingbird feeders in the yard, having set up two cylindrical mesh curtains he can raise and lower over the feeders from the distance of his chair. Susan calls a greeting from her porch, where she has staged her banding table, instruments, and notebooks. Liz and I take seats, and Susan slides a clipboard and data sheets to me. I'm to write what Susan relays. Liz will feed each hummingbird a sip of sugar water before releasing it.

We begin thirty minutes after sunrise. Lee brings the first hummingbird in a mesh bag, clips the bag into a contraption like a small umbrella clothesline, and rotates it toward us. Susan slips a head-lamp magnifier over her long silver hair. She begins reading off letters and numbers. I struggle to get the right ones into the right columns. The bird weighs the same as a penny. Then Susan lifts a tiny band no larger than the *O* on this page, reads off the number to me, and fits it on to the bird's leg. When I look up from the data sheet, Lee is there with another bird.

During breaks in the trapping, I watch for butterflies among the blooming *Anisacanthus* shrubs and salvia while we talk about the politics of mines. I wonder what Susan's data sheets will show as the mines turn the mountains inside out. More feather wear? Less fat on breastbones? Fewer birds? I count dozens of pipevine swallowtails and queens but no two-tails. A gray hawk screams from the cottonwoods.

Five hours later, we quit. Liz releases the final hummingbird, which rests momentarily on her extended fingers then zips away. Thirty-three hummingbirds. "Fairly light," Liz says. She will repeat the process every two weeks during migration (March through October). "Our biggest day was 140 hummingbirds," she adds. I imagine a whirling umbrella clothesline. A hummingbird centrifuge. A spinning world creating hummingbirds because it's the right thing to do.

In the afternoon, I wander through town looking fruitlessly for butterflies. I consider indulging in one of Cecilia San Miguel's Old-World handmade wood-fired, blessed-by-Our-Lady-of-Guadalupe chorizo, cilantro, and jalapeño pizzas at the Velvet Elvis. Instead, I take the long way home through the thunderhead-capped Huachuca Mountains for another search for the ridge-nosed rattlesnake. At the forest road turnoff to Scotia Canyon, I run into the Texas couple and several Arizona Game and Fish Department officials. Tony and Arianna are in trouble.

Back in Bisbee, I unpack the Kia and chat with my neighbors Hayley and Todd, looking up from the trunk to see a two-tailed swallowtail drift by. "I don't believe it!" I tell them. "I just spent a day looking for the thing, and there it goes. I should check the grill of my car!"

"So that's the state butterfly?" Hayley says.

"Yes. My nemesis."

Later, I check my e-mail and there's a note from Hayley. When I open the attachment, her photograph of the swallowtail fills my screen.

"Found this guy in my yard," she writes.

Pluto Lives Here

FLAGSTAFF, ARIZONA'S FIRST INTERNATIONAL DARK SKY CITY

ELEVATION: 6,910 FEET | FOUNDED: 1881 | POPULATION: 65,870

I drive through a desert upland country of blooming saguaros, passing the last state flower on the last saguaro on I-17 exactly 250 miles northwest of home before topping out of Black Canyon onto Black Mesa. The saguaro is on the left at Milepost 250.

Soon, descending into the Verde Valley, I catch my first glimpse of the San Francisco Peaks, Fremont and Agassiz and Humphreys climbing each other's backs with the latter reaching to the very top of Arizona. The 12,633-foot peak is a future destination with my hiking compadre, Chuck LaRue. The familiar triangular fractal of the mountains tells me I've crossed into northern Arizona, from the blistered land of cacti to the country of rock-dusted piñon and ponderosa. Land of Navajo and Hopi and Hualapai, of Vibram-soled plateau walkers.

An hour later, I pull into the town of backpacks and cargo pants, arriving a few days early in preparation for the solar eclipse on May 20. I figure I can work in two destinations in one by combining the end of one week with the beginning of another, in this case, Flagstaff and Grand Canyon. Call it a fudge, a bend of the rules I set for myself. Flagstaff is 340 miles from Bisbee. If I'm going to chase more than southern Arizona, I'll have to chain some trips together.

The voice of Flagstaff is the sound of a freight train coming your way. I charge across the BNSF Railway tracks and, like Jackson Browne, stand on the corner of Phoenix Avenue and Beaver Street at the original alignment of Route 66. A very pink 1963 Mercury Monterey takes a look at me, but there's no girl in a flatbed Ford in sight. (The town boasts that

Browne originally wrote the famous line in "Take It Easy" about Flagstaff, not Winslow.) The classic car of the open road with the rear breezeway window is parked outside the DuBeau Hostel. I walk along a low fence of upturned sandstone slabs and step into the lobby, crossing over wood floors past photos of Marilyn Monroe and Elvis Presley.

"I'm Marie," the woman at the desk says with a British accent. "Welcome to the oldest hotel in Flagstaff."

"Really!" I say, having just wandered in to look around. "I had no idea, but this seems to happen to me a lot these days."

Marie explains A. E. DuBeau came from Los Angeles in 1929 to build his motel along Route 66 for "a better class of motorist." For DuBeau, this meant motorists who wanted enclosed garages with steam heat to coax to life stubborn car engines in winter, the kind of motorists who sleep in their cars on cold nights, no doubt. DuBeau never bragged about amenities like heated rooms, but he was proud of the in-room toilets.

When I ask about the best place for a late lunch, Marie sends me across the street to the Beaver Street Brewery for "a pint of local brew." Perfect! Part of experiencing any place in Arizona is drinking the water, which I prefer flavored with malted barley and hops. Beaver Street Brewery, despite the name, is not a brewery but a brewpub. Microbreweries, like the nearby Lumberyard Brewing Company, brew beer for distribution. Brewpubs brew beer on site for consumption on the premises only. (I learn all this from the menu.)

I order the most full-bodied, hoppiest India Pale Ale they have: a Lumberyard IPA with a rating of ninety IBU, or "International Bitterness Unit"—I'm not making this up. The IBU is a scale from one to one hundred that measures bitterness based on the concentration of alpha acids from the hops. The copper-colored, piney flavored ale goes well with the pub's own burger: Angus chuck blended with garlic, fresh basil, sundried tomatoes, and topped with Havarti.

Formerly, my beer of choice was always Tecate, but a few years ago, I discovered an IPA while fly fishing on the Bitterroot River in western Montana. Now, I drink IPAs everywhere I go and so far haven't matched Missoula's Big Sky IPA, whose Simcoe hops push through the bitterness into a refreshing citrus flavor. Sipping my Lumberyard IPA, I decide to chase the best IPA in Arizona. I'm not sure I can. I'm not sure I can locate a beer that evokes leaky waders, drifting flies, and Bitterroot cutthroat under an expansive cobalt sky. But I'm willing to try.

After lunch, I walk south along Beaver Street past layered native sandstone and basalt fieldstone lifted into historic structures. When I look up, I'm standing behind Biological Sciences at Northern Arizona University, the place where I took my first college courses in biology, the place where I chose to become a naturalist. That was thirty-six years ago. I was a peach-faced seventeen-year-old when I moved to Flagstaff in 1976, hauling a few belongings—mostly my bass guitar—to Tinsley Hall dormitory in the back of my blue 1968 Toyota Land Cruiser. That fall, I settled in Flagstaff—or "Flag," as we called the college town. Between studying trigonometry and slime molds, I lounged at Granny's Closet and danced on Friday nights to Styx and Heart cover tunes at Shakey Drake's. I sank skis into powder on the slopes of the San Francisco Peaks at Snowbowl, rode a water chute at Slide Rock in Oak Creek Canyon, and left bootprints along the trails of the Little C Gorge and Grand Canyon. Flagstaff became my home. I had connected with those original Bostonians who came here exactly one hundred years earlier during our nation's first centennial, stripped a ponderosa pine of its branches and bark and raised the Stars and Stripes on a makeshift staff.

Outside red-walled Old Main, even the skateboarders wear cargo pants at what was originally intended to be a territorial reform school. I circle back around to the Wettaw Biochemistry Building, searching for evidence of a past life, and find it in the exterior walls. Several of the lower buff-colored Coconino sandstone blocks hold side-by-side footprints the size of quarters. I touch one of the 260-million-year-old surfaces, fitting three fingers into the tiny ridged dimples with toes. The animals were probably *Chelichnus*, squat, four-legged, mammal-like reptiles from a time when the planet was one giant landmass and a vast sea of sand covered northern Arizona. But I feel warm sand slumped into a crescent at the heel of each foot as if only yesterday some horned lizard climbed the steep slope of a wind-blown dune.

I walk north along San Francisco Street toward the Train Station and Visitor Center, along homes and businesses built of pitted, lichen-splashed basalt, some from the 1920s. The station, however, like many historic buildings in town, is made of local sandstone. Bloodred blocks of Moenkopi rest on the stronger dune-born Coconino. It's a recent renovation that replaced part of the 1889 construction, which had suffered from erosion of the softer stone. Wettaw Biochemistry has a similar design. After fire destroyed the original wooden station several months after it was built, the railroad switched to materials being quarried in the Moenkopi Formation only a mile east of downtown: Arizona Red flagstone. A new industry, second only to Flagstaff's lumber production, was employing Scottish stonecutters to harvest and lift thirty-ton blocks onto boxcars for shipment across the West.

Flagstone. The word probably comes from the Middle English term *flagge* for *turf*, or from the Old Norse *flaga* for *slab*. But for me, *flagstone* is the stone from Flag. If I were to continue north across the tracks, I'd run into the Babbitt buildings with their blockwork in moon-gray volcanic dacite and Moenkopi sandstone. Then I'd see the Coconino County Courthouse, the finest example anywhere of Arizona Red construction. Finally, going east along Birch Avenue, I'd find another kind of stone altogether, the irregular-chunked Kaibab limestone that served to insulate a 1946 ice house.

Basalt shingled with lichens, sandstone pocked with animal tracks—many of these structures might be lessons in biogeography, the study in the distribution of species through space and time. And none more so than the Historic Ice House with its seabed walls crammed with half-moons of extinct brachiopods and clams and the coiled horns of snails and chambered nautiloids. From shimmering two-hundred- to three-hundred-million-year-old slabs of fossilized tropical seafloor and desert dune and flooded river bottom to dark lumps of six-million-year-old lava flow to speckled rubble of a half-million-year-old volcanic dome to the one-thousand-year-old fragments beneath my feet, frozen lava rain from one of the planet's largest cinder cones—to walk through downtown Flagstaff is to walk through northern Arizona's geologic history.

Flag. Home of the Lumberjacks. A timber town hewn from stone and tucked into the shadow of Arizona's highest mountain peak. With the right primer, you could read the whole Colorado Plateau's life story in the rocks of Beaver or San Francisco streets. You could be flung back to Permian times yet not have to deal with the giant cockroaches. One hundred and thirty years founded on hundreds of millions. Flagstaff bends my perception of time, like starlight curving around the gravity well of a brilliant star.

As the stars come out over the world's first Dark Sky city, I take the steep road to Mars Hill and the Lowell Observatory, one of the oldest observatories in the United States. *Mike Brown better not show his face around here*, I think, as I pass the *Home of Pluto* sign at roadside. The Caltech astronomer is responsible for the demotion of our ninth planet to the new category of "dwarf planet" after he discovered Pluto wasn't the only icy rock at the far edge of our solar system. He thinks the hate mail from schoolchildren is tough. I wonder how Arizona could allow some guy from California to steal our planet.

"A real sore point here!" says Jeff Hall, the observatory director, when I rudely ask him for his definition of a planet. We're outside the auditorium where he's just given a lecture on everything anyone has ever wanted to know about solar eclipses. He looks young—too young to be an astronomer—in his blue button-up shirt and brown nest of hair. He's all arm movements and story as he tells me about solar prominences and hydrogen-alpha filters, spots, storms, and transits of Venus. He works on Lowell's Solar-Stellar Spectrograph, which monitors the sun and sunlike stars. But what he's most excited about is the new Discovery Channel Telescope.

"It's very exciting!" he says. "A tremendous gamble for us. But twenty years ago, we made the decision to be a research institute, not just a museum."

Twenty years ago you were in junior high, I think.

"It uses active optics. The mirror got its precisioning where you're from—the U of A."

The 4.3-meter Discovery Channel Telescope is Lowell's flagship research telescope and will be used to answer such questions as how our solar system formed. In another part of the Steele Visitor Center, a twenty-three-year-old graduate student from NAU shows me the Blink

Comparator that Clyde Tombaugh used to discover Pluto eighty-two years ago. The machine is blinking away, creating a two-frame movie, its electromagnet clacking back and forth between the glass photographic plates that Tombaugh took six days apart.

"Take a look," she says, and I peek through the brass eyepiece. A tiny white speck in a black field of hundreds of white specks jumps a few millimeters back and forth—Pluto!

"Dwarf nothing," I tell her. "Only an intellect vast and cool and unsympathetic would call it that. It's still the ninth planet to me."

Clyde Tombaugh discovered Pluto fourteen years after the death of Percival Lowell, the Boston mathematician and astronomer who came to Flagstaff in 1894 to build his own private observatory to chase an obsession with Mars. A Kansas farm boy who had aspirations to be an astronomer but no money for college, Tombaugh constructed his own telescopes, grinding his mirrors from glass blanks and making drawings from what he saw on the surfaces of Mars and Jupiter. In December 1928, he sent his drawings to the Lowell Observatory, asking for advice. They offered him a job. It seems the observatory needed an amateur astronomer to work long hours at low wages in a cold dome looking for a hypothetical object called "Planet X."

On February 18, 1930, only a year after he left Kansas for Arizona, Tombaugh sat at the eyepiece of his Blink Comparator as it worked one horizontal strip after another through its two identical photographic plates he'd recently taken. In a field of thousands of stars near Delta Geminorum, something moved. An image popped in and out. After checking his plates for possible errors, he became convinced. He hurried down the long, narrow hallway to the director's office. "Dr. Slipher," the still-wet-behind-the-ears Tombaugh said nonchalantly, "I have found your Planet X." Vesto M. Slipher had been looking for it for twenty-five years.

Percival Lowell had first started the search for Planet X, and the planet's name "Pluto" recognizes this in its stylized astronomical symbol P and L. Lowell believed Uranus and Neptune had displaced orbits due to the gravity of an unseen planet. The search continued after Lowell's death in 1916 (Tombaugh would have been ten), when Dr. Veston M. Slipher became director of the observatory.

But it is Mars that Percival Lowell is remembered for. My mind's picture of him always has him seated in his black suit and dwarfed by the monster 24-in. Alvan Clark Refractor, wool flatcap reversed on his head, right eye peering into the eyepiece as he concentrates on the waterworks of the Red Planet. His theories that an advanced but dying culture had built canals to tap the polar ice caps of their desert world didn't always sit well with the astronomical community. One of his assistants, Andrew Douglass, had a falling-out with him and left astronomy for archaeology, establishing the world-renowned dendrochronology (tree-ring) lab at the University of Arizona. But even as astronomers ostracized him, the public loved his ideas.

In his 1895 book, *Mars: Is There Life on Mars?*, Lowell writes, "We have learnt that the very same substances with which we are familiar on this earth, iron, magnesium, calcium, and the rest, are present in the far-off stars that strew the depths of space. Nothing new under the sun! Indeed, there is nothing new above it but ever-varying detail." He believed that astronomy teaches that we are mere details in the evolution of the universe, that we may never find our twins, but we are destined to "discover any number of cousins scattered through space."

I can't think of Percival Lowell without hearing Carl Sagan repeating "Barsoom" in my head. The beloved scientist had a fascination with the Edgar Rice Burrough's books about John Carter and Dejah Thoris, the princess of Mars. To think that Burroughs and H. G. Wells and even Ray Bradbury had gotten their inspiration from Lowell. He was probably as important in his time as Carl Sagan was in mine for filling people's minds with wonder about the Red Planet.

Outside the Clark Telescope Dome, a small crowd gathers around a guide who assists us with a 16-in. Dobsonian telescope. We take turns looking at the Whirlpool Galaxy (M51) and its companion, both glowing pinwheels in the eons-long throws of collision. I see two ships passing one another, leaving wakes that ripple the stars.

When my turn comes at the Clark Refractor, I step inside the circular room, its curving walls of planked ponderosa and bucket-shaped "dome" rotating on twenty-four 1957 Ford truck tires. Godfrey Sykes (soon to be associated with Tucson's Desert Laboratory) and his brother Stanley claimed they could build anything. The local bicycle makers designed and constructed the dome for Percival Lowell.

The tour guide aligns the six-ton, thirty-two-foot rolled-steel and glass telescope with the effort of two fingers, aiming it through a slip in the dome to magnify a point of light 282 times normal. "You can adjust the focus here," he says, laying a hand on the control knob. My right eye comes to rest where Lowell's did a century ago.

The image is stunning—the buff orb and moons, the dark Cassini division in the rings. It is almost as stunning as my first look at Saturn in my backyard when I was twelve, randomly pointing my new 4.5-in. reflector at stars while staring bleary-eyed through the ocular and twisting the focus. I remember my sudden astonishment and the unexpected joy of recognition. What I saw hanging in the blackness of nothing were golden rings of light.

Later, I stand in the dark of a new moon, a moon that even now swings closer in its orbit to slide across the sun and throw its shadow into the abyss of Grand Canyon. From this tiny observatory courtyard on this tiny pale blue dot, Sagan's "mote of dust suspended in a sunbeam," I scan a swath of stars from Saturn across the ecliptic to the southwest, stopping on the red dot of Mars. *Barsoom.* I imagine Percival Lowell's canals crisscrossing its ochre disk like a mirror reflection of one of my own blood-veined retinas. "That we are the only minds in space," he wrote in 1895, "it takes indeed a very small mind to fancy." Indeed.

A Ring of Fire Above the Rim

GRAND CANYON

ELEVATION: 7,000 FEET | FOUNDED: 4 TO 6 MILLION YEARS AGO |
POPULATION: 10,000 (TODAY)

Today, at 5:25 p.m., the moon will make first touch at the disk of the sun. For the next hour, it will slide diagonally over the sun's face to annulus, forming a thin ring of molten gold in the western sky above Grand Canyon, silencing the birds. I will be one of an estimated ten thousand people at the rim viewing it.

This morning I'm watching the sun. I carry a Mayan suspicion about solar eclipses, what the ancient Yucatán people called *chi' ihal k'iin* or "to eat the sun," as if a serpent were swallowing an egg. If I were pregnant, I'd be wearing red underwear and a safety pin, just in case. The Maya know about eclipses. They've painted red and black glyphs on lime-glossed *Ficus* bark at precise dates. They've correlated synodic lunations, something I can barely pronounce, much less grasp. I'm guessing they predicted the day and time of today's eclipse on their 5,125-year Long Count calendar, which runs out in December. (I always have trouble finding new calendars, too, but I'm sure, like me, they'll have one by next February.)

The 90-mm Meade Coronado Solarmax telescope with a hydrogen-alpha filter magnifies the glowing orange ball to the size of a grapefruit. The ball is angry. The sun spews ribbons of fire at two and three and seven o'clock, fuming at the unseen but approaching serpent. Astronomers at Lowell Observatory were talking about the occurrence of these prominences with language like "never seen one like it in my life."

I look again through the eyepiece. The limb of the sun roils with hydrogen plasma, streaming into fantastic plumes, filaments, and coils. The view is possible because the telescope filters out all wavelengths of light but a narrow band at the red end of the spectrum (656.21 nanometers). The six-thousand-dollar telescope belongs to Tom Taylor, and I'm sitting in the morning sun on the porch of his beautiful off-grid home in the middle of a wind-swept prairie fifty miles south of Grand Canyon. Tom built the place himself, and now he and his partner Amy run it as a bed-and-breakfast for astronomy and photography buffs. They call it A Shooting Star Inn. When he's not hoisting ponderosa pine timbers into place or laying ceramic tile in his 4,200-square-foot lodge, he's writing and recording music in his upstairs studio. He's photographing models in a corner of his pine-walled living room or studying gaseous nebulae in his front-yard observatory.

Last night, Tom showed me his 14-in. Meade reflector, directing the mount to lock in on Saturn then several Messier objects, including the Globular Cluster (M13) and Ring Nebula (M57), a gorgeous, fruit-loop-like shell of leftover dust and gas from a red giant that exploded seven thousand years ago. Nearly every observatory reflector in the world uses optics like the ones in his advanced Ritchey-Chrétien telescope, including NASA's Hubble Space Telescope. I spent two hours shivering in line to see the telescopes at Lowell Observatory when I could have been shivering here with Tom as my guide to the universe.

Like a young Clyde Tombaugh, Tom ground the glass for the mirror of his first homemade telescope in junior high school. Later, he studied astronomy at the University of Arizona, lectured for Kitt Peak National Observatory's public night program, and worked at the UA's Steward Observatory. These days he uses the expertise he gained at these observatories to turn people on to the night sky from his own yard.

After Amy's fresh blueberry pancakes, Tom hands me a CD called *The Cosmic Rocket Band.* He and a friend, Ron Brown, wrote and produced the music. "For your ride up to the Canyon," he says. I slip the disk into my CD player as I pull onto the highway. An acoustic guitar strums and I hear Tom's voice sing, "Have you ever been in the dark of night / Stared up at the stars so bright / Tried to catch a glimpse of a shooting star. . . . Let's take a ride / Across the universe tonight . . ." I've met a true Renaissance man, all cropped hair and gray goatee.

I make Grand Canyon Visitor Center in the early afternoon, catching Brian Day's program, "In the Shadow of the Moon." The director of communication and outreach at NASA's Lunar Science Institute is a big man with white hair and beard, vivacious for his size, and he whips the crowded auditorium into a frenzy. His enthusiasm is contagious. I want to join him on his next mission, counting meteors for NASA's upcoming lunar dust explorer.

Now he talks eclipse. He explains that today's annular eclipse is a rare event when the moon is farther away from the earth so it appears small and doesn't cover the whole sun. "At peak, the moon will block ninety-four percent of the sun. We will see a spectacular ring of fire."

I'm already there. I feel the "primal thrill" Carl Sagan spoke of: "this astronomical light show when, in solemn darkness, the eclipse echoes back to the dawn of man." I step outside into crowds of people. I'm on a "Totality World Tour," according to all the blue T-shirts. And the world is present, given all the accents I hear wearing bright hats and shorts, forming lines around the sprouting tubes of telescopes.

I talk with Sara Meschberger, a University of Arizona communications and linguistics graduate, who has accompanied an astronomy club out of Phoenix called Stargazing for Everyone. She stands by a hydrogen-alpha telescope. "Tonight I bring out the big scope," she says. "I have a Dobsonian that's taller than me, and I'll be showing you deep sky objects, star clusters, and galaxies." Sara has been teaching the public about the universe since she was eleven. She has flown in microgravity aircraft like NASA's "vomit comet" and launched high-altitude balloon payloads. Currently, she is vice chair of an organization called Students for the Exploration and Development of Space (SEDS), which believes in a space-faring civilization and works toward that future. I'm guessing she's a huge *Star Trek* fan.

During the next few hours, the visitor center parking lot fills with people and instruments, scores of telescopes all pointed toward the sun, some with stepladders to eyepieces, others with color LCD monitors. Bipeds among tripods. The star party begins, and for the moment, the focus is on one star. There's Susan O'Connor from the Tucson Amateur Astronomy Association with her 60-mm H-alpha and 10-in. Meade like a five-gallon paint bucket. And Dave Armstrong from the Tacoma Astronomical Society, who built his own Dobsonian-style telescope and hauled it from Washington with his son, Dan. And hundreds more.

Without diminishing Grand Canyon, we could declare a new alternate nickname for Arizona: the Dark Sky State, which should replace the less-accurate, extractive, and unsustainable Copper State. Astronomy has a past *and* a future in the Grand Canyon State.

Near evening, I walk to the rim near Yavapai Point, climb over the edge where swallows cut through the sky, and find a cradle of rock. From my heart-stopping vantage point a mile above the canyon floor, the entire length of Bright Angel Canyon points its wrinkled finger to the distant blue ridge of the Kaibab Plateau. So much crumpled-up space to be forgotten in. So much told and so much more to tell. Here, water uncovers stories told by rocks in languages as basic as the elements within them. Syllabics in silicon. Dialects in carbon and oxygen.

And now this geologic wonder joins one of galactic scale. The earth and the heavens feel poised at the brink of something. I'm draped in canyon light among the clicks of insects ticking off the seconds. Even the very mass of air before me sits still and waits. I hang my legs into the Grand Abyss, my cardboard "eclipse shades" in hand, a Pink Floyd tune running through my head: "All that is now / All that is gone / All that's to come / and everything under the sun is in tune / but the sun is eclipsed by the moon."

First Touch. Sunglassed faces turn full into the west. People gather and stare. A spectrum of skin tones and cotton shirts shines out of hollows among the green of pine and yellow sandstone all along the rim. Voices diminish with the light as a black nick in the sun slowly turns the orb into the white horns of Taurus.

My heart thumps in my throat as I snap pictures. I forget to breathe. The Douglas fir twisting out of the rock before me shifts its needles into high definition. Every rock and leaf, every spire and gorge and every dark hidden hole becomes what it should be, as if it were all painted on a vast canvas from the mind and hand of Bierstadt. Then, everyone bound together by the celestial event begins to cheer. One voice rises from the throat of the canyon.

Annulus. Pink Floyd in my head now sounds like Johnny Cash: "I fell into a burning ring of fire / I went down, down, down and the flames went higher / And it burns, burns, burns, the ring of fire / The ring of fire."

Grand Canyon narrows you to essences. If water is the first element of consequence in this place, then the second is earth gouged out layer by layer under a landscape of air. Water, earth, air—and now fire. Four elements. I count a fifth as well. The quintessence of awe.

Driving away from South Rim in the dark, I join a comet's tail of car lights as we move out of a rise of forest and canyon and fly backward into the world.

Two hours later, I unroll my sleeping bag beside Oak Creek. I finish my two-destination trip to northern Arizona with a Big Sky IPA for dinner and crawl into bed under my own big sky tossed with stars. Tomorrow I'll do a bit of research on the creek with my fly rod and then head for home, catching my usual late lunch in Tucson. Jesús will be waiting at his cart at the Chevron station at Kino and Ajo with a glorious Sonoran hot dog (God's food), which I'll order loaded. I can already taste the bacon-wrapped dog in its toasted bolillo, the grilled onions, beans, cheese, roasted chiles, and ripe avocado split into silky green crescents like phases of the moon.

JUNE

Apache Trout

Risen from the Ashes

PHOENIX

ELEVATION: 1,150 FEET | FOUNDED: 1868 | POPULATION: 1,469,471

"I never really liked quiche until I came here," Karen tells the innkeeper at Maricopa Manor just off Central Avenue.

"A lot of people say they don't eat quiche," says Joan Eveland, lengthening her *o*'s and *a*'s like a true Wisconsinite, "until they start eating their partner's. The recipe is the original innkeeper's recipe, which has passed down from innkeeper to innkeeper over the years."

I've just driven two hundred miles from Bisbee in 112-degree heat to meet Karen in Phoenix where she's attending a professional conference. It's the first week in June, and if we must be in Phoenix in June, then we'll stay at her favorite inn north of downtown and eat its historic quiche.

Joan shows us in to the Siesta Suite, and we cross the Saltillo tile, drop our bags on the king bed, and head straight for the whirlpool tub. I turn on the cold water. The Maricopa Manor is a gem in this desert town. Agricultural engineer Byron Showers and his wife Naomi built the place in 1928 when only sixty thousand people lived in Phoenix. Camelback Road was a dirt two-track leading to a farming hamlet called Scottsdale. The couple wanted a house in the country where they could escape from the city on weekends. They created a home that marked the history of the ground beneath it. The Showerses named Maricopa Manor for the peaceful native people who lived and farmed along the Salt and Gila Rivers. The pair of adjoining homes they called "Dos Casas," honoring the first permanent residence in Phoenix, a two-room adobe with a roof of cottonwood poles, arrowweed, and mud, built in the 1860s by an Englishman named Brian Phillip Darrell Duppa. It's the oldest house in Phoenix and still stands today behind a chain link fence near Central Avenue and Grant Street. I've seen the adobe—a squat brown toad of a house with tiny black pupils for windows, crouched beneath towering monuments of glass and steel. It looks like a desperate act to recall the past in a city faced toward the future.

"Lord" Duppa, a tall, lanky scholar of the classics and fluent in five languages when sober, is often credited for naming Phoenix. But Arizona's official historian, Marshall Trimble, says the recognition should go to Jack Swilling, who found the description in his *Webster's Dictionary* and "thought the name suited the place." Swilling, a red-headed, Indian-fighting former Confederate officer out of Wickenburg, saw the valley's potential and started the Swilling Irrigation Canal Company. Then he began rebuilding and improving the five-hundred-year-old Hohokam canals. Swilling's Ditch, as people called it, irrigated crops and carried water for the drinking, bathing, laundry, and spittoon-washing of fifty residents—the Dutchman Jacob Waltz certainly among them—literally rising out of the ashes of the Hohokam civilization.

In the morning, the resident orange tabby named Dreamsicle lazes in a patch of sun under the citrus trees. Our breakfast arrives outside our door with a quick knock while we soak in the tub (again). Pulling on robes, we retreat to the patio with the basket and unpack fresh fruit, coffee, and juice. Two white ceramic cups hold quiche with mushrooms (Karen's) and green chile (mine). Still the best quiche we've ever tasted.

Maricopa Manor is Karen's idea of comfort. I prefer hotels with pipes that go bump in the night. When licensed in 1989, the homestead and guesthouses became the first and oldest bed-and-breakfast in Phoenix. Fine. I can check the place off my list for the year. Tonight, however, we sleep in the Hotel San Carlos.

After breakfast, Karen takes off for Scottsdale and her conference. I head for the state capitol and the Arizona Capitol Museum. Under Winged Victory on her copper dome, two five-foot pedestals of petrified wood stand outside the building. The state fossil, as some claim, does indeed reside at the capitol. A tile mosaic of Arizona's state seal marks the center of the rotunda floor. "Ditat Deus"—God enriches the rich, or something like that. It's beautiful, but it looks wrong. Tony, a museum volunteer, tells me there's a mistake with the seal. "Two of the five *C*s are missing." Arizona has five, the historic drivers of our economy: climate, copper, cotton, cattle, and citrus. The mosaic shows the rising sun above the mountains. Bisbee prospector George Warren with his shovel. Irrigated fields . . . Tony is right. No cow. No citrus trees.

"Someone pointed it out to the artist after he unveiled it, and he said, 'Hey, I just made what you guys said to make.'"

I look at the seal and smile at the irony. Arizona has replaced those Cs with a couple of others I can think of. A structure behind George's right shoulder is either a correctional facility or a casino. And then there's George Warren himself, an alcoholic who died penniless. Every poor drunken coot should be so immortalized.

I walk down the hall to the State Symbols Room. This will be better than the Arizona-Sonora Desert Museum for seeing all twelve symbols in one place, if I want to count plastic, stuffed, and otherwise fake symbols. Which I don't. It's already June, twenty-two weeks into the year, and I have only four symbols, officially. The photograph-in-their-natural-habitat self-inflicted criteria is weighing on me. But at least here I can see what I'm up against. Three-dimensional, lifelike models of each symbol hang from the walls all the way around the room. A locked glass display case holds a polished cross-section of petrified wood, a dinner-plate-sized chunk of turquoise, a bola tie with turquoise clasp, and a Colt .45 Single Action Army revolver, the "nonfunctional gun donated by Colt's Manufacturing Company LLC." I've heard that the company lobbied hard at the legislature for our newest symbol—which says what about Arizonans? That we're a bunch of yahoos?

Then I learn something about the bola tie. The original braided leather style was invented by a cowboy silversmith in Wickenburg in the 1940s. I had previously bumped Wickenburg from my list of destinations once Jessica announced her marriage date. Now I'm determined to shoulder it back in—somewhere. My proximity alert sounds off. Phoenix's Heard Museum has a temporary exhibit featuring the history of the tie that includes examples of the inventor's "slide for a necktie." His name is Victor Cedarstaff. The neckwear has a natural habitat!

Before I leave, I write a note for the suggestion box. I'm partial to the prickly pear margarita for the state cocktail, and the Sonoran hot dog as the official food group, but today I decide to support the drive for the chimichanga as the state food. It must be time for lunch. I drop in my suggestion, the paper folded and rolled neatly like a tortilla into the shape of a burro.

It's 2:00 p.m. and smoking hot outside. With windows down and the air conditioner blasting a wall of heat hot enough to melt skin, I drive toward Chase Field and park next to Alice Cooperstown sports bar/rock-and-roll museum. *Welcome to Alice's Diner*, a sign reads. Alice Cooper was one of my favorite rockers during my pimple years when every local AM radio station played his "School's Out" hit this time of year. I hum the words, "No more pencils, no more books, no more teachers' dirty looks" as I step into the place where jocks meet rock.

Jerseys hang from the ceiling and giant televisions circle the walls. Among the memorabilia are framed gold records, concert posters, stage props, and musical instruments—including an Epiphone acoustic guitar signed by members of the Dave Matthews Band. And there on the menu is the rock star himself in his classic dripping black eye makeup.

Before there was KISS and its gender-bending cartoon characters with more show than substance, before Ozzy Osbourne bit the head off anything, there was Alice Cooper. The band invented the shock-rock genre with its on-stage theatrics. In terms of music, the band delivered. Alice Cooper, the stage name of the lead singer, Vincent Furnier, could write, play, and sing. This wasn't only electrocutions and guillotines, snakes and blood, but solid, riff-driven hard rock and vocals. Alice Cooper raised the bar on what fans began to expect from a rock concert.

The band is Phoenix homegrown. In the mid-1960s at Cortez High School, Vincent Furnier formed a group called the Earwigs, then later the Spiders, with four of his school buddies. Furnier's penchant for mixing music with sports goes all the way back to those days, as most of the musicians were also track stars. Furnier himself could run a mile in four and a half minutes. The Spiders played cover tunes—songs from the Rolling Stones and the Yardbirds—at high school cafeterias and pizza pubs. They opened for the Hollies, the Byrds, and the Mamas & the Papas. In Tucson, they recorded their first original song, which was played on local radio. "The station received hundreds of phone calls requesting the song," Furnier later recalled, "most of them placed long-distance from Phoenix by our families." "Don't Blow Your Mind" became the number three song. The band did a short stint in Los Angeles as the Nazz. Then, after suffering a life-threatening car accident, Vincent Furnier rose from the dead as the parents-horrifying Alice Cooper.

I'm tempted by his Big Unit, a two-foot-long hot dog named for former Diamondbacks pitcher Randy Johnson with "more meat than you can eat." But a girl with straight black hair and Cooper's trademark makeup talks me into the Cabo Wabo fish tacos. It's hardly a decision. Alice Cooper's girls could sell me anything, but what I'm really here for is the SanTan Hopshock—since I'm after the best IPA in Arizona. SanTan Brewing Company hails from the old Valley National Bank building in nearby Chandler where Anthony Canecchia brews his craft beer. The Hopshock, which appears in front of me instantly, shows a warm copper color and its pine-citrus flavor definitely pushes through the hops like the Big Sky IPA. An eighty-five on the IBU scale. This is close! Right up there with the Lumberyard IPA. A contender for sure.

I eat fish tacos and sip beer to Ozzy's garbled lyrics coming through the speakers. No competition. No comparison. No more Mr. Nice Guy. It's Alice all the way.

In the late afternoon, I pick up Karen in Scottsdale and we drive to downtown Phoenix, the "Urban Heart of Arizona." Tonight, we're staying where that heart began beating, the place where people say the native inhabitants worshipped a god of learning so the town built Arizona's first school, the Little Adobe. Later, a brick schoolhouse replaced it—Central School, the fourth brick structure in Phoenix. Finally, in 1928, enter Dwight Heard. While also working on his famous museum of Native American art and culture, the philanthropist, rancher, and newspaper magnate raised his luxury hotel. The San Carlos was the first hotel in the city to offer elevators, steam heat, and air conditioning. Each room had its own circulating ice-water tap, amenities for which the San Carlos charged a dollar more than other hotels in the area. People loved the San Carlos so much, it is said they built the city around it.

Keith checks us in to a "room with a view" on the infamous seventh floor.

"Supposedly, a young woman died there?" I ask.

"Leone Jensen. She jumped from the roof." Keith hands me a book about the hotel with the story. It happened shortly after the San Carlos opened and newspapers at the time described her as a "pretty girl of the extreme blond type." She wore an evening gown and Oxford shoes and leaped with her hat in her hand. She was distraught about a lost love, jilted by a bellboy.

"Her ghost is occasionally seen at the foot of someone's bed, her dress billowing around her in an unfelt breeze." Keith adds: "The crew from *Ghost Hunters* is coming next month. The San Carlos is the third most haunted hotel in the United States."

A photo of Gary Cooper hangs on the wall above our headboard. "Do you think he slept in this bed?" I ask Karen. On our way to our room, instead of taking the elevator, we climbed the stairs floor to floor and searched up and down the hallways for rooms named for famous guests. Clark Gable preferred a corner room on the fourth floor so he could watch people from his window. Marilyn Monroe liked to be near the pool on the third floor where she could swim at any hour without interruption. Mae West's suite on the second floor still has period furniture and décor, plus a private parlor where she entertained visitors. At various times the likes of Gene Autry, Betty Grable, Humphrey Bogart, and Jayne Mansfield visited the San Carlos.

Karen suggests that if we're going to sleep with famous people, we should eat with them as well. She's made reservations for dinner at Durant's, the renowned steakhouse and watering hole where stars like John Wayne, Clark Gable, and Jane Russell ate rib eye and sipped vodka martinis or whiskey. No Cabo Wabo fish tacos or Big Unit hot dogs for her.

"Park around back," she tells me as I approach the restaurant. "The locals use the back door." We've never been here before, but she's done her research.

I feel awkward walking through the kitchen, but there's red carpet on the floor and grill master Ernie Canez greets us with a big smile. He asks us about Bisbee when I admit to him we're not from Phoenix. He's worked at Durant's since 1959.

The place is packed. Our hostess seats us at a table in a dark, plush dining room of red carpeting, red vinyl, and red-flocked wallpaper, a pattern and style chosen by the late Jack Durant himself to duplicate the feel of a high-class Chicago chophouse or a New York speakeasy. While

Karen orders a calamari appetizer, I look over the wine list and study the history of the place and the man who created it.

It seems Jack Durant is a legend in his own town, one of the best kind because the legend comes from infamy. His is a tale of drinking and gambling, of quick temper and generosity. He was a professional ball player. Later he ran a house of ill repute. He was sentimental enough to marry five times. While living in Las Vegas, he operated a casino, being the only man, they say, whom gangster Bugsy Siegel trusted. Yet, he fled Vegas to escape the Mafia. When he landed in Phoenix, he became a restaurateur. That was 1950, and his steakhouse became, in his own humble opinion, "the finest eating and drinking establishment in the world."

This is definitely Karen's kind of place. My carnivore wife, a woman who prefers her steak bloodless, originating from a package of Styrofoam and plastic wrap and unrecognizable as the doe-eyed animal from which it came. She's all over the calamari, amused by the "lemon sleeve" as she squeezes the juice over tentacles and all. She makes quick work of a loaf of soft, salty Durant's bread, which is "infused," she says, "with butter, garlic, and minced leeks."

While we dine, Karen gives me a running commentary on the antics of a couple sitting in a booth behind me. "Looks like a date, and he's plying her with wine. Oh, they've opened another bottle. She's leaning on his neck. She's already had plenty to drink. Can you hear them? I'd say he's pretty pleased with himself."

Tonight, we chase one of Arizona's five Cs: cattle. As Karen finishes her prime rib, I'm staring at what remains of my so-called Humble T-bone. I want to pick it up and chew on it. Instead, we order dessert, a trey of crème brûlée, each as light and warm as breath exchanged by lovers. I sip a Patrón café. Nothing like tequila and coffee to finish off a fine evening.

Jack Durant died fifteen years ago, but his restaurant carries on the way he'd want it to. He may have left everything—the house, the furniture, and the cash—to Humble, his English bulldog, as was his way. But this plain-looking steakhouse on Central Avenue is his legacy, a legacy of giving people what they want—a taste of the Goodfellas life.

Back at the hotel, we get ready for bed. At the bathroom sink, a sign below a single silver spigot says that this is the original chilled water faucet from 1928. *Thank you for enjoying part of our history.* I turn the knob—nothing. Not a drop of cold water. No enjoyment. There is, however, the modern convenience of three-dollar bottles of warm water sitting on the desk. A note in a binder reads, "While we maintain stringent cleanliness standards, some elements are original fixtures and may exhibit signs of experience." Signs of experience! "I'm not getting old," I tell Karen. "I'm just showing signs of experience."

I look out the window to the street seven floors below and think about twenty-two-year-old Leone. A car moves slowly along Monroe Street. There are voices everywhere in these walls. After dark, the place becomes rich with stories, rich with expectations. This is the place where one person brought all her expectations and left them on the pavement.

The next day, I go looking for coffee. I head south on 1st Avenue from Monroe, cross Adams Street past Renaissance Square, take Washington Street to Jefferson. The quiet Saturday morning soaks in, rising up through my sandaled feet as a rhythm of footsteps against sidewalk. It's warm but hardly worth the sweat. Although many businesses are closed, people walk dogs, or exercise in shiny, curve-hugging Lycra. Others sit at tables, chatting over coffee concoctions. Cars toss engine sounds off the canyon walls of buildings. This, I think, is the voice of Phoenix. Not the weekday rush of suits and ties, but the weekend murmur of neighbors. I order a café latte and join the conversation.

At midmorning, Karen and I check out of the Hotel San Carlos. I'm on a mission. I want to make one last stop on Central Avenue to complete my Phoenix destination, which has become a Phoenix Central destination. From the elite elegance of quiche to prime rib, I now want to make good on the promise of chimichanga.

"Is this the original Macayo's Mexican Kitchen?" I ask the seating hostess as we walk through the heavy wooden doors.

"This is it!" she says, fetching me a pamphlet with the restaurant's history and directing me to a register. "Will you sign our petition for making the chimichanga the state food?"

"That's why I'm here—for the so-called original chimi," I say, writing my name beneath a long list of names. Then I add: "You know that El Charro in Tucson says they invented it. . . ."

"That's a filthy lie!" one of other greeters says, smiling at us.

We take seats near a large plastic macaw wearing a sombrero. Karen orders a prickly pear margarita for me while I look over the menu. It's a mix of history and recipe, and I fill my journal with notes. A timeline along the bottom margin begins with statehood and moves through the marriage of high-school sweethearts Woody and Victoria Johnson (Macayo's founders), the opening of the first restaurants, the chile shortage that caused Woody to start his own chile operations in McNeal, Arizona, and the 2009 visit of President Obama and family.

Woody's story about inventing the chimichanga sounds both apocryphal and very familiar: "Legend has it that one day in 1946," the menu says, "Woody Johnson . . . accidentally dropped a meat-filled burro into a fryer, creating what is now a staple of Mexican restaurants across the Southwest." This sounds like Monica Flin's claim at El Charro. I thought Johnson's daughter Sharisse said her late father created it when he began frying up leftover burros to sell the following day. . . . Hmm. The mystery thickens, like flan.

I've tasted chimichangas across southern Arizona at Mexican food joints with names like Santiago's, El Minuto, Casa Molina, El Charro (the country's oldest Mexican restaurant), and even a grilled-cheese-sandwich chimi at Café Piedra Roja. All fall short of Pancho's chimichanga. But now I'm hearing rumors about a Globe restaurant having the best green chile in the state and a chimichanga that's unlike any other. I'm there. The Chimichanga de Macayo definitely floats to the top of the deep fryer.

Chasing Gods

KITT PEAK NATIONAL OBSERVATORY

ELEVATION: 6,880 FEET | FOUNDED: 1958
POPULATION: 2 DORMITORIES OF SLEEPING ASTRONOMERS
ON ANY GIVEN DAY

On an early June afternoon, I wait on a rugged desert peak the O'odham call Ioligam, or "Red Stick," for the twisted, iron-stemmed manzanita that grow here. A raven tips her dark wings to the white temples of the mountain, riding the wind with the effort of outstretched primaries. *Raven* is *curocu* in the tongue of my Native American friend, Phoenix Eagleshadow.

I look south toward the lifted thumb of Baboquivari, sacred peak of the people who have lived in its shadow for two thousand years, and think about the last time I visited there with Phoenix. She wanted to offer her hunting bow to I'itoi, creator spirit and elder brother of the O'odham, and I agreed to be her companion for the long, sun-blasted day of hiking and ceremony. She said she chose me because of my dusty smell. "You remind me of a hill I like to sit on where I can sing to the wind." That was exactly nine years ago, and proper bathing still mystifies me.

We left Tucson at 5:00 a.m. and drove to Sells, then south on Indian Route 19. Phoenix—whose middle name is Psyche—chatted with her brother, who rode along in the backseat at various times. I couldn't see him. I couldn't see any of Psyche's relatives and acquaintances in the spirit world. Recently, she had become involved with someone named Gabriel. "Psyche," I asked her, "is this a person I can see with my eyes?" It was a question I asked her often, and this time I wanted to know because she said they'd gotten married. "Probably not," she said. "He's one of the warrior angels, the sexy dark one. Gabriel, the archangel."

We had just graduated from the MFA program in nonfiction at the University of Arizona. Psyche's writing often included these kinds of stories, for which some of her professors and fellow students criticized her. They thought she should switch to fiction. They couldn't understand that, for Psyche, there was no line between nonfiction and fiction, between reality and myth. I learned to never doubt her stories.

We climbed a trail among blooming coral bean, skyrocket red against the chlorophyll-wrung grasses and oak. At I'itoi's cave, the smoke from votive candles blackened the rock ledge. People had left offerings: photographs, prayer sticks, colored beads, and silver trinkets. Psyche collected mugwort, which grew around the cave entrance, bundling together the gray leaves. Then, under the pediment of Baboquivari Peak, she strung her bow and took out an abalone shell holding cornmeal and pollen. She offered the mixture to the four cardinal points.

Then she handed me a feathery sprig of the mugwort. "In thanks for strength," she said, her dark eyes shining. She sat quietly facing south and burned the remaining herb with dry sage, the smoke clinging to her skin and smelling of High Mass (some might say *high school*). Next, she knapped an obsidian point, placing it in a black medicine bag tied around her neck. After rubbing the bow with mugwort and sage and casting more cornmeal and pollen to the wind, she laid it on the ground, sprinkled it with water, and began to sing.

Ravens answered from the mountain. Psyche greeted them in her language as they winged around us, sending blessings to someone she called Grandfather Raven. Watching her that afternoon, I thought: *I have no ceremonies in my life. I have no faith in anything.* Psyche would just quote Tennyson: "There lives more faith in honest doubt than in half the creeds."

"I'itoi's got himself a very fine bow," she said, after placing the bow in a juniper tree—only the dead leave bows on the ground. "That's if Raven doesn't come and steal it first."

Near the center of the O'odham world, Kitt Peak rises into the thin blue air at the center of the astronomical world. Here, the planet's largest collection of telescopes—twenty-three optical and two radio—tug at and unravel and follow the singular threads of the universe's story. Today, I'm participating in an event the tale of which has been told only six times in history. An event that has ended the careers and lives of astronomers who've sacrificed all at the chance of witnessing it, a story that established the very shape of our solar system—the transit of Venus.

In her book, *Chasing Venus: The Race to Measure the Heavens*, Andrea Wulf follows the adventures and misadventures of a score of eighteenth-century scientists from six countries as they travel to remote places around the globe to measure the passage of Venus across the face of the sun as predicted by Edmond Halley in 1716. The British astronomer calculated that on two dates—June 6, 1761, and June 3, 1769 (transits always occur in pairs)—Venus would appear as a black circle moving across the sun's disk. Knowing he wouldn't be alive then—unless he lived to be 104—he nevertheless called on future scientists to join in an endeavor to record from both of earth's hemispheres the exact time and duration of the transit, achieving, Wulf writes, "what had hitherto been almost unimaginable: a precise mathematical understanding of the dimensions of the solar system, the holy grail of astronomy."

Andrea Wulf's book explores personalities, rivalries, and obsessive passions of men in knee-britches and powdered wigs, scientists like Sweden's Pehr Wilhelm Wargentin and France's Joseph-Nicolas Delisle and America's Benjamin Franklin. It's quite a tale. Catherine the Great, wanting to recast Russia as an enlightened nation, ordered eight expeditions to cover the second transit and included naturalists, taxonomists, hunters, and painters along with astronomers. James Cook sailed all the way to Tahiti only to have his telescopes stolen while building his observatories. The British Royal Society and the Académie des Sciences in Paris, whose two countries were at war, sent their astronomers into the path of cannon fire.

My favorite of Andrea's stories is the one about a "not very well-to-do" Frenchman with a very long name that I'll shorten to Guillaume Le Gentil. A member of the Paris Académie, the thirty-four-year-old minister-turned-stargazer was the first in the transit race and the last to return. His destination was Pondicherry, India, but after more than a year of trying to reach it, monsoon winds and the Seven Years' War left Le Gentil to attempt measurements in the Indian Ocean on the deck of a rolling ship. It didn't go well.

Undaunted by the failure, Le Gentil decided to wait it out for the second transit—in eight years. A true naturalist, during the interim he studied the region's geography, flora and fauna, stars, winds, and tides. He built an observatory at Pondicherry. Then, when June 3, 1769, finally arrived, so did the clouds. That day, Le Gentil wrote in his journal that he had risked everything "only to be a spectator of a fatal cloud which came to place itself before the sun at the precise moment of my observation. . . ."

Deeply depressed and suffering from dysentery, he returned to Paris empty-handed to find his heirs had declared him legally dead and had "enthusiastically" plundered his estate, his wife had remarried, and he'd lost his seat at the academy of science.

"That is the fate that often awaits astronomers," Le Gentil said at the end of his eleven-year odyssey chasing Venus. It could've been worse. Another Frenchman, Jean-Baptiste Chappe d'Auteroche, observed the first transit in Siberia but never returned from seeing the second in Baja California. Only one member of his party survived an outbreak of yellow fever. It's no wonder astronomers don't sleep at night.

"Great title," I tell Andrea Wulf when I catch up with her at the visitor center. "I've been chasing a few things myself. Like the solar eclipse at Grand Canyon."

"I've never been there," she says with a palpable English accent. "I have a few days in Arizona. Where should I go?"

"North Rim, if you have time. But the South Rim is amazing, too. Everyone hikes the Bright Angel Trail, but I like the Hermit Trail for a day hike."

Andrea was born in India but grew up in Germany before moving to Britain where she studied history at the Royal College of Art. "I don't own a telescope. I'm a historian," she says as we step outside where observatory staff has set up filtered binoculars and telescopes. We're minutes away from the start of the transit, and dozens of people have gathered at the viewing stations on the patio outside the visitor center. "We've set up a hydrogen-alpha telescope at the McMath-Pierce Solar Observatory," a docent tells us. "There's a prominence right where Venus will appear—be cool to see that!"

I leave Andrea with the group and take off toward the McMath with Baboquivari Peak rising at my right shoulder. Three people stand inside the white dome housing the Meade Solar Telescope Array, and as we arrive, one of them calls, "First contact!" I look into the eyepiece and see a black fingernail notched into a boiling red field.

Fifteen minutes later, Venus slips completely inside the disk, a black pea against the sun's glowing softball. I'm watching an event that won't recur until 2117—won't be seen again by me or anyone else alive today. I stand at the point where immeasurable spheres converge. A star path from where I can take the measure of my world.

"I'm very excited to be here during the transit of Venus," Andrea says at the beginning of her book presentation, pushing a long stand of blond hair behind one ear. "Normally, I have to explain what the transit of Venus is . . . but I don't think I have to do that here."

I settle into my chair to listen to her talk about men in knickers chasing the planet named for the god of love and beauty—the only planet in our solar system named after a female—all for the love of science. The love of discovery.

Later, a group crowds a spit of rock called Sunset Hill to catch the last images of the sun as it sets over O'odham lands with Venus in transit. Some peer through scopes while others cluster to talk about the region's geology or the clear view to Mexico. People find seats in a rocky outcrop, each one wearing solar glasses, the reddening sun on their faces.

"Oh, look," a green-shirted staff member named Geronimo announces and points to a swiveling dome. "SARA is waking up. Some professor is working from his laptop." SARA, Geronimo explains, stands for Southeastern Association for Research in Astronomy, a consortium of institutions that remotely operates the 0.9-m telescope and its sister telescope in Chile. With a depth perception gained by having two eyes separated by thousands of miles, the SARA telescopes allow astronomers to measure the orbits of asteroids, especially those that cross the orbit of earth. "In my opinion," Geronimo adds, "SARA is the most important telescope on the mountain."

After showing us the Belt of Venus, a rosy band above the eastern horizon with the curving shadow of the earth beneath it, Geronimo gives us a walk-in-the-dark tour of Kitt Peak's observatories. From the 4-m Mayall (the most prominent two-hundred-foot observatory, which I can practically see from a hundred miles away in Bisbee) to what Geronimo calls the "Rich Guy Telescope," or "RGT" (the only privately owned telescope on the mountain), I hear a string of superlatives: the "sharpest," the "world's largest," the "greatest," the "most," along with several "the first ever to's." Kitt Peak is the hub of the astronomical world.

Finally, Geronimo's radio comes to life. "Where are our guests?" a voice asks in a tone that says, *What have you done with them?* We're overdue to report to the visitor center. In the gathering darkness, observatory domes brighten like moons breaching the peaks. Motors pull on steel cables. Metal gears moan. Pythagoras's music of the spheres. Like the nine-headed Hydra opening its many slitted eyes, the mountain is awakening.

Kitt Peak is named for Philippa Roskruge Kitt, the sister of George J. Roskruge, our first Pima County supervisor. I had driven past the Roskruge school in Tucson earlier today—something I do quite often—on my way to Kitt Peak. But this time the marquee out front on the street caught my attention:

In Loving Memory
Former Student
Ray Bradbury
1920–2012

Ray Bradbury died today. On the day of the transit of Venus—on the day of a once-or-twice-in-a-lifetime celestial event, the man who for me brought the mythical heavens to earth, passed on at the age of ninety-one. I grew up with Ray Bradbury. Not in school, but in his books. His first was a sequel he wrote of Burroughs's *The Gods of Mars*. He was twelve years old and a student at Roskruge Elementary School. Burroughs liked to end his John Carter books with cliff-hangers, so it's easy to see why a budding science fiction writer might be inspired to complete a favorite story. I did the same in grade school—stories about the first people to visit Saturn who discover the rings are composed of previous space travelers, or about a misfit geek who builds a spaceship out of school-yard trash cans and stolen plumbing and launches himself into space to escape his tormenting peers. Mrs. Tream, my eighth-grade English teacher at Canyon Del Oro Junior High, once wrote on one of my "compositions": "This is the way

Ray Bradbury got started." I like to think that Ray Bradbury had a Mrs. Tream—maybe the same Mrs. Tream; she seemed ancient to me!—who wrote on one of his early stories: "This is the way Edgar Rice Burroughs got started."

As a boy, I imagined a future when the entire human race would one day look like Ylla, the golden-skinned Martian with eyes like yellow coins. Only yesterday I read in the *New Yorker* how Bradbury had said *The Martian Chronicles* wouldn't exist except for the impact the John Carter of Mars books had on his boyhood. Bradbury was influenced by the science fiction stories of Edgar Rice Burroughs, who had been influenced by Percival Lowell, who drew his Martian canals while staring through his Clark telescope on Mars Hill.

"I would go out to the lawn on summer nights," Ray Bradbury writes about his childhood in Tucson, "and reach up to the red light of Mars and say, 'Take me home!'"

Welcome home, Ray.

This place is the navel of the world, according to the O'odham. Near here is the opening in the earth from where the people emerged wide-eyed like John Carter into an inconceivable world. The heavens feature prominently in O'odham cosmology. Elder Brother gave them spectacular desert sunsets simply for their enjoyment. First Born made the sun to light the darkness and the moon and stars for the people to follow. Coyote created the stars of the Milky Way galaxy after stealing a bag of white tepary beans and scattering them across the sky.

One thing universal among humans is that we create stories to explain the nature of our reality. Out of dust we are made, says the book of Genesis. From the mud of the earth, Elder Brother formed the first people. Philosophers and poets say we are stardust, recalling what scientists say about the elements in our bodies having been forged inside a long-dead star. Some call this myth-telling, others scientific theory. And still others choose not to draw lines.

Geronimo showed us a telescope that first revealed the spiral shape of our home galaxy, the Milky Way. Coyote, apparently, liked to chase his tail. Geronimo then pointed out another telescope that astronomers Vera

Rubin and Kent Ford used to discover firm evidence of dark matter. The Dutch astronomer Jan Oort had suggested in 1932 that only an unseen "dark matter" could account for the orbital velocities of stars in our galaxy. A year later Swiss astrophysicist Fritz Zwicky came up with the same idea of a dark theoretical substance to explain the missing mass in the orbital velocities of galaxy clusters.

Dark theoretical stuff. Matter *and* energy. Mystery that shapes our world. Ninety-five percent of what fills the universe is mystery. We can't see it or measure it except for its effect on what we *can* see and measure. The theory of dark matter explains why the universe behaves the way it does, the way people use story to explain the unexplainable. Myth sometimes *is* reality. My friend Psyche would say that what Rubin and Ford discovered on this mountain more than thirty years ago was the handiwork of I'itoi.

Tonight, Kitt Peak astronomers traverse holy ground to gaze upon the handiwork of awe. And awe, writes the poet James Galvin, is the only thing that makes life worth living. This high mountain allows us multifaceted glimpses of the same mystery— and perhaps an answer to the oldest question asked by humankind. *Where do we come from?*

Chubasco

LEMMON ROCK LOOKOUT

ELEVATION: 8,820 FEET | FOUNDED: 1928

POPULATION: 2, INCLUDING GUS THE DOG

In the third week in June, meteorologists are predicting a 30 percent chance of thunderstorms. *Seems too early for the monsoons*, I think, when I hear the Tucson weather report. *We're still a week away from San Juan's Day.* El Día de San Juan, June 24, is the traditional start of the monsoon season. On this day in 1540, according to legend, a thirsty Spanish conquistador named Francisco Vázquez de Coronado prayed to John the Baptist for rain. When the heavens opened, his army was saved, and his soldiers promptly jumped into the flooding rivers in celebration.

Southern Arizona and Mexico have honored the day—which falls around the summer solstice—with processions and ritual baths, blessings of soil and seeds and crops. In Tucson, processioners carry a statue of the Baptist from the Santa Cruz River down Avenida del Convento, kicking off the monsoon season with food and games and art. Tucsonans say if it doesn't rain by San Juan's Day, it won't for six more weeks. June 24 is also Richard Shelton's birthday. Sometimes I call it "Saint Dick's Day."

Under blue skies, Karen and I wind along the Mount Lemmon Highway, rising out of a landscape of red-lipped, fruiting saguaros and one-hundred-degree heat. In *Finding Butterflies in Arizona*, authors Richard Bailowitz and Hank Brodkin claim the two-tail is widespread in the state, that it favors mid-elevation canyons and its large size and "gaudy" yellow-and-black pattern make it hard to miss. Sure. Karen reminds me not-too-gently that I've already seen one in my yard. The authors say the best bet to see it is at Molino Basin. So, we check out the oak- and boulder-strewn drainage for two-tailed swallowtails—I've only checked off four state symbols this year. The only thing I'm on track with is visiting eight out of fifteen counties!

Nothing. Nada, zip. No butterflies. Of any stripe.

At the southernmost ski resort in the United States, we stop for brunch at the Iron Door. The Mt. Lemmon Ski Valley restaurant is named for a Jesuit gold trove originally called the Lost Escalante and made famous by Harold Bell Wright's book. The story goes that Jesuit missionaries had discovered rich veins of gold in the canyon below us under Apache Peak. (I recall my Campo Bonito map that indicates the location of Spanish "chests and jewels" in caves on the peak.) Prior to their expulsion from Spanish territory in 1767, the black robes concealed their treasure in a specially constructed vault and sealed it with an iron door, intending to return. Apaches later destroyed the settlement, scattering the Indians who worked the mines, and the gold was forgotten. The most interesting part of the story is that long after the Jesuits were gone, a military commander camping near here while chasing Apaches found placer gold in the same drainage. The place became known as Cañada del Oro.

The restaurant's Sonoran Desayuno sounds perfect to me—layers of tortillas, eggs, refried beans, cheese, and salsa. Nelson, our server, takes our orders with a fake Swedish accent. Then he switches to French. "I'll be anybody but who I am," he says when I comment about his phonetic inventory. When he brings me the Tabasco sauce, his accent is Cajun. "The cook just hung himself," he says. "But we revived him and he's back at work." Our many-accented server and host drives up from Tucson each day. He can't afford to live in a ski resort, he says. "Especially since after the fire, they rebuilt Summerhaven as a rich suburb of Tucson."

Nine years have passed since the Aspen Fire. The worst blaze in the hundred-year history of Summerhaven destroyed eighty-five thousand acres of forest and more than three hundred homes and businesses. When it was over, Ski Valley had survived, but not the mountain community. Cabins burned to the ground. The Alpine Inn was a pile of rubble. The Mt. Lemmon General Store lay in ashes. The old sawmill, dating back to Summerhaven's beginnings and owned by the pioneer Zimmerman family, was gone.

Author Suzanne Hensel, a resident of the mountain who was present that afternoon of June 17, wrote a few days later: "This fire has taken more than buildings made of wood and nails. It has taken away the past, a big piece of the mountain's history, a testament to the people who came before there was a highway, before it was easy."

A large stuffed bear rides the ski lift. I want to take the lift up the mountain to hike the trails, but Karen gives me a hundred reasons why she won't, beginning with a lack of proper lift inspections (hers), wind, lightning, and the ever-present force of gravity. "I'm pretty sure they've replaced the Model A-powered rope tow," I say, thinking about the original Saguaro Ski Club and its membership patch showing a skier wrapped around the giant cactus.

Instead, she wants to chase the best fudge in Arizona. Sounds suspicious to me. She proposes fudge as the official state confection. Elise, a cheerful redhead at a place called The Miner's Sweet Tooth, sets us up with chocolate walnut (Karen) and rum raisin (me). I ask Elise if she lives on the mountain, hoping to get my usual question answered, but she says she lives in Tucson. Like Nelson, the place is beyond her means.

"The conspiracy theory," she says, lowering her voice and drawing close to us, "is that the Zimmermans, who own most of the real estate, let the fire burn to clear out the riffraff."

Fortified with fudge, we *drive* up to the nape of Mount Lemmon to hike the Meadow Trail. The 9,157-foot peak is the highest in the Santa Catalina Mountains. It was named for botanist Sara Allen Plumber Lemmon, who explored this range for plant species with her husband on their honeymoon in 1881. These are the same routes Karen and I hiked as newlyweds in the early 1980s while leading groups for the YMCA camp into places with names like Lemmon Creek, Romero Pools, Pusch Ridge, and Wilderness of Rocks. This is where we brought our own three daughters on their first backpacking adventure, when the girls slyly loaded my pack to eighty pounds with steaks and potatoes after I bought freeze-dried meals. "You'll love the ice cream," I told them. "It has a twenty-five-year shelf life." (Kasondra reminds me often that she's "ruined for life" concerning cheesecake because I introduced her to Mountain House freeze-dried blueberry cheesecake.) This open, sunny meadow is the place I survived my first lightning storm inside a sodden sleeping bag beneath a rain-porous tarp.

These days, Karen no longer prefers the downy comfort of a sleeping bag on bare ground under a throw of stars. She wants a king-size bed under a solid roof, breakfast included.

Along the trail, a wooden gate holds a piece of pipe and a cast-iron skillet lettered in white: *Door Bell Gus & Dave.* Posted hours indicate visitors are welcome. I bang on the pan.

"Come on up," says a voice.

We climb the rock stairway to the top, where a brown and white dog greets us.

"This is Gus the dog," says fire-spotter David Medford, wearing green trousers and a blue U.S. Forest Service T-shirt. "You're welcome to look around."

Dave invites us into his summer home, a fourteen-by-fourteen-foot shack perched on the lip of a cliff. A bronze plaque says that the Civilian Conservation Corps (CCC) constructed Lemmon Rock Lookout Tower in 1928 and that it is the oldest fire lookout still in use in the Coronado National Forest. Since 2010, this is where Dave and Gus—the only true residents of the mountain I've met today—have lived for the five months of the summer fire season. Dave is working on a master's degree in forestry at Northern Arizona University.

"You're doing the Ed Abbey thing," I tell Dave inside the shack, seeing his knotty-pine kitchenette and single bunk. A copy of *The True Story of Smokey the Bear* rests on a nightstand. Three walls of windows allow a spectacular view of the Pusch Ridge Wilderness and the mountains beyond. The sky islands crowding this corner of Arizona, all crumpled khaki beneath a darkening ocean of sky. Dave shows Karen how to work the Osborne Fire Finder, a lazy Susan–like device that dominates the center of the room. As she peers through the sighting hole and lines up the cross hairs on the distant white domes of the Steward Observatory, he reads the coordinates and reports: "This is Lemmon Rock Lookout, dispatch. We have a fire approximately four miles out at azimuth 106.5." He then pulls out the range maps. "You don't want to be wrong about the mountain that's burning," he says.

As reports begin coming in on his radio, Dave adds, "We also track thunderstorms. Right now we have lightning strikes in the Whetstones,

Rincons, Santa Ritas, Pinaleños—the whole forest is getting activity, and I'm stuck out here on a rock watching the show."

"Do you know if it's monsoon?" I ask.

"It's up from the Gulf."

Taking no account of Saint John the Baptist, for the past five years, the National Weather Service has used a calendar to signal the start of the monsoon season: June 15. Previously, the NWS marked the date as the first of three consecutive days when the average dew point reached 54 degrees or above. This at least had the possibility of falling on the twenty-fourth. Now, we can have a monsoon season without a single thunderstorm, if we should be so unfortunate. Today is day two of the monsoon season, which officially lasts until September 30.

Technically speaking, a monsoon—from the Arabic word *mausim* meaning *season*—is not a thunderstorm but a seasonal shift of wind, for us, one that arises—most meteorologist now say—from the Gulf of Mexico *and* the Gulf of California. As the desert heats up in the early summer, the rising continental air mass creates a thermal low that draws in oceanic air laden with moisture. The usual westerlies dip south and circulate into our region as southeasterly winds—a pattern that once had meteorologists thinking our monsoons came only from the Gulf of Mexico.

Now things get interesting. Columns of rising hot air, miles wide, penetrate the upper layers of cool, wet air, boiling over and into brilliant thunderheads that corkscrew upward tens of thousands of feet. These generate raging snowstorms high above the bone-dry landscape. Updrafts accompany terrific downdrafts. Dust billows, sometimes lifting into one-hundred-mile-wide apocalyptic storms called haboobs. Lightning flares. If we're lucky, rain pummels the ground. If not, hope evaporates, the thunderheads trailing wildfire and dust beneath purple rags of virga like so many dried-up promises. These localized, sometimes violent thunderstorms are better described as "chubascos," Spanish for *squall*. Our monsoon wind brings a season of chubascos.

I hear a groan of thunder. The wind shoulders in as clouds like black irises glom onto Mount Lemmon. Could it be happening? The first monsoon thunderstorm of the year and we get to watch it from Lemmon Rock Lookout? The bell sounds and another couple arrives.

"This all came in only a few hours ago," one of the women says. "It's all new, unexpected."

We introduce ourselves, and then thunder cracks above us like a sudden rockfall. I feel its echo in the rock beneath my feet, a shuddering from my legs to my spine. Julie and Nancy clear out. "You're braver than we are," Julie says, following her friend back down the steps. Gus ducks inside the tower. Dave goes to work with his binoculars, stepping onto the rim of the cliff. His radio squelches with noise and voices and I scribble down what I can make out: "One hundred fifty-three strikes . . . Happy Valley . . . Marsh Station."

"Rumbling good now," Dave says.

"My lightning detector was going nuts," his radio says. "I had to turn it off."

"Mount Bigelow . . . prevention or patrol?"

"Prevention has one hundred gallons of water," Dave explains about the hotshot fire squads. "Patrol has no water and only reports the location of fire."

Karen is nervous and wants to leave. She has no desire to hike with lightning striking at her heels. "We're safe right here," I say, unconvincingly, "with the spotters and the radio giving us updates." I remind her of what Dave had told us earlier, how he gets hit by lightning but feels nothing inside the tower. "He calls it 'exciting.'" I'm self-detonating my argument.

"You can spend the night," Dave says.

His offer charges me, but I know Karen is probably thinking: *And sleep where, exactly?*

The rain comes as we hike back to the car. Dark clouds toss shafts of brilliance that leave shadows on my retinas. Below us, the mountainside funnels the storm into Lemmon Creek, which becomes Sabino Creek, which empties into the Rillito River on its way to the Santa Cruz and Gila and Colorado Rivers before joining the sea from where it came. I can see the entire jumbled, sinuous route from the bridge in my mind, played out as a game of Pooh sticks. If the ocean created clouds in order to explore the land, it also created rivers for the return home.

Other hikers scramble past us. We slow our pace, reveling in wet summer skin like a pair of red-spotted toads. Where we pause along the trail overlooking the storm-shrouded Wilderness of Rocks, another hiker asks us where we're from.

"Can't you tell?" I ask as he hurries by. "Right here," I turn my face to the rain and raise my arms. First monsoon chubasco at the edge of the planet. From our high vantage point, the monsoon is a living, breathing conveyor, carrying the geologic organism of rain: Mexico slides into Arizona, which in turn rushes back into Mexico in a pulsing, thrashing penetration of elementals—air and water meets fire and earth.

Hydrologically, this is the top of the world. The monsoon rains do not end with a cloudburst over our heads. They are part of a dynamic process that extends from the sky to the very mantle beneath our feet. The mountains are falling and rising again—granite spires and monoliths erased by water's hydrogen bonds one grain at a time, shifting and altering landscapes, metamorphic core complexes to undersea sediment, the Santa Catalina mountain island to the floor of the Sea of Cortez. The rain-swept stones we stand on at Lemmon Rock will one day rise as dunes in El Gran Desierto on their way to becoming the next mountain archipelago.

Water is a holy thing in the desert. I've come across stone pools in sun-cracked, shadowless borderlands that were no larger than a baptismal font or carved marble stoup. Shallow tinajas scattered among miles of sand like grace sprinkled from an aspergillum. Seeds screwed into my socks would germinate at the sight of them. The desert raises water to the level of sacrament, blessed by wind and the bone dust of those who have come and never left, those who have knelt and wet their brows with water enough for two fingers.

You can always recognize the desert dwellers when the rains come. They never run for shelter. Their doors fly open and they leap into the downpour, even flinging themselves into washes and rivers in wild abandon. For me, our season of chubascos powerfully illustrates Mexico's influence on the state. We all drink the water in Mexico. From our culture of food and fiestas, language and history. From the San Juan's Day festivities to my Sonoran Desayuno "breakfast" to the very weather itself, Arizona *is* Mexico.

The Great Two-tailed Swallowtail Butterfly Hunt

TUCSON'S TOHONO CHUL PARK

ELEVATION: 2,520 FEET | FOUNDED: 1985
POPULATION: 500 RESIDENT PLANT SPECIES

I stay the night in Tucson after my weekly writing workshop at the University of Arizona Poetry Center, and this morning Karen calls to tell me she's seen a mountain lion in the yard.

"No way!" I say. "Not fair!" In all my travels, I've never come face-to-face with a mountain lion. I've never had an *encounter*. Only a glimpse from a distance. On the day I remain in Tucson, one noses up to the fence with intentions of eating our pet turkey.

"I can't believe you are so lucky."

"The window was open. It was as big as the length of the pen. I was twenty feet away. I don't feel very lucky."

I'm in town to complete this week's destination by visiting Tucson's "secret gardens" and at the same time search for the frustratingly elusive two-tailed swallowtail. I'm also—more to the point—low on funds. (Who could have guessed that each chair for Jessica's wedding would cost $2.50? And why do weddings have to be so huge? Who *are* all these people?) A week away from being halfway through this project and the Chevron card is on ice.

It's the fourth week in June and 107 degrees in Tucson, the monsoon season having done little to mitigate the heat. My bible for *Finding Butterflies in Arizona* says the best places this month to look for the species include Oak Creek Canyon and Hannagan Meadow. "The White Mountains at nine thousand feet or above are bursting with butterflies." Sounds lovely, but today I'm stuck in the stinkin' hot desert on one of the fiercest days of the year.

Five minutes from where I grew up, from where I took my first lessons about the tenaciousness of cactus spine, from where I had more faith in locating stagnant canyon pools than carrying canteens (and doubled that faith by drinking from those pools), from where I slipped my first gopher snake inside my shirt to hide it from my parents, I pull into the parking lot at Tohono Chul Park.

Cicadas grate against my eardrums. The state bird sounds off from an unkempt mesquite tree, ratcheting a nut from its bolt. I smile, recalling an article I read about some of the choices the states have made for their official birds. The writer runs through the list of states, criticizing nearly every selection and offering his own suggestions. I agree with his sentiments: "Seven cardinals but no hawks?" Yes, and way too many mockingbirds and meadowlarks. But I take issue with his comments about Arizona's choice, which he calls "a stupid state bird." He writes: "The cactus wren is like the only boring bird in the entire state." Apparently, he doesn't know about our white-winged doves. Instead, he suggests we adopt the red-faced warbler. Red-faced warbler?! Now what does that say about Arizonans? Aside from the name's connotation, some may take exception with a bird that crosses the border every year without documentation.

"How stupid do you have to be to get bit in the neck by a Gila monster?" asks a park docent. I walk into a crowd of people under a ramada enjoying a nature talk. Ed Moll discusses the foolishness of people with reptiles. "And what about the guy who wanted to see how many times he could pass his finger through its mouth? There isn't antivenin for Gila monsters!"

I'm just in time for a lizard walk with "Snake Boy." When I ask, he says he got the nickname from a twelve-year-old neighbor girl. He wears a tan cap with a picture of a Gila monster. Our first encounter is a speedy whiptail lizard, my favorite feminist reptile. Then, a macho, blue-bellied desert spiny that perches on a rock and flexes his biceps.

"Know why they do push-ups?" Snake Boy asks. "Because lizard gyms are too expensive!"

Near the Demo Garden we run into a six-foot coachwhip snake, undulating and darting like a live electric wire. "Red racer!" shouts Snake Boy, jumping into some salvia and chasing it directly onto the sidewalk and into the crowd. We scatter into the shrubbery. At the tortoise enclosure, we cool off under several spreading sycamore trees, walnut and hackberry. There's a noticeable temperature drop, but it could be just the sound of running water. When Snake Boy retrieves a tortoise from its den, one of the children complains about waking it up.

"It's show time," he says. "It's his job—what we're paying him for."

The tortoise promptly empties itself all over his shoes in a noisy splash of liquid. Everyone laughs and Snake Boy tries to recover by talking about water storage and defense mechanisms in tortoises. "It's only water," he says.

"A tortoise canteen," I say. "Go for it."

Snake Boy puts the tortoise back. He isn't thirsty.

On a butterfly tip from another docent, I walk toward the Desert Living Courtyard. The xeriscape of native shrubs and wildflowers, potted succulents and cacti was once the parking lot for the Haunted Bookshop, now a gallery and education center. The Tucson landmark closed in 1997, finally succumbing to the rise of the bookstore superstore after twenty-two years in business. It was a place you might find authors like Larry McMurtry, Barbara Kingsolver, and N. Scott Momaday. It was where I first met naturalist-writer Susan Tweit a year before it closed.

The Haunted Bookshop was the dream of Richard and Jean Wilson. The five-thousand-square-foot store employed twenty people and every one of them knew all sixty-two thousand titles packed into the shelves, from best sellers to the most obscure books in print. The Wilsons came to Tucson in 1962 when Richard, a geologist and graduate of Yale and Stanford, began teaching at the University of Arizona. The couple started buying properties that would ultimately become Tohono Chul Park. The largest portion came from the homestead of Robert and Eugenia Bagnell, who donated the land directly to the north for Saint Odelia's, the Catholic church where I served as an altar boy during its ground-breaking ceremony. In 1979 the bookstore opened and the Wilsons began work on the adjacent land.

"At first, we just went out and put down some lime to make a path and marked the names of some of the plants and bushes," Jean Wilson said about those early days, "but then it started to snowball." The trail grew into a loop that meandered half a mile through the desert, around haciendas and Spanish colonial courtyards with grapefruit trees and date palms, past corrals where I have a childhood memory of tending the Wilson's horses. Today, Tonoho Chul Park encompasses forty-nine acres of premier Arizona upland community. Among the saguaro and paloverde and creosote, the place is home to three hundred species of succulents and cactus, one hundred fifty kinds of shrubs and trees, and fifty different wildflowers. Tohono Chul holds the largest public collection of native night-blooming cereus in the country. On bloom night, the dead-stick cacti, La Reina de la Noche, perfume the air and light up the trails for hundreds of visitors. The Haunted Bookshop and the Wilsons are gone now. But the park they conceived as a pleasant addition to their bookstore remains as one of the world's greatest botanical gardens.

Desert pupfish crowd the pond, the males turning sky blue with desire. I smell sweet desert honeysuckle among the blooming plants: Baja fairy duster, salvias, verbena. All butterfly attractants. Clusters of bright pink flowers cover a small, shrubby perennial. When I ask, a docent says its *Melochia tomentosa*, "a dove plant from the chocolate family and an excellent nectar source for butterflies." I track down skippers, yellows, and sulphurs, even a pipevine swallowtail, but no two-tails.

When a large yellow and black butterfly drifts high overhead, I follow it to the Performance Garden and the world's largest foothill paloverde tree. Thickets of hummingbird trumpet and butterfly bush, however, don't tempt the butterfly from the sky. It's probably a look-alike giant swallowtail and not my target species anyway. One tail or two? I can't tell. A hooded oriole shoots by as if someone has thrown a ripe mango in my direction. A bright iridescent blue-and-green broad-billed hummingbird perches on a low twig and mocks me with its dry, laughing *tisk, tisk, tisk*. I manage a single photograph of a queen butterfly. Then I step inside the museum shop of the Exhibit House and buy a *picture* of the swallowtail.

I've heard that beer attracts butterflies. Pour a splash into a saucer and sit back to watch the action, they say, as butterflies drop out of the sky to sip some suds. I've tried it at the risk of wasting good swill and it doesn't work. The truth is: butterflies come at their own whim, with their own rules. They're never late. Things begin when they arrive. Where moths are ascetic monks, cloaked in browns and grays and moving silently in moonlight, butterflies are royalty, arrayed in splendor, always splashing onto the scene. They have names like monarch and viceroy, queen and emperor, and yes, even painted lady. They demand to be worshipped.

I head across town to the Tucson Botanical Gardens to continue my search for the two-tailed swallowtail butterfly. This is becoming something akin to a pilgrimage, a religious quest, what some might call an obsession. Today, it's an obsession with sweat. *Butterflies of the Southwest* by Jim P. Brock, the book I bought at Tohono Chul Park, claims that the swallowtails favor mid-elevation riparian woodlands, rubbing it in with "even the most casual of observers may notice this grand butterfly soaring down a Southwest canyon." But the guidebook also says they occasionally venture into cities and towns—so I'm hopeful.

At 3:00 p.m., I sit in a pool of blue shade poured on to red brick. My arms hang limp, hands draped over my notebook, smudging ink. From behind "Edna's Shed," a white-winged dove calls furtively: *You cook like stew. Cook like stew.*

The potting shed is dedicated to Edna Johnson, the Swedish housekeeper and friend of the Porter family. She is responsible for planting the grapefruit trees, which means I can blame her for all the citrus-loving giant swallowtails I'm chasing around the Butterfly Garden.

This place was originally the home of Rutger and Bernice Porter, who moved here shortly after their marriage in 1931. Rutger had studied agriculture at Rutgers University (where else?), and Bernice was a graduate of Vassar. Both had come to Tucson for the dry climate. Bernice's father had arthritis and

Rutger suffered from recurring bouts of pneumonia. The two met after Bernice's father hired Rutger to landscape his El Encanto home.

At this corner of Grant and Alvernon (then a dirt track called Maple Boulevard), Rutger started his Desert Garden Nursery and built a three-bedroom adobe house among the flat expanse of creosote. The couple raised three daughters while running the nursery and staying active in the community, particularly with the arts. In 1964, at about the time of Rutger's death, horticulturist Harrison Yocum founded the Tucson Botanical Gardens. But the plant society didn't have a permanent home, and Yocum's extensive collections floated between his own personal gardens and greenhouses at what was then called Randolph Park. The timing seemed right for a convergence. Bernice Porter was looking for a way to save her house and gardens. "We just didn't want to see this place go down under a bulldozer," Bernice said at the time, an echo of Jean Wilson's words concerning Tohono Chul.

In 1974, the Porter home and wildlife sanctuary in the middle of the city became a center for horticulture and education, the Tucson Botanical Gardens. "This story of the past," Bernice Porter wrote before her death in 1983, "is only a brief prelude to the increasing interests of the present and those which lie ahead. Tucson happens to be a crossroads for people, but it is possibly more so for plants."

I walk the circuit from Edna's shed and the herb garden toward the Sensory Patios, the gardens for cacti, for xeriscaping and native crops, for butterflies, birds, wildflowers, and even a garden for "moonlight." Five and a half acres laid out with seventeen specialty gardens, fountains, and quiet oases. But the place is deserted. The world around me is slow and dried out. Sensible people are home resting under their swamp coolers and drinking mint juleps. Instead, I'm wandering among sunlight and thorn with camera and notebook.

"This is the largest Mexican bird of paradise I've ever seen," says a tall man with dark hair and glasses who steps out of the Zen Garden.

"Yeah," I say, surprised by his sudden appearance.

"Oh, you're watching the butterflies!" He's more excited than I expect from a guy who reminds me of my high school physics teacher.

"I'm hoping for two-tailed swallowtails but seeing only the giants."

"We get them here very rarely. You'll have to go to Molino Basin for the two-tailed."

Molino Basin! . . . He's read the book. "I've already been there, a few weeks ago. So, you know *Finding Butterflies?*"

"I know the authors. Hank Brodkin and I were just scouting in the Huachuca Mountains for this fall's Lepidoptera conference in Sierra Vista. I'm John Rhodes. I'm curator of the Garden's Butterfly Magic exhibit."

John Rhodes! I came looking for a butterfly and found something equally amazing—a lepidopterophile. A butterfly lover. I've never met the man, but I know about him from his work with SASI, the Sonoran Arthropod Studies Institute, an environmental group devoted to all things creepy-crawly. A retired teacher himself, John often presents to schools, providing live insects, spiders, scorpions, and other invertebrates from his own collections. His enthusiasm is so engaging that my daughters not only picked up his bugs but chased the boys with them.

"If you're interested in butterflies," he says, "you should come to the NABA—North American Butterfly Association—conference in September."

There's a conference for butterfly people?

Like the Wilsons and the Porters, John Rhodes is a worshipper of things wild. Like a lot of things happening to me this year, our meeting could be only serendipity. But I find it more wondrous to believe that our meeting could be proof of Edward Lorenz's "butterfly effect." Somewhere in the world—Brazil or Beijing, perhaps—the flapping wings of a quantum butterfly stirred enough currents in space-time to bring us together at the Tucson Botanical Gardens on this gloriously hot afternoon in June.

Chasing the Apache Trout I

WHITE MOUNTAINS

ELEVATION: 11,421 FEET AT MOUNT BALDY
POPULATION: 12,429 APACHES AND 2 MILLION TROUT

A week later and the Chevron gods are speaking to me again. To celebrate, I map out a six-hundred-mile loop through eastern Arizona and the White Mountains. The Kia Rio is loaded with food and camping gear, my fly rod tucked in next to my fishing vest. I'm halfway through the year and still on target with my weekly destinations. This week's goal: Apache trout, the state fish. I also have wolves on my mind.

In the predawn darkness, I beeline north from Bisbee to Tucson to Oracle, catching sunrise among the mammoth saguaro cacti north of the town of Mammoth. Then Dudleyville and Winkelman, the state's smallest (population 350) incorporated town. From Globe, home of Arizona's first first lady, Rose Mofford, and the place where sultry Lynda Carter went to high school, I climb to the gorgeous white-water gorges of Salt River Canyon, then on to Show Low and the Pinetop strip mall. At McNary, I turn off the highway into Chabetou Groceries and Sundries ("fishing worms sold here") for information and a tribal fishing license. In case I don't know what the second highest community in Arizona is about, a record-sized Apache trout hangs mounted on the wall behind the register.

After the woman writes out my three-day permit, I ask her for directions to the Alchesay-Williams Creek National Fish Hatchery, source of the Apache trout recovery.

"Take the dirt road behind the store," she says, pushing back her long black hair and pointing to the wall.

"Not Hon Dah and Highway 73?"

"That's the long way. This road is better."

She gives me directions the Kia can't follow. It takes an hour to reach the hatchery.

"I wouldn't drive that on reservation roads," a young Apache teenager tells me when he sees the Kia. His name is Byron, and he's three weeks into his summer job caring for the fish. "I have to feed the young fry inside every thirty minutes. These here get food twice a day." He opens the padlocked gate to a hangar-sized covered enclosure of tanks like Olympic swimming pools. "Take a quick peek," he tells me.

"My God!" I say, looking into the water. "Five or six pounds?"

"More like seven or eight."

The trout are huge, dark bodied and fast. They swarm the deep water, bringing it to near-boil. These are the breeders, three-year-old Apache trout, Byron says. Nearly seven hundred females and a thousand males that each year produce over two million fertilized eggs. This is the center of the Apache trout universe.

Of the three native trout species that once swam the clear, cold headwaters in Arizona's north country, two—the Colorado River cutthroat and the Gila trout—are now largely gone from the state. Only the Apache trout thrives, inhabiting dozens of lakes and streams in the White Mountains. It lives nowhere else in the world.

In the middle of the last century, the White Mountain Apache Tribe recognized the importance of the fish and began protecting the streams under their sacred mountain. Mount Baldy still held pure populations. In cooperation with the Arizona Game and Fish Department and the U.S. Forest Service, the tribe studied the status and ecology of the fish, and identified possible places to reintroduce the species into its former range. A propagation program began in 1962, and in two decades, biologists at the Alchesay-Williams hatchery had grown a healthy brood stock from wild-caught Apache trout. The tribe started planting the offspring of these trout in a few reservation streams and lakes. The program was so successful that, in the early 1990s, officials began replacing the half-million rainbow trout—a nonnative competitive fish then regularly stocked on the reservation—with Arizona's only surviving native trout.

I remember when the change came. Instead of pulling Crayola-flanked fish out of these high mountain waters, I began hooking golden-hued gems. Instead of the white flesh of rainbows, I tasted the rich pink meat of a trout fortified with river insects.

Byron walks me over to the building where the millions of trout eggs are hatched and raised to fingerling size before being moved to the outdoor production units or raceways. On the way, he tells me about living in Hon Dah, about how he likes the wildlife—elk, bear, pronghorn—and the cold weather.

"Last winter we had snow up to my window!" he says, smiling broadly under his black Boston Red Sox cap. "Me and my little brother slid off the roof of the house with our sled!"

"What about the fishing? Where do you like to go?"

"North Fork of the White. At the turnoff to Hawley Lake," he offers.

"Me, too!" I say. "I'm headed that way—been fishing there since I was a kid."

I leave Byron to his feeding regimen and push through the door of the hatchery, stepping into a hard wall of sinus-clearing, eye-watering fish stink. The smell of it clings to my skin, soaks into my hair. The taste of caviar on my tongue. Long, narrow troughs like church pews fill the room. Ushers of plumbing stand erect down a center aisle. The place hums the monotonous chorus of machinery. I peer into one of the tanks and its swirling blackness. The sheer mass of fingerlings appears greater than the volume of water. They swarm the tank like too much spinach fettuccine cooking in a pot.

From the hatchery building, the trout go to the raceways, where they grow to adult size before being released to the wild. Ravens chortle from the pines, one reason netting and chain link surround and cover the outdoor tanks. Byron had said that bears also raid the hatchery.

While collecting fish with a long pole net, another Apache teen greets me with a slight nod. His long black hair cascades over a black hoodie. His facial hardware—brow studs, lip barbells, nose rings—glints in the sunlight. Juwon has heard about the crazy writer looking for the source of the Apache trout. He tells me that he and Byron trade duties, feeding, medicating, transferring, and planting the trout as part of a Youth Conservation Corps program. "They teach us how the fish are raised and maintained," Juwon explains about the new shift to sustainable conservation. "I like learning about how we're saving the Apache trout."

Olive-spotted golden trout shoot along the raceways. These are not the river-plowing grotesque. They are not the waterborne that prowl the bottom in stone casings or skitter over the surface. Or the stumbling shell-bodied or even the furred and web-footed. These are the finest of aquatic evolution. Their fins and scales hardly leave an impression. They don't swim; a river runs through them. Their movements go unrecorded by water. They are momentum in solid form. All organisms—from the slow-witted and vermiform to the quickened and carnivorous—are subject to an inalterable genetic plan. It's the way things are. But some can rise above their DNA, the five-hundred-million-year history carried in their cells . . . rise above their very nature.

Sunlight's warmth follows the trace of veins beneath my skin, raising my body heat. But the trout remain the same, quietly matching water and stone.

I ask Juwon to spell his name—"Very unusual," he says—and he types mine into his iPhone. He's a pleasant kid, informative and interested in what I'm writing about. I notice that he no longer wears his metal jewelry, only a silver nose ring. Sometime during our conversation, he's pulled it all out. He and Byron both care about the work they're accomplishing here, and it shows. They, more than the trout themselves, are the future of the species.

Juwon gives me directions to his favorite stretch of river. "Take your fly rod," he says.

I drive to the White River Crossing on the North Fork and follow a dirt road that contours the river. The pine forest is wet. Each needle, every leaf of aspen and oak and wild currant drips with expectation. In moments, my Teva-sandaled feet search the water's depths for purchase, blindly slipping among slick, cold rocks for solid ground while my mind connects with the river. Caddis flies rise. I feel the pull. The call of the rewilded.

Fly fishing a stream narrows down my world to the elk hair tied on a single dry fly. This is about focus more than meditation. The action of the rod and arc of the line. The way the tippet drifts the fly to precisely the place you set your eyes. Time goes still on the river and there's only the metronome motion of the fly rod. This is about fishing more than catching. This is how you find solidarity with the flawless trout.

I took my first serious lessons with hip waders in the great forks of Montana's Bitterroot, perfecting my backcast and my presentation to the river's native cutthroat, the taste of Big Sky IPA on my lips. But it's these tiny, rare Arizona streams that I love, the shinning cascades spilling from the Mogollon Rim, whose headwaters hold ancient and suspicious trout the color of Oaxacan chocolate. And the deep-forest, step-across creeks under Mount Baldy with their live-wire brookies. I grew up with these Arizona waters.

Working this fork of the White River is like visiting with a childhood friend. Every bend recalls a familiar game: hopscotch, hide-and-seek, keep away, kick the can. I've watched this channel change with age, each season its topography wearing new creases and scars not unlike my own. I see new bridgework. I remember fishing here with friends as a teenager and bringing Karen to camp among the alder and willows during our first year of marriage. Our new orange tabby kitten left clover prints in the morning snowfall. I taught Karen how to fly fish, and with a flick of her wrist, she learned to hook a woolly bugger into the skin at the center of my back. Oliver Wendell Holmes Sr. says that memory is a net that one finds full of fish when taken from a brook, "but a dozen miles of water have run through it without sticking."

Two hours with my fly rod and I don't catch any Apache trout, only two small rainbows, which I release. Still only four out of twelve state symbols on the year. No matter. I have time—and soon to come, the East Fork of the Black River. By now, the monsoon rains will be stirring ridge-nosed rattlesnakes and emerald-colored Arizona treefrogs. And there's nothing like standing alone in this wild river country. Alone except for the raucous Steller's jays and the possibility of wolves. The noisy jays remind me that these forested ravines could take the howls of half a dozen wolves and multiply them exponentially. Amplification by canyon. Aldo Leopold says only the mountain can listen objectively to the howls of wolves. You can't be objective when you hear their voices rise as if along the nape of your neck.

It was Leopold, assigned to kill wolves for the U.S. Forest Service in the early 1900s, who recognized the predators' importance to an ecosystem. Trophic cascade. Those at the top affect those at the bottom: elk and alder, beaver and bird. Wolves kill, and in doing so, give life. Today, we know that even rivers perk up in response to wolves. I'm not sanctifying wolves, but it's astonishing to think of them as cooperatives in the salvation of the Apache trout.

At sunset, I begin looking for a place to camp, hoping for a dry night and, if not the sweet taste of trout, then the harmonic sound of wolves.

JULY

Arizona Treefrog

POINTS OF INTEREST TO DATE: 90 | TOTAL MILES: 9,178

Chasing the Apache Trout II

WOLF COUNTRY, EAST FORK OF THE BLACK RIVER

ELEVATION: 8,000 FEET | POPULATION: 9 WOLVES AND 1 WRITER

South of Big Lake, naked black trees stand skeletal against an oyster-shell sky. In places the spruce and fir still show green. Then the forest returns, untouched, only to retreat again to bristling charcoal. I drive through a gerrymandered map of forest peeled back by fire and laid desolate. The largest blaze in Arizona's history, the 530,000-acre Wallow Fire torched this part of the state for the entire month of June in 2011. I'm worried, and I feel the weight of it on my chest. "Beneath any landscape," writes author Craig Childs, "is a desert."

But this is not a desert yet. This is a place of return, of life restored side by side, once the wildest, now wild again. This is where in only the last couple of decades, the Apache trout and Mexican wolves have come home.

Along the forest road, I navigate the low undercarriage of the Kia Rio over dozens of diagonal water bars the size of overturned sofas. Signs warn that *Low Clearance Vehicles Are Not Recommended.* I press on, scraping bottom. I have a narrow window of less than a week before the monsoon thunderstorms begin pelting these mountains. When the rains come, the roads go—water bars or no—as deep layers of ash turn to mud like slick, wet cement, and whole hillsides tumble and roll before relaxing into the next angle of repose. By the Fourth of July, the U.S. Forest Service will close the entire region.

At 5:00 p.m., I make my campsite with a couple hours of light to spare. I'm alone. Although the Wallow Fire swept through the undergrowth, giant ponderosa still forest the deep canyon. Willow and alder still thicket the banks of the river. This is good. The clear water will hold trout. Even better, five days ago telemetry in the area located the Bluestem Pack.

On March 29, 1998, eleven captive-raised Mexican wolves, the rarest subspecies of gray wolf in the United States, were released here in the

Apache National Forest near Campbell Blue Creek. The last wild Mexican wolf in Arizona was killed in 1970, although few had been seen since the 1950s. The release did not go well. Left alone, the wolves were fine, doing what wolves do, hunting elk, having more wolves. The alpha pair of this, the Campbell Blue Pack, even produced the first wild pup of the recovery program.

But by the end of the year, in what appeared to be an organized effort of sabotage, most of the wolves were dead or missing. But wildlife officials would not be denied. The following year, in the midst of the controversy—the lawsuits from the New Mexico Cattle Growers' Association, the angry threats from ranchers—the government brought in *Dances with Wolves* author Michael Blake and released twice as many wolves in five packs covering two states. Wolf recovery by shock and awe.

The Bluestem Pack arrived in June 2002. Nine wolves—an alpha female named Estrella and her mate, a two-year-old male and female, and five pups—took to a home range that spread out over the national forest and into two adjacent Indian reservations, even making forays into the ranges of other packs. After seven years, Estrella left the pack and her daughter became the alpha female. A year later, a hunter illegally shot Estrella, bringing an end to a legacy that included twenty-two pups—six of which became leaders of other packs. At her death, she was the oldest known Mexican wolf in the wild.

Reports say the Bluestem Pack survived the Wallow Fire with pups in tow. And this year, as one of the most successful wolf packs in the program, the Bluestem has denned again. Today, about sixty Mexican wolves in eleven packs roam these woods, from the Apache-Sitgreaves National Forests, the San Carlos Apache and Fort Apache Indian Reservations in Arizona to New Mexico's Gila National Forest, the so-called Blue Range Wolf Recovery Area. Last year, at least thirty-four pups were born to these packs. Three hundred additional wolves live in captive-breeding facilities—all of them descendants of five Mexican wolves captured in 1973.

After setting up camp, which for me amounts to rolling out my sleeping bag on to the pine duff, I pull on my fishing vest and walk to the river, threading my fly rod through a mesh of alder branches tight enough to screen bear. I tie on a #18 parachute Adams and get a strike on my first cast, the fish retreating in a swirl of dark water and yellow underside. Apache trout! Moments later, I land a nice brown trout. Then, finally, a ten-inch Apache. The official state fish of Arizona, symbol number five for the year, and officially . . . my breakfast.

At 7:30 p.m., the light fades. A Clark's nutcracker caws from looming pines. I eat a dinner of Triscuits (dill, sea salt, and olive oil) and Jarlsberg, crawl into my bag and switch off my head lamp. An eggshell of moon casts the forest into shadow, turning every burnt stump into a bear . . . or wolf. I think about the two wolves from the original Campbell Blue Pack that showed up at the camp of some hunters and, as they watched, began dismembering a deer they had killed. Careful. I try not to release my trepidation into the woods where it could take on steel-white teeth and claws as hard as obsidian. If I have one fear of wilderness, it is encountering eyes in the darkness. That brooding thoughtfulness behind the stare from a mind that pursues only furious certainty. The kind of stare that penetrates shut eyelids. I try to comfort myself with the thought that a mountain lion is more likely to make a meal of me. Then I start hearing a soft padding in the gray ash and seeing pairs of green eyes.

At 3:00 a.m., my brain shakes me awake to the imagined howls of wolves. Or were they imagined? I can't be sure, but I hear nothing now—except for a Grateful Dead song playing in my head: "I said my prayers and went to bed, that's the last they saw of me. / Don't murder me, I beg of you, don't murder me. Please, don't murder me." I sleep with my eyes open. Sometime between the blackness of moonset and the birdsong of dawn, I dream of wolves. There is movement among trees, like the shadows of shadows slipping past each other. And breathing, a wet, deep-chested huffing. I dream of wolves with my hazel eyes open.

In the morning, I find tracks near my camp. Everywhere are the cloven prints of elk, like giant plant stomata plump with moisture. Bighorn sheep, too, from a cluster of ewes that came to the river for water the evening before. These tracks I remember. But then I see the palm-sized imprints: four toes and a center pad. "*X* marks the spot," I hear my daughter say as she points out the diagnostic cross pattern of canine pads. Jessica is an expert animal tracker, part of the work she does for Sky Island

Alliance. She has seen wolf tracks here. She has seen wolves here. I'm not sure if these are wolf or very large dog. I just know I didn't see them yesterday. I take photographs of Os and Xs, and print my own letters on paper to remind myself to ask Jessica how to read the language.

To see a wolf is to see an animal two million years old. This is when the ancestor of *Canis lupus* parted ways with what would become the coyote. But the story of the wolf is much older, older than the dinosaurs, as mammals go—at least the gopher-sized insect-eaters that slept in the shadows of dinosaurs and only came out at night.

What we begin to recognize as "wolflike" appears in North America after the great extinction of sixty-five million years ago, when a group of slow and clumsy carnivores called creodonts gave way to the carnassials with their specialized teeth for shearing flesh. Ten million years later or so, this group of carnivores split into the two great divides: the Cat Branch (cats, civets, mongooses) and the Dog Branch (dogs, raccoons, bears, weasels, seals, walruses). From this latter branch, the first canid, a fox-sized "dawn wolf," took to the trees, walking on padded toes or stretching out its long, supple frame among the limbs.

In the following epochs—Oligocene, Miocene, and Pliocene—while the cats honed their basic stealthy ambush form, the dogs explored many variations on a theme, molding and remolding their bodies into a cornucopia of predators. While one line tested out flippers and tusks, or a massive bulk with huge heads and marrow-extracting jaws, another tried longer legs and compact feet, a shorter tail and broader snout. During the early Pleistocene, nearly two million years ago, we see the development and diversification of the North American wolf.

Now comes the rise of *Canis*. *C. edwardii*, the first wolf. *C. rufus*, the red wolf. *C. armbrusteri*, a giant wolf and sister to the dire wolf, *C. dirus*, the largest bone-crushing wolf ever to exist, which became extinct only eight thousand years ago. And *C. lupus*, the modern gray wolf. Some researchers think the progenitor of the gray wolf crossed the land bridge to Eurasia and evolved there into *C. lupus*, crossing back again into North America where they shared the continent with dire wolves. Both had established themselves here as the first Native American people, trailing their domesticated dogs, came over Beringia around eighteen thousand years ago. Human packs living and cooperating with canine packs.

Being pack animals ourselves, we either have an alliance with wolves, or we compete with them. In the beginning, before we drew out and formed from their stock our canine familiars, it was all alliance, hunter to hunter. Today, I'm afraid, it's mostly competition. We speak the same language, but like so many other human traits, we'd rather polarize than compromise. The politics of predators like the politics of insects. No compassion. No concession. But the nature of wolves lies outside whatever we think of them, beyond competition or compromise, beyond our science and our myths. They are as real as the sound of their voices through the trees, as vital as breath. Their way is as evident and mysterious as a trail of blood in the snow.

With my limit of six Apache trout in the cooler, I drive the spruce- and fir-forested road fifteen miles to Alpine, Arizona's highest community at 8,050 feet. In Alpine, you could find yourself scraping frost from your windshield any day in July. But not this day in July. The woman behind the counter at The Tackle Shop sells me a bag of ice for the fish.

I point the Kia toward home and drive south on U.S. Route 191 for Hannagan Meadow. A slab of "Lollipop" Dion's homemade mouth-puckering lemon-meringue fudge rests on the seat beside me. My fingers stick to the steering wheel and rain blurs the windshield. Fine weather for the Arizona treefrog, and these forests could be the place to see one.

According to a marker by the side of the highway, I'm driving the Coronado Trail. Route 191 runs the length of eastern Arizona, from the U.S.–Mexico border at Douglas to Utah. This portion, a quiet 123-mile scenic byway from Springerville to Clifton, is said to be a former Native American footpath followed by the Spanish explorer-conquistador Francisco Vázquez de Coronado in 1540–42 as he searched for the Seven Cities of Gold. There's a reason the road is quiet. It drops six thousand feet from pine forest to desert grassland in a winding, gut-twisting, adrenal-gland-dumping route of more than 460 curves, switchbacks, and shoulder plunges. It is the least-traveled federal highway in the country. Bring water and a good book in case of breakdown. Twenty minutes may pass before the next car comes along.

Twenty years ago, this was U.S. 666. But Arizona highway officials asked the feds for another number designation, arguing that people kept stealing the signs. It's still called the "Devil's Highway." At Hannagan Meadow, I pull off the road. A yellow sign at the trailhead warns:

CAUTION
FIRE DAMAGED AREA
TRAIL NOT CLEARED OF HAZARDS
USE AT YOUR OWN RISK
WATCH FOR FALLING TREES/BLOCKED ROUTES
ERODED TRAIL
CHANGING WEATHER/FLOODING

I have a choice between trails for Fish Creek and Ackre Lake, and I take the latter, stepping among bracken fern and white-fleshed aspen whose leaves hold shining constellations of droplets that wet my hair and clothes. The forest is thick and green in recovery from the Wallow Fire. Still, burned and broken trees mark my route, whole trunks intersecting my path or cleaved off at midsection and lying askew like I'm walking beneath the beams of a village of burnt-out A-frames. The dispassion of wildfire. The indifference of gravity. I breathe the cool blue resin of spruce in cloud-dampened skin.

The desire of fire is sketched across this forest in mosaic. There is a calculus in the pattern of burn: Some trees remain green and standing;

others are blackened and at repose. Fire reveals itself to the forest. It harbors no hypocrisy. There is no question of its intention. Fire means whatever it does. It reeks of what it has consumed. But in its wake, it leaves the seeds of something new. This is not the destructive work of randomness. It is the beauty of madness.

I walk through a creation of Jackson Pollock, an abstraction of woods where my daughter Jessica recently found her first Arizona treefrog, a photograph of which she enjoys tormenting me with. I've never encountered the amphibian before, and now the pressure is on to see one this monsoon season as I search for the remaining seven of Arizona's official symbols.

In 1985, the Arizona Game and Fish Department featured a "Wildlife Awareness" program. Students studied hundreds of animal species to determine four finalists in each category for the official state mammal, reptile, fish, and amphibian. Thousands of Arizona schoolchildren then cast their vote, choosing among ringtails and javelina, rattlesnakes and tortoises, trout and chub. In the amphibian category, the vibrant and vivacious Arizona treefrog received 11,622 votes, beating out the Colorado River toad (now the Sonoran Desert toad), red-spotted toad, and the spadefoot. Toads, it seems, being all warty and bug-eyed, aren't as kissable as toxic-skinned frogs.

On August 13, 1986, the Arizona treefrog became our official amphibian. A tiny beetle-eating nugget that comes in two mineral shades—Globe malachite and Bisbee copper. Herpetologists' eye candy. The frog that lives among the fir and pines of Arizona's White Mountains and quacks like a duck. At least that's what my field guide says. I, however, can't be sure since all I hear on this wet-forest afternoon are the Morse-code tappings of sapsuckers.

U.S. Route 191 pulls me south through cloud-hung emerald forest laced with stands of charcoal. I have plans to follow the highway to its terminus at Douglas, passing through the open-pit landscape of Clifton-Morenci and then the Gila River farmland of Safford with its many oh-so-tempting hot mineral springs with names like the Essence of Tranquility. There's nothing like a long soak in 103-degree arsenic-laden water to loosen tangled muscles after nights of sleeping on the ground. But first, I have one more stop to make on the Mogollon Rim.

Near Milepost 223, I park next to a dead rainbow-quilled conifer: the Arrow Tree. The huge pine sports hundreds of colorfully fletched arrows and, I imagine, the steep hillside below it sports thousands more. Elk hunters challenge each other with who can place their arrow highest in the tree. But this entire barkless side—bottom to top—is a pincushion. Steel broadheads and aluminum high-impact arrows aren't cheap. I could pay the gas for this trip by collecting all the missed shots, although I'd more likely break a leg trying to negotiate the terrific downslope. The tree is amazing—how many elk tags are filled in this unit? Not many by the look of it.

I hear you. As a hunter of frogs and butterflies, I feel your frustration. I could loose a few arrows of my own. You call it the Arrow Tree. I call it the Monument to the Skunked.

Wedding Day

SWEET CHILD OF MINE

POPULATION: 250 GUESTS

God promised men that good and obedient women could be found in all four corners of the earth. Then he made the earth round. The ancient Greeks had it easy. Tossing an apple to a woman was considered a marriage proposal. If she caught it, she accepted. If she ate it, you were doomed. This week, instead of driving to an Arizona destination like Wickenburg or Casa Grande, I take the Kia Rio for a wash and upholstery shampoo in Tucson. My wife and three daughters head for the hair stylist, again. I spend a hundred dollars, but it's quiet and relaxing. Tension dissolves at the massage of the machine, the leavening of foam, the loosening of grime.

For the past few days, I've had one job: Do what I'm told. Easy as tossing apples.

At 6:00 p.m., I deliver Jessica—a giant white ball of satin with blond head, stuffed into the back of the Kia—to the Riverpark Inn. I can hardly put one foot in front of the other as we follow a bouquet of flower girls down the aisle. She's the last of three daughters to hold me up by the arm on this walk. Jaguar man Sergio Avila performs the ceremony. Then we eat, we drink, we dance. Somehow, for the father-daughter dance, my selection of the Guns N' Roses song "Sweet Child of Mine" gets translated into a George Strait tune. But the highlight of the evening arrives with the Motown vocalist and performer Burnie Starks, a friend of the girls since grade school. Burnie and I sing "My Girl" to my three daughters. Afterward, because he *understands*, Sergio gifts me with a bottle of mescal he's carried with him from Zacatecas.

Earlier in the day, during a lull in the flurry of hair appointments, arrivals, arrangements, and last-minute Father-of-the-Bride assignments, I took a walk on the new Gutierrez Bridge next to the Riverpark Inn. Five years ago, while I was researching my book, *Dry River*, I hiked this part of the Santa Cruz and spoke with people planning something called Tucson Origins Heritage Park, part of the Río Nuevo project to create a historical interpretation of this river-slashed place, Tucson's birthplace. I fell in love with the plan. Thousands of mud bricks were already rising into the torreón of a Spanish presidio in downtown. I imagined a similar reconstruction of the two-story Convento with its copper bells lifted into the azurite sky, its chapel and workshops and kitchens, the cottonwood-draped acequias carrying river water past the Carrillo house to the grape arbors and Kino orchards of the mission gardens under "A" Mountain. But as the years went by, and all I saw of the plan amounted to an adobe wall, it seemed Río Nuevo hadn't gotten into bed with the birthplace idea.

All that changed on the bridge. Seeing it for the first time, I thought: *This is what Río Nuevo is supposed to be.* Art and culture and history realized in the utility of concrete and steel. The bridge is named in honor of Luis Gutierrez, the city manager who envisioned Río Nuevo as a celebration of the city's connection to its river, its people, and its past. In the elegant lines of the architecture, the bridge symbolizes the greatness of our community, of our diversity.

I climbed the stairs leading to the pedestrian deck, each step embedded with replicas of Hohokam pottery shards, a design known from the nearby excavations of our earliest settlers. Under the sweeping arcs of the canopies, perforated with wedding-heart leaves, I walked through the dappled light of a cottonwood gallery into Tucson's past: twelve landmarks sandblasted into the deck, from Father Eusebio Kino's entrada to San Cosmé del Stjukshon (Tucson) to the University of Arizona's Phoenix spacecraft landing on Mars.

And more, something astonishing: history's sundial reaching out with light and shadow. On specific days and times, an alignment between the sun and the bridge illuminates the past. Like when on every February 19 at 8:45 a.m., the shape of a propeller appears on the engine of Charles Hamilton's biplane, the first aircraft to fly over Tucson. Or on October 14 at 8:45 a.m., when the letters "TPBCo" come to rest on a picture of the Tucson Pressed Brick Company.

It was at this last image near midspan that I met a sun-weathered Hispanic man as he crossed from the other direction. He stopped when he noticed my interest. "My father," he told me, "worked his whole life at the brickyard—right over there." He pointed to a vacant spot above the west bank of the river. He then swung his arm toward the base of "A" Mountain. "I was born there."

We talked for half an hour. He told me what it was like growing up here, going to school, raising his family on the Santa Cruz River. I explained how I'd raised my daughters on a nearby tributary of the river, and how my oldest was getting married that day only a few hundred yards from where we stood. When I asked him about the new bridge, what it meant to him, he said: "I walk across it every day. It's how I get to everywhere."

Hope and Serendipity in Apache Country

HAWLEY LAKE

ELEVATION: 8,200 FEET | FOUNDED: 1956

Near sunrise, a white mist boils off Hawley Lake's iron skillet. A light rain begins to fall, but a banked fire spreads heat into the cabin. I stand on the porch, sipping coffee. Beyond the line of ponderosa pine, an osprey rides a trout swimming high over the flat water.

Then, for the first time in my life, I hear them. After millions of years of evolution, of nature sculpting organs, muscles, bones, and the orderly electronics of instinct to create a perfect animal, I hear my first wolves. When it begins, in the seconds it takes for my brain to resister "wolves," the blood pools in my chest. I feel no warm surge of pulse. Light slides over my skin as their calling moves through the forest like an unexpected hush. A single throat joined by a harmony of throats. It is the sound of angels mourning their immortality. The furious desire of wolves howling. For the next moment, I stand half in and half out of the world. Then it ends as suddenly as it started, my foot still lifted, poised midstep over the threshold of a connection.

Karen and I have come to Hawley Lake on the Fort Apache Indian Reservation to join her uncle for a few days of trout fishing. Jim Prothero is a novelist and singer-songwriter with a hooked nose, bald pate, and Glenn Frey's voice. When he's not strumming Eagles tunes, he teaches English at San Juan Capistrano, where he lives with his wife Gail and daughter Sarah. The Protheros' home, twenty minutes from the southern California beaches, is where my family lands in summer. This July, however, Jessica's wedding has brought us all together in Arizona.

Three-hundred-acre Hawley Lake rests atop the remnants of the volcanic eruptions that created the White Mountains twenty to thirty million years ago, mountains that Pleistocene glaciers carved into headwalls and cirques, moraines and tarns. Only two areas in Arizona have seen such alpine glaciation, the other being the San Francisco Peaks near Flagstaff. This was the time of Arizona's ice sheets and mastodons, of Paleo-Indians and dire wolves.

Twelve thousand years later, in 1956, the Apache tribe decided to dam Trout Creek and create Hawley Lake as a reservoir for irrigation and recreation. (The name honors Albert M. Hawley, the Fort Apache Bureau of Indian Affairs superintendent at the time.) The BIA convinced the tribe to offer non-Indians leases for summer home sites on twenty-five-year terms as an economic boost. Problems soon developed, however. First, Arizona's largest utility saw the dam jeopardizing the continuous flow of water to the sprinkler heads and swimming pools of greater Phoenix. The Salt River Project (SRP) sued the contractor. The tribe proceeded to construct the dam anyway, setting up barricades to prevent outside interference. With an injunctive order in hand, SRP officials brought in a busload of armed deputies. The Apaches circled with their own weapons drawn. It was a standoff of the classic Old West kind, cowboys and Indians, only this time the cowboys lost, retreating without firing a shot as the cameras showed up. So the dam rose and the lake filled. The summer cabins of Phoenicians began dotting the lakeshore.

In the following years, issues arose between the Apache tribe and the leaseholders. The annual income from the four-hundred-plus leases couldn't even pay for the garbage collection, which the tribe was responsible for under the lease agreements. When the tribal council tried to renegotiate, the Hawley Lake Homeowners' Association rebuffed them. As a result, when the leases came up for renewal, the tribe elected to let them expire.

I've read the lawsuit that followed. The Homeowners' Association argued that the BIA had a duty to protect their property from "marauding Indians," that the United States must ensure the "integrity, honesty, and fairness" of transactions between Indians and non-Indians. The HOA tried to get Hawley Lake removed from the reservation and turned over to private ownership. In the end, some owners burned their cabins and others moved them or donated them to the tribe.

Today, you can rent a cabin from the Apache tribe for a reasonable price, depending on its location and the size of your group. For your money, you'll get fully furnished rooms and a kitchenette and spectacular views without television or telephone interruption. Maybe even the howls of wolves. There's also garbage collection.

Along the road to our cabin, a crowd of people gather in the rain to watch the garbage Dumpsters. A large black bear has climbed into one and is extracting his lunch.

Rain. Again. Hawley Lake is one of the wettest places in Arizona. Thirty-eight inches of precipitation (about seventeen inches of rain and as much as fourteen feet of snow!) may fall in any given year. It is also one of the coldest. Hawley Lake holds the all-time low for Arizona, recorded on January 7, 1971, when temperatures plummeted to forty degrees below zero. Two weeks later, Prospect Creek, Alaska, recorded the coldest temperature for the United States: negative eighty degrees.

On a balmy summer morning by comparison, Uncle Jim and I rent a boat for some trout fishing. I row. He guides. Jim has a particular spot in mind. In three hours, we catch nine keepers, including a thirteen-inch rainbow, the largest fish Jim has ever hooked at Hawley. Not bad for a nine-dollar tribal fishing permit.

Only recently has the Apache tribe taken more control of its lands and wildlife. Whereas my culture's legacy will probably amount to little more than a eighth of an inch of polypropylene in some limestone strata, the Apache people seem more mindful of the land. They have one word— *ni'*—for both the land and the mind.

Hawley Lake was only the beginning. When I fished here as a child, my license fee went directly into the state coffers. Not any more. Today, my tribal fees support programs like the recovery of the Apache trout. The tribe also has its own trophy elk hunts. It is the first tribe officially involved with the Mexican wolf's reintroduction. The Fort Apache Reservation is home to the Tsay-O-Ah, Maverick, and Paradise wolf packs. It was one of these three packs I heard calling this morning.

I mention the wolves to Larry and Jackie, who arrive at our cabin in the afternoon as the rain comes furious and hard. "I heard them early this morning, too," Jackie says. Larry Begay is Uncle Jim's college roommate from Northern Arizona University. Larry and Jackie live in an off-grid home, powered by sun and wind, on the Navajo reservation near Grand Falls and have invited me to stay with them when I visit Arizona's "Niagara" later this year. This is our first meeting. Jim, Larry, and Jackie make this trip to Hawley Lake every summer.

We sit around the fireplace on plush sofas and talk about books, trout fishing, and getting too old for tent camping.

"Especially with wolves," Karen says.

"Or Bigfoot," Larry adds.

"Bigfoot? You're kidding," I say.

"There was one at Hon Dah two or three winters ago. People found tracks in the snow, and a woman named Mary May Harvey saw it looking through her window."

I'm surprised. Bigfoot here? In the White Mountains? I'm reminded of Travis Walton's story of alien abduction in these mountains in 1975, popularized by the movie *Fire in the Sky*. Only a couple of weeks ago, Walton spoke about his new theories on why he was taken into the spacecraft, that it was an accident of circumstance. "I got too close," he said in the interview. His case is one of the best of its kind ever documented. Six people witnessed his abduction.

But Larry is talking about the so-called Mogollon Monster, which witnesses first reported in 1903 as an eleven-foot creature having "long white hair and matted beard that reached to his knees." A good description of some of my relatives. My friend, the nature writer Robert Michael Pyle, has walked with Bigfoot. Bob favors listing the species under the Endangered Species Act.

"Mary May's story brought in TV crews," Larry says. "Bigfoot hunters. They interviewed some residents, took some pictures. But they spent more time at the casino and drinking at the bar than looking for Bigfoot."

As the rain lifts, we head for Larry and Jackie's campsite: Karen helps lay out the ingredients for dinner—beans and beef, shredded cheese, diced tomatoes and onions, chopped lettuce—while Larry drops perfect rounds of bread dough into hot oil. "Jackie's specialty," he says about the tacos. "My job is turning them." Soft flour coats her fingers and the front of her sweatshirt as she tosses the dough back and forth between her hands.

"My job is eating them," I say, grabbing a plate and loading up the fry bread. In a moment, I have a problem, which I solve by tearing the thing in half and folding it.

"There's no easy way to eat them," Larry says, as I twist my head and wrap my mouth around the taco.

After dinner, we warm ourselves around Larry's fire, a bright, incandescence of cedar from Navajoland. We talk about our NAU years, about Grand Falls, Tucson, chimichangas, and Sonoran hot dogs. Jim says he's never tried one. Larry and Jackie say they've never even heard of the bacon-wrapped food group of the borderlands.

"No?" I say. "Never been to El Güero Canelo?—probably the best in Tucson!" I mention how Daniel and Blanca Contreras started with a taco stand and now have three restaurants. "They brought it from Mexico to Tucson. The Sonoran hot dog may have been conceived in Hermosillo, but it was born in Arizona." I have work to do, I figure.

Then, something calls from the darkness and we go silent.

"Sounds like a bird—a duck," Jackie says.

"Yes, a duck! Do you have a flashlight I can borrow?" I hunt along roadside pools, waiting and listening for the call, which always quits as I approach. Pools of rainwater lie still and dark. The flashlight throws shadows into dripping ponderosa.

After fifteen minutes, I spot something with tiny golden eyes. I shine my light on it, kneel into the water, and grab at a clump of grass. With the creature squirming in my palm, I hurry back to the campsite and peel back my fingers. I can't believe it! A thumb-sized bright-green frog. Chocolate eye stripes run the length of its sides—an Arizona treefrog! Jackie gets her camera and takes pictures while Karen holds it in her hand against the brown of her jacket. I stand back and watch, amazed. Serendipitously, the state amphibian has come to me. It is beauty. A wayside sacrament. Some say that poetry lies, that numbers are as close as we get to the mind of the divine. But math, even symmetry, isn't necessarily beauty, and beauty, says Ralph Waldo Emerson, is the handwriting of God.

Beyond the circle of our campfire light and late into the night, the treefrog croaks. The sound moves across its puddle like waves from a dropped pebble. A sound reaching out for others but finding none. The croak comes again, unanswered. The frog obeys something that requires it to sing even if it were the last frog on the planet. It's not, I'm sure. Somewhere out in the darkness are other treefrogs. It is a song with the full-throated urgency of hope behind it.

The Wisdom of Serpents

HUACHUCA MOUNTAINS

ELEVATION: 5,803 FEET | POPULATION: INNUMERABLE MOSQUITOES

At the end of July, thunderheads rake virga across the sky islands of southeastern Arizona. I navigate the oak and pine creek bottom of Scotia Canyon in the Huachuca Mountains with Walker Thomas, former snake hunter and a man who once lived in a cave.

I met Walker years ago when he joined the creative writing workshop I direct at the Poetry Center in Tucson. He shared a story he published in *Outside* magazine in 1988. In it, he writes about imagining himself in flight with a Townsend's big-eared bat he shares the cave with, about the bears and skunks, foxes and ringtails that have become his companions. "I have come to feel less an intruder," he says, "more a functional part of the environment. Life goes on around me, gaining from me where it can. Wherever we are, we become part of the nature that is there, despite ourselves."

We've made two attempts to reach his cave. Both failed. Neither one of us is young. Now in his sixties, Walker no longer has the steel-fibered muscles and bottomless stamina he had in the 1980s when he could out-hike a horse and rider, uphill. Even then, with eighty pounds on his back, it took him most of the night and part of the next day to reach his home—the cave where he lived the last few years of his eight-year stay on the mountain.

Earlier this year, I asked Walker if he would accompany me on my hunt for Arizona's official state reptile. I knew that he wouldn't mind spending his days monkeying up steep canyonsides and his nights sleeping on the ground in the rain. When I picked him up today, he handed me a "snake stick" he had made by breaking off all but one of the tines of a garden cultivator. "You're going to need this," he said.

The monsoons have released every leaf and blade from the foresummer drought. With darkness coming to the canyon, the Mexican blue oaks take on a gloaming luminescence. Apache and Chiricahua pine poke black needles into pinprick starlight. I breathe in deeply. The woods are seasoned with decay, sprinkled with overripe mushrooms and shelf fungus, with worm and beetle dung measured out and crushed between fingers, then splashed with mountain lion urine. The oak duff smells of barreled wine.

We don head lamps and carry backpacks with cameras and water, snake sticks in hand. Walker is in his element. He points out the blue eyeshine of male wolf spiders, his excitement as fresh now as when he wrote about the phenomenon thirty years ago. Water pools at every creek crossing, the depths undulating with horsehair worms and leeches. A single firefly winks on and off as it turns figure eights over flat water the color of spilled oil. The woods feel magical in all this blueness. Here are creatures with fantastical names like pygmy nuthatch and brown creeper, cave myotis, coatimundi, and ocelot. *Here*, I think, more hopeful than certain, *are the planet's rarest pit vipers, the ridge-nosed rattlesnake, all slit eyes and war paint.*

Of all the world's thirty-six species of rattlesnakes, thirteen live in Arizona, more than in any other place. I've seen most of them. I kept rattlesnakes when I was much younger. Glass cages holding western diamondbacks, blacktails, and Arizona blacks, western, speckled, and tiger rattlesnakes crowded the walls in my bedroom. I'd handled the Mohave greens at the summer camp where I worked, giving impromptu show-and-tells with fangs jackknifed, oily venom running down my arm. My first introduction to the sidewinder came at nine, shortly after moving to northwest Tucson. I discovered it resting among its coils on a bank of the dry Cañada del Oro wash. The sidewinding horned rattlesnake is my totem animal, according to my friend Phoenix Eagleshadow. She says this is because the snake never deceives. It wears its nature on its sleeve, so to speak. It can be nothing but honest about what it is—a poisonous reptile. (I didn't know it was that obvious. . . .)

But there is one I have never seen in the wild—the mountain-dwelling rattlesnake with an upturned snout painted like an Apache warrior. And like the Apache of history, it favors these rugged mountain islands in the southeastern corner of the state. It stirs for only a few short months in a few isolated wooded canyons after the rains begin.

Monsoon stirrings. Serpent risings. Each year in India, near the end of the monsoon season, when rising water drives them from their holes, serpents are celebrated with Naga Panchami, the Festival of Snakes. For Hindus, a plague of snakes means it's time to rejoice in the well-being of the people. Even in the Sinai Desert, when the Israelites complained of a similar plague, Moses lifted up the serpent and those who looked upon it were healed.

Snakes also appear often in Aztec mythology, especially rattlesnakes. The Maya called them "vision serpents" and believed they were a conduit to the spirit world. Many cultures throughout history connect snakes with wisdom. This makes me think that one of our greatest myths is the serpent's deception of Eve. We're the ones deceived. Eve wasn't fooled. She sought out the serpent. Curiosity drove her. She desired wisdom, and she pursued it. She wanted a revelation of her world.

We bed down under broken clouds and a canoe of moon that skims along their backs. The night is warm, and I forgo my tent, preferring to sleep under an expansive sky. Poorwills call from the creek bottom, and I drift off to their twin-note lulls. During the night, I pick out the calls of three different owls: a great horned, pygmy, and western screech, all hoots, toots, and bouncing whistles.

At 5:30 a.m., the kingbird alarm clock goes off. *Noisy birds!* I think, rolling over. But my eyes flick open when I hear the barking of an elegant trogon. *Trogons!* I'm up. I fix oatmeal and coffee while Walker experiments with his new backpacking stove. He finally gets the gas mixture right and heats water for his Mountain House freeze-dried bacon and eggs. Mountain House is proof that you can eat anything at least once. I decline his offer for a taste.

We start out hiking up canyon from where the Arizona Trail crosses the creek, the two of us spreading out along adjacent sides of the drainage. Parrotlike trogons and zone-tailed hawks, both prizes of bird watchers, call out from the canopy, the first voicing its presence, the second its agitation at *our* presence. Clark's spiny lizards shoot through the dead leaves while alligator lizards eye us from beneath their rotting logs. A good sign. Ridge-nosed rattlesnakes feed on lizards—at least the slow ones. Near the top of the canyon at the edge of a pond, I step in thick grass that releases half a dozen leopard frogs, which leap with legs splayed and splash into the dark water and disappear. We don't see snakes of any kind.

Back at our campsite, Walker and I prepare for a wet night. Just as the rain begins to fall, a couple drives up in a car with Texas license plates. "Do you know anything about the snakes?" the driver asks.

"That's why we're here," I answer.

The woman in the passenger seat seems excited by what I say. "We just tried Sunnyside Canyon. The road is rough." The driver's name is Tony, and he's a herpetologist. His girlfriend, Arianna, works with giraffes. Her T-shirt says: *Herd Nerds and Giraffes: Together Neck and Neck.* They have a ridgenose in their collection.

As they drive off, I collect my wet sleeping bag and begin setting up my tent. "How crazy is that!" I tell Walker, who's considering abandoning his soaked gear altogether and sleeping in the car. "People—*professionals*—looking for the same rattlesnakes we are!"

The next morning, Tony and Arianna return. We team up and spread out, scaling the opposite ridge, zigzagging across talus slopes and stomping though the underbrush. Walker is pleased about our new friends, and I listen with amusement to his and Arianna's conversations. "I have to apologize," I hear him say at one point. "I keep getting a whiff of myself."

"It's okay," Arianna replies matter-of-factly, "I work with large mammals."

I laugh. Walker is the most social of hermits. The sixty-seven-year-old milk-drinking substitute teacher loves people. While he lived in a cave, he spent his weekdays as a gym instructor and college student, making friends and falling in love, even dodging *two* marriage proposals! *Two!* Hermit indeed. He's dragged more than one woman up that mountain with him.

Halfway up the ridge, our enthusiasm is flagging. I hear too much conversation and not enough scouring of hillside. Then I see movement. Dark bands slip beneath an agave. I cry out "rattlesnake!" and drop my pack. "Rock rattlesnake, I'm pretty sure," I say as the others gather.

Tony kneels at the base of the agave and parts its dry leaves with his hands. "I see coils," he says. "Yes! Banded rock!"

Walker slowly retrieves the reptile with his snake stick, and we take a few minutes to admire and photograph it. Then we leave it alone. It's not the ridgenose, but it's close.

"First one I've seen in the wild," I tell Tony.

"Me too," he says.

We make the summit by noon without another encounter. In an hour, we're back at our campsite. Tony and Arianna head for the campgrounds at Parker Canyon Lake to clean up. They plan on trying another canyon tomorrow. "I'm sorry," I tell Arianna before they leave. "But I looked everywhere, and I didn't find a single giraffe."

Two days later, I return to Scotia Canyon. I'm headed home to Bisbee after a couple days of hummingbird banding in Patagonia with my friend Liz Bernays, taking the forest road through the southern Huachuca Mountains and hoping to spend the few hours before dark hunting for the ridgenose. At the turnoff to upper Scotia, I recognize Tony and Arianna's vehicle, stopped behind an Arizona Game and Fish truck. Tony sits in the front passenger seat.

I park in the road and walk up to Arianna in her car. "What's going on?" I ask, thinking they're having a conference.

She's hysterical. "They caught us with . . ." she sobs. "They're arresting him!"

"No! God, Arianna, I'm sorry," I tell her, looking up as a uniformed official walks toward me. Tony and Arianna were collecting protected snakes *without a permit. I've stepped too close to the water's edge*, I think. Frogs of suspicion, as the writer Terry Pratchett might say, are leaping into the pond of my gullibility.

"Do you know these people?" the officer asks me.

"I met them a couple days ago. They gave me no indication they were collecting, only photographing. I think they're okay. . . ." I try to explain, though I'm starting to have doubts. As I began to defend the two, a second officer writes down my license plate number. Arianna screams: "Leave him alone! He had nothing to do with it!"

"It's okay," the officer says to me, finally. "He's just getting a citation."

Tony, however, never leaves the vehicle, and when the officers drive away, Arianna follows behind them. I spend the rest of the afternoon poking around and wishing I had at least asked to see the snake.

At the end of September, Walker and I return to Scotia Canyon for one last try at the ridge-nosed rattlesnake. It's my fourth attempt. Last month, I camped in Lower Scotia after arriving at 10:00 p.m. Dew coated my sleeping bag as soon as I rolled it out. All night I listened to the pings of screech-owls and poorwills while U.S. Border Patrol vehicles splashed through the creek where it crossed the road. By morning, a perfect corona of dew shone on my pillow around my head, beneath a perfect cloud of deet-loving mosquitoes. I counted thirty-seven bites. I spent the time alone, hiking the canyon in search of patches of snake-warming sunlight as monsoon clouds gathered over the mountains. The day turned out to be snakeless.

This morning, again in Lower Scotia, I'm loath to leave my sleeping bag and its tarp covering in this steady drizzle. But I can hear Walker moving around, and the all-night rain hasn't dissuaded the mosquitoes. By noon, we're soaked. We head for Parker Canyon Lake, hoping the mercantile at the marina will sell us another tarp or two. When we arrive, four Game and Fish vehicles are parked out front. I single out one of the officers. "You don't have to answer me if it's a problem for you," I begin, "but I'm wondering what happened to the couple you caught with rattlesnakes last July."

He looks me over. "Yeah, Texas husband and wife . . ." He hesitates to say more.

"Boyfriend and girlfriend, actually. We met them, had no idea they were collecting." I explain that I'm writing a book, chasing the state symbols, and looking for Arizona's official reptile. "Did they have a ridgenose?"

Another pause. "Yes. He threw the snake under his seat. Then he lied about it. The Border Patrol had been watching them for days."

Jeez! I think. *Were they watching Walker and me, too?*

I feel bad for Tony and Arianna, but at the same time, I'm thinking, *What did you expect? This is what you get when you mess with Arizona wildlife!* I want to drive to the Lone Star State and retrieve all our stolen rattlesnakes. All I know about Texas and rattlesnakes is that Texans eat them. Arizonans don't eat our state reptile, just our state fish.

"I could use the business," Scott Kerr, the store owner, tells me after the officers leave. He overheard me mention my book. He says he bought the store in 2010 as an improvement to operate on Forest Service land. He plans to expand. He and his partner live nearby on ten acres, and this is their dream. "So make Parker Canyon Lake one of your destinations."

"It already is," I say.

Just then a young Hispanic boy comes through the door with a live bluegill dangling from his fishing pole. His dad follows, and there's general excitement about the boy's first fish.

"I need some ice," he says, swinging the fish around the room. "And more worms!"

The next day, refreshed from a night of hot food (oh, the bruschetta at Bisbee's Screaming Banshee Pizza!), warm beds, and dry clothes, Walker and I return to the southern Huachuca Mountains. One final day of snake hunting. We check out Oversite Canyon first and then abandon it for lack of running water. Bear Creek Canyon looks more promising,

and we spend the morning combing the underbrush and rocky outcrops along pools that look like shining beads on a string. Longfin dace dart through amber water on translucent fins. An algae-furred Sonoran mud turtle plows through the muddy stream bottom. *What about this for a state reptile?* I think. They could've picked any other reptile. Like the Gila monster I found last March. It's pretty, sexy, and lives in Arizona. *What about the bloody Gila monster?*

Sycamore Canyon is dry except for a few sinking pools crowded with butterflies like chips of paint at reveille: cloudless sulphurs and tailed oranges having "puddle parties." Scores of Arizona sister butterflies cruise the creek drainages on chocolate wings. I check every flutter for the infamous two-tailed swallowtail. Among the dozen or so species—none.

By noon, we arrive at Upper Scotia Canyon. Ground zero for ridgenose (if the Texans didn't collect them all). We follow the Arizona Trail into a now-familiar woodland. Sunlight angles through the oaks, turning the dry leaf litter into rich flakes of golden-brown that crunch underfoot. I see ridge-nosed rattlesnakes everywhere I look in my mind but not in the places I turn my eyes. Three hours of hiking, poking into crevices, swatting at mosquitoes yields nothing. No snakes of any kind.

Some say that to experience the wild, you must be in the moment, observant to your immediate, mosquito-clad environment. Some say you must let nature come to you. Take the Thoreauvian stroll into the woods. You have to meet nature at least part way. But if you want more than a casual acquaintance, nature has demands. She desires to be pursued. She requires it. Rather than living at home like a traveler, your home should be mostly empty. If you want intimacy, you have to get out there, engage the place, devote time to it, pay the price with hunger and chill, sunburn, blister and thorn. Max out your credit cards, strain your relationships. Obsess. Take risks—it isn't wilderness unless something in it might poison you or feed on you. It isn't nature unless it can kill you. You have to earn it. Pay your dues. Then, and only then, you might get lucky. Like great art, one of the purposes of nature is to disturb, to jar us out of our complacency in the world.

Back at the car, we pore over maps, considering the best route to one last canyon and one last search before light fades and my efforts to find the snake come to an end. But the forest road we choose proves impossible when I drive to a washout ditch the Kia can't negotiate.

"We should just walk in from here," I tell Walker, wanting to get out of the car before we lose daylight altogether.

"Let's try this other road," he suggests, pointing it out on the map.

I'm not so sure, since it takes a longer way around, which means more time spent riding in the car rather than hunting for snakes.

A quarter mile down the road, I see a suspicious shape moving over the gravel. I hit the brakes and skid the Kia over the snake, straddling it with my tires and coming to a stop on the other side of it. Walker is already out of the car with his stick. Before I can unbuckle my seatbelt, before my hands and heart recover from the adrenaline spill in my blood, he says: "It's a ridgenose!"

Of course it is! The snake pulls into itself and spring-loads. *God, it is beautiful!* I drop to my knees, camera in hand. Wide hazel irises consider thin black pupils. My reptilian brain signals "flight" while the rattlesnake's says "fight." But the only rattling is in my joints. Cool and collected, the reptile waits as I shutter through a thousand photographs.

"The irony of it all," Walker says, finally.

"Yes," I say. "The beautiful irony . . ."

Two months. Nine weeks of hunting on four separate occasions, six days, thirty-six combined hours of scrambling up mountainsides, turning over rocks, rolling over logs, shoving our hands into holes . . . and we find the rattlesnake in the final hours of the last day as a pattern of scales among tire treads in the middle of the road.

It is a gift. Another of Emerson's wayside sacraments.

Nature doesn't reveal herself too easily. We have our science and our myths, but nature has a way of picking us clean of answers. The way of nature is sometimes beyond our reasoning, but that is the mystery, what makes any revelation of hers an act of grace. Nature's way is as hard as the stab of stone underfoot and as wondrous as the coils of a serpent in the road.

AUGUST

Ridge-nosed Rattlesnake

POINTS OF INTEREST TO DATE: 104 | TOTAL MILES: 10,728

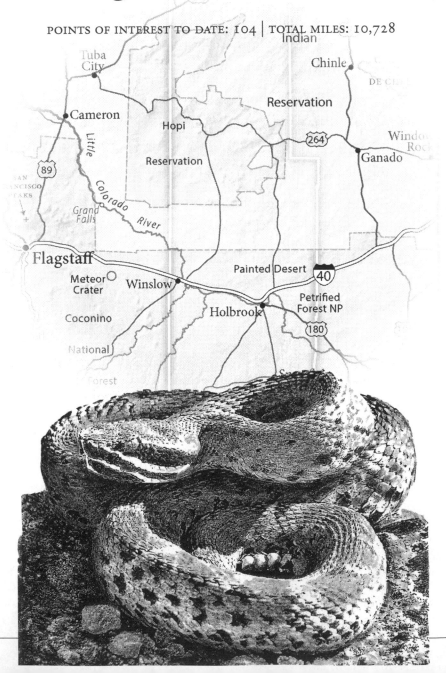

Our Lady of the Traveling Cross

HOLY TRINITY MONASTERY

ELEVATION: 3,691 FEET | FOUNDED: 1974 | POPULATION: NUMEROUS
MONKS, NUNS, OBLATES, AND PEACOCKS

In the first week of August, thirty-one weeks into my Big Year, I drive north along Highway 80 toward the Mormon community of St. David and the Benedictine monastery called Holy Trinity. On the side of the road, a dead raccoon lies on its back. To an uplifted paw, someone has tied a colorful Mylar balloon. It reads: *Get Well Soon.*

The last part about the balloon isn't true, I confess—although it's real in my imagination.

I pull into the monastery and park next to the Shrine of the True Cross, a seventy-foot Celtic cross that stabs at a sharp blue sky. A peacock screams about its immortality from some hidden place. Pipevine swallowtails cut low over a square of grass, wings held up by layers of air pungent with marigold and juniper. An Inca dove cries "No-hope. No-hope." But I don't believe it.

Inside the chapel of Our Lady of Guadalupe, the siren calls of peacocks penetrate the rammed-earth walls. Votive candles release the fragrance of incense and wax, the smoke twisting upward into the peeled ponderosa vigas and cedar shakes. An altar of native mesquite rests atop the twisted trunk of a black walnut tree harvested at the monastery. At the back of the sanctuary, the figure of a brown-eyed Christ appears on hand-painted Italian tiles, looking more glorified than crucified upon his split redwood cross. Paintings of Saints Benedict and Bernardo Tolomei take up positions on either side, places usually reserved for thieves. All this art—the paintings and mosaics and carvings and cast-bronze candle holders, from the red oak and tile floors to the beveled glass windows—is the work of the monastery's oblates and laypeople.

I genuflect awkwardly and take a pew in the back, finding myself alone with my own profane thoughts. This is always the danger with sacred space. Unencumbered with the world's many distractions, technological and otherwise (gas pumps with TVs!), the mind unplugs and turns inward, where it may wander among the landfill of regret. And who wants to go there? But this is also how we reach the place of brilliance. The unobstructed place of the imagination. The real danger with what some call the extinction of sacred space is the loss of the creative. Poet, writer, and Benedictine oblate Kathleen Norris says that to attach oneself to place is to surrender to it and suffer with it. It is in the suffering that a place becomes sacred.

Inside the Holy Trinity Bookstore I meet Carol Kline, a residential oblate. She's been affiliated with and served this community since the beginning. "I'm interested in the history of the monastery and the Celtic cross," I tell her.

"What do you want to know?" she asks. "I think we have a booklet here somewhere."

While she hunts among the shelves, I learn from her that the monastery began in 1974 when Bishop Francis Green of the Diocese of Tucson wanted a Catholic renewal center in this part of Cochise County—some might say this part of Mormon country. This would have been shortly after my confirmation at St. Odelia's when the bishop gave me the customary *pax tecum* and slap on the cheek. (Karen says he didn't hit me hard enough.) In the fall of that year, Father Louis Hasenfuss, O.S.B., arrived to lay the groundwork for the ninety-two-acre monastery, starting with the construction of Our Lady of Guadalupe Church.

Today, three communities live here—the white-robed Olivetan Benedictine monks, the sisters of the Holy Family Convent, and the residential oblates. About 750 additional oblates serve from outside communities, some even from overseas. A growing group of RV people arrive seasonally—the "Holy Hoboes." But it's the cross I've heard so much about, and the reason for my visit. My eyes are always drawn to it as I drive along the highway. Carol Kline says the cross came as a gift—one of two gifts offered on the same day in 1996 to Father Louis. He saw the pair of gifts not as a coincidence but as a sign from God.

The first was also a cross—a sliver of the actual cross of Jesus—a relic passed down from Pope Pius IX to Baron de Kestella, general of the Swiss Guard (who saved the pope's life), to Joe Testin, the baron's great-great-nephew. A few hours after Joe Testin's visit to the monastery, Sierra Vista oblates Gerald and Patricia Chouinard asked Father Louis if they could erect the Celtic cross on the property.

The Chouinards were having problems with their neighbors. A few years earlier, after completing their home in the Huachuca Mountains high on a hillside above Ash Canyon and being inspired by a religious pilgrimage to Yugoslavia, the couple commissioned the fabrication of a lighted seventy-foot cross to shine from their property over the San Pedro Valley. Plans for a chapel were drawn up. Permits for the monument were acquired. The local residents, however, were not so spiritually inclined. They organized, collected funds, and filed a lawsuit to stop the project. Opponents began calling it "visual pollution." When the Chouinards' permit was finally revoked, the couple filed an appeal and waited for the outcome. In the meantime, the giant cross came to the Holy Trinity Monastery. In the fall of 1996, after the Chouinards spent fifty thousand dollars in legal fees and other costs, the court reinstated the permit. This time, Jerry built a *seventy-five*-foot cross at the shrine next to his home.

My proximity alert goes off. Our Lady of the Sierras is something I've got to see.

A gray cassock drapes the hunched shoulders of the Huachuca Mountains, where last June a wildfire destroyed twenty-nine thousand acres. Thunder rolls down Ash Canyon like the voice of Morgan Freeman. From the lower parking lot, I follow a path of brick and wood upward along the burned hillside and the newly remade Stations of the Cross. I pause behind another visitor named Steve. He has a hole in his right earlobe so large that I can read the first cross's cast-bronze plaque through it: *Jesus is condemned to death*.

Halfway through the stations, I arrive at the river-rock chapel, also recently reconstructed. The thirty-foot Madonna, her head encircled with a crown of twelve stars, stands with her right hand uplifted to the cross (and, some say, to Mexico five miles to the south). The cross, a thirty-ton construct of concrete and fiberglass fitted over structural steel, blocks much of the western sky. Its circular transom perfectly eclipses the cloud-shrouded sun.

A Mexican family joins me. They span at least three generations, from a gray-haired woman to a seven-year-old in a pink dress. The girl sits in her wheelchair, looking up at the statue of Mary. A breeze off the mountain tosses her long black hair. Most of her Spanish I don't understand, but the words sound holy, like the language of heaven.

More pilgrims arrive. More of the faithful to see the miracle. To pray for one of their own. I climb the steps to the last Stations of the Cross. Each one pulls me backward like gravity through my childhood altar-boy years: preparing the credence table, filling cruets with water and wine, carrying the processional cross to voices rising with hymns. I smell the burning resin from a censer. The smoke of charcoal and frankincense. "Let my prayer come like incense before you," the Psalmist prays, knowing his offering can have no sweet savor without sacrificial fire.

The aftermath of fire is everywhere in this place, but so is newness. Out of the black earth and scorched tree stumps come leaves of green. At the final station, *Jesus is laid in the tomb*, my emotion rises unexpectedly, surprising me in its intensity. The Monument Fire of last summer swept through here, taking every blade of grass. It took every oak tree, all fourteen Stations of the Cross. It gutted the chapel with its 170-year-old hand-hewn oak beams. But it did not touch the Madonna or the Cross. Often we make a place sacred *because* of a miracle. But sometimes we make a place sacred and the miracle follows.

Chasing the State Butterfly (Again!)

CHIRICAHUA MOUNTAINS

ELEVATION: 9,760 FEET AT CHIRICAHUA PEAK
POPULATION: 375 BIRD SPECIES AND A MULTITUDE OF PHDS

Eighty-eight miles northeast of Bisbee, I park at the Portal Store Café & Lodge. Rock House Road takes me past several *Birders Welcome* signs to a giant flowering acacia heavy with iridescent blue-black pipevine swallowtails. For a book project that is becoming *Chasing Southern Arizona* or *Chasing Some of Arizona*, I've come to the Chiricahua Mountains to chase the two-tailed swallowtail, state symbol number eight for the year— if I'm lucky.

Inca doves cry "No hope," and this time I believe them. I walk along Spider Lane among sycamore and cottonwood, the humidity and August heat like a woolen blanket around my shoulders. Dry cobbles pave Cave Creek. Cloud butterflies and sulphurs drift by, some Mexican yellows, but no swallowtails. Clown-faced acorn woodpeckers cackle at me from the trees.

I drive to the South Fork Picnic Area, having decided to work my way up the canyon to Onion Saddle, then Pinery Canyon on my way home. The fee is five dollars, so I stuff my last ten-dollar bill into the envelope and push it through the slot. Then I break out lunch, half a jar of melted peanut butter, some stale saltines, and an apple. The Mexican jays see me coming.

"Are you hungry?" I ask, holding up a cracker. One of the birds snatches it from my fingers with a stunning blow. Shrill cries cut through the forest, and more birds mob the table. "This is going to get bad, huh?" I say, abandoning my lunch to the jays.

I hike South Fork of Cave Creek Trail, scanning the creek bed, the oaks and pines, for drifting flakes of yellow and black. I've forgotten to check the grill of the Kia for butterflies. Places are burned over from last year's Horseshoe II Fire. Red tape on one dead pine reads *Killer Tree* with a black skull and crossbones. *Because it's going to fall on someone?* I'm more worried about the fresh pile of bear scat in the trail. Bells and pepper spray, they say, work best against bears. And you can always identify bear scat because it's chock-full of bells and smells like pepper spray.

I walk among brown creepers and painted ladies, nuthatches, sapsuckers, and fatal metalmarks—mixing my butterflies with birds as if they were metaphors. I could be describing some seedy inner city district after dark: "Check out the chickadee with a great blue hairstreak! And the cuckoo with the dogface!" Like Thoreau—but maybe not the way he meant it—my whole body is one sense. I imbibe delight through every pore.

At Maple Camp, I sit with my feet in the creek. The water is cool, not stone cold, but at least it's wet. I consider climbing in and letting the butterflies come to me. A nice soak to loosen the salt and grime and my stiffening muscles. Nature's Jacuzzi. Then, I hear the *keow*ing of trogons, elegant trogons with the long coppery tail. The pursuit and prize of Cave Creek. Bird watchers from all over the world come here to see them. But not today. I'm alone in this canyon. When the tropical birds arrive—one of them fig-beetle metallic green with a belly like crushed raspberries—my paradise is complete. The two birds practice their vocals and flit about with the undulating wings of butterflies.

Lorraine at the Nature Shop at the Southwestern Research Station asks me to post my trogon sighting on the whiteboard. "People are having trouble finding them," she says. I ask her about current projects going on at the station, and she says Earthwatch is collecting caterpillars right now. The group is studying ways caterpillars feed on specific plants that make the larvae unpalatable to parasites. My entomologist friend, Liz Bernays, says new research shows that caterpillars and other insects like moths, ants, and fruit flies, can actually self-medicate. The animal pharmacists change their behavior to eat plants with certain chemicals that relieve symptoms caused by parasites. Some may even offer medication to their sick offspring. I imagine houseflies keeping their little maggots home from school.

"And," Lorraine adds, "Wade Sherbrooke is back. He returns every year to work on horned lizards." She hands me his book, *Introduction to Horned Lizards of North America.*

"Ah," I say, flipping to the inside flap, "the horny toad bible." One endorsement says that the book will give everyone "a new appreciation for these magically bizarre animals." Yes, magical indeed. Although Karen can stroke them almost into a purr, it seems like every time I pick one up, the lizard puffs itself up, takes aim with one swollen eye, and squirts me with blood.

"I also have two of your Chiricahua books," she says, handing them to me to sign.

From the Nature Shop, I walk past the living quarters for the researchers. They say this side of the Chiricahuas has more PhDs per square mile than anywhere else in the country. The board trail through the demonstration reclamation wetland offers me a lungful of swamp gas, courtesy of the scientists. I bench myself in front of the nectar feeders anticipating my favorite blue-throated hummingbird. I see blackchins, rufous, broadtails, and broadbills. A male magnificent zips out of a juniper, bringing the total to five species. Then, a high-pitched whistle signals the arrival of the bluethroat, which towers over the others, its wings all aflutter.

Between their stop-action solid forms, the birds are a blur of color as if unchained from the plodding restraints imposed on the rest of us by time and gravity. Wings thrum between twenty-two and seventy-eight beats per second, depending on the size of the hummingbird. The frequency is distinct enough to identify some birds by sound alone. A plucked string on a bass guitar being tuned to its species' resonance. I hear an open E in the bluethroat's wings.

I see myself in hummingbirds. Their boldness. The way they get into your face, plunging in with parted beaks. The same way I might reach out and take hold of a sudden insect or stick my arm down a snake hole.

Hummingbirds are dramatic by nature. They thrive on excitement. Their base act of feeding is worthy of the stage. It is a frenzy of competing beaks—of swordplay more than food gathering, the birds acting as if tomorrow's sun will never rise. I could watch them, as I often do, until evening draws the last curtain on them. The little rufous hummingbird at the feeder weighs less than a nickel, yet today it flies the return leg of a three-thousand-mile journey from Alaska where it breeds to its wintering grounds in southern Mexico. Six thousand miles every year. With hummingbirds, expect the miraculous.

Later, I drive over Onion Saddle to Barfoot Park through burned-over hillsides blooming with purple verbena, scarlet betony, and the yellows of mountain oxeye. A butterfly bouquet, but I'm on a sidetrack to the talus slopes for twin-spotted rattlesnakes. With my recent successes in finding both the banded rock and ridge-nosed rattlesnakes, the lizard-eating subalpine twinspot would make a nice trey for the year. Lichens in blues and yellows encrust the broken rhyolite in a jumbled field that lies collapsed against the mountainside. A cool wind rises out of the valley and picks up speed once loosed from the pine forest. Lizards scurry at my stumbling approach. With every step, the rock slide shudders. I should be wearing boots rather than Tevas.

As I pick my way across the talus, something black and yellow flashes by. Am I imagining things? Then I see it again, low over the rocks. A two-tailed swallowtail! *You've got to be kidding!* I think, slipping to my butt while fumbling for the camera. Rocks skitter. Something rough scrapes against one ankle. I look up and the butterfly is gone. Only lichens color the rocks. I will spend the rest of the day debating with myself whether or not to count it.

The Kia climbs out of the PhD side of the Chiricahuas and coasts down the GED side of the mountain, winding through Pinery Canyon and out into Sulphur Springs Valley to Turkey Creek and a highway mottled with the dark stains of horse lubbers. Here lives Petey Mesquitey. I have one last stop at the banks of the ol' *guajolote*.

A sign at the closed gate says *Keep Out*. Another reads: *By Appointment Only—No Drop Ins*. A third warns, *Dead End* with a picture of a rattlesnake. This is the place. But Petey isn't home, as far as I can tell. He may be already off to the Bisbee Farmers Market, where he and his wife Marian are regular fixtures on Saturdays.

I hesitate. Shall I hop the gate? I could be wrong, but after seeing one of his CD covers, with Petey you're just as likely to find him wearing blue jeans and a white button-up shirt with a live cicada brooch as to find him wearing nothing at all. My shyness gets the best of me.

Peter Gierlach goes back to my college days in Tucson when his country swing band, the Dusty Chaps, was playing places like Poco Loco and the Stumble Inn. I wasn't much into honky-tonk, but some of the girls I dated were, along with members of the garage band I played bass guitar with. These days, although he still plays a mean squeeze-box with the occasional Dusty Chaps reunion, most people know Peter for his weekly radio spots on Tucson's KXCI 91.3 FM. In *Growing Native with Petey Mesquitey*, he turns his three decades as a local horticulturalist into five-minute spurts of humor and song and poetry about the plants and animals that live among us. "I'm not makin' this up!" he's fond of saying. Petey can start with the scientific name for the kangaroo rat and finish with a sea chantey. "The kangaroo rat don't ever sweat / build a mound little *Diplodomys*, build a mound / and he prefers dust to getting' wet / build a mound little *Diplodomys*, build a mound. . . ." A longtime friend of Ed Abbey before the writer's death in 1989, Petey is an environmental activist of a different sort. He's changing southern Arizona one song, one story, and one potted plant at a time.

"Licked any toads lately?" I ask Petey at his booth at the Bisbee Farmers Market.

"Sorry I missed you last night," he says, his Kentucky drawl as thick and white as his giant horseshoe biker 'stache. As a consolation he hands me a sprig of mugwort to burn and rid my house of "bad spirits."

"Will it kill scorpions?"

"No," he says. "But their sting won't hurt!"

Today Petey is selling advice, again—for ten dollars, a price greater than his potted salvias and *Anisacanthus* shrubs. When I see the sign, I say: "I only want your bad advice."

"That'll be twenty dollars, then," he says with a laugh.

This is the place to come for a laugh—Petey could make more with his humor than his advice, maybe even his nursery sales. My yard is filled with his plants, which the deer seem to prefer. He's told me he trains the deer to eat his plants so I'll buy more. This late in summer, I wonder if he doesn't offer classes to the caterpillars as well. When I show interest in his single five-gallon Chiricahua black cherry tree, he informs me that people like it because it's the host plant for the two-tailed swallowtail.

"Thanks, Petey," I say. "The state butterfly. The reason I was in the Chiricahuas."

"You didn't see one?" He acts surprised while rubbing it in.

"I couldn't get the photograph I wanted. Do you have any larvae on the cherry tree I can raise to adults?" We talk about the state symbols I've seen so far this year, and those I haven't.

"I can't help you with the Colt .45," he says. "But maybe the ringtail."

A few days later, Petey e-mails me his KXCI segment called "Literary Ringtails" about a pair of the animals who live in the attic of the county library branch. "Every morning some books would be found on the floor," he says. "They seemed to be looking for something. . . . Those ringtails had been pulling books off the shelves and reading through the night." His voice and words move into rhythm and rhyme as he describes what the ringtails were reading, books on rodents, their favorite food, and cookbooks, too. "Today we're cooking *Diplodomys* dumplings and Rodentia stew," he says in a perfect imitation of Julia Child.

The librarian, Petey claims, solves the issue by giving the ringtails library cards. "Peter never lets the truth get in the way of a good story," says his wife, Marian the Librarian.

Indian Traders and Skinwalkers

GANADO AND THE HUBBELL TRADING POST

ELEVATION: 6,386 | FOUNDED: 1876 | POPULATION: 1,210

From Bisbee, I drive north four hundred miles in eight and a half hours to the Hubbell Trading Post at Ganado with bald tires and a hundred dollars in my pocket. It's the third week in August, and come what may, I'm breaking away from southern Arizona and shooting straight for Navajo country. An invitation I can't pass up. When I first met Jim Kristofic last March at the Tucson Festival of Books, I mentioned to him that Ganado was on my list of destinations. "I'll be working there this summer," he said. "Bring a sleeping bag and you can stay with me."

At the visitor center, a Navajo woman sits at a loom working on a gorgeous rug of the "Ganado Red" style that Juan Lorenzo Hubbell made famous. Her name is Ruby Hubbard, a master weaver who has spent five months on the double diamond design with its rich accents of black and gray. Her last rug sold for five thousand dollars.

Becky Begay at the desk hands me a brochure for a self-guided tour, and when I introduce myself, she says, "Oh, Jim told me you were coming. He will be back soon." She smiles and points out features of the post on my map, telling me about the history. "Feel free to look around." Next to her is a large stack of Jim's book, *Navajos Wear Nikes*. I laugh when I see Becky's and Ruby's footwear.

Today, the trading post is just as much a store for groceries and jewelry, baskets and rugs as it was in 1876. Only the merchandise is new. I walk along walls of mortared sandstone to the barn and blacksmith shop. An ancient double door of wood planks opens into a dark cavern, the largest barn in northern Arizona when it was built in 1900. A dust-covered buckboard and buggy rest beneath a high ceiling of pine beams overlaid with poles and thatched with straw and cornstalks. It smells like the cracked leather and sweet horse dung of history.

"Would you like to see a hogan?" a man wearing green asks. His name is David Naegle. He's worked maintenance for the National Park Service for the last couple of years after being a drill sergeant in the marines for seventeen. "I grew up in Ganado," he tells me when I ask him where he's from. "I was happy to come home. This place is like an oasis for me."

He drives me in his Ford F-350 pickup to a mud-domed structure of hand-hewn timbers. A log-roof hogan with seven sides and no windows—a female hogan. "It's been here as long as I can remember," David says, unlocking the wooden door.

I duck my head and step inside. The air is cool. The intricate corbelled pattern in the ceiling draws my eyes to the center opening, the smoke hole for the center fire that represents the North Star. I stand inside a miniature universe, a replica of the outer universe. This is more than a structure. It is a place for making sense of the world, a place to live in harmony with the cycles and forces of life. Traditional Navajo say they remain attached to the hogan as if by a string. And from that point, they look at the world.

"I can take your picture." David instructs me to sit at the west side and face east. It is the "seat of honor." When he shows me the photo on my camera, I'm sitting cross-legged in the dirt with half a smile on my face. I look like a *bilagáana* tourist.

Soon I find Jim in a NPS ranger uniform surrounded by Navajo children. "Hey!" he says. "Good to see you! We

have chili for dinner!" He's been working at the trading post all summer, leaving his wife Christina in Pennsylvania where Jim teaches high school English in the "off season." Jim returns to Ganado every summer. He's working on an oral history project, interviewing and writing about the people who've lived their whole lives along the banks of this tributary to the Little Colorado River, the Pueblo Colorado Wash.

With wavy brown hair and turquoise eyes, Jim looks about as Navajo as I do. When he speaks, however, you understand he has a history with this place and its people. He laces his sentences with words in Diné, the language falling from his tongue like water off slickrock. He was seven years old when his mother packed him and his younger brother into a Dodge Caravan with all their assorted pets—a cockatiel, a Persian cat, and a Great Pyrenees dog—and drove them to an adobe bungalow in Ganado in three days. His mother was a nurse with dreams of a western life among Indians. When a reservation hospital offered her a job with moving expenses and a house, she left Pittsburgh for good.

Reservation life, however, did not begin well for Jim. His Navajo peers called him *bilagáana bilasáana*, "white apple," and almost daily picked fights with him, with his *bilagáana* little brother, even with his *bilagáana* dog. But eventually Jim made friends and adjusted. Today, he says he feels more comfortable with the Navajo people than with many aspects of his own Anglo culture, especially with the concept of credit cards and property ownership.

"This apricot tree is one hundred and three years old," Jim tells me. "Grown from a seed spat out by don Lorenzo Hubbell himself." We're standing in the inner courtyard of the Hubbell home immediately behind the trading post. "Or so they say," Jim adds.

The tree twists into the sky. I follow its gangly branches with my eyes, thinking: *I love this stuff.* Jim leads me through the 1902 adobe showplace home, a main hall with five flanking rooms that incorporated an earlier mud-walled structure (now the dining room). We pass through the kitchen with its long, low kneading table. "The cooks had to feed thirty-five or forty workers—lots of bread, beans, chile, and beef going through here. . . ."

This was the nucleus of the Ganado community. The place where Hubbell became something of a feudal Spanish lord. He was born in 1853 in New Mexico, to a Connecticut Yankee and the granddaughter of a Mexican governor. Twenty years later, he was self-educated, speaking three languages, and employed at the Navajo agency in Fort Defiance. He came to this place around the time of the witch scare of the 1870s, serving as an interpreter to help restore the peace. A witch had been killed in the doorway of a trading post at nearby Ganado Lake, effectively finishing any business with the superstitious Navajos. Hubbell bought this store and property from a trader named William Leonard so as not to lose all the Navajo trade. Soon, the region's landscape gave up its soil and timber and pink sandstone as Navajo and Mexican craftsmen raised the high, solid walls of his new trading post.

Inside the hacienda living room, Navajo rugs spread over wood floors. Native American baskets extend across the ceiling among pine vigas. An elk mount spreads its antlers over most of one wall. It faces a bison on the opposite wall. Bookshelves hold titles from Shakespeare and Poe. I'm stunned by the elegance. Of all the old traders, Hubbell had flair. "Theodore Roosevelt stayed here after Hubbell arranged for him to see the Hopi snake dance," Jim says.

I stop at the serrated pattern at the margin of a rug. "Hubbell is responsible for the Navajo rug as we know it today," Jim says, "as a work of art." He explains that early on, the trader recognized and encouraged quality in the workmanship, even suggesting colors and patterns. He paid the weavers by the rug rather than by the pound as other traders did. "Ganado Red became popular because one of his biggest customers was the Fred Harvey Company. In 1923, Hubbell sold sixty thousand dollars' worth of Navajo rugs. Unheard of at the time."

Scores of drawings of Indian profiles hang on all the walls: E. A. Burbank "Red Head" sketches that the portrait artist made in Conte crayon. Geronimo and Sitting Bull look over the room where Hubbell died. Jim shows me one marked "Chief Many Horses, Navajo, 1907." "He was the eldest son of Ganado Mucho, and his descendants still live here." I recognize the name. The friend of Hubbell is buried on the hill behind the trading post where Lorenzo lies next to his wife, doña Lina. David Naegle had told me the graves are unmarked, as is the Navajo way.

The Hubbell family continued operating the trading post until 1967 when the Park Service purchased it after it was designated a national historic site. It's one of the first of forty-four in Arizona (and number five of the dozen on my list). NPS considers it to be the best surviving example of an Indian trading post in the United States. It still *is* an Indian trading post. Locals still bring their handcrafted artwork to sell and trade, as the

Hubbell family intended. The first duty of an Indian trader, don Lorenzo Hubbell believed, was to look after the welfare of his neighbors. It was good business, and it continues to this day.

In the spare kitchen of the ranger quarters, a three-bedroom house near the trading post, Jim prepares homemade chili from beans and fresh diced green peppers. He dips cups of flour from a sack of Blue Bird and kneads it with baking powder and water into dough for "tortillas"—what I would call fry bread—frying the flattened disks in an iron skillet.

"We aren't having mutton?" I ask.

After dinner, Jim shows me the town. It's dark. The moon, a waning crescent, has already set. No matter. I'm reminded of a hike in the dark with another friend, Paul Bogard, when he was researching his book, *The End of Night*. Walking near my home without flashlights, I unintentionally terrified him with stories of my mountain lion sightings.

We hike east along the highway, then climb a fence and cut across a desert of sagebrush and piñon, heading for the Presbyterian mission with its hospital, nurses' home, power plant, and Old Manse, his childhood home. Jim tells me that the original settlement was called Pueblo Colorado, but when don Lorenzo Hubbell bought the trading post, he changed the name to Ganado in honor of Ganado Mucho ("Many Cattle"), the Navajo clan leader known to the Diné as Tótsohnii Hastiin, "Man of the Big Water Clan." Jim knows the names and dates and history, and I have a hard time keeping up with his stories. "No one knows this stuff," he says. "It took me years to learn it—one of the reasons I want to get this oral history book published."

"What is it about Ganado?" I ask.

"People come—missionaries and traders—but they have a hard time leaving. It's the community, a self-sustaining community, and like the Hubbells, they want to be part of it."

They want to live and die here, I think. *But they can't.* The Hubbells may be the only white people buried on the Navajo reservation.

We walk in silence along the same streets, in the same darkness, beneath the same spreading canopies of the Chinese elm of Jim's youth. And I know what's coming. Because I read about it in his book. Jim points to the barbed-wire fence he and his friend Ferlin Shondee climbed, and beyond the fence, the house they hid in, trying not to imagine the creature sprinting after them, "its shadow trailed by the coyote skin flapping over its back in mid-leap."

This was the place of my first living nightmare. The house is as dark now as it was on that night twenty years ago. Jim is hesitant to talk about it, and I don't press him, except with my silence. "I guess it's okay," he says, finally. "As long as we don't call it by name."

Is this fear or respect? I'm not sure. Maybe both. He's talking about *yee naaldloshii*, a skinwalker. Before I read Jim's book, I'd never even heard of skinwalkers, Navajo witches that can take on the form of an animal, shapeshifters that use their supernatural abilities to harm others. Then I picked up the novel by Tony Hillerman.

Jim's story begins when he and Ferlin got caught out in the Pueblo Colorado Wash after sunset. "No man's land." The place where Ganado Mucho and his sons had hunted and killed scores of suspected skinwalkers during the 1878 witch scare.

Then the trees began talking to them.

The boys ran for the green streetlight at the Old Manse and made it inside, but no one was home. When the dogs began growling and barking in the backyard and something thumped against the roof tiles, the two bolted for Ferlin's aunt's house a quarter mile up the road. In the darkness of his aunt's kitchen, Jim ran his fingers over Ferlin's shoulders and back, searching for any cursed bone chips inserted under the skin by the *yee naaldloshii*. Then Ferlin checked Jim. For skinwalkers, writes Jim, don't care about skin color.

I rise early the next morning to coffee perking in a blue enameled pot set on the stove. Nothing speaks better of friendship. Jim leaves for Pennsylvania in a couple days, and he's already packed. I'm headed for the Petrified Forest National Park and my ninth state symbol. Before I depart, Jim rummages through his gear and pulls out a folded bandana. "For your travels," he says. I unfold an Arizona flag. I spread it out beneath the rear window of the Kia Rio where it will stay the remainder of the year.

Getting My Kicks

HISTORIC ROUTE 66 FROM PETRIFIED FOREST TO METEOR CRATER

ELEVATION: 5,080 TO 5,710 FEET | FOUNDED: 1926

Wild buckwheat blooms over a vast yellow expanse that suddenly drops away into a gouged-out, rainbow-hued landscape of the Painted Desert. I stand on the shore of an ocean drained away and filled with sky. A wrinkled and dimpled badland of bentonite clays layer-caked in cyan, vermilion, and plum. Home to North America's earliest dinosaur fossils and the greatest concentration of petrified wood on the planet.

I haven't seen any native petrified wood yet, but I have encountered the park's giant reptiles: not *Smilosuchus* or *Postosuchus* or even *Stagonolepis*, but *Crotaphytus collaris*, the collared lizard. From Kachina Point, I drive along the park road toward Blue Mesa and the forest of logs that Dave at the visitor center recommended. "It's my favorite place to visit," he said.

"One question," I asked, knowing I'd be the millionth visitor to ask it. "Are the trees standing?"

From the 1940s Fred Harvey pueblo-style Painted Desert Inn (national historic site number six!), I stop at each pullout and get out of the car to survey the landscape: First, Pintado Point, then Nzhoni, Whipple, and Lacey. Whipple Point honors U.S. Army Lieutenant Amiel Weeks Whipple who, in 1853, first noted the great quantity of petrified wood while surveying along the thirty-fifth parallel for a railroad. President Theodore Roosevelt would later set aside parts of the stone forest as the country's second national monument after Devils Tower in Wyoming. Then, in 1962, Congress designated the monument a national park.

Ten miles of road later, cones of carbon clays, iron siltstones, and white sandstones rise on the west: the Teepees. I see dark cylinders lying partially buried in flat earth the color of monsoon clouds. I pull off the road and walk. The air has weight. The sun blazes against my neck. Each

footfall sends up plumes of dust as if stepping on dry
puffballs. I recall that I'm thirsty. After ten minutes,
I stand beside the largest agate I've ever seen. A
shining red-barked stump lifts out of the puzzle-
piece ground. I could count its marbled
rings, but instead I take a seat. *Araucarioxylon
arizonicum*. Arizona's official state fossil in its
natural habitat.

Two hundred million years ago, this was a
vast floodplain braided by streams that tumbled
from distant pine-clad mountains touching the bottom of the sky. Triassic
dragonflies as large as songbirds zipped among cycads and ferns. Spiked
reptiles shoveled forage from the ground along riverbanks crowded with
broadleaf and evergreen trees.

These trees may have become the Petrified Forest we see today. But I
like to imagine another theory—that the forest resulted from a catastrophic
volcanic eruption similar to Mount St. Helens: a pyroclastic blast uproots
and flattens a montane forest. Mudflows transport gigantic rafts of peeled
and stripped trees, burying them under hundreds of tons of sediment. Then
begins the slow molecular exchange of cellulose for silicates. Wood into
stone. Ash and mud, laden with oxides of iron and silicon, manganese and
cobalt, cut off oxygen and slow decay. Over time, the minerals crystallize
within the porous tissue, growing into jewels of clear and smoky quartz,
yellow citrine, and purple amethyst while preserving the original cellular
framework of the wood. Eventually, wind and water erase the deep layers
of ash and mud and bentonite clay to expose fallen logs of solid quartz
weighing 168 pounds per cubic foot, broken into gleaming sections by
eons of uplift geology. In this scenario, what happened here in Triassic
times was really more the preservation of a logjam than of a forest. But
somehow, Petrified Logjam National Park doesn't have the same ring to it.

I pass the early afternoon hiking at Blue Mesa among the carcasses
of fallen trees. Whole logs of shining agate lie over the ground as if an
ocean had retreated and left them there in their astonishment. I share the
company of people speaking a language not my own. What we have in
common is the heat and a retinal experience that requires no words.

On the drive out, four sleek pronghorn cross in front of me. They move as one body, like syncopated thrust. I stop for a fifth, a straggler, a large male with dark fishhook horns and hanging tongue. A tan shawl drapes the shoulders of his white coat. At twenty feet, he pauses, and with his round, wide-spaced eyes pins me to my seat in my own astonishment.

Bisecting Petrified Forest National Park east to west, a line of unwired power poles traces a raised roadbed of sagebrush just north of I-40. I'm looking at the remains of the most famous highway in the world. A fossil of Main Street, America. The Mother Road. What once connected Chicago to Los Angeles with 2,200 miles of billboards, neon signs, burger joints, and Bates Motels: Historic Route 66.

The remnant Route 66 crosses I-40 outside the park and parallels the interstate, heading west toward Holbrook and Winslow, my next destinations. From the Petrified Forest, I follow the route where I can, sometimes in the Kia, mostly with my eyes. The interstate has largely obliterated the old road, but there still exists a weave of weather-worn, vestigial alignments and frontage roads that were part of the original highway. For fifty miles, my meander is punctuated with a dilapidated stage station and a wigwam motel, roadside museums, dinosaur parks, trading posts, and rock shops. Lots of rock shops. In Holbrook,
the rock gardens seem to be escalating a war of the ridiculous, erecting ever larger Godzilla-like allosaurs, Flintstone brontosaurs, or promoting monster fossil alligators. "Wild Bill" is a 2.9-million-year-old former resident of Florida, who apparently has retired his bones to Arizona.

When I see a billboard for the "World's Largest Petrified Tree," I pull off of I-40 onto Route 66 and the Geronimo Trading Post. The parking lot smells of hot diesel fuel and fried chicken. Diesel fried chicken!

"It's fifteen feet high and buried nine feet in the ground," says a man named

Sterling who's working the counter and surrounded by trinkets and kitsch. "The rest is lying next to it, all two hundred feet." Sterling tells me that Carl Kempton, the owner for forty-five years, bought it from the railroad. Workers had uncovered it while laying track a mile from here.

Outside, the blond trunk of the tree rises above a cluster of sturdy tepees made of plywood and covered with white rolled roofing. This tree *is* standing upright. But there's something strangely wrong with it. It's also upside down.

My trip along the historic road wouldn't be complete without stopping in downtown Winslow where Route 66 became the first divided highway in the state. The corner of Kinsley and 2nd Street has been on my bucket list for some time. I sit on a bench across the street from a life-size bronze statue of a man in Levi's with a guitar resting on his right boot toe. A storefront reflection of a blond woman driving a flatbed Ford pulls up behind him—the John Pugh mural as realistic as the cherry-red Ford parked on the street. The Eagle's signature tune, "Take It Easy," plays from hidden speakers. Really? Like 24/7? No, actually it's only my timing. The song is just the first track on their first album from 1972. "Witchy Woman" follows.

Locals say the statue is neither Glenn Frey nor Jackson Browne, co-writers of the classic open-highway ballad of the American Southwest. (Frey came up with the key lyric in the second verse: "It's a girl, my lord / In a flatbed Ford / Slowin' down to take a look at me.") To me, with that short, center-part haircut, he looks like a young Randy Meisner, the band's bass player and high-harmony vocalist. They say he can hit notes that only dogs can hear.

People come and go, many posing with the statue for photos. I've heard hundreds visit each day. The park, which opened in 1999, is helping to revive Winslow. A trio of visitors stands in the street, attempting to line up the painted Route 66 sign in the center of the intersection with the statue and a camera on a tripod. The woman wears more skin than clothes. Someone in a pickup—not a blond—lays on the horn. Traffic slows. A Coors Original tractor trailer breaks and screeches to a stop. *Don't let the sound of eighteen wheels make you crazy.*

My suggestion when visiting "Standin' on the Corner" Park in Winslow: *Stand on the corner*, not in the street. This is a *highway*, after all. As the first bars of "Hotel California" play from the speakers, I walk down the dark desert highway to hotel La Posada. It is Karen's gift to me. One night in the sprawling pink-stucco Mary Colter Spanish-colonial hacienda and the last of the grand Fred Harvey railroad hotels. *Hotel Arizona.*

I pass through the rose garden and terrace with its canal and bridge and enter what once was the rear door back when the entrance of the hotel faced the tracks. I check into the Betty Grable, one of the rooms of the original hotel. New Mexican tinwork hangs on the walls, the art of Verne Lucero. Navajo rugs spread over saltillo tile. Diesel locomotives shake the foundation.

In the later nineteenth century, traveling by rail was a harrowing experience. Station stops allowed only twenty minutes to serve two hundred passengers. According to Winslow historian Mary-Ann Lutzick, the food was overpriced and often rancid, amounting to not much more than weak coffee and beans. "Roadhouses would charge the next passenger for the very same uneaten meal. Fred Harvey wanted to attract rather than repel customers."

An immigrant from England, he got his start in food service at seventeen as a pot scrubber and busboy in New York. It was an auspicious beginning. For by his death in 1901, his company operated forty-seven restaurants, fifteen hotels, and thirty dining cars along the Atchison, Topeka and Santa Fe line. Fred Harvey, they say, conquered the West with a beef steak and decent cup of coffee.

The man was a visionary. When people at the time considered waitressing "morally suspect," Fred Harvey hired women and called them "Harvey Girls." His restaurants, the first chain restaurants in the United States, also employed the first female work force in the country. And there were rules. Harvey Girls would remain unmarried and be educated to at least the eighth grade. They would wear uniforms to "diminish the female form," use no makeup, and live together in dorms under supervision. For this, the girls received room and board and $17.50 a month.

Mary-Ann Lutzick says that the rules didn't relax until after World War II. (The company lasted until the death of Harvey's grandson in 1965.)

When I talked to her recently, she mentioned the mythology surrounding the Harvey Girls, the stories and bad movies. "One girl became a madam because there was better money to be made," she said. "Another became a cattle rustler. Will Rogers said that Fred Harvey kept the West in food and wives. Thousands of sons were named Fred or Harvey." Mary-Ann says he is the reason she lives in Winslow.

In the morning, I take my coffee in the Sunken Garden in the company of rosemary, salvia, hollyhock, and juniper. Water trickles through a giant stump of petrified wood into a pool bordered with gleaming chunks of the same. The fossils were hand selected from the Petrified Forest by the architect, I recall, before such pilfering was illegal.

In 1903, the Fred Harvey Company hired a chain-smoking perfectionist and one of the few female architects of the time. Mary Colter had the audacity to tell stories of history, culture, and art through her designs in the presence of some of the world's greatest landscapes. She merged Hopi, Zuni, Navajo, and Mexican themes into her use of native rock and rough-hewn wood, completing almost two dozen projects for the Fred Harvey Company. But it was La Posada that she considered her greatest work, a masterpiece she created from the buildings to the gardens to the furniture and china, right down to the quilted aprons on the maids' uniforms.

Finished in 1930, La Posada saw twenty-seven years of grandeur, its staff of a hundred catering to the likes of Howard Hughes and Charles Lindbergh, Will Rogers and Albert Einstein. But with the wane of railroad passengers, the hotel finally closed. The Santa Fe auctioned off the furnishings, gutted the buildings, and turned the place into cubicles for its division offices. Then the railway slated it for demolition. In the mid-1990s, the National Trust for Historic Preservation put the hotel on its endangered species list.

I stand in front of a Tina Mion painting called *The Last Harvey Girl.* The oil shows two aged women. One of them—Ruby McHood—supports herself with a cane while offering me a cup of tea. Beneath the painting rests a bouquet of roses and a handwritten note: "Our last Harvey Girl Ruby died Sept. 1, 2011, at 8 p.m. She was 97."

I've wandered through the gardens and ballroom, the arcade, library, and foyer. Tina Mion paintings—some haunting, others humorous—hang throughout the place. I'm not staying in a restored 1930s hotel. I'm a guest in someone's home.

Allan Affeldt and Tina Mion bought the endangered hotel in 1997, moved in, and began renovations on their twelve-million-dollar project. "It was a wreck," Allan says. "Our friends all thought we were crazy." But today, not only has the couple saved a magnificent work of art and a part of Arizona's history, they've revived an entire community.

On a flat desert highway, hot wind in my hair. Rim swell of an impact crater, rising up through the air. . . . In the forty-five years I've lived in Arizona, I've never visited Meteor Crater. And now, directly in front of me, the entire dirt-red landscape lifts into a pale sky. I could be traveling on Mars. But what lies ahead is the first proven meteor impact on *our* planet.

Barringer Crater: Where space meets planet earth. This is where fifty thousand years ago a chunk of space rock the size of a house slammed into northern Arizona and blew out a mile-wide hole deep enough to cradle downtown Phoenix. The blast ejected thirty tons of meteorite fragments mixed with giant blocks of sandstone and limestone over a seven-mile radius and for twice that distance incinerated every Pleistocene sloth, mammoth, and incredulous bear-sized beaver.

Kim Merrill asks where I'm from. She's a third-generation native Arizonan, studied history and literature at NAU, and works for Meteor Crater Enterprises and Barringer Crater Company, both private family-owned businesses. We walk along the rim trail and she talks history of the impact. "The meteor came from that direction," she says, pointing to the east. "From New York to here in five minutes. The earth basically turned over on itself."

I look over the edge. A thermal rises into my face carrying the smell of pulverized stone. Some child has dropped a pink sandal.

"We have nuclear weapons that do twenty times the damage as this," Kim says.

"Why?" I ask, not expecting an answer.

Kim explains that meteor craters have much in common with nuclear sites. It was the discovery here of a rare form of silica—created only by a nuclear explosion or an impact event—that proved Meteor Crater was of extraterrestrial origin and not the result of a volcanic eruption. A mining engineer named Daniel Barringer first suggested the impact theory in 1903. He staked a claim and spent the next twenty-seven years drilling for what he estimated to be a one-hundred-million-ton iron meteorite, a lode worth a billion dollars. He never found it, and his idea remained controversial.

Then, in 1960, Flagstaff resident, geologist, and hopeful astronaut named Eugene Shoemaker confirmed Barringer's theory after finding a rare "shocked quartz" at Meteor Crater and several nuclear test sites. The work earned him a Princeton PhD and the Barringer Medal for advancing the understanding of impact phenomena, just the beginning of his many accomplishments as a planetary science pioneer. Shoemaker said that his greatest disappointment in his life was "not going to the moon and banging on it with my own hammer." After his sudden and tragic death in 1997, a vial of his ashes, wrapped with brass foil showing a picture of Meteor Crater, was slammed into the moon by way of NASA's Lunar Prospector. He is the first and only (to date) person buried on another celestial body.

"When Gene Shoemaker trained the astronauts here for the moon landings," Kim tells me, "one of them tore open his spacesuit on the rocks. NASA decided it needed to make a better spacesuit. Also, the Jeff Bridges's movie *Starman* was filmed here. We couldn't get the spaceship into the crater, so we used special effects."

Back inside the visitor center, I lay my hand on the wrinkled iron surface of the Holsinger Meteorite, the largest fragment known of the original 150-foot diameter meteor. "It was found two miles away in Canyon Diablo and weighs 1,400 pounds," says Kim. "As valuable as this is, we don't bother bolting it down."

When Kim leaves with another tour, a skeptic with a white Colonel Sanders beard voices his uninformed opinion. "They don't know what that crater is," he says to his impromptu captive audience (me). "They never found a meteorite. They never found anything." All this talk about moon landings and extraterrestrial rocks is bothering him. "That the space agencies of the world are involved in a conspiracy is depressingly obvious if you look at the evidence."

Ah, I understand. A flat-earther. Like with *Starman*, this is all special effects. Shoemaker's ashes are rolling over in their lunar crater.

Land of Gorges, People of the Fourth World

GRAND FALLS

ELEVATION: 4,700 FEET | FOUNDED: 20,000 YEARS AGO

At the end of August, I maneuver the Kia's bald tires over a Pleistocene lava flow, gingerly crunching basalt rock that looks like hard chunks of black foam. With my head sticking out the window, I search out the smoothest route, cringing at every pop and crack, fearing the worst. I'm four hundred miles from home. Forty miles from the nearest town. I need to get a spare.

I park at the edge of a seething abyss. A brown mist rises into the desert air. On my right, the Little Colorado River appears flat and placid, the color of chocolate milk as it curls over a baked mudstone plain. On my left, the river roils into a deepening gorge and doglegs northeast before sinking into layers of earth like the spines of stacked books. Behind me, seven miles away, the dimpled cone of Merriam Crater rises out of a spewed pavement that spreads to the very ground beneath my feet.

For millions of years, this part of the Little Colorado was much less theatrical. The river quietly devoted its energy to reaming out a deep canyon through layered mudstone and limestone as the crustal block beneath the Four Corners region lifted into the Colorado Plateau. Water wrestling with rock and time. Then, about twenty thousand years ago, an eruption sent a tongue of lava toward the river gorge. The lava thundered two hundred feet into the mostly dry ravine, creating a river of molten basalt that flowed both upstream and downstream for a dozen or more miles, topping and overfilling the ravine at this point. Grand Falls began as Lava Falls. Born of fire and water.

As the liquid rock cooled, it dammed the Little Colorado as effectively as the great concrete plugs at Glen and Black Canyons on the greater Colorado River. Seasonal rains charged the river. A lake of sediment began to swell behind the dam until at last the Little C breached the dam and spilled once again into its former channel in a tremendous cascade that continues on occasion to this day. From atop the lava dam, I trace the great sweep of river as it bends around the basalt plug and drops over an arching staircase of Kaibab limestone.

Wendell Duffield says the best vantage point to see the dam is from the falls—"but not when they're running!" He is the author of *Chasing Lava*. A self-described "pink-cheeked septuagenarian" and sometimes "ripe old septuagenarian" with a PhD in geology from Stanford, he retired from the U.S. Geological Survey and NAU and now lives on an island in Puget Sound. "I moved here after thirty-two years in Flagstaff," he told me. "And I already miss Flag terribly."

He came to northern Arizona to be what he calls a "hard-rock" geologist, "which has nothing to do with one's preferred genre of music. I simply wanted to study rocks hard enough to sing back when struck with a geology hammer." After my daughter Melissa, Wendell is the second person I know to mix rocks with rhyme. When I asked him for a personal story about the falls, he sent me his poem, "The Story of Grand Falls."

> First came the canyon, so deep and so wide.
> Water ran through it, with plants on the side.
> Then came the lava, real runny and hot.
> It spilled in the canyon and filled up the spot.
> Next came erosion that washed rocks away,
> To make a new canyon that we see today.
> Finally came students to study this stuff,
> With help from their teacher
> And a geologist named Duff.

Grand Falls is higher and browner than Niagara Falls, if not carrying the same volume—at least today. I detect no recent monsoon cloudburst over Mount Baldy. The flow hardly compares to the great gushing of Grand Falls the last time I was here. Then, the presence of it filled the senses, the jet-engine roar as the arc of the river swept entire cottonwood trees over the edge, their stripped branches flailing and gripping at each riser and tread of the staircase. The shudder of the landscape beneath our feet. A smell like earth turned out of a grave that bit into our sinuses. The boiling debris, more solid than liquid, that rose in the channel and tumbled away. Tit for tat on a geologic scale, as if there were intention: a river conforming to the will of the canyon until the canyon becomes the will of the river.

My friend Chuck LaRue had driven Jessica, Melissa, and me to see the flooding and to practice with an atlatl, a carved wooden shaft Paleo-Indians once used to throw stone-tipped darts. Chuck is a master at this primitive technology. He had crafted the spear-thrower, modeling it after one on display at the Museum of Northern Arizona. The darts he shaped from giant reed, fletching them with turkey feathers and tying on greasewood foreshafts with points made from the distal ends of deer tibia. We passed the afternoon slinging darts at imaginary mastodons being driven by pueblo-dwellers into the gorge. Jessica had an ancient knack for distance and accuracy. Melissa, not so much. I just watched my back.

The atlatl, I've decided, is my new suggestion for the state firearm. Right up there with the Hopi throwing stick—weapons of real honor. Both less *fire* and more *arm*.

Jackie and Larry Begay arrive on schedule. From Grand Falls, I follow the dust plume from their pickup across the Navajo reservation to their home a few miles away. Larry, who gave up a pre-med program at NAU because he discovered he loves construction, built the place himself, including an expansive redwood front deck for perfect evenings of stargazing under exquisite skies. The house is off-grid. A bank of photovoltaics and a small wind turbine supply enough power for a modern kitchen and a fifty-two-inch flat-screen television. Larry trucks in water.

Jackie spreads the table with her delicious Navajo tacos. "We don't eat this every day," Larry tells me, in case I think they might, since the last meal I ate with them at Hawley Lake was the same. "Only with guests. I like having guests."

Early next morning, I walk out onto the quiet windswept mesa, a landscape of thirst. Hardly a shrub pokes up out of the black rock pavement. Some might call it desolate. "I lived in Mesa for thirty-two years," Larry told me last night. "I feel more at peace out here." Larry had grown up in Utah with a Mormon family. Jackie, who works for the Indian Health Service, grew up right here. "I herded sheep as a child," she says. "My grandpa always brought me lunch."

We drive across the mesa headed for the Little C. Sheep browse among sparse rabbitbrush. When a black-and-white dog guarding the flock spots the truck, it charges after us and Larry guns the engine. "Does that every time it sees me," he says. He parks at the edge of the world where the land gives way to sky, and Jackie shows us where we can climb down. She points to caves where eight-hundred-year-old pots rest untouched since the day they were placed there. Above the cliffs, two golden eagles look like cutouts against the unreal blue of space.

In a couple of hours, we join the river where it scoops out sheer red walls from a flat land. Jackie remembers a cluster of ruins and takes us there. Larry's never been here before.

"You want to climb up there?" he asks.

"If it's all right."

"Go ahead. We'll wait for you here."

The deep sand at the base of the cliff sucks at my boots; my footsteps leave red liquid tongues. My heart thumps and my lungs burn with the effort. Then my legs. Thump and burn. Liver-colored draperies of desert varnish hang from the rim as if some ancient had a decorating flourish and too much material to work with. What you can do with a mineral wash of iron and manganese and a hundred years . . . Inside the cleft of rock, heat radiates from stone to skin. My sunburn complains. Swallows' nests cling beneath the overhang like tiny adobe ruins. *Which builders arrived here first?* I wonder. *Who learned from whom?* A keyhole doorway leads me into a darkened room among walls of stone fitted in a mortar of mud. The air smells like mummy dust. Eight centuries enter my pores, fill my arteries and veins. I wait for my eyes to see. The place might speak, but right now it is alive with silence. No one is home.

Agrarian people once grew corn, beans, and squash along these river benches and alluvial fans. They hunted deer with atlatls, formed pottery with imaginative, geometric designs, and traded with other tribes for seashells and parrot feathers. They built canals for irrigation, catch basins and reservoirs for water storage, roads and line-of-sight towers for communication. The Ancestral Puebloans were a sophisticated people. Today, we know them as the Zuni and Hopi.

From my rocky perch above the Little Colorado River, a raven slides by at eye level, one obsidian eye tethered to a pair of hazel. It has a look of disdain. I've lived half a life in this place of mountains and desert, but I'll always be a transplant. There are times like this when I feel most acutely how much I don't belong. The only connection I have with these Puebloans are the Scotch-Irish genes I carry from a people who lifted stones to wall themselves in against a perceived or real darkness in the world. We have the same history of retreating into stones.

SEPTEMBER

Petrified Wood

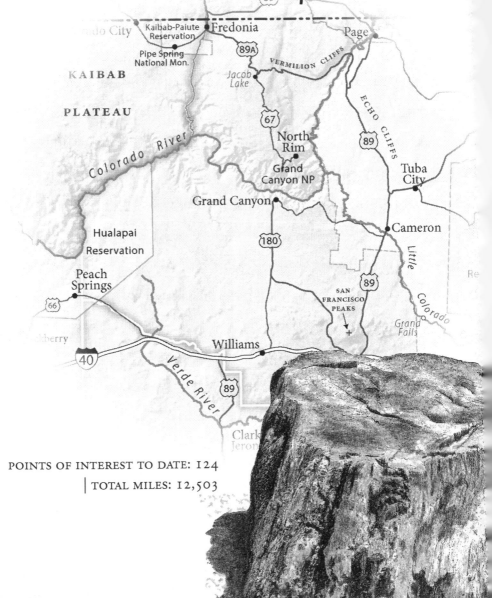

POINTS OF INTEREST TO DATE: 124

| TOTAL MILES: 12,503

Lost in a Vortex

SEDONA

ELEVATION: 4,326 FEET | FOUNDED: 1902 | POPULATION: 10,031

In the first week of September, Karen and I drive to red rock country, land of sandstone and spirits, named in honor of the wife of settler T. C. Schnebly—another name inscribed on the very hills. Ours will be a few days of soul searching. Karen will seek enlightenment through a creek-side massage. I will find inspiration at the end of a fly rod.

At the village of Oak Creek, I slip the Kia into a traffic circle. My head snaps right three times looking for the way out. "Which way?" I ask, going around to the point where I entered. "That way," Karen says, without indicating anything, believing I can read her mind. Shortly after, I'm circling again in another traffic circle, roundabout, whatever . . . then another. I begin counting roundabouts and soon can't keep track. Eight . . . ten . . . a dozen? We begin our spiritual odyssey on Labor Day weekend in Sedona, trapped in a vortex of circling motorists.

We make the Creekside Inn at Sedona bed-and-breakfast at sundown. Dennis shows us our room, the trails to the creek, the gazebo. A quiet place of grass and lantern light. Cedar shakes ripple darkly over walls of native stone. The B&B is a gift from our middle daughter Kasondra, who also paid for Karen's massage, which we hope will alleviate her two-week-running migraine.

In the evening, we walk to the galleries and shops on Sacajawea Plaza and something called "Moonlight Madness on Main Street." At the Center for the New Age, Melinda offers to sign us up for a UFO tour at Boynton Canyon. "Tonight!" she says. "We use military-grade night-vision goggles. Last night we had eleven unexplained sightings. Twelve the night before."

"I could probably explain them," I say, "if that's helpful."

Victor, a man with white hair and beard as crazy as his eyes, is doing readings. He clasps my hand in both of his. "She may not come back," he says, pointing with his eyes to a woman he just sent upstairs to his reading room.

Down the street, a young woman calls to us. "Visiting Sedona? I have maps!" Then: "You look like a million dollars!" She must mean Karen. My shirt doesn't even have sleeves, nor my pants, legs. I haven't shaved in days. Karen wears a silk scarf, black skirt and blouse, and turquoise jewelry, a gift from daughter Jessica. This is the second "visitor center" where we get the hard sell. Brynne calls herself a "rock nut" and fantasizes about finding her own meteorite. "We're in the iron triangle," she says. But tonight she's selling timeshares. Sedona Pines Resort. The Gateway to Adventure. She plies us with free wine tastings, jeep tours, rides in a UFO, and such. "All you have to do is attend a presentation at Sedona Pines." We laugh, tell her she's wasting her time, but she assures us we're perfect. *Perfect marks*, I think. When she offers us a free ticket on the Verde Canyon Railroad— which is on my list for this year—my interest peaks. "I can get you first class."

"Okay . . ." We're game. But the sale devolves as Brynne begins asking for details, like major credit cards. "We use Visa debit," Karen says. "We have zero credit-card debt."

"I have a Chevron card," I offer, "and a library card I borrow with."

More questions. Brynne types furiously at her keyboard. She's still sure she can make this work for us. But in minutes, the verdict is in: we don't qualify. "You two still look like a million dollars to me," she says.

At Mooney's Irish Pub we order "Late Night Food": "Everything closes after nine in Sedona," says our host, chef, and bartender. We eat chips and salsa in Styrofoam cups. "Sedona is a vortex for tourist dollars," I say to Karen, sipping an Oak Creek Amber Ale. "We come here to have our spirits uplifted, and we nearly sell our souls to a timeshare. No street music. No performances. No curbside barbecue. The only madness in the moonlight tonight is the marketing."

The next morning our hosts Dennis and Jody serve us eggs Benedict. Karen, not being fond of eggs, asks for just "Benedict." I chat with the couple about our evening with the money-changers in the temple. Karen has been reading a book she found at the inn called *Spirit of the Stones: A Retrieval of Earth Wisdom* by Amalia Camateros. She had a similar experience with Sedona during her first visit. "She found a small retreat center with a room for rent," Karen says, her nose in the book as she turns the pages, "but felt nothing relaxing about it. People here were lifeless, out of their bodies. Sedona was no different than Los Angeles. She calls it a 'spiritual shopping mall' pitching everything from vortex tours to visiting sites known for UFO activity."

"Yep," I say. "She's pegged it."

"They were offering to take people to meet aliens," Karen reads, "when they, in terms of their relationship to the land, were aliens themselves."

I like the alien part. I see an H. R. Giger alien, seated in the lotus position, bony tail circling its frame. "Find your center," the caption reads. "And burst forth through its chest."

At midmorning, we arrive at our first vortex. A ninety-foot dune-colored cross—my second giant cross this year—rises skyward from red stone: the Chapel of the Holy Cross. For the first time, Karen's headache is gone. We climb the long, curving concrete ramp through high outcrops of sandstone to the chapel entrance. Off to the right, a crowd has gathered. People stare over the edge to the valley two hundred feet below. I hear "Oh my God!" several times. Many take photographs with family members smiling before the multimillion-dollar eyesore. They're saying it's the mansion of Loan Cosmescu, the inventor of Lasik surgery. I become a tour guide for the profane: "If you stand over here, you'll see his million-dollar koi pond."

Karen and I sit in one of the back pews beneath a seventeenth-century hand-carved statue of Michael the Archangel with drawn sword. A recorded choir sings from some hidden recess in the nave. The chapel is smaller and sparer than I remember but carries charm in its simplicity. The ghastly beautiful black corpse of the crucified Christ is missing, replaced by a sculpture of a masked face.

I've read that the Chapel of the Holy Cross has one of the strongest vortices in all of Sedona. People say they feel inspiration and joy within the walls, an energy that evokes love, harmony, and oneness with all that exists in the world. Vortex or no, I could easily burst into tears. We sit in the back watching the visitors. Asians approach slowly and bow with folded hands. Hispanics cross themselves and genuflect before taking a pew. Anglos step into the sanctuary to pose at the altar and take photographs.

"The sacred *and* the profane," I write in my notebook.

A spiral stairwell in the narthex takes us down to the gift shop beneath the chapel. "It was too controversial," says Val, the woman at the register, when I ask her what happened to the cross. "People said Christ's body didn't decay. Marguerite didn't want to upset anyone, so she took it down. She died in 1988, and no one knows what happened to it."

Sometimes the purpose of great art is too disturbing.

Marguerite Brunswig Staude was the dreamer behind the Chapel of the Holy Cross. The idea first came to the sculptor in 1932 in New York City when, with the Lenten ashes from St. Patrick's smudging her forehead, she caught a glimpse of the Empire State Building under construction. She saw the form of a cross rising out of its scaffolding. Back at her California studio, she roughed out a sketch of a church and showed it to the son of the great architect Frank Lloyd Wright. Wright agreed to help her with the architectural design. "We scanned plans of Gothic cathedrals and searched for a way to bring the modern back to the classic background from whence it came," Marguerite would later say. After a year of work, the model of a cruciform church emerged. It became reality in 1956. The following year, an article in the *New York Times* said the chapel "represents the ultimate in fitting a structure to its site," inspiring a trend in design that continues among Catholic churches to this day.

This trend I can appreciate. But gift shops in the basement? Karen shops for cards. The cash register rings. I'm bothered by the commercialism, the rampant consumerism. I recall our daughter Melissa's senior trip to Vatican City. How disillusioned she and her Hispanic classmates became after seeing all the hawking of trinkets outside St. Peter's Basilica.

I fight the holiday traffic to get to the next vortex on my list. Karen tells me that Amalia claims the native people never lived in the Sedona area. "They only came here for a short time because they understood the nature of the place. Sedona was never intended to be inhabited, only visited for ceremony and prayer. For a new perspective. The vortex by nature is destructive. She calls it a 'cosmic washing machine.' If you stay too long, you become a twisted juniper."

"A twisted juniper?"

"She says all the juniper trees in Sedona have twisted trunks because of the vortices."

When we arrive at Bell Rock, Karen's headache has returned. We walk along a red path through flowering nightshade and juniper. I look over the trees suspiciously. They seem normal. The only things twisted are the tour helicopters whirling overhead. We commune with noise.

"You guys are dumb-asses," a cyclist in green and black spandex says as he approaches.

"A voice from the rocks?" Karen asks me.

"Not you guys," he says. "Those guys." He points with his head to a couple of tourists scaling the side of the cliff.

My vortex guidebook claims that the popular sandstone butte, which looks more like a sunburned breast than a bell, has an electric energy that releases the inhibitions of our more serious adult selves. *Just what I need!* Some people experience profound physical healing or increased vitality. Others may have an overwhelming desire to play on the rocks like children.

"According to Amalia," Karen tells me, "Bell Rock is home to an Anasazi shaman who imparts wisdom from the rocks for those who seek it. Maybe they're looking for him."

"They'll need it. Better first ask him for the knowledge of a safe way down."

\- - -

While Karen takes in her creek-side massage, I drive a sinuous road high into Oak Creek Canyon with my fly rod. I pass the crossing where at twelve I landed my first rainbow, and my mind begins unreeling more than four decades of memories with this place. This afternoon, I'm alone. Hardwoods lean across the water, dappling sunlight in a light rain. The sweetness of blackberries fills the air, stains my lips. Their canes leave hooks in my legs, while I put a few in the mouths of Oak Creek's wild brown trout.

In the morning, I sip coffee while watching a great blue heron be a perfect mime of stillness. It lifts away from the creek on New Age wings. After breakfast, we head for the Cathedral Rock Trail: one last vortex for the twisted mind. For the first time in weeks, Karen hasn't started her day with medication. I'm frustrated, however. The trailhead parking lot is full. We must take another road and hike a trail on the opposite side of the famous landmark.

We start well, but then Karen promptly wanders off-trail. We bushwhack on slickrock, all hope of regaining the trail fading as we push on and on. In a place where the very rocks lean to the center, we scale Permian sandstone. Straight into our first twisted juniper. The gnarled tree winds up out of the rock. A creek burbles below us. Cicadas whirr. Vultures hang in the air, wings held in their practiced *V*. The season's last monsoon thunderheads rise, curl, and blossom out of every red-rock spire. The buttes remind me of Spanish missions whose walls hold an iconography read only by the light of stained glass.

I breathe in, relax into sun-warmed stone, and scribble notes. Of all the scrambled manzanita and prickly pear, only the juniper pirouettes through time. A revolution. And then it comes to me. The mystery of the vortex. The vortex isn't so much a "cosmic washing machine," as Amalia says. Something that swirls around you, breaks you down, upsets your life. It's more like a gyroscope, where spinning means balance. To live in this place—to live anywhere—you must find the center. The eye of the hurricane. The calm within the storm. The axis of the spin. Sedona encompasses spiritual energy *and* natural beauty, as if God's finger were stirring the landscape. It's best to burst forth from the center of the maelstrom.

Amalia would say the rocks revealed this to me.

She never seems to resolve the "spiritual shopping mall" conundrum. In the end, she buys into it. A note stuck into the front of her book advertises her services for guided nature tours. Maybe this is her answer. Enriching others rather than getting rich. Christ drove the money-changers from the temple. But he didn't stop them from buying and selling. They moved their operations elsewhere—like a gift shop outside the temple. We are, after all, material as well as spiritual beings. Perhaps this, too, is the center of things, the eye of the conundrum where stillness reigns. Like purchasing Christmas cards at the Chapel of the Holy Cross. Or prayer beads at the Vatican. As Karen says, "Where else should you buy a rosary?"

Bottle-Shocked I

VERDE VALLEY WINE COUNTRY

ELEVATION: 3,147 TO 3,545 FEET | FOUNDED: 1865
POPULATION: 26,243

The best way to experience the Verde Valley is to taste the earth beneath your feet. Sip the spring water that runs through it. Savor the fruit of its sedimentary and volcanic soil. The best way to experience this place is in its wine as it flows through your veins.

I'm already feeling it. This ugly bag of mostly microbes, as Michael Pollan might call me, is on the ferment. The javelina are leaping in the vineyards at Page Springs on lower Oak Creek. Karen and I are visiting the tasting room at Javelina Leap, a family-operated boutique winery owned by Cynthia and Rod Snapp. Tall, blue-eyed Allyson Bright tells us they took the "leap" from Stags' Leap, the Napa Valley winery whose Cabernet Sauvignon won first place in the 1976 "Judgment of Paris" blind taste test, the competition depicted in the 2008 movie *Bottle Shock*.

Allyson introduces us to Christina Hemingson, the general manager, who invites us to see the operation. Giant vats of fermenting grapes crowd the "wine vault." Racks of oak barrels rise among racks of wine bottles. Here, after picking and de-stemming, forty-four tons of Arizona grapes are fermented, pressed, aged, bottled, and labeled to become 2,600 cases of Arizona wine.

Christina hands me a glass of 2011 Barbera, a thirteenth-century Italian varietal grown from thirty-year-old vines in Santa Barbara. She describes the wine as "big." A robust, full-bodied red bigger than Merlot. "It will stain your teeth!" Karen sticks her nose in the glass and calls it "musky." I sip—not a hint of sweetness. The tannins do handstands on my tongue. "Deep and rich with a peppery finish," I say, as if I know what I'm talking about.

But it's the 100 percent Arizona wines I'm interested in, so Allyson suggests I try their 2011 Merlot. "People say it has a fruity forward with a smoky cocoa finish," she says, half filling my glass with the dark red wine and stamping my tasting sheet with "Cheers!"

The Zinfandel is next. Javelina Leap produces an Arizona Zin that's 100 percent Arizona grapes from nine-year-old vines growing in their Dragoon vineyard. But the winery also has younger vines right here from which they make their Estate Legacy Zinfandel. The winery knows Zinfandel. Wine-hikers named their 2005 the top Zinfandel at the 2007 Zinfandel Advocates and Producers (ZAP) festival, calling it "voluptuous" and saying, "Who could have thought that a Zinfandel from Arizona would take the checkered flag from California?"

With the taste of Arizona red wine on my lips, I ride in the passenger seat while Karen drives us on to Oak Creek Vineyards & Winery for their Merlot, Syrah, and "pet" Zinfandel. Then we're off to Page Springs Cellars (where Karen will stop handing me cash for wine flights). Vintners will tell you that every palate is different when it comes to describing taste. So, I've been practicing my wine descriptions, imagining sampling flights, and getting more and more preposterous.

With the first glass of white, I start out carefully: "The perfect triage of fruit forward," I say. "Rose petal and melon show up in a linear sort of way, with cherry following an oblique tangent of geometry on the tongue." Move on to the rosé of Merlot: "An unctuous, persistent textural quality in the mouth that keeps it bolstered by sandy mesquite bean on the palate. A good, cleansing tannin that clings like Irish Spring." Then, a nice, medium-bodied Tempranillo: "Ruby red in the glass, spicy on the nose, approaching chiltepine in the eye." And finally, if I haven't been ushered to the door, a bold Syrah: "There is a smoking beefcake about this wine that I would tend to enjoy on a bearskin rug around the holidays. Wants to be paired with black leather in a bad way."

This could be an effect of too much wine tasting.

Three weeks later, in early October, Karen and I continue my wine-tasting tour of the Verde Valley by visiting Arizona's largest winery, Alcantara Vineyards. Near the confluence of the Verde River and Oak Creek, a long winding dirt road cuts through chalky hills draped with row after row of vines. Then it drops us among Italian cypress in front of a villa in Tuscany.

"We're seven years young and about 85 percent sustainable," says a woman with dark hair and green eyes when I ask about the place. Her name is Jennifer, and I envy her perfect tan as she hands me a tasting sheet of seventeen wines. I hesitate, get out my notebook, and ask about the vineyard's specialties. "I'm writing about Arizona's wines," I add cautiously.

She runs a finger down the list, checking off her favorite wines while describing each one: a 2011 Pinot Grigio ("My personal favorite as far as whites are concerned right now"), a 2011 Viognier ("100 percent estate produced"), a 2009 Merlot ("Sweeter on the palate than most Merlots"), an NV Grand Rouge ("My favorite red"). She stops at the 2010 Zinfandel. "Welcome to Arizona," she says. "This is unlike any of your California Zins. It really says *Arizona*—it's a huge reflection of our state."

Easy. I ask to taste all five of her selections. But I already know I'll be leaving with a bottle of the Zinfandel. Sipping wine, I follow Karen out back to take in the views of the river and the limestone terraces beyond. Fountains and flagstone surround lush green lawns. A sign lists five reasons to drink wine: The arrival of a friend. One's state of thirst. To evoke cleverness. Excellence of the wine. Or any other reason.

When a sweet Chesapeake Bay retriever comes to visit us, he has his owner in tow. "His name is Charlie Brown," she says. "He's a rescue dog." We introduce ourselves, and she says her name is Barbara Predmore. "Alcantara is my grandmother's maiden name. She believed in not doing anything unless it benefits others." Barbara was raised in Saudi Arabia. Her father was an oil man—a "Bedouin," she says, a big smile crossing her oval face. She and her husband Bob started the vineyard in 2004, "taking the two-million-dollar challenge" by planting nineteen thousand vines on twenty acres after years of research and study and relying on a family connection to vineyards in Napa Valley. "We wanted to show how rural Arizona can develop. Anybody here can become what they want to become. Isn't that the American Dream?"

For Barbara, it's always been about family and community. And about making wine that compares to the best in California and Europe. "Wine wants to pair with something—art, music, culture—and it takes you into something deeper. Relationships. Wine has a positive effect on people. You take a sip and you slow down. You see color. You hear music. You start listening to each other. That's why we started this place."

That stargazing wine-bibber Galileo once said that the sun, "with all those planets revolving around it and dependent upon it, can still ripen a bunch of grapes as if it had nothing else in the universe to do." The Verde Valley seems to know this. Its climate (hot days and cool nights) and volcanic and limestone soils make it a perfect place for grapes. Some claim these special characteristics even place it among the best wine regions of the world: Spain, Portugal, Italy, and Bordeaux, France. "The wine industry in Arizona is relatively young," writes Randall Weissman in the *Chicago Tribune*, "but it offers consumers a chance to visit wineries while they are still developing. The winemakers know their terroir and their grapes. They may never produce the next Screaming Eagle Cabernet, but don't be surprised if they start producing world-class competitors to Châteauneuf-du-Pape in a few years."

The Rise of Arizona Red Wine.

"I should like wine," Karen says as she drives along the chalk roads of Alcantara. "But I don't care for the way it tastes. Like something left too long at the back of the refrigerator. You know. It tastes . . . fermented. What I really like is the *idea* of wine!"

"Me, too," I say. "Wine is one of civilization's best ideas to immerse yourself in."

Tripping the Strip

THE ARIZONA STRIP

ELEVATION: 7,900 FEET | FOUNDED: 1858 | POPULATION: 8,095

After a night of "dispersed camping" among an expanse of many-headed yellow sunflowers above Oak Creek Canyon, we beeline north on Highway 89 to the top of Arizona. Karen and I have $120 to spend for a week in the middle of September on the North Rim. No wine. No B&Bs this time— it's all camping (with an air mattress). But the Kia has new tires!

At Tuba City, I pull off the highway and follow a sign that says, *Dinosaur Tracks*. I've been here before, many times, and it's one of my favorite stops on the way to the North Rim. Two hundred million years ago, large two-legged, flesh-eating dinosaurs called theropods crisscrossed a once muddy floodplain leaving behind hundreds of claw-toed tracks. We meet Leonna and her nephew Benny at their American-flag-draped plywood booth where Leonna sells silver and turquoise jewelry. "These are the tracks you find here," Leonna says, showing us a miniature model of the twin-crested *Dilophosaurus*. Paleontologist Sam Welles uncovered two fossil skeletons of the twenty-foot dinosaur near here in the 1940s and a third twenty years later.

Benny offers to be our tour guide, pouring water into several prints of a trackway that run across the mudstone next to the booth. Three-toed tracks jump out of the red rock, and we follow them out into the sunblasted flats. Benny, a young Navajo man with pleasant smile and reams of stories, has been doing this since he was fourteen. "This is the real Jurassic Park that you are walking on," he says.

Early Jurassic, I think, but I'm being technical. I already know the science. What I want is the Navajo story, the kind the guides told my children when I brought them here years ago. Benny Yazzie is up to the task. He shows us a five-foot allosaur track, conveniently outlined with small stones in case we might mistake the footprint for the surrounding rock. "And over here are its bones," he says, pointing to half-exhumed rock that looks vaguely like an elephant pelvis. "This is the ribcage and chest. You can knock on it and see that it's hollow." Benny demonstrates and the sound is a xylophone from the *Lion King*.

I love it. I wonder if Benny is thinking: *If they believe this, they'll believe anything. Time to take it up a notch.* We move on until Benny stops at a cluster of cow-pat stones. "This is what comes out after they eat us—coprolites. In English, they call it 'droppings.' And these over here are pterodactyl tracks." A trail of curled slashes like lost quotations marks the stone. I hand Karen the camera and take notes. "Explosive evolution," I write. "Evidence of Navajo Thunderbird." I think about modern sightings of the flying reptile as reported across the Nation.

"What do your people say about this place?" I ask.

"We call it *Naasho'illbahitsho Biikee*, 'Big Lizard Tracks.' It is where, long ago, monsters battled against the Twin Heroes." The twins are part of the Navajo creation story. During the time when the Holy People created the Diné in the Fourth World, monsters ruled the land. Then, the first human, Changing Woman, married the Sun and gave birth to twin boys. A war between the Twins and the monsters took place. The twins threw lightning bolts and eventually prevailed, destroying the monsters so the people could inherit the Earth.

"Every place the Twin Heroes killed a monster, it turned to stone," Benny explains. "If you want to walk more, I can show you some meteor craters."

"Like the one that wiped out the dinosaurs?" I ask. *Talk about global war.*

We hike north across sand dotted with orange globe mallow and flecked with black like chocolate sprinkles. Pointing toward a green swatch along some low bluffs, Benny says, "That's Moenave. Where I grew up." Soon a rise in the landscape becomes the rim of a perfectly circular crater. It's one of several. As if chunks of the Barringer meteorite slammed into the earth and left pocks the size of backyard swimming pools.

"And over here are some dinosaur eggs," Benny says, indicating three white nodules, half protruding from smooth rock. One of them is broken open, revealing what looks like fossil yolk. Thunderbird eggs. "And we'll wrap it up here," he says.

We head back for the booth, where we give him some cash and thank him for his stories. While Karen purchases a "cedar-bead" necklace made by Leonna from Grand Canyon juniper berries, I talk to Benny about my book project. Before we leave, he hands me a bright green Post-it note that says: *Tour Guide Benson Yazzie Tuba City* with his e-mail address.

There is something very right about a world that created dragons. I drive down the dirt road of myth back to the highway of reality where my images of thunder lizards and thunderbirds become theories of monsters. The geneticist Richard Goldschmidt coined the term "hopeful monster" in the 1930s. He suggested that evolution is not necessarily gradual as Darwin claimed but that large changes as seen in the fossil record were caused by large mutations. Evolution as an endless list of special cases, some say. Eye-migrating flatfish. Naked-headed vultures. Or perhaps even dinosaurs sprouting feathers. Evolution is God's process of beauty.

In 1972, paleontologists Niles Eldredge and Stephen Jay Gould refined the theory, calling it punctuated equilibrium. This kind of evolution acts on whole populations rather than individuals and takes tens of thousands of years of reproductive isolation for new species to appear, which is still fast, if not as instantaneous as dinosaur eggs hatching out monstrous birds.

As much as I like the idea of hopeful monsters, I'm not happy with the theory of punctuated equilibrium. It reminds me of human existence. We live with long periods of boredom, interspersed with a few bright spots of excitement, followed by even longer spans of being dead.

Skirting along the color-washed monocline of the Echo Cliffs, we head north to Navajo Bridge. The gray- and purple-banded Vermilion Cliffs rise into a sky so blue and hard to look at it's like biting on aluminum foil. I have condors—the real thunderbird—on my mind, since North America's largest bird frequents the 726-foot steel span over Marble Canyon.

Or spans. There are two Navajo Bridges. A new, wider bridge was completed in 1995 and mirrors the historic eighty-three-year-old structure, which remains open for pedestrians. Thousands of people came to the original christening, accomplished with a bottle of ginger ale since it was Prohibition. For the second dedication, a bucket of Colorado River water sufficed, this still being Mormon and Navajo country.

I descend onto the bridge, checking off one of Arizona's longest and highest for the year. When I look left, there, perched on the railing ten feet away, is a California condor. Karen and I both yell as I hit the brakes. The giant black vulture slowly pivots and drops over the edge, spreading its ten-foot wings like something out of the Pleistocene.

"You can't stop on the bridge!" I hear Karen shouting when my mind returns to the Holocene. On the other side, I pull into the visitor center parking lot and grab my binoculars. We race out onto the old bridge in time to see two condors stalking their shadows along the cliff wall like obsidian cutouts against a Martian landscape. Then, they pause in midair and swoop toward us at eye level between both bridges. My mouth drops open, but there are no words. I hear the rush of pines in a windstorm.

A tag number on one of the condors shows *13*. A quick check with my NPS "condor chart" tells us that this is a six-year-old male, hatched at San Diego Wild Animal Park and released here two years later. He's one of only 226 wild condors living in Mexico, California, and Arizona. Later this month, wildlife officials will release three more at the Vermilion Cliffs, the seventeenth public release in Arizona since the first in 1996.

"What a beautiful success story," Karen says, our eyes riding the birds as the pair drifts upstream above the Colorado River. There were only twenty-two known in the world in 1987 when the last free-flying condors were taken into captivity to save as much diversity of the gene pool as possible. Captive breeding programs at San Diego, the Los Angeles Zoo, and the Peregrine Fund's World Center for Birds of Prey in Boise, Idaho, slowly increased their numbers, mostly due to the birds' ability to double-clutch. Reintroduction into the wild began in early 1992. The California condor is one of the world's rarest bird species. Only 405 exist on the planet, of which seventy-eight spread their wings over these rugged wildlands of northern Arizona.

"Did you see the condors?" I ask Sarah, whose working the desk in the Navajo Bridge Interpretive Center.

"Oh, yeah," she says. "We have to chase them off the railing to keep people from stopping on the bridge."

I feel Karen poke me in the ribs.

"They run from us when they see us coming," Sarah adds, laughing.

I say: "Did you know that the state bird of Arizona is the California condor?"

Darkness closes in as we locate camp deep in the Kaibab National Forest. Karen chooses the site, the place for the tent, even the tent's orientation. It's always been this way. I learned long ago that I have no say in where my wife sleeps. While I set up the tent and inflate the mattress, Karen makes dinner by lantern light.

In the morning, a goshawk wakes us. Then an equally loud squirrel starts in. Both sound like they're in the tree above us. I make coffee and grab my notebook, binoculars, and camera. With the success of yesterday's condor sighting, I'm now hoping to see a Kaibab squirrel, which Karen has been telling me all about having memorized the scene from the 1997 movie *Fools Rush In*. The character played by Salma Hayek tells the story as a metaphor for her relationship to Matthew Perry's character. A family of squirrels living on the plateau become separated.

"Over time, the two families became different." I hear Hayek's rich Hispanic accent. "Each one adjusted to their environment. The ones to the north are dark, bushy-tailed, and have bigger ears. The ones to the south are leaner, meaner, and much prettier. Even though they look different and they act different, they are the exact same squirrel. They just grew up on different sides. And this canyon between them."

Punctuated equilibrium! Very romantic.

Kaibab squirrels are a subspecies Abert's that became geographically isolated from the common ancestor of both on the North Rim about ten thousand years ago after the end of the last ice age caused stands of ponderosa to retreat to higher elevations. The difference in the squirrels is really more about the pine trees than the Grand Canyon. Instead of locating a Kaibab squirrel, I spend the morning tracking, photographing, and being out-foxed by a fox squirrel.

From the "Mountain Inside-Out," the Paiute name for the plateau, we drop into the arid lowlands and miles upon miles of blooming purple sage. "Riders of the purple figwort," Karen says. Outside Fredonia, we pull into Judd Auto Service for drinks. "Good Mormon name," I say. Beneath the sky-blue letters, bright yellow words read: *Lotto * Guns * Ammo * Beer.* "About covers all the vices," I add. "Check to see if they have any adult videos."

Karen finds something better. From a rack in the curio shop, she holds up a T-shirt: *Utah Big Love: I'll Share My Man But Not My Beer!*

At Pipe Spring National Monument in far northwestern Arizona, we meet Paiute ranger Bennjamin Pikyavit. His long gray hair is twisted into a pair of thin braids and pulled behind each ring-adorned ear.

"The Mormons built a stone stronghold over the water they found here. We called it Matungwa'va—'Yellow Dripping Rock.' It is the only water anywhere." Benn explains that the Paiutes lived at Matungwa'va and planted corn, beans, and squash and always returned after hunting and gathering trips. Then in the 1860s, Mormon settlers named it Pipe Spring and brought thousands of cattle to graze the grasslands of the Arizona Strip. "The monstrous beast called the cow," he says, "was part of the church-owned enterprise called a 'tithing ranch.' There was an immediate cultural gap. Indians didn't understand why Mormons could shoot deer but Indians couldn't hunt cattle. Pipe Spring became the clash of three cultures—Mormon, Paiute, and the federal government."

The name comes from a legend of marksmanship. In 1858, the brother of Jacob Hamblin, being goaded about his shooting ability by his companions, put a bullet through the bowl of a pipe at fifty paces without breaking the sides. Pipe Spring is named for "the pipe that Bill Hamblin so skillfully shot through." The place *should* be named for the unsuspecting instigator smoking the pipe!

With Benn's encouragement, Karen and I wander through the museum and then over to "the fort." We pass the site where James Whitmore, the first Mormon pioneer at Pipe Spring, built his dugout and corrals in 1868.

Then we walk through twelve-foot gates and solid sandstone walls two and a half feet thick into the courtyard of Winsor Castle. A high, wide veranda splits the first story from the second and half circles the courtyard. Bedrooms fill the upper story. Their windows are narrow gunports.

I recall that Jacob Hamblin stayed here regularly. He was a Mormon missionary to the lost tribes of Israel, in this case, the Paiutes, Havasupai, Navajo, and Hopi. He explored this part of Arizona from 1858 to the 1870s, locating Mormon settlements, befriending the Indians and learning their languages, and serving as an advisor to John Wesley Powell before his second expedition into Grand Canyon. Hamblin also negotiated with the Paiutes for the safety of Powell and his men. He regarded Native Americans as his equals, believing they were no more superstitious "than many who call themselves civilized." Concerning their religious rites and ideas, he thought they were "as consistent as the Christian sects of the day."

Winsor Castle was also a way station for Mormon couples traveling the "honeymoon trail" to the temple at St. George, Utah, to get married. "Many had to share a bed with a complete stranger," I hear a ranger named Ellie say to a tour group. ("A new spouse?" Karen says to me under her breath.) For years, Pipe Spring was a polygamous underground. Women hid from federal marshals at Winsor Castle to save their husbands from prosecution.

On a door lintel, I point out to the ranger the many tally marks carved into the sandstone. "First wife, second wife, third wife . . ." she says, laughing. We follow her into the spring room where water spills from a pipe into a hollowed-out log, flows across one end of the room, and exits at a corner drain on its way to the ponds.

"Hey, a pipe spring!" I say. The water feels cold. I raise a cupped handful to my lips.

"Don't drink the water," Ranger Ellie warns me. "Pipe Spring revenge is second cousin to Montezuma's revenge."

"Oh," I say, shaking out my hands. "Those poor honeymooners."

Once again deep in the Kaibab Forest, we camp among aspen, fir, and blue spruce, our tent tucked into a wild nest of fallen and standing trees. A light wind ruffles its fingers through high branches of needles and leaves.

The night is cold, but we stay toasty in our dome tent among all the peeled-open sleeping bags, comforters, and blankets piled so high on our mattress that we can hardly move. I close my eyes on the Kaibab Plateau and drift to sleep on a limestone bed thousands of feet thick beneath my back.

On the morning of our last day on the Arizona Strip, I walk beneath the forest canopy among emerald mounds of moss and dry mushrooms, over a landform that betrays every drop of water, shrinking away at its touch, dissolving limestone to form deep passages and caverns that sometimes collapse into sinkholes. A squirrel chatters from its lookout high in the trees. My toes sink in pinewood duff. Puffballs erupt underfoot with tiny explosions of filé powder. "The smells of childhood morning days," says writer Peter Matthiessen, "that tug my heart."

A couple hours later, Karen and I walk along Bright Angel Point on the North Rim. The first people we see, sitting on a bench with the whole Grand Canyon before them, are staring at their smartphones. Both of them. I think: *You have the best view on the planet and you're staring into a zombie screen.* I want to shake them.

At Grand Canyon Lodge, an enormous pine-beam ceiling stands before an equally enormous Navajo rug. I recognize the Ganado Red style. The rug is ten feet by twenty-seven, and it took two years for Many Horses's niece and her daughter to weave. A letter from Lorenzo Hubbell to Henry Ford says: "I am of the opinion that I have the largest handwoven Navajo Indian rug that has ever been made in America." Hubbell thought Ford could use it for advertising purposes. "Three cars can be placed side by side upon it," he wrote.

From a window seat in the dining room, we order chocolate layer cake and Grand Canyon coffee. Our server wants to take our menu, but Karen hasn't finished reading it. He's unsure of this strange couple smelling of camp and woods. He brings two forks and a pair of straws. The coffee rises through my sinuses, quickest route to the brain. "We just spent our last twenty dollars, but it was worth it," I tell Karen, feeling the double arterial dump of caffeine and alcohol. Triple dump with the sugar.

At the desk for canyon mule rides, we meet a woman who's working on a pen and ink drawing of aspens. "All I do is sit here," she says, "and

I've run out of rubber bands to shoot at people." A sign in front of her says: *Hello, my name is Vickie if you like me, Bernice if you don't.* Bernice, she says, is her boss. Vickie is full of information and wit. We tell her we're interested in hiking along the rim and she says, "You've chosen the good side. I call that"—she points south—"the Dark Side."

She recommends we hike the Uncle Jim Trail, a five mile loop to a viewpoint that overlooks the canyon and the North Kaibab Trail switchbacks. The trail honors Jim Owen, who worked as a game warden for the Kaibab Forest and reputedly rode with Jesse James. At the time, there probably wasn't much difference in the jobs. We pause to allow a string of mule riders to pass. Then continue on the mule-poop trail. At the viewpoint, a bench of Kaibab limestone overlooks dark clouds sliding across a blue sky. Rising to meet them are layers gouged out by time and gravity and sculpted with texture and form. Here, water is a lapidary's diamond saw, cutting into and exposing earth's geode with its multifaceted geometry the color of amethyst. Our feet dangle over history and revelation.

"I could get used to this," Karen says.

On our way back to the lodge, a squirrel the color of charcoal crosses the trail and climbs into a ponderosa. It has a large white tail. "Did you see that?" I ask Karen, who's already guessed what it is. "Our first Kaibab squirrel!" The mammal pauses mid-trunk, its body suddenly rigid as if its brain were thumbing through ten thousand years of genetic memory to locate a file called "human." Then the silver ghost is gone.

Near sunset at Bright Angel Point, we're looking down on the tops of pine trees. Karen's face is white. She grips the back of my T-shirt as we walk the narrow path. "I don't like heights," she says. "Heights with gravity." We find a comfortable niche among the rocks where a few other people have gathered. We chat, waiting for the event to unfold. Then, a hush draws through the crowd as the canyon dims. Something sacred is happening.

On our final morning, we wake to thirty-seven degrees and dewfall. The aspens have turned from green to golden in only these few short days. A tiny spider hauling an egg case crawls up my bare leg. I'm in no hurry to leave. Fourteen more weeks and there'll be no more chasing anything but words on the page.

Six hours later, we pull into the Cameron Trading Post. Karen scrounges for a few coins, enough for Indian fry bread, which we dress up with our own shredded cheese, beans, and salsa and eat sitting on the lip of the Little Colorado River Gorge. A pair of tourists walks over while we're having lunch and takes our picture. I think of the T-shirt we found at Marble Canyon that said: *In the Desert, One Forgets to Count the Days.* After so many days of dirt, we must look like part of the landscape.

It's All About Altitude

HUMPHREYS PEAK

ELEVATION: 12,633 FEET | FOUNDED: 200,000 YEARS AGO

In the last week of September, I slip out of my tent before dawn in the high reaches of Oak Creek Canyon. I catch three brown trout, keeping the largest, and fry it up with a mess of crispy pancakes while Karen sleeps. Her breakfast—I prefer coffee. She's off to Flagstaff today for a three-day conference. I'll meet up with my hiking compadre, wild man Chuck LaRue, and together we'll tackle 12,633-foot Humphreys Peak, the very rooftop of Arizona.

I've known Chuck for nearly thirty years, and we've hiked many trails across Arizona, from the Chiricahua and Catalina Mountains to Monument Valley. He appears in two of my five books. He's lived his whole life on the Colorado Plateau. Educated in BIA schools and Northern Arizona University, he's taken greater lessons in this austere and seductive slickrock country. He's always sending me photographs of thousand-year-old black-on-white Puebloan pottery he's found (and left untouched) on some remote cliff face. He's the quintessential naturalist, historian, and guide—a wilderness technologist with a bologna sandwich. He reminds me of the preeminent desert-rat/archaeologist Julian Hayden in a fedora and sturdy hiking boots.

When we drive the short distance from his house to the Museum of Northern Arizona, he's my personal curator. He's fashioned replicas of split-willow figurines and atlatls from handling the museum's artifacts. He's worked out how to straighten reed shafts for arrows and darts using grooved stones, how to rough out an oak branch with a hatchet and bend it with heat into a Hopi throwing stick. His garage is jammed full of sotol stalks and bear grass, tules and reeds and cordage bundles, skulls, hides, and roadkill.

One of the coolest things Chuck taught me is how to make fire with materials commonly found in the desert, although I can hardly work the seep-willow spindle into its yucca-stem fireboard and get an ember without blistering my hands. If you've seen Rae Dawn Chong in *Quest for Fire*, you've seen Chuck spin up a fire—only he does it with his clothes on. He is my go-to guy for adventuring in northern Arizona, and I'm fortunate to be his friend.

I arrive at his place near noon, but Chuck has given up on me. It will take four hours to reach the summit, he explains, which means it will be dark before we're off the mountain. I persist anyway, standing on his doorstep next to slabs of mudstone rippled with fossil watermarks. "Isn't the trail only four miles?" I ask. *What do I know about hiking above nine thousand feet?*

"Heck," he says, finally. "We don't have to go all the way. It's not like it's a date!"

The three of us, Chuck and I and Spot, Chuck's energetic beagle, pick up the Humphreys Peak trailhead at Arizona Snowbowl Ski Resort. What starts out as a pleasant walk through yellow-flowered meadows—cowpen daisies, Chuck says—soon turns rough and steep. I'm expecting this, since we have more than three thousand feet to climb, but I'm still reminded how much I hate switchbacks. It could be worse, I suppose. Not long ago—the mere drop of a sand grain in the hourglass of geologic time (about ten wobbles of the earth's axis)—this trail would have had to cut a twisted route twice as high to reach the summit.

San Francisco Volcanic Field is a Rhode Island–sized area of cinder cones, lava vents, flows, and domes, and one ash-and-lava layer cake, San Francisco Mountain. The region has seen six million years of fiery upheaval, the most recent at Sunset Crater less than a thousand years ago. San Francisco Mountain, what locals call "the peaks," comprises an open ring of six of them. The highest peaks, turning clockwise from the south— Fremont, Agassiz, and Humphreys—make up the familiar skyline. If you drew lines into the sky following the slope of each peak, the lines would intersect at the vertex of an imaginary cone almost four thousand feet higher than the present mountain. Had the cataclysm of two hundred thousand years ago not occurred, we would be scaling one of the five highest volcanoes of North America. What we see today, however, is the remnant of a sideways explosion—much like Mount St. Helens—

that Pleistocene glaciers later smoothed over. The San Francisco Peaks: sculpted by fire and ice.

Some people say the mountain got its name because you can see San Francisco from the summit. (My parents actually told me this when they dropped me off at Flagstaff for college!) Call me a romantic, but I like this explanation much better than the actual one about Franciscan monks naming it in 1629 in honor of their patron saint, Francis of Assisi. The Navajo, who consider the mountain sacred, call it Dook'o'oosliid, the Summit That Never Melts.

Along a trail paved with evergreen needles, Chuck starts listing conifers found here—ponderosa, limber, and white pine, Douglas, white and corkbark fir, blue and Engelmann spruce—I lose count at nine species. Then he points out bristlecone pine, showing me its five needles per bundle—the "foxtail pine." "It's the only place in the state where they grow," he adds. *They must be the oldest trees in Arizona,* I think. Although they do not grow to the extreme ages of some Great Basin bristlecones (five thousand years), one in the area was documented at 1,438 years—old enough to hide a stone projectile point from an Anasazi atlatl dart.

I recall that the presence of bristlecone means we've entered Merriam's subalpine conifer forest, what he called the "Hudsonian Zone," named for its similarity to plants found around the Hudson Bay of northern Canada. In Merriam's system, altitude means latitude.

More than 120 years ago, the zoologist, ornithologist, and a founder of the National Geographic Society, C. Hart Merriam, came to these mountains and devised a classification system based on characteristic plants found at certain elevations. He called the concept "life zones." Although largely replaced today by a more comprehensive "biome" or "biotic community" model, many ecologists still recognize its usefulness, especially in the West. Despite its limitations, the life-zone system remains one of the most dramatic ways to show plant and its associated animal diversity, particularly in our Sky Island region.

I imagine "Hart," in his great shaggy walrus mustache, climbing up and down this mountain to draw his maps of the four life zones he saw here and chastising the unruly trees that invariably didn't conform to his nice model.

Where cinders crunch like Grape-Nuts underfoot, a trailside sign reads: *11,400 feet*. I've made it to Merriam's sixth life zone, the highest biome in the state, the southernmost in the United States, and the only alpine tundra found in Arizona. This cold, treeless plot of fractured rock harbors a few matted plants like a thick-leafed, yellow-flowered groundsel (*Packera franciscana*) that grows nowhere else in the world. It's as if I've climbed to the arctic tundra of Alaska, and I'm only eighty miles from a saguaro cactus.

I'm beginning to feel the altitude. My pace has slowed and I take more breaks to breathe the thinning air. Chuck and Spot disappear far up the trail. From the saddle at 11,800 feet, the dark head of Agassiz Peak rises into the stratosphere on my right, Humphreys's naked dome on my left. Sweat chills my skin, more sweat than what seems necessary. Chuck and Spot the Wonder Dog are waiting for me. I take their picture, but I can't breathe and the nausea is rising. "Go on up, Chuck," I say. "I'll stay here and . . . upchuck."

After the two vanish again, I look over the mountain to still myself before trying the summit. So blue. Even the bare rocks are blue. Sunlight carries no warmth, no radiance. Every outcrop on the edge of the world leans outward in vertigo, as if gravity had once reversed itself. I could inhale the entire sky from up here—and throw up the entire planet. Like this stratovolcano at one time, everything on the inside wants outside. Ejecta. Hot, gaseous venting from the bowels of the earth. Projectile volcanism. Explosive flux.

A girl wearing nothing but running shoes, a thin T-shirt, and shorts, and carrying a water bottle shoots past me. A body of pure thrust. Now I'm feeling sick *and old*. I climb another two hundred feet and collapse. I can go no farther. Chuck and Spot glide high along a ridgeline under the flank of Humphreys Peak. The rocky trail is their springboard. Supple spines and leg muscles carry them upward. Leaf-blower tracheas slam oxygen into red blood cells the size of jujubes. In moments, the two are specks on the summit, while I suck air through a cocktail straw.

I'm so close. I can see it, almost touch it. A twenty-minute stroll—normally. But I must turn back to where I left my insides at trailside.

A half hour later, Spot finds me below the saddle. "He was worried about you," Chuck says, as he comes up behind him. "Then he got excited when he picked up your scent where you turned back. I couldn't keep up with him."

I rub Spot's ears, happy to sit next to him. "You guys are amazing!" I manage to say. "I think my desire had reached the summit before my body."

Farther down the trail, we join two women, probably twice my age and all walking sticks and gray hair. They're returning from the peak. "Oh, you didn't make it?" one of them says when she sees me. *Does it show?* "Don't worry. You can try again next year."

Later in the evening back in Flagstaff, Karen and I meet Chuck and his wife, Sarah, for dinner at Beaver Street Brewery. Chuck wears a cap with a picture of a ringtail. He knows the mammal is one of the three remaining state symbols I've yet to see this year, and he needles me with the hat and his wide grin.

"How's the altitude sickness?" Sarah asks. She's a clinical manager of pediatrics.

"Better," I say. "Better now that I have more air above me than beneath me. The nausea is subsiding enough that food sounds good again. I'm going carefully, starting with something light, like liquid bread."

I order a Lumberyard IPA. The brew's motto epitomizes my day puking out on Humphreys Peak: "It's All About Altitude!"

Karen has been force-feeding me crackers since my return. She says she loves the Navajo word for the mountain: "Summit That Never Melts." Now she asks me about the Navajo word for "Summit You Never Reached."

OCTOBER

Ringtail

POINTS OF INTEREST TO DATE: 152 | TOTAL MILES: 14,917

Bottle-Shocked II

THE ALE CHASER, JEROME, AND THE VERDE CANYON RAILROAD

ELEVATION: 5,246 FEET | FOUNDED: 1876
POPULATION: 444 AND A FEW UNDEAD

People once called Jerome the "wicked city," the "town too tough to die in the first place" (sorry, Tombstone). These days they say Jerome is where Mayberry meets Woodstock—or *Animal House*. It's hard not to compare Jerome with Bisbee. Both copper towns were first staked by civilian army scouts chasing Apaches: German-born Al Sieber (1876) and Irish-born Jack Dunn (1877); both towns are propped up on thirty-degree mountainsides at five-thousand-plus feet; both were financed by Douglases. Dr. James A. actually passed up Jerome for Bisbee, but his son, James S. "Rawhide Jimmy," would invest in Jerome thirty years later. And both towns were saved by hippies after the mines closed. I'm biased, of course, but I say Jerome is where Mayberry meets Bisbee.

In the first week of October, Karen and I pull up to the 1898 Connor Hotel. Fortunately, the place is recently remodeled with period furnishings. "Each room now has a bath," says the desk clerk. "Unlike the original hotel, which only had one in the hall." Her name is Dinah Perkins, and she says she's from the Bates Motel. (*Perkins? As in Tony Perkins—Norman Bates?*) She looks the part with her long gray hair twisted into a bun and her dark Victorian high-neck lace blouse buttoned up her throat. She talks history: the Connor is the first hotel in Jerome built of solid brick after the town-gutting fires of 1897 and 1898. "Your room has a settee that's a hundred years old. I bought it in New York myself."

The day it was made, I guess.

We climb a carpeted stairway, feeling the whole structure leaning to one side. A ghost tour parts to let us pass and the guide says: "The boy says to his parents that he's seen a man in old clothing upstairs." A dim hall leads to our corner room with its tin ceiling, fireplace, and brass bed. I don't see any ghosts, but I still check off haunted hotel number six for the year.

"We have reservations at the Asylum," I tell Dinah on our way out for dinner. She hands me a flashlight and mumbles something about stairs and a dark road up the hill. She's walked this route before. The Asylum is part of the Grand Hotel, "a restaurant on the fringe," according to a brochure I pick up in the lobby. Karen taps on my shoulder and points to a sign: *Bates Motel. No Vacancy.* I check for Norman on the infamous cherry-red couch, in a stairwell that smells of antiseptic, and in the oldest self-service elevator in Arizona and maybe the United States, a 1926 Otis. "Don't take any showers," I warn Karen.

She looks suspiciously at the spider webs and gaudy Halloween décor. "If there ever was a place where the walls between the living and the dead were thin—this is it."

The Asylum restaurant takes its name from the third-floor ward for the insane at the United Verde Hospital, one of the most modern hospitals in the West when it opened in 1927. The hospital closed in 1950 as the mines played out and stood empty for more than forty years until Bob and Debra Altherr bought it and renovated it as the historic Grand Hotel. If the San Carlos is the third most haunted hotel in the United States, the Grand must come in close behind it. The place is rife with strange stories stemming from the days when the hospital, its insane asylum, and its tuberculosis infirmary lost on average one patient every day.

I check off my seventh haunted hotel and then look over the wine list. The six-hundred-dollar bottle of 2001 Robert Mondavi Cabernet Sauvignon Reserve is tempting, but I choose instead the Arizona Stronghold Tazi, telling our server Rick that I prefer local wines. We both order the renowned butternut squash soup. An hour later, the soup arrives. "They weren't kidding when they said be prepared for a relaxing evening over a glass of wine," Karen says. Dinner comes twenty minutes after that. We now have no other plans for the evening.

"You'd have to be insane not to order dessert," Rick says. He knows the history of the hotel, and we prod him for stories like the "death rooms" where patients drew their last breaths; or the "woman in white" who appears standing on the balcony and wakes guests with a wagging finger; or Claude Harvey, who died in the basement pinned under the Otis elevator. Claude, a.k.a. "Scotty," was the maintenance man in 1935. He's the most famous ghost in the hotel.

I ask if he's had any ghostly experiences. He says he doesn't want to spook the guests.

"But we're not guests at the hotel," Karen says. "So we want the stories."

Rick tells us about one late night when he had only one guest in the hotel. "I was in the lobby, all alone, and I felt two fingers on my neck. You know this place was a hospital, right? Something dressed in white and carrying a clipboard was taking my pulse! I said, 'Okay, I'm not ready yet. But thanks for checking.'"

In the morning we meet Sandy Colin, mother of the owner, Anne Colin, who bought Connor Hotel when it was a flophouse a decade ago and remodeled it. She encourages us to walk the town: The Jerome Winery and its twisting vines as thick as my arm and clusters of dark purple grapes. Gisele's Café and Bakery with its cinnamon rolls, éclairs, and pastries as "edible art." A sign at Nellie Bly's says it used to be called Jennie's Place, an 1898 brothel owned by the legendary Madam "Belgian Jennie" Bauters. When she was murdered in 1905, she was said to be the wealthiest woman in the Arizona Territory. "The redistribution of wealth via the oldest profession," I say. "But I doubt Madam Jennie will ever appear in a book called *Arizona Women Who Made History*."

On Hill Street, a flower garden teems with orange- and black-mottled butterflies. "Painted ladies," I say.

"Well, that's appropriate!" Karen laughs.

"We appreciate you being early," says the woman at the Verde Canyon Railroad ticket counter when Karen and I arrive at the Clarkdale depot. "We have four hundred visitors today."

"Four hundred?" I say.

"Yes. But they won't all be in your car."

The ales part of Ales on Rails is in full swing. Smiling young women stand behind tables lined with bottles. So many beers to choose from. Verde Canyon Railroad even has its own private labels: Copper Rail Ale, Pullman Pale Ale, and Tunnel Down Brown Ale.

I sip through my beer lingo, describing whether the brew is malty or hoppy or balanced and if it has body or not. I'm definitely in the "hop-head" category of beer aficionados. Karen reports on color. "This one looks like suede," she says. We've splurged for first-class tickets, and when we climb into the Wickenburg Car, Becky, our personal attendant, brings me a prickly pear margarita. "First class," she says. "You don't have to behave yourself." I feel Karen's eyes burning through the back of my skull.

The Verde Canyon Railroad is a time machine. Thirty-eight miles of swaying side to side as you ride into Arizona's past. From the vintage FP7 locomotives—only twelve remain in service in the country—to the 1930s–40s Pullman-Standard and Budd Stainless Steel coaches, to the historic 1929 caboose, the train is a relic of a time when passengers rode the rails in trains like Santa Fe's *El Capitan* from Chicago to Los Angeles. Even the route was hand-dug, blasted, and mule-carted in the year of Arizona's statehood.

The machine's four-hour round trip is truly Wellsian. We slip past a slag dump where for forty years streams of molten waste from the Clarkdale smelter buried forty acres of river bottom forty feet deep, right up to the edge of the tracks. I lift my eyes to the Black Hills beyond and imagine Miocene lava flows at their crests. Over the next mile, we race forward in time from the basalt volcanism and landform-heaving block faulting that formed the Verde Valley ten million years ago. High on a cliff face, a pattern of dark rectangles resolves into human-made structures of stone and mud. The bad-ass housing of Sinagua cliff dwellers. People who made coming home an extreme sport. Nine hundred years ago, these farmers raised parrots as pets and traded cotton fabrics and red-clay pottery with people as distant as Mexico. They lived at the perfect intersection of human and nature.

After five miles, the machine winds deep into the Verde River Canyon. Cottonwoods, sycamore, walnut, ash, and willow trees thrust up a green broadleaf canopy over the river. A scene unchanged since the river first flowed through the canyon. Mountain lions and gray fox still hunt the woodland. Black hawks and golden eagles still nest along the cliffs. Bald eagles sweep overhead on wings that cast shadows like thunderheads.

At Perkinsville, we arrive on time a hundred years past. The ranch and its pastures, station buildings, and bunkhouse feel unchanged since A. M. Perkins drove in his herd of cattle here and settled. Then, we reverse to the future. The train, the beer, the margaritas lull us to sleep. We return to our own time at the Clarkdale depot. Except that I'm sure I pass a ghost of my younger self.

In the late afternoon, we drive back to Jerome for dinner at the Haunted Hamburger: "Locally owned, operated, and haunted by Eric, Michelle, Nicole, Eric Jr. Jurisin, the dead, and the undead." I've wanted a copy of Nicole's book, *How Do I Get to the Haunted Hamburger?*, since I learned about the place. The Jurisin family lived in the basement—Nicole was three years old—after selling all they had to buy what was then a broken-down boardinghouse. The place got its name during the remodeling when tools went missing, then reappeared. There were weird rose-water smells.

We take a booth upstairs next to a window. To the north across the valley, the San Francisco Peaks reach into the last rays of sunlight and ignite in the darkening sky. Not a bad view to finish off our day, sipping iced tea. My haunted burger should come with a chest spreader for my jaw.

Outside our window, the town spreads itself along the shadowed mountainside. Lights wink on as gloaming comes. My favorite picture of Jerome is a 1950s scene much like this one: buildings stacked on top of each other scaling a hillside. In the foreground and off to the right is a sign that says *Jerome Population 15,000*. Only the number is crossed out, along with the next three numbers in decreasing amounts: *10,000, 5,000, 1,000*. All crossed out. What remains at the bottom of the sign are the white-lettered words: *Ghost City*.

There's Nothin' Like Mutton

FOUR CORNERS MONUMENT

ELEVATION: 4,866 FEET | ERECTED: 1912
POPULATION: 300,000 NAVAJOS

In the middle of October, Karen and I drive north 430 miles to Pinky's food stand where I order the special: squash mutton stew. This is Window Rock, capital of the Navajo Nation, on our way to Four Corners Monument. While we wait at a table for the food, a friendly Navajo man next to us in white cowboy hat and blue denim button-up asks us where we're from. I tell him Bisbee, expecting I'll have to explain where it is.

"I've been to Sierra Vista but not as far as Bisbee," he says. "I love southeastern Arizona." He tells us to be sure to visit Canyon de Chelly on our way to Four Corners, giving us advice on where to go and what to see. I say that Canyon de Chelly is on my list of destinations and that we'll be returning next month.

Karen retrieves our lunch from a woman at the kitchen window. I look at the Styrofoam bowl of watery stew. "It might help if you practice savoring meditation," she offers. She won't even attempt the mutton, but she's read about the Zen way of mindful eating. She ordered fry bread with grated cheddar. No meditation needed there.

This food is a gift from the earth that will nourish me in special ways, I begin the meditation. *I thank the sagebrush that fed you, the shepherd who raised you, the butcher who . . . you know.* I breathe in. Inhale the hot, greasy steam. Lift the plastic spoon to my lips. Feel the slick broth cling to my tongue, to the roof of my mouth. Karen watches me. "Rank it high for authenticity and low for culinary excellence?" she asks.

It is surprisingly tasteless. I add crushed red pepper. Now all I taste is crushed red pepper. I chew squishy yellow squash and rubbery brown wads of gamey fat. I'm mindfully aware that this is god-awful. But the Navajos are clearly enjoying it. Everyone is eating today's special with obvious relish. Perhaps my response would be different if this was a recipe of my mother's. I don't have a history with mutton.

Window Rock's Navajo Nation Zoological and Botanical Park is tucked into great uplifted monoliths of red sandstone crosshatched with a history of dunes. Karen and I tour the visitor center and museum, built to resemble a giant hogan. Among the dioramas of Diné life, culture, and cosmology, we examine mountain lion quivers and Navajo mud pottery. We browse the gift shop's books and T-shirts. I hold up a blue one with yellow double-arches that says, *McMutton*. Karen models another showing a black and yellow warning sign across the front. Inside the triangle a covered wagon bursts into flames.

We enter the park and follow a trail to the eerie bugling of a bull elk. The dark animal is enormous. A tree grows out of its head. The chain link fence seems an afterthought, more to keep people out than to keep it caged. We feel the same about the bighorn sheep, the mountain lion and Mexican gray wolves and black bear. I look for "Gummer," the old toothless coyote who was a resident here many years ago.

A giant model of a two-tailed swallowtail flits above the porcupine enclosure. We practice our Navajo: *ma'ii* (coyote), *tábaah ma'ii* (raccoon), *tazhii* (wild turkey), *atsátsoh* (golden eagle). I'm surprised and pleased to see that my friend Jim Kristofic has adopted a sandhill crane (*délí*) to help the park feed and care for it. It's name is Carrie. Since the Navajo don't have a word for "pet," I wonder how this kind of animal sponsorship translates.

The seven-acre park is home to fifty species of animals native to the Navajo reservation and important to their culture. All are rescued animals that couldn't otherwise survive in the wild. The park, however, hasn't been without controversy. In 2000, the outgoing president of the Nation closed it and ordered the animals released after Navajo deities visited two women and said that by keeping caged animals, the people were disturbing the natural order and not living according to traditional ways. No one questioned the visitation, but complaints about the closure still came, mostly from children. Meetings were held. Options discussed. The incoming president decided to keep the zoo open but not expand it and allow the animals to live out their lives there.

Today, the zoo—the only one in the United States owned and operated by a tribe—continues to receive, treat, and care for orphaned and injured animals. Striving for balance in nature is at the core of what it means to be Navajo. The world community is everything, and in this, the Diné embrace all life. The Navajo prefer to see this place not as a zoo of caged animals but as a sanctuary for nature and spirit.

Arizona's northeastern corner is in the corner of nowhere. After a long drive across a Navajoland rubbed raw by wind, we arrive at a slab of granite and brass that marks the only place in the United States where four states meet. Four Corners. My second "corner" in the state for the year after Pipe Spring. Flags representing Colorado, Utah, New Mexico, and Arizona, along with the four tribal nations of Navajo, Hopi, Ute, and Zuni, circle the monument. Surrounding that is an arc of jewelry and taco stands. Then, 360 degrees of blasted red rock.

A family of four attempts every state, playing Twister. Children practice gymnastics, performing handstands, front walkovers, back bridges in four places at once. Wind snaps at the flags, imprinting swirls into our fingertips, as the Navajo say, embedding itself and its load of sand into our lives. I plant my butt in four states and open my journal.

Recently, the National Geodetic Survey (NGS) reported that the monument is off by a third of a mile, exactly 1,807.14 feet eastward, according to chief surveyor David Doyle. Apparently, this has been known for more than a century, although you couldn't have guessed it by all the public frothing. Government surveyor Ehud Darling first established the location in 1868, marking it with a slab of sandstone. Seven years later, Chandler Robbins located another place a short distance farther east. As it turns out, Darling may have been correct. Yet Robbins's survey became official when in 1925 the U.S. Supreme Court established the monument. Thus, the spot where I'm sitting is the "legal" location of Four Corners. It *is* Four Corners, despite the misplaced geography. In surveying, says the NGS, law trumps science. Monuments rule.

The controversy reminds me of the supposed center of the continental United States near Lebanon, Kansas, where there's a monument with a chapel. Only the marker is not the center of the country but at a location half a mile away because the geographical cross hairs actually fall in the middle of a pig farm and the owner refused to sell his land.

But what is geography anyway but human-made lines on the landscape? Six thousand years of peg-and-rope geometry, plumb lines, alidades, and astrolabes, compasses, theodolites, laser range finders, and GPS—all for the purpose of defining (sometimes imperfectly) boundaries for land ownership. We westerners find such comfort in drawing maps so that we might know our place. The Navajo—not so much. But maps can be as ephemeral as water pockets on slickrock. Like here, where the land is never still. It heaves beneath us. The Colorado Plateau is a 130,000-square-mile raft, tilting to the north and rising as much as an inch or so every hundred years on an upwelling ocean of mantle. The NGS should place a gyroscope at Four Corners.

If the Supreme Court says so, what does it matter where lines cross a shifting geology? Perhaps the court will correct another survey error and rule that the Continental Divide does indeed pass through Bisbee. We have the monument to prove it. And monuments rule.

Twenty-five miles east of the Navajo community of Kayenta, the sun sinks behind Monument Valley turning it to flame. The 1,400-foot volcanic plug of Agathla Peak holds up a purple and neon sky. On advice from a Navajo youth at the Chevron station, we stop for dinner at a restaurant shaped like a hogan: the Blue Coffee Pot. Jo Donna, wearing a Blue Bird flour sack as an apron, suggests the house special. She describes it as "mutton strips rolled in a tortilla." I order a Navajo burger instead (beef and fry bread). Karen chooses a hot roast beef sandwich with mashed potatoes. Two Anglos eating.

"The coffee is great," I tell Jo Donna when she brings our plates heavy with food.

"We put dirt in it," she says, laughing.

"Ah. Real Navajoland coffee."

"We are the Blue Coffee Pot."

The vintage blue enameled percolator symbolizes the relationship between the Navajo and the Anglo, my menu says, one of "change and friendship as people shared a cup of coffee with anyone attracted to a campfire."

The next day I'm drawn from my room to the sound of water on stone. Outside the Cameron Trading Post lodge, I sit among tiers of mortared sandstone as intricate and multilayered as any Navajo rug. Ash trees filter the morning sun in a courtyard where salvias and primrose, marigolds and rose shimmer with insects and light. I smell water and rock. All feels perfectly balanced. The lodge folds itself into this space, the wood and stone construction organic to it in color and texture. The Navajo are weavers of more than yarn and loom.

Even the sound of truck tires on steel feels integral to this place of cross-culture and commerce. Cameron, our last stop on our tour of Navajoland, is as vibrant today as it was a hundred years ago when the swayback suspension bridge first stretched across the Little Colorado River Gorge and the brothers Hubert and C. D. Richardson raised their two-story trading post. A month ago on our way to the North Rim, we met a Navajo woman who showed us around the original trading post hotel and talked about what it was like to grow up here. "I learned to weave from my mother," Virginia told us, showing us rugs of wool, dyes, and designs she had drawn out of the very ground beneath our feet. "People like to meet the artist who creates such things. Then they buy them."

Her mother, Juanita Dohi, also used to weave here, up to the time of her death in 2007. "She sold the very last rug she made. It's at Wayne Newton's house. One day he came by and bought it from her."

"You don't have any rugs from your mother?" Karen asked her.

"No. They're all gone."

Karen still talks about the irony: that Juanita's rugs were so valuable her own daughter couldn't afford to keep her last one. I tell her we should drive to Las Vegas and have a talk with Wayne Newton.

Before we leave for Bisbee, I find stacks of Blue Bird flour in a corner of the trading post store. "If it's not Blue Bird," Virginia had said, "your fry bread won't puff up." I buy a ten-pound sack and a blue coffee pot. I can't afford Virginia's rugs.

The Navajo are a ritual people, as shown in their handwoven blankets, their wedding baskets crafted from tightly wound sumac strips, their ceremonial bows, quivers, and drums. And they live within a panorama of equal ceremony: a sweep of barren red rock, gouged and twisted by an old movement of water. This is a landscape of walls and drop-offs. But there's also a symmetry of rock and sky where gravity pulls everything down into space and creates emptiness as an art form. Although I will never become an eater of mutton or own a Navajo rug, I still feel a connection to this country where the land and its people express themselves through art. I had sought a new way of seeing this place. What I found was its relevance.

The Rise of Arizona Wine

WILLCOX

ELEVATION: 4,167 FEET | FOUNDED: 1880 | POPULATION: 3,698

"If food is the body of good living," they say in Willcox, "wine is its soul." *And tequila is its spirit!* I think. "How about this one?" I say to Karen. "Give me wine to accept the things I cannot change, beer to change the things I can . . ."

"And tequila so you don't care about the difference?"

"You've heard that one."

We've just driven eighty miles north from Bisbee on the heels of climbing a thousand steps at the annual Bisbee 1000: the 5K that feels like a 10K (and costs you 100K for knee replacement). I'm looking forward to some flights of wine at this year's Wine Country Fall Festival.

On our way to Railroad Park, we walk past the Willcox Commercial, Arizona's oldest continuously operated retail store and the place where Geronimo shopped for tooth decay. The mercantile claims it is "the safest place to trade since 1880." *Sure,* I think, *but probably not because of the occasional visits of a Chiricahua Apache leader.* Tanya Tucker also shopped here. The "outlaw" country music artist is just one star that Willcox lays claim to. Another is Marty Robbins, whose museum is next door. Juanita Buckley, president of the Friends of Marty Robbins, says the singer/songwriter/NASCAR-racer was born in Glendale, but he may have shopped here, too.

Willcox is, however, *near* the birthplace of Rex Allen, who was born in 1920 on a ranch forty miles north at Mud Springs Canyon. The ghost town of Bonita could make a stronger claim than Willcox to his birthplace. The famous country and western musician was the last of Hollywood's singing cowboys. He starred in nineteen movies in the early 1950s, beginning with *The Arizona Cowboy,* a title soon applied to Allen himself, although he later regretted making the film. "I'd like to find the damn negative of that thing and burn it," he once said. "It was the most horrible thing ever made. Boy, was it bad."

His film success led to several recording hits, songs like "Sparrow in the Treetop," "Crying in the Chapel," and later in his career, "Streets of Laredo," which sold over three million copies. Allen also acted in television shows and narrated Walt Disney's Wonderful World of Color nature films. I remember him as the narrator of *Charlotte's Web*.

His son, Rex Allen Jr., wrote Arizona's "alternate" state song, adopted in 1981. Father and son often performed the song together: "I love you, Arizona / Your mountains, deserts, and streams / The rise of Dos Cabezas / And the outlaws I see in my dreams . . ." *Outlaws!* Sheriff Joe, eat your heart out. Rex Allen died in 1999 after collapsing from a heart attack in the driveway of his Tucson home. He was killed when his caretaker accidentally backed over him.

We walk past the Rex Allen "Arizona Cowboy" Museum and Willcox Cowboy Hall of Fame to the Rex Allen Theater, next to the Rex Allen windmill, Rex Allen gazebo, and Rex Allen alleyway. After that, boarded-up buildings make up much of the town. Across the street at Railroad Park stands the life-size bronze image of the singing cowboy, Stetson on head, guitar in hand. "He asked that his ashes be scattered around his statue," I tell Karen, sharing my newfound information. "The sculptor even molded a bronze heart with veins and arteries and placed it inside the chest cavity so Allen's heart will always be in Willcox. His pony is here, too. KoKo the Wonder Horse, buried at our feet."

Rex Allen may be at the center of Railroad Park, but today the hundreds of people gathering here have come for the wine. More than sixty wines, in fact, from a dozen local wineries. With apologies to the famous dead, this is the future of Willcox.

Green grass and a swarm of white canopies front the twin knobs of Dos Cabezas to the southeast. The funky blues of Bisbee's own Buzz and the Soul Senders and the smell of barbecue fill the air. With fifteen dollars' worth of tickets, I head for the Dos Cabezas tent. I pick the 2010 Primativo, a Zinfandel described as "the Kool-Aid man bursting through a wall of fruit and crashing the party in your mouth." It actually tastes better than its description.

Next, it's Page Springs Cellars Mule's Mistake. Then, Lawrence Dunham Vineyards Sky Island and the wineries of Grand Canyon, Keeling Schaefer, Coronado, and Carlson Creek . . . I attempt to keep track using a scorecard that Justin Ove at Arizona Stronghold gave me. "I made it so you could rank your tasting," he told me. "On the flipside are directions for what to look for, how to smell your wine, how to taste it." I'm supposed to give each sip "a good churn" on my palate. "Think mouthwash," he says. My mouth is as fresh as it gets. My sips go straight to swallows.

Before Karen and I depart with our five bottles of Arizona wine, we talk with Peggy Fiandaca, president of the Arizona Wine Growers Association and owner of Lawrence Dunham Vineyards. Peggy and her husband, Curt Dunham, had what they describe as a mind-bending, life-changing Arizona wine-tasting experience that led them six years ago to buy forty acres in the Chiricahua Mountains and plant a vineyard. Soon, they started making world-class wines.

"Arizona is a rising star, especially with the Rhônes," she says, explaining that the grape varietals from southern France—Petite Sirah, Grenache, Viognier—are suited to Arizona's rocky soils. "The state's highest score from *Wine Spectator* is eighty-nine. We'll be in the nineties soon. And, we now have Aridus, a custom crush facility—state of the art—in Willcox."

The wine company converted an abandoned apple warehouse with sorting, de-stemming, and crushing equipment from Italy. From crush to case, the facility provides everything to make wine, except the grapes. It's a bring-your-own-grapes operation.

"We want to grow the raw crop then turn it into a product right here," Peggy says. "It's better than cotton, which is shipped out. With more than twelve vineyards and eight hundred acres of vines, Cochise County is primo for grapes. No other industry is growing like this in Arizona."

If the state once had a love affair with unsustainable copper, cotton, and cattle, then wine could be its new seduction. Even "Mr. Arizona," Rex Allen, tried out three marriages.

Still a Population of One

RUBY

ELEVATION: 4,186 FEET | FOUNDED: 1912 | POPULATION: 1

The end of October. Ten weeks to go, and I still need three more state symbols: the bola tie (Wickenburg?), the Colt Single Action Army revolver, and the ringtail. I'm sure I can get the state mammal at Madera Canyon, where I've seen it before. And Karen likes the idea of spending a few days at Madera Kubo with our friends Richard and Cora. Even better, I can add the ghost town of Ruby to the excursion. I contact Pat and Howard Frederick, two of Ruby's owners, and Howard agrees to meet with me there tomorrow.

Late afternoon, I toss peanuts to a flock of turkeys near the back porch of Madera Kubo #4. Karen spreads the table with breads and cheeses and fried chicken. Cora arrives with a fruit salad. Richard carries a Bud Light.

"I have beer!" I say. "But it's all IPA."

"That's why I bring my own," he says.

We eat, talk about our kids, wine, my travels. When I look up, a burly raccoon lurches across the porch in front of the sliding glass door. "Chupacabra!" I say. "The state mascot!"

"There's been a coati hanging around," Cora says when we hear a thump and then rapid pattering across the roof. The hummingbird feeder swings without a breeze. *Skinwalker?* It is Halloween. I climb onto an oak stump and peer over the rooftop into the darkness. Something moves toward my face. I snap a picture and a blurred image fills the LCD display. It has glowing white eyes.

In the morning, pairs of ratty-winged Arizona sister butterflies drift along the canyon road. I drive south toward Nogales and the Ruby loop turnoff near Rio Rico. In an hour, I'm winding through some of the wildest, ruggedest, most eye-pleasing high desert grasslands at the bottom of Arizona. The Tumacácori Highlands. A thicket of crumpled hills weighed down by light and shadow. Tawny land where northern jaguars come to be alone.

At Sycamore Canyon, I pull off the road and step into my own plume of dust. I lose the sweatshirt and take a break beneath a fat blue sky. This is one of my favorite places in the state, despite the border issues. The last time Karen and I camped here, a border patrol agent drove up and asked what we were doing.

"Uh . . ." I said, indicating our tent and fire, "camping?"

"It's not safe," he said, adding some warnings about the prevalence of Mexican immigrants.

"We're fine," Karen said.

"Well, we're bivouacked just up the road if you need us."

As he drove off, I told Karen that he must be fantasizing about the Ruby Mercantile murders in the 1920s. "One of the largest manhunts ever in the Southwest—and he's still on it." We watched him attempt to circle his truck around a large oak and promptly crash into it.

I meet a tall, lanky blue-eyed man at Ruby's padlocked gate. "I knew Sundog when he lived here," I tell Howard Frederick about Ruby's solitary resident, who seemed left behind by the sixties. "Ruby: Population 1— Sundog! But the sign is missing."

"We've had some colorful caretakers," he

says. "It takes a certain kind of person to live out here. We had to let Sundog go."

As we walk to the new caretaker's residence to meet Michael Thistle, Howard tells me about some of the earliest caretakers—people like Jerry, who would charge visitors a twelve-pack of beer for the entrance fee. And Peppermint Patty, who took to tearing down the walls of Ruby's historic buildings for firewood. "Stan Christopher built a boat here," Howard adds to the list of artists and hippies. "It was a thirty-six-foot ocean-going sloop with a cement hull. Took him three years to finish it, and then he hauled it off on a flatbed truck and sailed it out of San Diego. Christopher was quite an artist. We still have some of his oil paintings of Ruby."

When we arrive at the caretaker's Winnebago, the door pops open and out steps Michael, wearing only his boxer shorts and a smile. "I have the amazing power of prophesy," he announces. "I read pasta. I had just put it on, and when it was ready, I knew you'd be here."

Called Montana Camp in the 1870s for the cracked thumbnail of a peak rising in the south, Ruby is named for the wife of store owner Julius Andrews who established the post office in 1912. During its heyday in the 1930s, when Ruby became Arizona's largest producer of lead and zinc, and number three in silver, 1,200 people lived here. The Eagle-Picher Lead Company built dams, piped in water, generated electricity, and ran the Montana Mine around the clock. The mine's fine white tailings still lie beyond the town's lake like a Mexico beach.

The operation shut down in the 1940s, leaving Ruby as one of the best preserved ghost towns in Arizona. These days, Howard and Pat Frederick are working hard to maintain that preservation. We walk up "Snob Hill" to Ed Crabtree's home where the mill superintendent lived with his wife Thelma. "It was the only place in Ruby with indoor plumbing," Howard says. "Water came from the Santa Cruz River sixteen miles away."

I've read that Crabtree was responsible for the town's drinking water supply, which he kept so chlorinated that coffee was undrinkable. The couple also placed the legs of their baby cribs in kerosene-filled coffee cans to keep the scorpions and spiders out of their children's beds.

Next we visit the office and infirmary of Dr. Julius Woodard, a tuberculosis sufferer who was also the company doctor. During the ten years that Woodard cared for the people of Ruby, he delivered scores of babies, performed surgery while administering his own anesthesia, set broken bones, and treated the usual miner's injuries and childhood illnesses. Apparently, he was the last physician in Arizona licensed to practice in multiple disciplines.

Then, Howard and Michael take me to what I'm really interested in: a 750-foot vertical mineshaft where 120,000 Mexican free-tailed bats spend the summer. At sunset, the bats rise out of the ground for a half hour like thick smoke. October, however, is too late for the show. I look into the dark hole. Howard says some bats hibernate here, that researchers have found five species besides the Mexican freetails. But the only thing rising out of the shaft now is the sinus-clearing smell of bat guano. "Sounds like a jet engine as they come in at dawn," Howard says.

On the way to the schoolhouse, the teachers' residences, and the jail (every town should place these together), Howard mentions to Michael that the *Ruby: Population 1* sign is missing.

"It disappeared in the last ten days," says Michael. "Maybe Sundog took it."

I laugh, picturing the hairy skeleton of a man hitchhiking with the sign over his head.

"Sundog had crossed out the *1* and added a *2* after he got a girlfriend," Howard says. "Then later he crossed out the *2*."

I laugh again. Loopy in Ruby! Sundog's love life by signpost.

I spend the evening back at Madera Kubo, prowling around the cabins and flesh-white sycamore trunks with camera and head lamp. This morning, a coati climbed into the fruit-heavy pyracantha shrub outside our cabin, a fine state mammal by my estimation, all coon-faced and monkey-tailed. "You walk out into your American woods and suddenly the branches part and there stands a unicorn," Chuck Bowden writes in *Frog Mountain Blues*. "That is the feel of sighting a coati." Now, a raccoon rifles through the leaf litter. It materializes into a coati twice the size and scrambles onto the roof. Twin blue orbs bob along the driveway—the eyeshine of a gray fox. It's a perfect night for unicorns.

At 9:00 p.m., I walk a canyon of glowing eyes. A hunter's moon throws shadows from the trees and my lamp makes them jump with every head turn. The canopy writhes with the drama of theater, and I am an audience of one. High in the leaves, something makes a huffing, coughing, rattling racket. I can't tell what it is, and it's creeping me out. Then I see black-and-white rings fastened to the long branch of an oak. *Ringtail!* I put my light on it and take pictures, but it's not watching me. Its wet black eyes zero in on something over my shoulder. I take more pictures, and now I hear crunching sounds behind me. I turn to look, and my light falls onto a hog-nosed skunk with a great white plume of tail coming straight for me.

So I finally check off the ringtail at Madera Canyon. Two symbols to go. What I didn't know then was that over the next months, the state mammal would be checking off me. A ringtail had already appeared in my backyard in Bisbee. But I didn't count it, of course, although I did get several nice photographs. I should've guessed something was amiss when the animal made it from the compost pile to our rooftop with a bread roll stuffed in its mouth and disappeared under the eave. "So many old and lovely things are stored in the world's attic," John Steinbeck writes, "because we don't want them around us and we don't dare throw them out." I, however, became bent on throwing this one out.

It began on a night as different from other nights as ringtails are from cats. On Christmas Eve, my three daughters and their husbands rescued a perfect tree from a Dumpster at a Christmas tree lot. We spent the rest of the evening decorating it with fine glass ornaments and lights. Embers in the fireplace spread their warmth into the room. Cinnamon tea simmered on the stove. A shrinking plate of pineapple empanadas sat on the table next to a newly frosted gingerbread house. All seemed as it should be.

At 3:00 a.m., a sound in the kitchen woke me. It was an elfin visitor but not the one with curled toes and pointy hat, dressed all in green. For the past few nights, something had been emptying the cat's food dish—and it wasn't the cat. Whole loaves of bread, torn from their plastic, were stuffed under the China cabinet and refrigerator. Dust on the windowsills held the exquisite prints of tiny hands, each with five bulbous fingers extended as if waving hello. The visiting daughters had been complaining about noises in the night, the husbands and I bonding over a flashlighted quest for answers.

In the dark of that Christmas morning, husband of the youngest daughter trapped the culprit in the kitchen garbage can. A ring-tailed cat—or ringtail. Close kin not of anything feline but of the raccoon and coati. A nocturnal feeder of meat and fruit, of cheese and crackers. *Bassariscus astutus larderus.* The cunning little fox of the kitchen pantry.

At daybreak, the girls' boys and I carried it in the can to a release site we had chosen down the road. Our feet crunched on gravel. The ringtail crunched on cat food. "Do you think it arrived in the Christmas tree?" one of the boys asked. I smiled as I pictured the animal clinging for life as its home hurled down the highway at eighty miles an hour on the roof of the car. "No," I said. "It probably lives in the attic."

When I removed the lid, it stared at us with large liquid-obsidian eyes. It had the pink ears and pointed face of a kitten. A black-and-white tail wrapped around its long body like a feather boa. *How many ringtails have I looked at all my life and never actually seen?* I thought, dumping it onto the ground and watching it scurry away. I named him "Steinbeck."

I spent the day plugging holes, covering vents, stuffing balls of foil into any chinks in the rock walls of our 1890s stone house. Any access to the attic. But the next night brought more of the same. I was startled awake by wine bottles being loosed from their rack. I stumbled around the house with a flashlight but found nothing. In the morning another ringtail, or the same one—my field guide says ringtails are solitary—had left tracks in the frosted gingerbread house and three green gumdrops were missing, leaving white sugary craters along one eave. The candy dish was empty, save for one twisted black "present" like a stubbed-out cigar.

Then I noticed the absent package of tortillas. I slid out the refrigerator and there was Steinbeck. The girls used brooms and voices to sweep him out the front door. He climbed into the oak tree and watched us from the long limb that bent over the house.

"Look! He's so cute," middle daughter said.

"Don't you feel sorry for him?" youngest daughter added.

"Poor wee thing," said my wife. "Where is he going to go now?"

"Sure," I complained. "He's all cute and cuddly up there in the tree. But what about at three in the morning when you're chasing him around the house? He's about as cute as scat in the candy dish. He can bloody well find a new home."

Steinbeck returned the next night. I climbed into the attic and discovered he had chewed a hole into the flexible heating duct. I set about clearing the space, shifting around boxes of books and writing files. I expected to find a little bistro table set with Grandma's Staffordshire porcelain and glasses of red wine. I wound half a roll of tape around the hole in the heating duct, and set a live trap baited with gingerbread just to be sure. As a final blow, I removed the outside door to the attic, leaving the space open to winter's freezing nights. *God may see the sparrow fall*, I thought, *but he doesn't do anything about it.*

A few evenings later, I was up late. The kids had returned to their lives and Karen was in bed. My obsessive need to check on every bump in the night substituted for sleep. Then, near midnight, angry screams filled the house. I tracked the noise to the closet of the guest room. There, high up where the heating unit entered the attic, I saw a face sticking through a hole where the ductwork had separated from the ceiling. Not the cute wee thing. It was a look of furious spite, eyes flashing and teeth bared. A spitting, screeching, ear-splitting picture that remains with me to this day.

I knew I had won. Being miserable, I had also made his life miserable. Screaming at me was his way of slamming the door on his way out. "Good-bye, Steinbeck!" I shouted, my words as sharp as ringtail teeth. The face disappeared and the house grew quiet again, quieter than it would have been had there been no ringtail. I never saw Steinbeck after that, although weeks later, while roaming the house with my flashlight one night, I found a stash of half-eaten pineapple empanadas stacked neatly under my dresser.

NOVEMBER

Bola Tie

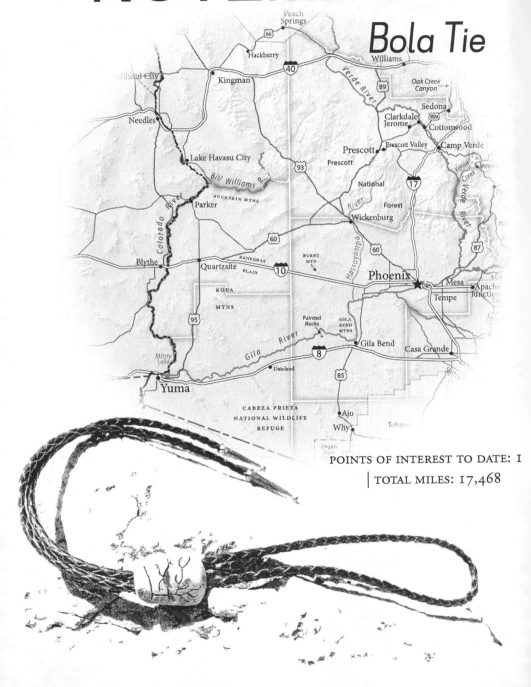

POINTS OF INTEREST TO DATE: 1

| TOTAL MILES: 17,468

On the Trail of What's Hot in Mormon Country

SAFFORD

ELEVATION: 2,917 FEET | FOUNDED: 1874 | POPULATION: 9,479

At La Casita Café in Thatcher, a replica of Leonardo da Vinci's *The Last Supper* hangs above a fireplace mantle crowded with ceramic figures of mustachioed and sombreroed Mexicans. "I hope this isn't *our* last supper," I tell Karen when she points out the painting. After mocking the popcorn ceiling and fake wood paneling, I turn over the menu to a picture of vaqueros riding bareback with reins flying. *Paso de la Muerte*, it reads. "Great," I say.

My resolve is wearing thin. How many chimichangas can one person eat in a year? In *Revenge of the Saguaro*, Tom Miller—who is quite the chimichanga aficionado himself—says "you know your chimichanga is authentic if an hour after eating it, you feel a log gently rolling around in your stomach."

According to my menu, La Casita got started in Globe in 1947 and still uses Mother Salustia Reynoso's original recipes. I order a green chile chimichanga with rice and beans. To remind me of where I am, a kid wears a sweatshirt that reads: *I'm a Mormon. I know it. I live it. I love it.* On the wall above his head hangs a Bud Light sign. We're having lunch with a few of Karen's coworkers. One of them is a local and recommended the Mexican restaurant.

"So far I've learned that Safford is the fire agate capital of the world," I tell the group of planners and consultants, "although a woman I just talked to at your offices said she's never heard that before—and she's lived here forty years."

"I've never heard that either, and I've lived here since 1990." John is a friend of Susan, Karen's coworker. He's from the Midwest, he says, where to go hiking you have to get some property owner's permission. "Here, I can go anywhere." I mention to him that the last time I visited Safford, I drove down the Devil's Highway from Alpine and stopped to see the Arrow Tree. He said he put an arrow in it.

"Why?" I ask, surprised to have met one of the skunked.

"Why do people climb Mt. Everest?"

"Because it's the fire agate capital of the world?"

John decides to test me about my newfound knowledge of Safford by asking me what else the town is known for. "Besides 'Home of the Salsa Trail.'"

"The telescopes on Mount Graham!" I say. "The Vatican and the LGBT!"

"What?" Karen says. "The Vatican's LGBT?"

"That's 'LBT,'" John corrects me. "Large Binocular Telescope—the most powerful optical telescope in the world."

"Yeah, that one," I say. "Lucifer is helping Vatican astronomers look for extraterrestrials," I add, quoting a recent news headline. Lucifer is an acronym for the infrared camera and spectroscope instruments on the Large Binocular Telescope, which Vatican astronomers are using along with their own adjacent telescope, the Vatican Advanced Technology Telescope (VATT). Lucifer can be chilled to a negative 351 degrees F., allowing near-infrared, Hubble-like views of star nurseries eight thousand light years away. For years, the Vatican Observatory has hosted researchers and conferences to examine the possibility of extraterrestrials and its implication for the Catholic Church. Now, Jesuit astronomers are using the telescopes on Mount Graham to watch for the arrival of an alien savior from another world. Papal astronomer Brother Guy Consolmagno, told *The Guardian* in 2010 that he would baptize an alien if he were asked. "Any entity," he added, "no matter how many tentacles it has, has a soul."

But will it have a taste for Mexican food? Before we leave, Susan asks about my chimi.

"I'm going to put it in my top three," I say, surprising even myself. "Up there with El Charro and Macayo's." The flavor was poetry—I had expected something greasy, but it tasted like it was baked—a pungent green-chile Velcro clinging to the tongue.

I harbor a fantasy that good food should have soul. That it should taste like a poem. There should be stanzas of flavor—smoke and wood, salt and oil, meat and vegetable—that come together to create something greater than the individual parts. A taste that becomes music with rhythm and texture. When asked what part of a poem should be the best, the poet

Alberto Ríos says, "It better be the part I'm reading." The same can be said for food. The best part better be the part I'm eating.

Karen and I stop along the roadside for ten pounds of freshly roasted chiles and then head for Mi Casa Tortilla Factory in downtown Safford. We're unwittingly following the "Salsa Trail," which mostly traces the valley of the Gila River, land of cotton fields and hot springs. The tortilla factory, along with a chile farm and a dozen Mexican restaurants located in eight towns spread over three counties, make up the 240-mile route to glorious heartburn.

"I wouldn't recommend it for a marathon," I tell Karen, rolling up warm chiles into a soft flour tortilla. "It should be called the 'Prilosec Trail.'"

With bellies full of Mexican food, we follow some printed directions and road signs to Essence of Tranquility natural hot mineral spring. The artesian well is off the beaten path. But we've been warned: "This place is out in the desert," Karen reads from my printout, "in the country. It is not a city, glitzy day spa as such. If that is what you are wanting, this is not the place for you."

"And here's my favorite part," Karen says, as I pull into a drive surrounded by towering walls of bamboo. "Just because this place is a more natural, earthy place, it is not a 'dirty hippy' place, although it almost always needs some sort of cleaning and/or maintenance done. This is a one person–run business. I do my best to keep it a nice place for ones to come to."

The entrance looks like a birdhouse emporium. No one is around. A sign below a slot in the front wall of the blue bungalow reads *Pay Here*. We follow a path along lattice panels and bamboo screens, past green lawns and potted papyrus, to one of six private (clothing optional) soaking tubs. The Waterfall Room. One hundred and three degrees of pure muscle-soothing, skin-dissolving chemical submersion. I'm not kidding. The list of the "inorganic contents" of the water flowing 1,632 feet out of the earth from a well drilled more than sixty years ago spans the periodic table. There are the metals—alkali and alkaline earth, transition, poor and metalloid (arsenic!). Then come the nonmetals like fluorine, chlorine, sulfur, and selenium. Eighteen elements in all, including the heaviest ones: barium, mercury, and lead (oh, my!).

Karen dips only her feet. I strip and soak everything. You only live this gloriously once.

On our way out, we meet the owner, Clarisse Drake. "Did you figure it all out?"

My wet shirt betrays my negligence in bringing a towel. But Clarisse loves to laugh and joke about the people who come from Bisbee. She thinks we're hippies, but I assure her we're the clean kind, at least now.

"Twenty years of doing this," she says, raising an arm tucked into a sling. "Rotator cuff has worn out on me."

"Too much overhead activity," Karen says, "and not enough in the hot tub."

"Or maybe too much fun in the tub," I tell Karen as we drive away. "I've heard there's an incidence of rotator cuff complaints from people taking supplemental selenium."

Three Generations of Baking Thingamajigs

GLOBE

ELEVATION: 3,510 FEET | FOUNDED: 1876 | POPULATION: 7,457

Globe. The city named for the shape of a silver nugget. "Glob," as Ed Abbey called it. "There's a town in Arizona called Glob. Named for a nugget," Abbey begins his story, "In Defense of the Redneck." I imagine the old curmudgeon didn't make many friends in these parts. But at least he stopped here for a beer. Globe was always something I drove through to get to somewhere else, like the White Mountains or Roosevelt Lake. It was the gateway to elsewhere, to anywhere else, although I might stop for gas if I had to, or a Big Mac. For me, the best thing about Globe was imagining going to high school with Wonder Woman Lynda Carter.

On this middle-of-November evening, Karen and I slip into the near-empty town to look for food. I drive past the McDonald's without a glance and pull into Chalo's Casa de Reynoso. We find a seat at a plastic booth. The Virgin of Guadalupe hangs above us on a wall next to a picture of a bullfighter. I'm reminded of Abbey's U-Et-Yet? Café.

On last week's run along the Salsa Trail, I tasted a baked chimi at La Casita Café in Thatcher. So, while Karen considers beef tacos, I order another green chile chimi—this one "spicy." Globe, they say, is all about Mexican food. I've heard their green chile is the best anywhere. In fact, we meet a couple who drove a hundred miles from Tucson just for the gollo burro, a flour tortilla filled with green chile pork, beans, cheese, and topped with butter.

"The burro was first created when someone rolled meat inside a tortilla to keep it warm," our server tells us when I ask about the famous burrito. "Look it up on Google," she says. "And it's 'burro,' not 'burrito,'" she adds, rolling the *r*'s perfectly. "A burrito is what you get in California or at Taco Bell."

Her name is Roberta, and she knows her food history. Her dark eyes narrow and she dismisses the chimichanga story I tell her about Macayo's and El Charro, waving an arm as if shooing a fly. "Chivichangas is nothing new!—that's what they call them in Sonora. In Mexico, they fry everything! We bake our chimichangas. We don't want the oil to soak in and change the flavor of the meat."

Did someone accidentally drop a bean burro into the oven? I ask her about a photograph of Salustia and Pedro Reynoso on the wall. She retrieves and unrolls a poster of Reynoso restaurants. There are a dozen names on it—I recognize La Casita in Thatcher. "We were there just last week!" I say. "I ate my first baked chimichanga there!"

"Salustia started the first restaurant with her three sisters in the 1930s. All of these sprang from these four women." Roberta's husband, Gonzalo Anthony Reynoso Jr., "Chalo," is the third generation. He started his place—the fourth restaurant on the list—in 1969. "Nobody wrote the recipes down. It was all in their heads. If something were to happen to him, this food as we know it would be done. When *Sunset* magazine came here, I wouldn't give the editor the recipes. I couldn't!"

A sense of place and history and culture you can taste, I think. Karen has been reading Michael Pollan's latest book to me during our travels. He could be talking about Chalo's Casa de Reynoso. As with all things, taste has its complications. A bite of chimichanga comes with layers, each one an echo of something elemental. The tortilla's wheat to the soil, the green chile's chlorophyll to sunlight, the cubed pork to the grain it fed on—all elements of earth, water, and sun. A recapitulation of the long contract between animals and plants. Between people and the earth. Sonorans. Arizonans. Chinese immigrants and egg rolls. Chimichangas are people! *Chimichangas are Arizona!*

Could it be that frying in oil masks this recapitulation, this complication of layers? And that the familia Reynoso knew this generations ago? Could a traditional chimichanga be baked? When my chimi arrives, I smell the sweet tang of green chile and cubed pork in piecrust. This is it. I'm back at Pancho's in Tucson when I was nine. Mariachis play from the Uno Mas Lounge in a room lighted by the largest known dripping candle. El Charro's and Macayo's chimichangas may have risen to the top of the deep fryer, but this one never fell in. Never fell from grace.

Roberta had told us that Mama Salustia had seven children. "She would not raise her children in Mexico. She wanted them brought up in the United States." Today, those children, and their children, carry on a tradition of Mexican food that has spread to seventeen restaurants in a dozen towns across Arizona. Pick any one of them. From Thatcher to Show Low, Mammoth to Phoenix, the House of Reynoso has the best chimichanga in the state.

We drive Highway 60 high above Globe, passing a very dark Apache Drive-In, the last single-screen outdoor theater still operating in Arizona. After sixty years, it, too, is slated to close next fall with a final showing of the iconic drive-in movie, *American Graffiti*. I wonder if Lynda Carter has a date.

Karen has rejected my suggestion that we stay at Globe's Noftsger Hill Inn (built in 1907) and has chosen more modern accommodations. "No more historic hotels!" she told me. "No more ghosts, cold beds, and noisy plumbing that doesn't work! *Historic* really means low maintenance. *Haunted* means old and run down." "But Governor Rose Mofford learned her ABCs there," I complained. No matter. She found a mansion on a hill called Dream Manor Inn.

Karen has been reading my previous chapters and commenting on the plethora of destinations with graveyards and haunted something or others. I hadn't noticed, but now I count half a dozen cemeteries and almost twice that many hotels. Add these to the collection of ghost towns I've visited and my book could be titled *Chasing Haunted Arizona*. Chase the past and you trail the dead, I could argue. But this is not my intention, although it may expose an unconscious fascination with death and the otherworldly. Maybe it's cultural. The Anglo in me sees the spiritual as entertainment, whereas others have an altogether different respect for the dead. Halloween trick-or-treating versus El Día de los Muertos.

The Kia's tires thrum over brick. I pass gardens, balconies, and lighted fountains and park before an expansive view of nighttime Globe and the dark open mouth of the Pinal Mountains. Owner and innkeeper Carl

Williams checks us in and gives us a tour. Then Karen fires up the bathtub Jacuzzi. *You won't find this in some ancient haunted hotel!* I hear her voice in my head. The place is a 1960s ranch house that the owner and his wife converted into a bell-towered bed-and-breakfast surrounded by Tuscan villas the color of earth. Our room, Villa 4, is the size of our home in Bisbee.

In the morning, we plan to visit Globe's historic district and take in the Oak Street Marketplace. First, however, we have breakfast with Eric and Marcy, a couple from Safford who were married here three years ago. They love the Essence of Tranquility hot spring, "especially after hard labor all day," Eric says. He works the mines for Freeport McMoRan in Morenci. We talk about Safford and Mexican food while Carl and his bubbly brunette wife Rebecca serve us omelets ranchero.

"I can actually say I've been kicked in the ass by Woody Johnson," Rebecca says, after I mention Macayo's and my quest for the ultimate in chimichangas. She's a native Arizonan and has worked in the food and hospitality business all her life. Now she runs her own place with her husband and four of their five sons. "Woody invented all kinds of things—like taco salad."

"Sure," I say. "But did he ever bake a chimichanga?"

A Living Monument

CANYON DE CHELLY

ELEVATION: 5,610 FEET | ESTABLISHED: 1931 | POPULATION: ABOUT 40
NAVAJO FAMILIES

At 460 miles north from Bisbee in the third week of November, I make one final venture into Navajoland, sans the mutton. I count forty-six weeks into this yearlong adventure, with six more to go. I've seen ten of the twelve state symbols in their natural habitats. I've just tasted Arizona's best chimichanga. I'm definitely on the downhill slide. Those who said I was crazy, those who doubted my resolve, can simply kiss my "Az."

I want to make a *Kiss My Az* bumper sticker for the Kia, but Karen says I'm being rude. Besides, she has issues with any kind of bumper sticker. "How about *Kissing Az* as a book title then?" I ask.

"If it's your autobiography," she says.

We've just arrived at the Thunderbird Lodge at Chinle, "where the water flows out" at the mouth of Canyon de Chelly. It's dark, but to the east a greater darkness rises through spider-legged cottonwoods to meet the night, and I feel its pull. Just a short walk from here, the entire landscape empties out. This is where the world dissolves. Somewhere out there, coyotes call, their voices flaring large and frenzied, unfettered even by canyon walls. I want to take a short flashlight hike.

The Thunderbird trading post was built in 1896 by brothers William and Samuel Day and their father, Samuel E. Day, a civil engineer from Ohio who came to the Southwest to homestead near Window Rock with his wife and three sons. The Days were a family immersed in Navajo culture, fluent in the language. Sam Jr. was one of the first to preserve Navajo sand paintings on wood using adhesives. He married a chief's daughter named Kate Roanhorse. Eldest son, Charles Day, ran a second trading post in Chinle. He served as a guide, interpreter, and photographer, documenting and helping to preserve the history and ceremonies of the Diné. In 1903, the Department of the Interior appointed him as the first custodian of Canyon de Chelly.

One of the stories Charles collected is called "A True Story of the Coming of the Railroad Over Fifty Years Ago." The typed manuscript begins with how in the Village of the Pueblos in the old adobe homes, children would gather around their aged great-grandfathers and wait for a story:

> "Listen children," they would say, knocking the earth with their finger. They would knock again and again and then listen to the ground. "Oh, great-grandfathers. What is going to happen to us?" we would ask. Then they would say, "They are coming nearer and nearer." "Who is coming nearer and nearer?" "A white man with his iron road."

The story continues with a warning to the children: "Some of you girls will marry white men and forget the Indian ways and claim the white man's ways." In the end, the author says that in only one way was her grandfather wrong, "As I married a chief instead of a white man."

I leave our room at midnight and walk a quiet, dark road with a couple of rez dogs. They think I have food; I'm happy for the company. Somewhere, the sickle-headed constellation Leo rises, but my view to the east is obscured by cottonwoods and clouds. Too many clouds. If any Leonids are splashing into our thin curve of sky, I can't tell.

In the morning, we meet Daniel Draper and his Chevy Silverado at the visitor center. His sweatshirt shows a tricked-out 4x4 truck with a deer stand rising high out of its bed. *Larry's Mobile Deer Hunting Tours*, it reads. *Spotlights are extra.*

"I met your brother the last time I came through here," I tell Daniel. "He said to look you up. His name is Tim something?"

Daniel laughs. "I tease him that we have different names because his father is Hopi!" He draws his hand across his forehead. "See? Take off your hat—your hair is real flat!"

Daniel and his brother run Twin Trails Scenic Tours. They grew up here, and both know the place intimately, its history, geology, culture. "A hundred and thirty-one square miles—I had this big of a playground when I was a little kid. Rode my horse everywhere." Daniel says. "I've been taking in tours since I was thirteen."

Karen and I climb into his beat-up Silverado and we're off. Soon we pass a carload of tourists stuck in the sandy creek bed. "You want to mess up your brand-new SUV," Daniel laughs, "hire a guide to drive it!"

"Oh, no!" I say. "Not in our little Kia!" and now we're all laughing.

"You know that I come from four clans from my grandparents. Spanish from my grandmother. Mescalero Apache from my grandfather, the people-who-walk-around clan. I'm a trickster, coyote clan, from my mother."

We're in for a wild time.

"There are two stories for how Canyon de Chelly got its name," Daniel explains as peach-colored walls of sandstone rise on either side of us. "*Tsegi*—pronounced *chay-e*—means 'rock canyon.' But my grandfather tells a different story, that the canyon is named for a person who lived at Junction Ruin called *chi'li' yazhi*, the 'small curly-haired man,' which sounded like 'de Chelly.' That's what my grandfather says. I tell both stories."

At a pictograph site called Kokopelli Cave in the Canyon of the Small Man with Curly Hair, a flute player rests on his back among other white froglike figures and handprints on the sandstone. "These are what we call dancers," Daniel says, explaining that the hands show both the positive and negative technique. "We find three colors that the Pueblo people mixed with tree sap."

The enigmatic Ancient Ones. From the earliest Archaic hunter-gatherers to the Basketmakers and their plots of beans and squash to the pueblo-building potters and weavers of cotton to the present-day Navajo themselves, people have always lived here. This place is a monument to them more than it is to some natural wonder. Here, people are the natural wonder.

Last summer's alfalfa and corn fields drape across the canyon bottom, surrounded by orchards of peach trees. An orange baler rests in the yard of a simple wood and stone house—the home of Daniel's aunt. "We stole my grandfather's chicken wire," Daniel says, reminiscing about his childhood pranks. "Tsaile Lake at the head of this canyon has trout, and sometimes they would escape downstream. My bother and I used the chicken wire to catch the trout. Then we built a fire and used the same chicken wire to cook the fish!"

We meet Daniel's aunt at Antelope House Ruin, our turn-around point at nine miles. Cara is a health educator and jewelry artist. Karen is drawn to her tables of silver and turquoise. "I should have brought more money," Karen says, trying on a large necklace.

I talk with her husband, Travis Terry, who sends flute music into the canyon with instruments he's designed himself, turning breath into song. His double and triple flutes are handmade from aromatic cedar in Patagonia, Arizona. And it turns out he's performed with my friend, percussionist Will Clipman. "I'm a chief tech for Pima Medical," he says. "My real job."

"I know about the 'real job' of an artist," I say. "My wife says my writing is a hobby. My real job is doing whatever she says."

Antelope House Ruin is named for the work of another artist, a Navajo man called Dibe Yazhi (Little Sheep) who lived here in the early nineteenth century. His drawings of four brown pronghorn grace the walls above the mud ruins where dark draperies of desert varnish spill from the canyon rim. The pronghorn stand among much older pictographs of white bighorn, and a "wheel of life" symbol, representing how nature is cyclical and that good fortune comes in and out of our lives. As a trading place of the Anasazi, Antelope House Ruin was a center for this ebb and flow over great distances, as seen in the buried macaw feathers and seashells.

Nature, it seems, reveals itself in this place. Most of us move through our days in straight lines, forcing what is elliptical into the linear. We shove hours of daylight into one season, then jerk them out in the next. But nature follows no calendar. It needs no adjustment to fit modern society's constraints because it is flawless.

On the drive out, Daniel passes us his smartphone to show us photos of his family. He has four children: three gorgeous daughters and an equally handsome son. "You've been busy," Karen says.

"Only when there is no hunting," he says. "It's the old traditional way, my grandfather says. The Navajo sweat lodge will give you better hunting—no sleeping with your wife." Daniel begins to sing a song in Navajo, saying that his grandfather wrote it for his son. It's a beautiful and haunting melody, though I don't recognize a single word. When he finishes, Daniel says: "It's about not dating girls who already have boyfriends."

In the late afternoon, Karen and I hike the trail to White House Ruin, a five-hundred-foot descent along switchbacks, stairways, and a tunnel to a sixty-room dwelling occupied a thousand years past. Sunlight slants on tilted rock, cross-bedded sandstone holding the shape of dunes born of prevailing north-easterlies from Permian times. In a world of striation and pitch, I lean into warm stone. Ravens croak among seams of blue sky and red rock. Unseen voices carry off high canyon walls.

Canyon de Chelly—a place where the landscape is as sharp as the taste of cayenne. And where the people are a living monument to a five-millennia-long chain of uninterrupted humanity, the longest in North America. Where we pause to rest, two Navajo boys shoot past us, racing each other down the trail, bounding over ledges of rock like antelope, black hair streaming from their shoulders with their laughter. I see two Anasazi boys from centuries ago, wearing buckskin and sandals instead of blue jeans and Nikes.

On the Road to Arizona's West Coast

WICKENBURG TO KINGMAN TO LAKE HAVASU CITY AND THE BILL WILLIAMS RIVER

ELEVATION: 735 FEET | FOUNDED: 1963 | POPULATION: 52,527

In Arizona, we have dry rivers, dead rivers, and one river that runs upside down. We have the Salt that tastes sweet, the Black that runs white, and the Colorado that is anything but. They say there are two easy ways to die in the desert: thirst or drowning. In the Hassayampa, you can do both at the same time. No, I haven't been drinking from the river and telling "hassayampers." Well . . . call it personal embellishment or panache. Call it creative nonfiction.

I drive west along Carefree Highway singing Gordon Lightfoot's 1974 song ("let me slip away, slip away on you"), crossing the legendary river of tall-tale tellers. I'm on my way to Wickenburg to locate the native habitat of the bola tie. It's part of a longer excursion that will take me to the rum capital of Arizona, a honeymoon suite that's also a bomb shelter and the burial chamber of a twelve-thousand-year-old giant ground sloth, a bridge carted stone-by-stone from London, and the site of the state's first and only naval skirmish (we lost). Who needs to sip from the Hassayampa when you have stories like these?

At the Desert Caballeros Western Museum in Wickenburg, I snap a photo of a picture of a somber-looking Henry Wickenburg (1819–1905). I think: *Not Henry Wicken? Then shouldn't the town be called Wickenburgburg?* The smell of old leather permeates rooms stuffed with saddles, ropes, riatas, and quirts, both historical and Hollywood. I find Clayton Moore and Gene Autry but no Victor Cedarstaff.

This past summer at a bola tie exhibit at the Heard Museum in Phoenix, I learned that the Wickenburg silversmith had invented the neckwear. (Some call it "bolo" tie, but I prefer Victor's spelling.) In 1949, the story goes, while riding in the Bradshaw Mountains after wild horses, a gust of wind dislodged his hat. He managed to retrieve only the silver-trimmed hatband, which he tossed around his neck. Someone liked the look. Inspired, he created and patented what he called a "piggin' necktie" because it resembled the small rope cowboys use to tie cattle by the feet. Apparently, few wanted to tie on one of these, so Cedarstaff changed the name to "bola" tie after noticing its similarity to the end-weighted, braided-leather cords called "boleadoras" that South American gauchos use to wrap up the legs of fleeing game and livestock. The guy had a one-track mind. But the bola soon became a fad among cowpunchers and TV newscasters because, surely, it never hurts to have an extra hog-tie at the ready.

A woman at the gift shop wants to sell me a bola tie when I ask about the inventor. "No," I explain again, "I'm looking for the Cedarstaff display."

"It's across the alley," another woman says. "At the Learning Center."

Native American baskets and pottery, spurs and more saddles, Buffalo Bill's dagger and Wyatt Earp's straight-edged razor crowd the walls. But in one corner of the room is a glass case of two dozen ties. Next to a photograph of a smiling balding man hang some of the gaudiest bolas I've ever seen. Their clasps hold slabs of petrified wood or giant scorpions in plastic resin in the shape of Arizona. But three small braids tipped with silver stand out. Two of the silver trapezoid slides have polished turquoise stones the size of a fingernail. Cedarstaff's earliest work. His best work. I carry a similar bola tie that was my father's. A simple silver keystone design with an engraved roadrunner beneath a turquoise-chip sky. It could be a Vic Cedarstaff creation.

Wickenburgburg. In a tiny western museum, right down the street from the jail tree in the town of the hanging tree. There you'll find our official state neckwear: the piggin' necklet, a.k.a., the bola—or, as I will always think of it, the cowboy hog-tie.

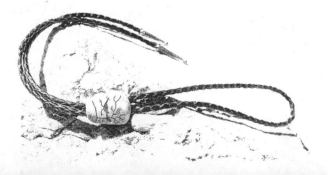

On Highway 93, I pass cottonwoods in fall jaundice and drifts of desert snow loosed from the shrubs of desert broom in seed. Soon, the first Joshua tree appears, a giant Hydra-like monstrosity that seems to eschew gravity with a dozen branches exploring every possible oblique angle known to nature. The nineteenth-century pathfinder John C. Frémont called it "the most repulsive tree in the vegetable kingdom." Okay, but maybe he hadn't encountered baobabs or boojums. I enter Arizona's own Joshua tree forest, tucked into the land of saguaros. Why would anyone travel to the Mojave Desert of California?

I see nothing in Nothing, Arizona, a "town" of four people, supposedly named by drunks who also called it the rattlesnake capital of the world. Nothing used to be something. The townsfolk—the entire population ran a gas station—erected a sign that claimed these dedicated people had "faith in Nothing, hoped for Nothing, worked at Nothing, for Nothing." Reminds me of the misspelled billboard just outside of Hope, Arizona, that says: *Your Now Beyond Hope.*

"Nothin' from nothin' leaves nothin'," I sing the Billy Preston tune. "You gotta have somethin' if you wanna . . . *make me pull over.*" I press down on the gas pedal, the song running in my head. I'm late for a date with rum. After crossing more dry rivers—Burro Creek (check off the fourth longest and highest arch span bridge in the state) and the Big Sandy—I jump on I-40 and head west, picking up Route 66 north to the airport and the Desert Diamond Distillery. This is the reason I've come to Kingman.

I meet Deborah Patt at the door, just in time to join a tour led by her father, Peter. The smell of molasses forms a solid wall in the fermenting room. A row of stainless-steel vats rises behind me—all connected with a maze of pipes to a giant thousand-liter copper still and two copper towers more than twice as tall as Peter. It's all tanks and plumbing and gauges and glass cylinders and dark portholes—like I've stepped into main engineering on the starship *Enterprise*. Or perhaps the main galley.

"The entire process is controlled here," Peter says, moving to a center console, "including cleanup. All touch screen. A German company, Bavarian Brewery Technology, installed the state-of-the-art equipment, making us the first computer-controlled distillery in the industry."

This is where art intersects with science, I think, as Peter explains the distillation process, how molasses becomes alcohol in twenty-four hours. How the still evaporates the unwanted "heads" (unlike moonshine) and takes the product up to 90 percent ethanol for rum, 95 percent for vodka. Desert Diamond makes vodka from their finest rum.

The art comes in the handcrafting, the careful blending with distilled water, the oak-barrel aging. The color, the flavor, the aroma, and the finish all come from the oak. "You can't pass any of this through the distillation process," Peter says. "We use American white oak—five hundred dollars a barrel."

I'm tempted by their make-your-own barrel program, but I live six hours away and couldn't give my personal five-liter oak cask the proper testing it would require during its aging. I doubt I'd have much product to show for in the end, anyway.

After the tour, Peter's wife, Mary Ann, offers me a tasting. I buy the mini-sampler. I ask Peter why he chose Arizona for his family company. "I first looked into Nevada," he says, "but it turns out Arizona's liquor laws are more lax. Besides, agave is a native plant in Arizona, and agave rum is our invention!"

"It's my favorite: sweet, smooth, better than anything I've tasted like . . . Bacardi." (I almost say Captain Morgan.)

"You know, we won platinum for our chip-aged rum—our first entry at SIP we ever made." Spirits International Prestige, Peter explains, is an annual competition. This year, their barrel reserve rum took one of the four gold medals at the San Francisco World Spirits Competition. "But the best part was getting the certificate saying we'd tied for first place with Bacardi. Can you imagine?" His sharp blue eyes are penetrating. "The best part is knowing that Bacardi got the same certificate saying they'd tied for first place with Kingman, Arizona!"

Late afternoon, I'm back on Route 66 heading north to Peach Springs, home of the Hualapai tribe and gateway to the Havasupai. Near sunset, I pull off the highway at a sign for Grand Canyon Caverns and park at an old, worn-down motel. I have a reservation, but the place looks deserted. No cars—no *late model* cars. No lights. After walking around in the dark, I find a doorbell and push the button. A young dark-haired girl slides open a tiny window.

"I'm here for the Sky Room," I say, but she's confused. She can't find my reservation and retreats into a back office to make a phone call. When she returns, she copies down my information and gives me directions to my room. I spend the next half hour driving along dirt roads trying to find it by moonlight. *Being lost*, I tell myself, *is part of discovery—and the reason I refuse to use GPS*. It isn't helping. When I return to the hotel, the girl tells me I should see it next to the corral. *What corral?* "Take the side road. You have to open the gate—the chain shouldn't be locked."

I finally locate it in the middle of a pasture, a raised platform of hewn logs silhouetted against a black sky. Clutching my sleeping bag, some Jarlsberg and crackers for dinner, and my rum sampler, I climb twelve wooden steps to my high bed. It's cold, this fourth week of November among the piñon pines of northern Arizona. I eat from inside my bag under an expanse of stars, washing the food down with one sip of rum after another. Then the vodka.

Sometime during the night, the sound of galloping horses beneath my bed awakens me. I slip on my glasses then draw the mummy bag tight around my head and face, exposing only my eyes. The moon has set. Hooves stamp. Nostrils snort. My nose runs. The stars hold to the sky like a suspension of powered mica. Two on the Bortle Scale, I think, maybe one. Only once have I seen stars so extraordinary: in Hawai'i on the Big Island with my daughter Melissa. We first thought our star party on the slopes of Mauna Kea was ruined when clouds appeared after dark. But with our naked eyes, we could see Messier clusters as if they were cotton balls. The clouds turned out to be stars, and the stars were casting shadows upon the ground.

Tonight, through my tiny goose-down portal, I see no horizon, only space. I drift light-years from earth. Orion lifts his bright sword at the end of my nose. The winter Milky Way is glittering dust upon my eyelashes. My God!—*It's full of stars!*

In the morning, I wake and discover my contacts are lenses of ice inside their case. *At what temperature does saline freeze?* Once my eyes thaw, I head for coffee at Grand Canyon Caverns, where I meet Paul Wilson beneath a life-size model of a *T. rex* skull.

He gives me the rules. No food. No touching. No touching food. We step into an elevator and descend 210 feet into the earth. The elevator shudders and I look at Paul, who smiles through his Ironman goatee. "My first week working here, the power went out," he says as the door opens into a dim limestone tomb. "I had to climb the stairs in the dark. Twenty-one stories. I'll do that only once."

"Good thing there are stairs," I say. "Imagine only a rope."

This is how the first visitors toured one of the largest dry caverns in the United States. For twenty-five cents, they would be tied to a rope and lowered by a hand winch while gripping a kerosene lantern. They came to see the bones of two troglodytes. The cavemen.

The story begins in 1927 with a woodcutter named Walter Peck, who on the way to a poker game took a shortcut and fell into a hole. With gold on his mind, Peck returned the next day with two friends, one of whom he convinced to do some exploring at the end of a long rope. When the volunteer spelunker returned to the surface, he held a sack full of what would turn out to be iron oxide. He also claimed to see human skeletons. After a disappointing assay report, Peck decided to recoup his investment in a worthless gold mine by selling tickets to anyone who dared to see the prehistoric cavemen. Dope on a rope.

We enter the large expanse of the Cavern Suite, a barely lit bedroom ensemble with loaded bookshelves, lamps, and chairs. "The largest, oldest, deepest, darkest, quietest motel room in the world," Paul explains. "You spend the night 220 feet below ground. The only sound is your heart beating. You are the only living thing in the caverns. The room comes with your own personal attendant who's there in case you freak out. . . ."

"My personal attendant better come with a powerful sedative."

Paul shows me a wall of flowers, souvenirs of the many weddings taken place here, five just this year, the last one on Halloween. They are perfectly preserved in the cave's year-round dry fifty-six-degree air. Among the blooms, I point out a particular pair of lacy undergarment. "We're going to be talking about that wedding lingerie for decades," he says.

In the Halls of Gold, a cache of pallets is stacked high with drums of water, boxes of crackers, MREs. In 1962, Paul tells me, President Kennedy designated Grand Canyon Caverns as a fallout shelter, and the military stocked it with emergency supplies. "It's enough to keep two thousand people alive for a month, and it's still good after fifty years. There are two flavors of candy. Good to know for the coming zombie apocalypse."

From the Snowball Palace, past the 1850 mummified bobcat, to the Mammoth Dome, Paul explains how long before Walter Peck created his tourist attraction, the neighboring Hualapai knew about the cave. It turns out the human remains found by Peck were Hualapai, two victims of a flu epidemic, buried here during a snowstorm the winter of 1917–18. Peck had put them on display as "cavemen," refusing to return them to the tribe. "He was a bad man," Paul repeats several times. "He sold the property in 1940 and died shortly after. When the elevator went in in 1962, we sealed the hole in agreement with the Hualapai to respect their sacred burial ground."

Paul swings his light into the chamber of the former entrance. Wooden scaffolding and ladders slip askew in a shaft now filled with debris a hundred feet above us. "This is also where they found the fossil of a giant ground sloth." He shifts his beam onto the cave wall. Dozens of white vertical lines mar the ochre limestone. "You can see where she tried to claw her way out."

A fifteen-foot replica of the one-ton creature rises from the cave floor. Mouth agape. Claws extended. This is what I came for—the last resting place of an extinct ice-age animal. I look again at the claw marks, at the hairy bearlike sloth, at a window on an Arizona long gone. Time feels thin here. I can see into the past as if by kerosene lamp.

Later that afternoon, I drive Route 66 to Hackberry, a place that could just as easily be called Petticoat Junction. (Do the girls here also bathe in the town's water supply?) Then Kingman and south across the creosote-smudged outwash of the Mohave Mountains toward Lake Havasu City and the London Bridge. Locals say the bridge is Arizona's second most visited attraction after Grand Canyon. I would have put the bridge behind Gertie, the giant ground sloth. Perhaps what they mean when they say "visitor traffic" is just "traffic." Walkers, bikers, motorists, an endless stream coming and going. A history of traffic could put the numbers over the top. The bridge was one of the most congested places in London in the 1890s when hundreds of vehicles and thousands of pedestrians crossed every hour.

I walk across the bridge looking for the head of William Wallace, but my history is off. I'll find no tangential connection to my Scottish ancestor, William de Lamberton, bishop of St. Andrews and supporter of Wallace. This construction, completed in 1831 by the Scottish engineer John Rennie, replaced London's six-hundred-year-old gateway across the Thames with its customary display of traitors' severed heads.

The mud nests of swallows cling to the stonework. Maybe they came from London as well? After Robert P. McCulloch, the shirt-sleeve- and saddle-shoe-wearing founder of Lake Havasu City and seller of chainsaws, bought the sinking bridge in 1968, masons numbered every granite block before disassembly and shipment to Arizona. Well, not *every* granite block. Just the facing stones, which were thinned by six or eight inches. Ten tons of the stones, with the 1902 balustrade and corbels, became cladding for a 930-foot-long, five-arched concrete frame built on a peninsula of Lake Havasu sand, later dredged with a canal and flooded. Arizona's London Bridge is more London Façade than bridge.

Jet skis and boats bob along a bricked waterfront of shops and restaurants. Lake Havasu City, the personal watercraft capital of the world. Brick chimneys rise among rows of peaked rooftops imbricated with cedar shakes. More English veneer? A gull crosses a blue sky. I relax. My first impression of the place—a strip mall populated by old white guys in ORVs—subsides. A young man fishes for carp with a fly rod beneath the bridge. "We're all the same," he tells me when I ask about people who live here. "You have to like the outdoors and adventure. You have to like the heat."

Yes. Last night I froze. Today I sweat. I need beer.

Just down the street is the Mudshark Brewery. The name hails from the famous Frank Zappa song about an iconic tale of rock 'n' roll bad behavior involving a mud sh-sh-shark and a red-headed girl. "And I'm gonna tell you, this dance, the mud shark, is sweeping the ocean!" I won't say more, except that maybe somebody's been sippin' from the Hassayampa.

"I've tasted your Desert Magic," I tell my server, but she insists I sample their seasonal handcrafted beer of the week, a Solar Red IPA, ninety on the IBU scale. "Perfect!" I say, and I order a tall glass with the Mudshark pizza special.

"Be right back," she says, flipping her long blond braid across her back as she spins around. Annie was born here, I soon learn. The doctor who delivered her also delivered her daughter. She and her husband love the Colorado River "beach life" and the wild burros that come through her neighborhood. "The poor maintenance guy spends his days shoveling burro poop!" Mostly, however, she stays for the weather: "I like it hot!" she tells me, smiling. She must. Lake Havasu City holds the record for the highest temperature ever recorded in Arizona: 128 degrees on June 29, 1994. Only eight degrees shy of the record for the planet.

When I'm ready to bust open, I tell Annie the hoppy, smooth IPA is my favorite Arizona beer. It is. Mudshark Solar Red is the closest I've come to trumping a Big Sky IPA. I guess there had to be a fish involved. She wants to send me off with a half-gallon growler. (I picture a galvanized bucket of brew in the passenger seat, growling with escaping CO_2 as I fly down the highway.) "I'll seal the cap with electrical tape," she says when I hesitate, but I decline the temptation. I have a long drive home. She brings me a box for half my pizza. On the bill, the Mudshark girl has signed her name and added: "Have a wonderful adventure!"

Near sunset, I cross the Bill Williams River at its confluence with Colorado and pull off the highway where Parker Dam backs up both rivers into Lake Havasu. This is the place where Arizona's historic navy first set sail in a classic tale of the ridiculous.

In 1934, Parker Dam began its plug of the Colorado River. The concrete arch-gravity construction rose in the shadow of the mighty Hoover Dam, which at the time was well on its way to becoming the largest dam in the world. Not to be outdone by its big brother 155 miles upstream, Parker Dam would become the deepest dam in the world. Three quarters of its height is buried out of sight below the riverbed.

The dam, however, was deeply troubling for Arizona. Its purpose was to divert Colorado River water into an aqueduct for the lawns, fountains, and swimming-pool culture of Los Angeles. As construction moved to *our* side of the river, Governor Benjamin Mouer, a grumpy-looking, stogie-smoking cue ball of a man, declared martial law and sent out the National Guard to put a stop to it. Arizona would not be some backwater to California. The guard commandeered a fleet of boats, wooden steamers owned by state representative Nellie T. Bush for her ferry business. Governor Mouer subsequently proclaimed her the admiral of the Arizona Navy and commissioned her great armada of two ships to patrol the river and "repel an invasion." Unfortunately, our first navy ran afoul of some cables and had to be rescued by the Californians. The affair ended with a Supreme Court injunction and the governor recalling his "machine gunners and infantrymen." Besides our bruised pride, the only casualty was one guardsman who died of pneumonia.

A dark, narrow trail takes me out on the long lizard tongue of the Central Arizona Project (CAP) peninsula and I find a seat at the terminal bench. The moon rides on my left shoulder. A last hint of sun backlights the rugged Buckskin Mountains. The warm air and a belly full of Mudshark pizza and beer, the black water of Lake Havasu lying flat before me—it's a perfectly sublime ending to this week's adventure.

Lights from the Mark Wilmer Pumping Plant throw parallel streaks on the still water. The mighty headwaters of the CAP. In Arizona, we talk about rivers that run upside down. This one runs uphill. Beneath the mountainside, the Colorado River is forced to the top of Buckskin Mountain, where a tunnel seven miles long carries it through solid basalt to a concrete-lined canal. More tunnels, pumping plants, inverted siphons, and 174 miles of canal deliver the river to Phoenix, 1,200 feet above its source. Ten more pumping plants and 140 miles of canals and pipelines raise it another 1,200 feet for the spigots of Tucson. Nature undone. Gravity overcome by coal.

The CAP is an epic story that winds through vast desert plots before climaxing in its urbanity and going down the drain in utter exhaustion at its conclusion. Some might call it a masterpiece of Homeric proportion. The Iliad and Odyssey of the Grand Canyon State. I say it is a fantasy of overallocated imaginations. There are many stories to tell about a place, and each one has its own truth. But as Homer writes, "There is a time for many words, and there is also a time for sleep."

3:10 to Yuma by Kayak

THE YUMA TERRITORIAL PRISON

ELEVATION: 138 FEET | FOUNDED: 1873 | POPULATION: 95,429

I drop my bedroll among the tules and mosquitoes of Mittry Lake near the Colorado River a dozen miles north of Yuma. So far, the deet has the bloodsuckers confused. So far. A full moon pulls away from the eastern rim of the world like molten wax in a lava lamp. The voices of loons mingle with the yodeling of song dogs. I'm concerned about the mysterious punctuations of routine splashes. Perhaps my sleeping bag is too close to the lake.

Dinner is cold bean burros, hunks of cheese, and coconut rum—all of which settles nicely into a belly full of "world famous" date shake. Yes, the fabulous Medjool date: rescued from extinction in Morocco and grown in Arizona for the blender and lactose tolerant. Don't bother with the straw. I can't resist Dateland.

The rum isn't Desert Diamond Distillery's agave rum, but it will do. It comes courtesy of Jerry, my compadre of ghost towns and graveyards and other places of ruin and the paranormal. Jerry would say "normal," not "paranormal." He deals with it every day.

"Had a psychotic patient last week," he says, his glasses aflame from the light of our campfire. "I was explaining about the voices, how they're not hallucinations but parasitic entities, when he suddenly turned beet red in front of me. I asked him what was going on and he said, 'You are protected. You have a yellow-white energy field around you.' I asked him if he could see the light and he said he could. This isn't the first time a patient told me I was protected from these entities. Sometimes I feel like this is all some strange science-fiction movie."

"You do have an aura about you," I say. "But it's probably only the rum."

Jerry not only took off work but volunteered his kayak for this adventure. And his truck, to which we lashed his kayak and loaded up with gear. For the first time in forty-eight weeks and twenty thousand miles, the Kia Rio gets a break. The plan for this, the fifth week in November: 1) Drive to Yuma County, my third "corner" and the last of the state's fifteen counties to visit this year. 2) Kayak the Colorado River between Arizona and California downstream to its confluence with the Gila River. 3) Explore the Yuma Territorial Prison.

That's the plan anyway. In the morning darkness, our camp is dewy and cool. Having fully crossed the carapace of night, an orb of moon hangs motionless in the bluing western sky. Clacks, squeals, and grunts from the sedges and rushes sound my wakeup. I smell green, the kind that floats to the surface on the buoyancy of decay.

We put in below Imperial Dam after locating a side channel of swift water that should thread us through a canvas of vegetation. "I have a bad feeling about this," Jerry says, paddling furiously from the bow to avoid getting us hung up in the branches. But soon, the irrigation canal dumps us into the broad sweep of the Colorado and we're on our way—entirely in California, according to my map. For the next few hours, we will weave in and out of Arizona on a river that obeys no boundary lines, although supremely controlled. Here, the Colorado—more imprisoned and dredged waterway than free-flowing river—no longer escapes its banks to spread across its former floodplain twenty feet above us.

A belted kingfisher rattles from the tamarisk. "No bow fishing," I say to the crested, spear-headed bird, recalling the posted sign we passed earlier. "Or you will be *vigorously* prosecuted." We paddle, replenish sunscreen, and watch the shore birds—all at the river's pace. There's no urgency, except among mosquitoes. Snowy egrets stand motionless in the shallows, intent on the flash of fish scales. Gulls drift on the water in rafts, intent on nothing. A squadron of cormorants flies toward us, their wing tips held in place only inches from the dark surface.

"Ground effect," Jerry says, explaining that the birds can glide for great distances with just the air pressure created between their wings and the water's surface.

"The effort of outstretched primaries," I say. "Pelicans are masters at powerless flight."

"Arizona has the best sailplaning in the world," says the sixty-two-year-old glider pilot. "Updrafts feel like a fast elevator. In twenty minutes, I can be five thousand feet above the desert floor."

In late afternoon, we draw out the kayak and find a campsite beside the river. While I collect scrappy wood for our fire, Jerry peels a mess of onions we gleaned from a farmer's field during the day. I think about Grubstake Darren and his fish and chips. Last week, on my return from Lake Havasu City, I learned that the Brit had left Quartzsite for Yuma to open his own restaurant. We're having pasta for dinner, with jalapeños and fresh roasted onion bulbs. And more rum. It wouldn't be a waterborne adventure without the rum.

After dinner, we stare wordlessly into the fire, the last of the rum soaking into our aching muscles. "Why is the rum always gone?" I ask Jerry, breaking the silence with my rhetorical question. A thickening vapor trail zigzags across the dark, as if a bright sailing skiff were leaving a wake in the sky. My skin is wet. Another dewfall. Birds sound off on the river. The quintessential sound of Yuma, I decide, is the squeaky-sneaker call of the American coot—the water bird, not the old white guy.

At midmorning the next day, we arrive at the Yuma Territorial Prison State Historic Park. My ninth and last state park—Arizona has thirty—for the year. Jerry, who knows the worst about prisons, wants to first visit the cemetery. A sign cautions us: *Dangerous insects and reptiles inhabit the area.* I think: *What an awful thing to say about a bunch of dead felons!* The graves are unmarked. A bronze memorial lists 104 "unfortunate souls" who "met their death" by "disease, accident, murder, suicide, and escape attempts." *Escape attempts?* I recall that even today when a prisoner dies in lockup, his final papers state a perfect irony: *Released to death.*

At the main entrance, a school group lines up for a tour. "That's right," I tell Jerry. "Teach them young about their future lives in the joint. By high school, everyone will call them criminals." I'm closer to the truth than I realize. Louie, the shift supervisor, tells us if we don't buy something in the gift shop, he'll have to lock us up. Prison humor. The place must be rife with it. From the guard tower, stationed above an eighty-five-thousand-gallon granite-walled water tank, I see the bend in the Colorado River where it once joined the Gila River before coursing past the prison.

An old photo shows the prison looking like Alcatraz on its rocky island surrounded by high water. Malaria and yellow fever should be added to the list of outbreaks of typhus, smallpox, scarlet fever, and rattlesnake bites.

The granite stone, quarried on site during construction in 1875, makes up much of the prison, including the cellblocks with their strap-iron doors and bunk beds. Prisoners also made adobe bricks from the earth beneath their feet, raising an eighteen-foot-high, eight-foot-thick perimeter wall that replaced an earlier wooden fence. Stone-cold cells held over three thousand men and twenty-nine women during the prison's thirty-three-year lifespan. What kind of hopelessness—or work ethic—drives a man to construct his own cage?

The place was where the good people of Arizona Territory kept its worst offenders: murderers and thieves, adulterers and polygamists. One man was sent here for the crime of "seduction under the promise of marriage." His victim must have been a judge's daughter. The prison even had its own prison within a prison. For gambling or littering, refusing to bathe or foul language, you could get the ball and chain, or worse. You might get bread and water in your underwear inside an iron cage in a cave carved out of the hillside. The "dark cell." Jerry seems disturbed by it. He looks like he's hearing voices rising out of the four rough caliche walls. "It feels like the holding cell I visited next to the Florence prison death chamber," he says.

The "Country Club on the Colorado," people in Yuma called it, resenting the pleasantries such as electricity, forced ventilation, running water, and books. In 1896, the *Arizona Sentinel* wrote: "One can go any day to the prison and see convicts singing and skylarking, joking, and all-in-all having a grand old time at the expense of the taxpayer. It is well known here that the prison on the hill is more a place of recreation and amusement than servitude."

"If you like it so much," says a recorded voice in the museum, "go on up! Everybody's welcome!" The museum features famous criminals like the jury-flirting, stagecoach-robbing wannabe-actress Pearl Hart, her Colt .45 on display. So is a photo of fifteen-year-old J. Hammal, who got one year for burglary. And Buckskin Frank Leslie, killer of Billy Claiborne of the Clanton gang. Buckskin Frank reputedly murdered Johnny Ringo as well. A guard's record book from 1906–8 shows two pages of notations— inmate names, numbers, crimes, places of origin. More than half of the entries are from my own Cochise County.

And then I see the photo of a beautiful young woman with dark eyes and an oval face surrounded by wavy brunette locks. A gold class ring rests beside her picture. *Class of 1930*, it reads. What? The woman, I learn, was not your ordinary kind of criminal. Born Valentine Arizona Cooper on February 14, 1912, "Zona" came into the world on the day our state came into the Union. Except for a short stint in San Diego, she lived an entire life sentence in Arizona until her death at ninety-one. Now her picture graces the prison museum.

It turns out that after the territorial prison closed in 1909, the new Yuma Union High School, needing facilities, moved into the vacant buildings. From 1910 to 1914, teachers taught classes in the cellblocks. Students held assemblies in the prison hospital. When the Yuma football team beat the Phoenix Coyotes on their home turf, the sore losers dubbed the Yuma players "criminals." Students and teachers wore the name with pride, and soon the school board adopted the mascot. From that time forward, Yuma High School has been the home of the Criminals. Zona Cooper graduated from Yuma in 1930. The first child born in the state of Arizona was a Yuma High Criminal.

This is something unexpected. Serendipity. But the year has been full of such experiences, which I owe to simply being present and observant. It fits the rules I've learned to accept in my travels: 1) I am in the right place at the right time. 2) Everything is a gift. 3) I haven't earned it nor do I deserve it. These rules govern not just my travels but also my life. From locating the state anthem in Douglas to running into a Dutchman hunter at the Superstitions. To finding the state amphibian in a roadside mountain ditch to running over the state reptile in the road. Some might call this dumb luck. What's certain is that none of it would have come to me without leaving the house. Well, except maybe the butterfly . . . and the ringtail.

On our way out of Yuma, Jerry's Magellan GPS speaks to us in a woman's voice. "You should have turned back there," the wife in my head says. Jerry pays it no attention. He drives in complete comfort. I scratch mosquito bites. It must be true. Apparently, some people are tastier to mosquitoes than others. Scientists claim that everything from our metabolism to our blood type (type O twice as much as type A), body temperature, and sweat, can signal the insects to feed. They can smell your breath from more than a hundred feet away. They're particularly fond of the ethanol you excrete while drinking. They know if you're pregnant.

When I arrive home, Karen will count 121 angry red welts across my torso. It must be the rum, because I'm pretty sure I'm not pregnant.

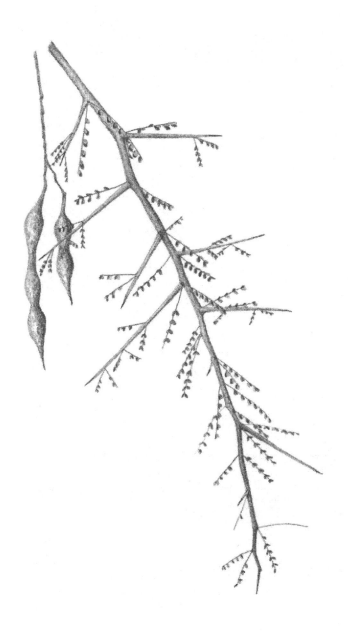

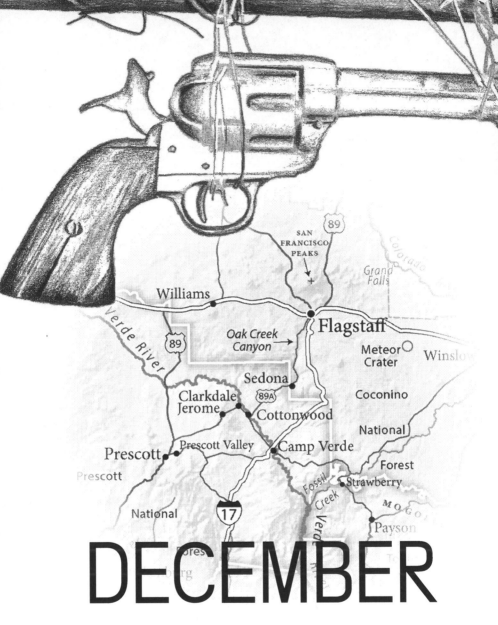

DECEMBER

Colt .45 Single Action Army Revolver

POINTS OF INTEREST TO DATE: 187 | TOTAL MILES: 20,693

Mockingbird Blues

SLAUGHTER RANCH AND THE SAN BERNARDINO NATIONAL WILDLIFE REFUGE

ELEVATION: 3,720 FEET | FOUNDED: 1884 | POPULATION: 2

In the first week of December, I drive to the historic Slaughter Ranch, fifteen miles east of Douglas along the Geronimo Trail. Just beyond the "Great White Slaughter Gate" with its *Z* brand, a small yellow sign at the right of the dirt drive says, *Wolf Crossing.*

I've come to this far southeastern corner of Arizona, my last corner of the state, with my friend, Tom Leskiw, a retired hydrologic technician and writer who, with his wife Sue, migrates from northern California to southern Arizona every winter. "You're doing an Arizona Big Year," Tom had said about my book project last January in the Dragoon Mountains. Tom has recently seen his seven hundredth bird species, an amazing feat when you consider he has only been birding for thirty years and has never been to Alaska. Now, my own version of a Big Year is almost complete. One month to go. Four destinations. One more state symbol.

Tom came for the birds. I'm here for the Colt, and maybe some connection to an Arizona legend, the gunslinger-turned-sheriff of Cochise County, the man Geronimo called "that wicked little gringo." The short, rock-solid ex–Confederate soldier, ex–Texas Ranger turned the Tombstone jail (and probably the Yuma prison as well) into "Hotel de Slaughter." At least for those he didn't put in a grave. John Slaughter favored the Winchester lever-action repeater and a 12-gauge shotgun as a lawman, but he always had his pearl-handled Colt .45 within reach. I carry a picture of him in his latter years, astride his horse, cigar in mouth, trademark obsidian-black eyes penetrating the camera lens. His engraved revolver is tucked into the pommel holster.

A weather-beaten barn. The sweet tang of cow dung in sunny heaps. We're the only visitors, but within minutes we meet Bob Krueger, the goatee-sporting caretaker. He's missing most of his teeth but still energetically launches into the history of the ranch.

"At this point, you're only six hundred feet from the borderline with Mexico," he says, telling us that the San Bernardino Ranch originally spanned both sides of the border as part of large Mexican land grant Slaughter had purchased from the heirs of Ignacio Perez in 1884. "Slaughter was there at the surrender of Geronimo. He started a cattle empire to supply meat to the border community. Today, we only have ten Texas longhorns, owned by the Johnson Foundation."

Floyd Johnson, Krueger explains, loved the Old West and had a dream of holding on to part of it. With the help of a close friend, Harvey Finks, he established the foundation to preserve rural ranches, stage stations, and homesteads. Like so many other ranches in the Southwest, the San Bernardino had fallen into disrepair. After John Slaughter's death in 1922, his wife Viola began breaking up and selling the land. In 1937, Marion Williams bought the U.S. portion, which the Nature Conservancy acquired in 1978. Five years later, the Conservancy deeded the eastern rangelands to the government and formed the San Bernardino National Wildlife Refuge. The western lands and the original homestead came to the Johnson Foundation, its first acquisition. The foundation created the Slaughter Ranch Museum, a national historic landmark and the eleventh such site in Arizona I've visited this year.

"Floyd Johnson never lived to see the place," Krueger says. "The homestead is now the only one remaining of Arizona's great nineteenth-century cattle ranches."

Before Krueger releases us to take the self-guided tour, I ask him about the *Wolf Crossing* sign we passed.

"I saw it cross the road when I went down to unlock the gate one morning."

"Mexican gray wolf? Which way was it headed?"

"North."

Tom and I walk down to the famous hackberry thicket, where a few years ago, a local bird watcher and guide named Richard Webster spotted a blue mockingbird—only the third one seen in Arizona, fifth in the United States. "We had three thousand visitors for the three months it was here," Krueger had told us. "Cars were lined up at the gate in the morning. Parking was crazy. People were throwing money at me, not waiting for change. We don't get many visitors these days."

We don't see any mockingbirds, only a single curve-billed thrasher watching us from the bare thorns with one yellow eye. Too common. If not the mockingbird, the place needs a rufous-backed robin or a Sinaloa wren. We continue hiking east, out into the San Bernardino National Wildlife Refuge and across a mesquite-tedious land, stopping to examine ponds choked with triangular-stemmed sedges, coots, and marsh wrens. Cottonwoods still cling to their yellow crowns, even this late in the year.

Then we stumble upon low mounds of stones among twisted mesquite. The Slaughter Ranch cemetery. All trails, it seems, lead to the dead. How many graves and graveyards have I encountered this year? At least nine. Not a single one in a churchyard but all tucked away into some empty, out-of-the-way backlot. Exploring Arizona means walking over buried lives. When the wind stirs, we eat the dead.

The thirty-two graves are unnamed, the few markers holding coils of rusted bailing wire or transoms slipping askew. Bob Krueger had said that a ranch foreman, three outlaws (someone named Childers, "Peg Leg" Finney, and Three-Fingered Jack), and twelve children are buried here. One of the mounds belongs to Apache May, the Slaughters' adopted four-year-old daughter who died tragically in 1900 after her dress caught fire.

I scan the distant ranges of New Mexico, the border to the south, the trucks crawling along Mexican Highway 2. A breeze carries the song of cottonwoods. This is a place where I, too, could leave my weight on the world.

Back at the ranch near the house pond, we locate the day's best bird: an eastern phoebe, a rare transient in winter. The sallow-breasted bird drifts like a leaf among the cottonwoods on the trail of airborne insects. I've seen the species only once before in my life.

John Slaughter created the pond in the 1890s, constructing an earthen and masonry dam to impound several artesian springs for the irrigation of his crops on both sides of the border. Today, the pond is home to endangered fish like the Yaqui topminnow, Yaqui chub, and Yaqui catfish, which the U.S. Fish and Wildlife Service is monitoring here. These three rare native fish come only as far north out of Mexico as this southeastern corner of Cochise County; the chub, in fact, is restricted to just a few places in the county and is known in Mexico only in San Bernardino Creek immediately south of us. It was in this creek, whose headwaters flow right through the ranch property, that the Yaqui catfish was first identified in 1896. About two hundred of the blue-gray Fu Manchu fish patrol the muddy depths of the pond.

"He must have really loved his wife Viola," Karen said to me earlier this year when we first visited Slaughter Ranch. "He built all this for her." She was eighteen; he was thirty-seven and recently widowed with two small children. We walked over the hardwood floors in the house, looking into each room, pausing to wonder at the Navajo rugs, the English Flow blue china, the embroidered pillow slips and bedspread, the 1895 Mason & Hamlin reed organ and wind-up Victrola. Hanging on the wall in the hallway, an old crank magneto telephone, the first in the territory, connected Sheriff John Slaughter to his office in Tombstone, the phone lines laid directly on the ground over the seventy-mile distance. Magazine articles and photographs along the walls depicted stories of family, John and Viola in various stages of life, son William, daughter Addie, their black servant "Old Bat" (John Baptiste), and their child, Apache May. These people were so full of life and had such an important impact on a young Arizona. And this is what we remember about them, printed on the pages of half a dozen *Arizona Highways* magazines.

Today, the house is empty and cold. The wind blows through its doorjambs in a rising and falling monotone. We've seen only two other visitors all morning at this monument to a bygone time. Now, even the caretakers of that time are leaving. If we so preserve the past that we can't live on it, how will we create it? We should celebrate it, not conserve it. The past isn't supposed to last. Most places exist on the former layers of themselves. As Faulkner famously said: "The past is never dead. It's not even past."

If the ranch closes to visitors, there may never be another rare bird sighting here. "I have seven hundred stories and more," Tom says about his years of bird watching. "All tangible, memorable, genuine. No tepid, pixilated, ersatz excuses for real encounters in real places. If the legions of those mesmerized by Wii and Xboxes only knew." They do, to some degree. They just choose the indoors over the outdoors. A virtual world over one with bone dust in your teeth.

On our drive out, I watch the margins of the road for northbound Mexican gray wolves. Northbound mockingbirds, too. For it's a future of blue mockingbirds, I realize, immigrants from Mexico, that could help save this place.

The Natural Habitat of Rattlers and Revolvers

RATTLESNAKE CRAFTS

ELEVATION: 4,924 FEET | FOUNDED: 1979 | POPULATION: 2

It was my psychologist friend Jerry who first told me about the rattlesnake gift shop. He found it while riding his motorcycle across the high desert at the southern reach of the Dragoon Mountains. This is how he spends his weekends, exploring Arizona's backcountry, and he's always sending me stories and pictures of his travels to some old abandoned hole in the ground.

"You won't believe the place," he told me. "It's in the middle of nowhere—thousands of rusting pieces of cool junk on display for those who wander by. I saw guns, too. Bet you'll find your Colt there."

After arriving at Tombstone and then following ten miles of dirt road, my route narrows and winds through a rangeland of spidery mesquite trees. Somewhere, I miss a turn and end up at the Gleeson Jail. Right in the center of town—or ghost town, one of several on the Ghost Town Trail. Some towns build churches at their centers. Not Gleeson. This four-walled sanctuary is now a museum, a labor of love of locals Tina Miller and John Wiest, who bought the property and the surrounding acreage. Tina collected period antiques to furnish the jail, and now on the first Saturday of the month, visitors can try on a pair of belly shackles or drag a ball and chain from their sleeping cot to warm themselves by the woodburning stove. Lovely.

Gleeson is named for John Gleeson, an Irish prospector who found large copper deposits here and opened the Copper Belle Mine in 1900. At its peak, the mine supported a community of five hundred people, and although the Irishman sold out in 1914, his mines continued to produce through World War I. Today, one restored miner's cabin shows a new coat of paint in lively colors of yellow and red under the usual corrugated tin roof. If Tombstone is "The Town Too Tough to Die," then Gleeson is "The Town Dying to Be Tough."

The sun angles into the distant Whetstone Mountains as I pull into John and Sandy Weber's Rattlesnake Crafts and Rocks, three miles from Gleeson. Wood and metal trinkets clink and clang in the cool December wind. Sandy greets me out front of a vintage trailer/gift shop, but she's on a mission. "Have a look around," she says with a smile. "What's in the trailer is for sale, the rest is not." Then she disappears into the desert.

Too cold for rattlesnake hunting, I think, picturing her posing with her husband, the flattened skin of a six-foot diamondback rattlesnake stretched between them. Soon John appears, wearing his trademark Stetson and full white beard. "How's the rattlesnake hunting?" I ask.

"Well, we've scaled it back a bit. Game and Fish has reduced the limit from four per day to four per year."

We talk about my own experiences looking for ridge-nosed rattlesnakes earlier this year, how a pair of Texans taught me about wildlife permits and regulations. "My wildlife biologist daughter reminds me that killing rattlesnakes without a permit is illegal. Most people don't know you can't shoot them or take a shovel to them even if the snake is in your carport or coiled on your front porch."

"We just turn them into lots of weird stuff," John says.

This is what John and Sandy have done for more than thirty years. In 1979, the couple left jobs and homes in Illinois to become rattlesnake hunters in Arizona. On summer evenings, when the air cools after a monsoon thunderstorm and the moon offers enough light to see by, the two search among the tarbush and creosote, probing their snake sticks under rocks and into tortoise holes. Until recently, on an average day, they might catch one rattler every nine and half hours. They turn every part—skin, bones, rattles, and fangs—into handmade hatbands, belts, wallets, knives, and the tastiest rattlesnake jerky you can pick from between your teeth.

John says he's still having fun, but he and Sandy are "getting pretty long in the tooth to be hunting rattlers." The truth is, in a few months, all of this will be gone. The end of an era for a couple who came to the desert to literally scratch a living out of it.

After he leaves, I look over their trailer-load of crafts, hoping to find Christmas gifts for my daughters and their husbands. *All wildlife in Arizona is protected*, I think, smiling at a story Jessica had told me recently. Except for birds, tree squirrels, and maybe rabbits, you can't intentionally feed wild animals either. My daughter had said that a woman sued Arizona Game and Fish after a coyote ate her poodle. The woman argued that the department should be held responsible for controlling its wildlife. Almost sounds reasonable. "They considered countering her lawsuit by fining her $1,500," Jessica said. "For illegally feeding wildlife!"

For the boys, I select a whiskey flask, key ring, and grooming kit—all wrapped in diamondback skins. For Jessica: rattlesnake rattle earrings. Melissa: turquoise earrings. Kasondra gets earrings, too—dangling shellacked globes of jackrabbit poop.

I drop the cash into the box provided, but I'm not here only for the shopping. I still need one last official symbol of Arizona. I hunt among the multitudes of weathered and weathering artifacts, primitive and western antiques, many of which the Webers have found around Gleeson and Tombstone. If a picture is worth a thousand words, a picture of this place, this so-called outdoor museum, is worth a whole new language. Spread out over an acre of hardpan, rows of sun-bleached tables and wooden racks warp under the weight of wired-in-place treasure: glass bottles of every hue and shape, cook pots and pans and cast-iron stoves, bone-white antlers and skulls and rust-red animal sculptures, arrays of farm tools and milking stools, powder horns and French horns and army bugles, wheelbarrows and metal armadillos, trombones, telephones, and pumice stones, mauls, awls, and whipsaws. . . . I try to write down the names of things in my notes, and I begin feeling like I'm lost in a Dr. Seuss land of Jing Tinglers, Flu Floopers, Tar Tinkers, and Who Hoovers, Gar Ginkers, Trum Tupers, Slu Slumkers, Blum Bloopers. The place overwhelms the senses, defies categorization. Is this a museum or junkyard? Or a graveyard of the unwanted and obsolete?

On the far side of one of the high fence racks, a grouping of tarnished firearms swings from twisted strands of baling wire. I recognize a German

Mauser pistol and what looks like a Winchester rifle, its stock like a piece of firewood. Other handguns I don't recognize. Then, backlit by a swollen red sun, a cocked revolver. The Peacemaker. Finally. And in its natural habitat. I pull the silver .45 bullet from my pocket where it's been all year, lift the weapon in its wire hammock, and stop. I won't chamber the cartridge. I let the .45 swing. Somehow this Arizona symbol seems more fitting not as a firearm but as an artifact. As an art form.

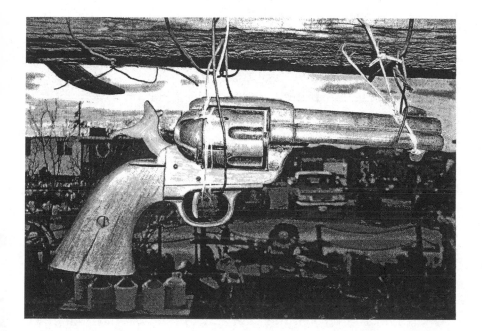

Arizona's Christmas City

PRESCOTT

ELEVATION: 5,368 FEET | FOUNDED: 1864 | POPULATION: 39,843

"Did I tell you I once saw Bigfoot?" Darrel says when a coyote plows through the snowdrifts in front of the sleigh. Darrel is our wrangler and cowboy poet who, with the assistance of dark-haired Lauren and a pair of nags, hosts our snowy adventure in the darkening pines of northern Arizona.

"The Mogollon Monster!" I say from out of the horse blankets wrapped around Karen and me. Melissa and her husband ride on the seat in front of us, both dressed in boots, woolen gloves, and knit caps. Although Iowa has yet to see snowfall, they've come prepared.

"I was under my horse, and I saw him staring off into the woods. When I got up, I looked in the direction the horse was looking and I saw him. Bigfoot! Eight feet tall and watching me from the trees. When he saw me looking at him, he turned around and went back into the woods. I found his tracks, but I wasn't going to follow him."

I tell Darrel about Bigfoot sightings recently in the White Mountains near Hon Dah, and he starts listing Bigfoot facts he's researched since his sighting. "I'm a believer!" he says.

And so begins the Christmas gathering of our daughters and their husbands at Little America in Flagstaff. The second snowiest city in the lower forty-eight states has proven itself true to form. Kasondra and her husband, coming in from Albuquerque, are also snowless. Our plan is to meet here among the hundred pines aglow with a million festive lights, each trunk, limb, branch, stem, twig, and needle bundle coiled with LEDs. We'll spend a couple days eating cherry pie and drinking Irish coffee in downtown Flag, then head to Prescott, "Arizona's Christmas City." By Christmas Eve, the eight of us will arrive at Bisbee.

Along with its Yuletide designation, Prescott also calls itself, "The Mile-High City." So, not to be outdone by this upstart of a town, Bisbee calls itself the "Southernmost Mile-High City." And then there's Flagstaff, officially the "Mile-and-a-Quarter-High City." Alpine should get in on this. At 8,050 feet, it could proclaim itself, "Arizona's Mile-and-Two-Thirds-High Unincorporated Community."

After days of sleigh rides, stargazing at Lowell Observatory, and corn chowder at Heritage Square, we drive through Oak Creek as shadows lengthen into canyons and snow begins to fall once again. Then Sedona, Cottonwood, Jerome, and over Mingus Mountain to downtown Prescott and the Prescott Brewing Company. (The route allows me to avoid the "living opportunity" of Prescott Valley, where Walmart eats Mayberry.) Across the street, beyond the life-size model of Santa and his sleigh, the Courthouse Plaza blazes with the lights of a hundred Christmas elms.

The kids order a "fajita fondue," an eruption of jalapeño cheese dip with diced tomatoes and green onions, spilling from the uncapped dome of a boule surrounded with tortilla chips. They should call it "heart-attack fondue." But I'm here for the brew, not the fondue. I consider a Black Sheep Ale, which our server insists "contains no sheep products," but can't pass up on the Ponderosa IPA. I sip it with dessert first: a peach bread pudding topped with Southern Comfort. Bread pudding and Christmas cheer. More than the lights and parades, the carolers and holiday performances, maybe this is the reason former Governor Rose Mofford proclaimed Prescott "Arizona's Christmas City."

In the morning, snow dusts the boulders of the Granite Dells. Someone has shaken powdered sugar over the crumpled Precambrian landscape as we slept. A rising sun ignites the far escarpments as our host, Gary Edelbrock, serves the family German pancakes. I sit with Alex, the golden retriever "who doesn't do any work," according to Gary. "All lies!" Alex tells me with his eyes. Among beamed ceilings and red-oak floors, I read about "Everybody's Hometown" in front of a fireplace of river stone. Prescott's picturesque landscape, "salubrious" climate, and cowboy-and-Indian lore have created one of the "most desirable and livable communities in the country," according to a publication by Frederic B. Wildfang and Sharlot Hall Museum Archives. *Salubrious? When was the last time I'd seen that word in a sentence?* "The outhouse will do me nicely," I recall from James Joyce. "It will be more salubrious."

Then I see a note related to Christmas. During the holiday, Prescott is home to the largest gingerbread village in the world. My POI proximity alert goes off. I imagine walking through a gum-dropped, sugar-frosted house like Hansel and Gretel.

After breakfast, the kids don their elf and reindeer hats and pile into cars. We sing "The Twelve Days of Christmas" along with the a cappella group Straight No Chaser on the CD player. The gingerbread village is at the Prescott Resort and Conference Center, part of the Yavapai-Prescott Indian Tribe. I can now count six Arizona tribes I've visited this year, more than a quarter of the twenty-two reservations that cover a quarter of the state's landmass. The village is walk-through, but in miniature. There will be no eating of sweets, no witches tossed into ovens. Under snowy mountain peaks, where the air is as fresh as candy cane, a train moves among a hundred gingerbread houses, from mansions and castles to cake-decorated huts and hovels. My teeth ache at the sight of it.

The girls' favorite hails from Girl Scout Troop 2532: little gingerbread tents set up in a green field of sugar, with a circle of gingerbread "girls" toasting miniature marshmallows over a blazing fire of candy corn.

Later, while the kids window shop in downtown Prescott, Karen and I walk the icy streets to the Sharlot Hall Museum. This one is on my list. Outside the museum stands the oldest log cabin in Arizona, built in 1864 and moved a half mile to this spot in 1934. Fort Misery. "Probably named by the poor souls who lived in it," I tell Karen.

Inside the museum, we stare at Sharlot's dress. This woman *was* Arizona. The thing—more chain mail than garment—weighs eight pounds. "It's made of copper links," says Jan Berrett, a museum docent. "Sharlot wore it to Washington in 1925 to cast Arizona's three electoral votes for Calvin Coolidge." The dress comes with a matching hat made from the meshlike skeleton of prickly pear cactus pads.

Last February, I stumbled upon a reception at the University of Arizona Poetry Center called "Sharlot Hall and Hattie Lockett: An Arizona Centennial Exhibition." Organized by Wendy Burk, the library supervisor, it was a celebration of the lives of two Arizona pioneers. The center was crowded with patrons and visitors. A cellist played classical tunes. Refreshments spread across a linen tablecloth. The Lockett family gathered with people around display cases of photos, journals, and original manuscripts of the two writers, both important voices at the time of statehood.

I'd never heard of Sharlot Hall and Hattie Lockett. I learned that they came to the territory in 1882 and 1897, respectively, Sharlot to Lynx Creek near Prescott, where her family built a homestead, raised horses, and mined gold. Hattie lived in Scottsdale, where she taught school at the age of seventeen. She later served as president of the Arizona branch of the League of American Pen Women and inaugurated Arizona Poetry Day in honor of Sharlot Hall. Sharlot, while honing her craft in prose and poetry, was appointed territorial historian in 1909, becoming the first woman to hold public office in Arizona Territory.

Some credit Sharlot Hall with the very shape of the Arizona. The story goes that she was so incensed with Congress considering admitting Arizona and New Mexico territories as one state that she ridiculed the lawmakers in poetry.

"No beggar she in the mighty hall where her bay-crowned sisters wait," begins Sharlot Hall's poem, "Arizona."

> No empty-handed pleader for the right of a free-born state;
> No child, with a child's insistence, demanding a gilded toy,
> But a fair-browed, queenly woman, strong to create or destroy.

"Arizona" has eight stanzas with eight lines each. Some congressmen, each of whom received the epic poem, probably went to sleep as it was read into the record. With lines like, "Ay! Let her go bareheaded; bound by no grudging gift / back to her own free spaces where her rock-ribbed mountains lift," I wonder if Sharlot was speaking more about herself than Arizona. But the poem may have quelled a movement. Imagine. One woman's heartfelt words prevented the formation of the great state of New Mexizona.

"Although the world has changed in the past hundred years," said Wendy Burk, addressing the Poetry Center crowd, "there is no reason that we cannot emulate Sharlot Hall and Hattie Lockett's belief in the power of words, in the power of poetry, to change individual and collective lives."

Prescott. The first permanent capital of the territory. Where Mayberry meets *Little House on the Prairie*. (Yes, deer and pronghorn antelope play here.) Arizona's Christmas City. Prescott's greatest gift to the state, however, was Sharlot Hall.

Blitzkrieg on the Border

NACO

ELEVATION: 4,610 FEET | FOUNDED: 1902 | POPULATION: 1,046

The last week of December. My fifty-second and final destination for the year. Karen and I drive eleven miles south from Bisbee to the twin border towns of Naco. I park across from the Gay 90's Bar, and we are immediately greeted by a man named Jesus Valencia.

"What's the best thing about living in Naco?" I ask.

"The peace and quiet," he answers immediately. Jesus hands me his card. He does brickwork, flagstone, drywall, stucco, roof repair, "and much more."

Peace and quiet, I think. *Sure, these days.* During Prohibition, these sleepy villages could wake the dead as people from Bisbee and Fort Huachuca poured across the border to satisfy their many thirsts, transforming Naco, Sonora, into what historian Marshall Trimble describes as "a bibulous Babylon, its bistros lighting up like Christmas trees beckoning pleasure seekers much the same way as the Sirens tempted Ulysses and his men." Sounds like a border patrol bivouac to me.

And if the drunken revelry of Americans wasn't enough, there were the skirmishes between *federales* and revolutionaries like Pancho Villa. Naco, Arizona, in fact, has the dubious distinction of being the only town in the continental United States to be bombed by a foreign power. The so-called Naco blitzkrieg happened in 1929 during the Escobar or Topete Rebellion, a religious/political revolt against the Mexican government, which had outlawed the Catholic Church. *Cristero* rebels had surrounded the garrison of *federales* at Naco, forcing them up against the U.S.–Mexico border. An Irish barnstormer and mercenary named Patrick Murphy (the rebel air force) agreed to blow the federal troops from their trenches using suitcases loaded with dynamite, nails, and bolts. The problem was that Murphy enjoyed spending his nights in Bisbee's Brewery Gulch. On four occasions, Murphy flew his biplane over the wrong Naco, tossing his bombs through the roofs of a pharmacy, a Western Union, a Phelps-Dodge mercantile, and a garage, blowing automobiles and canned goods from their trenches.

I've seen a photograph of the mangled Dodge touring car, which belonged to a Mexican officer who drove it to the American side to keep it safe. It was probably this last bombing run, which also injured an automobile mechanic, that forced Fort Huachuca to dispatch eighteen U.S. Army planes to deal with Murphy. One story says that, in the end, the Irishman was arrested but no charges were filed, and he was "subsequently released and disappeared into obscurity." But I like the version that says the air raids ended when *federales*, Indiana Jones–style with Springfield rifles, summarily shot Murphy from the sky.

The garage still stands, its front bay doors bricked in. Directly next to it is Rogers' Border Service. Ernie Rogers has lived in Naco since 1952. Now in his seventies, he still occasionally repairs autos in his shop. Karen and I peek inside the now-abandoned mining store through a door standing ajar from a busted padlock. The roof looks solid to me. Around the corner, along the side facing the customs house and Mexico, we walk past boarded-up windows and doors. In places where the beige stucco has slipped away from the wall beneath it, I find several perfectly circular chips the size of silver dollars in the redbrick. They look like impacts. Bullet impacts.

Karen and I cross the border to buy tortillas from our favorite *tortilleria* and visit with our favorite Naco, Sonora, resident, Augustine. When we return, we step inside the Gay 90's Bar, and a man wearing a Desert Storm Veteran cap whom I've never met before buys me a beer. His name is Jaime Valenzuela, and he's full of stories.

"I met Black Jack Pershing's great-great-granddaughter," he says as our bartender, Teri Tumbleweed, spreads out old black-and-white photos of the U.S. Army general, along with others of Pancho Villa, General Bliss "on the Mexican border," and a rapid-fire one-pound cannon called "Panchito."

"What about the photos of Ronald Reagan?" I ask, referring to the framed pictures on the walls of the president with Leonel, the owner of Gay 90's.

"He was going hunting on a ranch in Mexico. My brother Jorge found out that he was coming through the border here. Jorge and Leonel got the Reagans out of their car as they were waiting to cross! They walked right up, and they got right out!"

Just then, Leonel Urcadez walks in and joins us. "We always took the day off for it," he says. "The Reagans arrival at Naco—they came several times. They taxidermied the horse that threw Ronald Reagan. Did you know that? Remember when they flew him to Fort Huachuca after his riding accident? They still got that stuffed horse at the ranch."

We laugh. Sip our Tecates. Talk about the way it was when you could leave your door open and people took care of your place while you were gone. "We had family across the line," Jaime says. "My great-grandmother was from Mexico." Then Jaime buys us all another round.

The Gay 90's Bar: Naco's oldest watering hole since 1931, still the town center. *True West* magazine called it the "Best Name for a Hetero Bar in a Redneck Border Town."

On our way back to Bisbee, we stop for a late lunch at Turquoise Valley Golf, which claims to be the oldest continuously operated golf course in Arizona. What better place to finish my obsession with the state than to make one final stop—my two hundredth point of interest!—at a border-town business that's been going strong since Arizona's birth. I imagine golfers in 1929 pausing in midstroke to watch some crazy Irishman delivering luggage from his crop duster.

While we wait for our order, I wander around the restaurant and look over the photos of Jackie Gleason and Arnold Palmer on the greens. A giant freshwater fish tank fills the wall behind the bar. Then I find T-shirts for sale depicting a rattlesnake wrapped around the fifteenth-hole pin: *The Rattler Bit Me.* Turquoise Valley is home to the infamous 747-yard "Rattler," the only par six in Arizona. *Forbes Traveler* calls it the fifth longest hole in the United States. *Today's Golfer* ranks it among the tenth longest on earth. But this isn't what I'm thinking. I'm thinking about another story.

I don't play golf, not since high school, anyway, but my neighbor and friend Charlie LaClair has played some of the greatest golf courses in the world, from Pebble Beach to our own Turquoise Valley. He knows the Rattler. He's eagled it, though generally he makes par. Recently, over beers on his front porch, he told me about one golf game with two friends. As they came up on the fifteenth hole, they noticed that a large diamondback rattlesnake had gotten there first. It wouldn't allow them to play through.

"I'll take care of it," said one of Charlie's buddies. He walked over and picked up the snake only to have it bite him on the hand. Surprised by the snake's rudeness, he shook it off and flung it around the neck of Charlie's other friend. Both were Air Evacked to a Tucson hospital for antivenin treatment. I'll wager that Charlie bought them both a T-shirt.

I often say that you haven't experienced Arizona until you've been welcomed by the giant desert hairy scorpion. But I know a few Arizonans who can claim they've really lived—one who, post-snakebite, still wears sandals in the desert.

New Year's Eve

BISBEE

TOTAL POINTS OF INTEREST: 200 | TOTAL MILES: 21,603

On the last day of my Big Year, Bisbee gets slammed with eight and a half inches of snow. By 4:00 p.m., the sun slips behind the Mule Mountains and the oak woodland is hung with heavy clusters of perfect white. Sunlight scatters through the last rags of cloud beyond our southern ridge, turning the sky the color of smoke and flame. The world looks apocalyptic.

I build a fire. Karen lights a Saint Jude candle and places it on the fireplace mantle. The saint of hopeless cases, our patron saint. We start a pot of beef stew, bake cookies and bread, read books—we don't have television. We don't want television. A perfect day to stay home for a change. As Karen has said: no more chasing anything but words on the page.

Today, I think about George Warren, the Bisbee miner whose aged face often squints at me from a photograph on the wall of the Bisbee Coffee Company. A poor and destitute drunk representing Arizona. I do love irony. I make jokes about him, but why shouldn't he appear on our state seal? He's as much Arizona as anyone. And why isn't he accompanied on our state seal by a rancher rather than a cow? A farmer rather than cotton and grapefruit trees? It's the people behind the economic drivers— the people, men and women, doing the economic driving—who built Arizona. It's people who will remain tied to the land when the economic powers diminish, as they always do.

One hundred years now—2012. By the next centennial, we'll still have ranchers and farmers and miners, but I believe we'll recognize them more as stewards of the land. It's already beginning. You hear more and more about sustainable practices. Locally raised, grass-fed beef. Free-range chicken. Cell grazing and carbon farming. Holistic management and organic gardening. Permaculture, rainwater harvesting, and key-line design. Even green mining (recycling?). I'm reminded of Arizona's new wine industry, how it treads lightly on the landscape, using solar power, less water, local compost, and even recycles its French oak barrels. Vintners, they say, not only care about wine but also about all that accompanies wine to the table.

Copper, cotton, citrus, cattle, and climate—this is what founded our state. Now we must look to a future less extractive and more sustainable. I'll keep the climate (and add casinos, which at 1.7 billion dollars in revenue have surpassed cotton, citrus, and cattle together). Here are my five Cs for the next century:

1. CLIMATE. Sunshine is the perfect renewable resource.
2. COMMUNITY. Whether people love peace and quiet or seek wild adventure, most view Arizona as a great place to raise a family.
3. CONSERVATION. As our number one export industry, tourism packs an annual economic punch of 17.7 billion dollars. Wildlife watchers alone contribute 1.4 billion dollars. Ecotourism will be the major economic driver of the future.
4. COSMOLOGY. From city Dark Sky initiatives to mountaintop telescopes, Arizona will always be the center of the astronomical universe. We are home to the planet Pluto, despite what some Californian claims. Pluto should be our official state planet.
5. CULTURE. The economics of traditional food, clothes, jewelry, pottery, music, and dance. Both natives and immigrants will continue to bring innovation and investments to the Arizona enterprise. Just think. We are the birthplace of a cultural food staple, Arizona's quintessential cuisine: the Sonoran hot dog!

Arizona is an extreme place: geographically, geologically, biologically, culturally, even politically. The state shares the landscape types of all fifty states and can produce both the highest and lowest temperatures in the country on the same day. It spans blistering Yuma dunes near sea level through grasslands and deciduous forests to the treeless alpine tundra of the San Francisco Peaks. We have the highest agricultural community in the United States at Alpine and oldest continuously inhabited village (since AD 1150) in the United States at Oraibi on the Hopi Reservation.

The *diversity* of extremes, however, is what's important. In other places, where the extremes are attenuated or homogenized or erased altogether—or where one extreme is emphasized—Arizona revels in it multiplicity. Arizona is the shape of collision. It's a shame that our vocal political extremes get so much attention.

We are a mixed tribe—Native American, European, Asian, African, Mexican—bound together by artificial lines on maps drawn across a desert and mountain landscape. But we aren't so different. A linguist once told me that if aliens ever visited our planet, they'd say we all speak the same language. Most of us won't meet in real life, but here we are kin. What we have accomplished for ourselves, in our own lives—none of this counts. Instead, we measure our worth by the distance we travel for our neighbors, those nearby, those across the line. We measure our worth by reciprocity.

My friend Alberto Ríos, whose parents are Mexican and British, who grew up in the border town of Nogales, and who is Arizona's first poet laureate, says our borders are where we are joined, not separated. Like a membrane. Like skin that links us to the larger world. You experience this connection when you touch this place, and when this place touches you.

Arizona exemplifies the scenic, the strange oddities of wildlife and people, but it's also the intangible qualities that make our state unlike any other place *and experience* on the planet. Arizona harbors a geographical and emotional landscape that shapes our imaginations. We live on Arizona time, in our own time zone, one that saves no daylight. Who needs to save daylight when we have desert sunsets that torch the skies and bring us to pause midstride in awe? And nights that toss us from mountain peaks without horizons to vault among stars?

Wallace Stegner writes that the West was built on the geography of hope. We live on that geography. The Grand Canyon State. A geography of hope. A landscape of awe.

So, how far did I go to experience Arizona this past year? This is a question of so much more than distance. With an answer so much greater than what these pages hold. It has been a year of firsts. I learned to enjoy engaging with people! I discovered that if you want to really know the place where you live, talk to the people who call it home. Looking back over the year, I see that it was my connection with people that led to my best wildlife encounters: my first-ever ridge-nosed rattlesnake and Arizona treefrog, the rock rattlesnake, wolves, condors, and Kaibab squirrels. With people, sometimes crowds of them, I recorded ninety-eight species of birds, witnessed a solar eclipse and the transit of Venus, sat in a Navajo hogan. I ate mutton! People often asked me about my favorite destination. This was like asking what my favorite rock 'n' roll song is. The last time someone asked this, Karen provided my answer: "You better say that it's coming home to your wife."

Despite the hard miles of road (all 21,603), the lingering soreness in my gas-pedal heel, the many long weekends away from home, I am not quite ready to be done. There is no buffer between my time on the road and the next household plumbing project that lies ahead. *Chasing Arizona 2*? I love the travel, the experience of seeing new places, meeting new people, as much as I love Karen and our garden and our cabin in the woods. But this is my experience, my story. There's so much more of Arizona out there . . . right out our front door. It's a big place, and it's beyond any one person to tell it. There's plenty of room for others to explore and then write their own adventure stories.

Karen will want me home for a change, if only to recover our finances. The latest Chevron bill has already arrived. I sip a prickly pear margarita and look out the window. The Kia Rio waits under a mountain of snow.

Acknowledgments

This book began as an idea floated to me by the amazing Patti Hartmann, my former editor, now retired, at the University of Arizona Press. Although I had doubts, she made me believe in the project. She, too, doesn't believe in near-life experiences. And many thanks to Kristen Buckles, who ran with the idea and encouraged me to ride my insanity to the four corners of the state. And to the rest of the wonderful folks at UA Press: Kathryn Conrad, Allyson Carter, Holly Schaffer, Scott De Herrera, Abby Mogollon, Leigh McDonald, Amanda Krause, among others. You have my sincere admiration for the vision you carry for important literature in the Southwest.

To my fellow writers at the Poetry Center Writing Workshop: Walker Thomas, Gillian Haines, Whitney Vale, Billy Sedlmayr, Ralph Hager, Tyler Atkinson, Barbara Peabody, Steve Gladish, Klara Dannar, Jerry Whitney, Sarah Spieth, Bill McKee, Marilyn Gustin, Laurie Calland, and Merrill Collett, who read my early chapters during the evolution of this book and offered many exquisite insights about how I should not, in fact, write a guidebook.

To Lyn Levy, editor extraordinaire and master of track changes, thank you for taking on the whole manuscript in its draft stages, hanging with it—and always asking for more pages.

To my outdoor companions—Larry and Jackie Begay, Liz Bernays, Jim Kristofic, Chuck LaRue, Jerry Marzinsky, Tom Leskiw, Walker Thomas, Phoenix Psyche Eagleshadow—my utmost gratitude for sharing your adventures with me (and commenting graciously on what I wrote about you).

To Tom and Mary Jane at Patagonia's Spirit Tree Inn: My gracious hosts during the writing of my final chapters, providing me with local wines and luscious chocolate-covered strawberries out of season.

To Paul Mirocha, for your excellent maps and most engaging conversations about them.

And to my fine neighbors here on the old mule road: Todd and Hayley, Ron and Dee and Ron, Silvia, George, Claudia, and Charlie. Thanks for encouraging me to press on with the travel and writing, for watching over the garden and RainCloud, our ancient blind cat, while I was gone, for the wood for my fire to write by and the wine-and-cheese gatherings (captive audiences) to read to, for the beer (IPAs, Todd!)—mostly the beer—and your stories about this excellent place where we live.

And finally, many thanks to the author Terry Pratchett, whose humor punctuated the long periods of driving equilibrium during those times my wife sat reading in the passenger seat. And to Karen, who read every word of mine as well and crossed out only a few. And finally to my daughters— Jessica, Kasondra, and Melissa—who continue to join me on many adventures even while knowing they will end up in some silly story. They would agree with J. R. R. Tolkien: "It's a dangerous business, Frodo, going out your door. You step onto the road, and if you don't keep your feet, there's no knowing where you might be swept off to." I would add that the only real danger in this business is encountering the extraordinary.

Portions of *Chasing Arizona* first appeared in Jeff Clark's anthology *Wolf*, the *Vermilion Flycatcher, Rain Shadow Review, Blue Lyra Review, Desert Leaf, Isle: Interdisciplinary Studies in Literature and Environment, Terrain.org, Edible Baja Arizona*, and *Orion*.

Selected Bibliography

Baars, Donald L. *Navajo Country: A Geology and Natural History of the Four Corners Region*. Albuquerque: University of New Mexico Press, 1995.

Bailowitz, Richard, and Hank Brodkin. *Finding Butterflies in Arizona: A Guide to the Best Sites*. Boulder, CO: Johnson Books, 2007.

Barnes, Mary Ellen. *The Road to Mount Lemmon: A Father, a Family, and the Making of Summerhaven*. Tucson: University of Arizona Press, 2009.

Brennan, Thomas C., and Andrew T. Holycross. *A Field Guide to Amphibians and Reptiles in Arizona*. Phoenix: Arizona Game and Fish Department, 2006.

Brock, Jim P. *Butterflies of the Southwest*. Natural History Series. Tucson, AZ: Rio Nuevo Publishers, 2008.

Brown, Mike. *How I Killed Pluto and Why It Had It Coming*. New York: Spiegel & Grau, 2010.

Brugge, David M. *Hubbell Trading Post: National Historic Site*. Tucson, AZ: Southwest Parks and Monuments Association, 1993.

Camateros, Amalia. *Spirit of the Stones: A Revival of Earth Wisdom*. Holualoa, HI: EarthSpeak Publications, 2005.

Chronic, Halka. *Roadside Geology of Arizona*. Missoula, MT: Mountain Press Publishing Company, 1983.

Cleere, Jan. *Levi's and Lace: Arizona Women Who Made History*. Tucson, AZ: Rio Nuevo Publishers, 2011.

Cokinos, Christopher. *The Fallen Sky: An Intimate History of Shooting Stars*. New York: Jeremy P. Tarcher/Penguin, 2009.

Di Peso, Charles. *The Amerind Foundation*. Dragoon, AZ: Amerind Foundation, 1967.

Escapule, Betty Foster. *The Five Fosters: Cowboys, Ranch Life and Growing Up*. Tombstone: B&C Enterprises, 2007.

Froeschauer-Nelson, Peggy. *Cultural Landscape Report: Hubbell Trading Post National Historic Site, Ganado, Arizona*. Santa Fe, NM: U.S. Deptartment of the Interior, National Park Service, 1998.

Gardner, Renee. *Southern Arizona's Most Haunted*. Atglen, PA: Schiffer

Publishing Ltd., 2010.

Haak, Wilbur A., and Lynn F. Haak. *Globe*. Images of America: Arizona. Charleston, SC: Arcadia Publishing, 2008.

Hagedorn, Hermann. *The Magnate: Biography of William Boyce Thompson*. Superior, AZ: Boyce Thompson Southwestern Arboretum, 1977.

Haynes, Vance C., Jr., and Bruce B. Huckell, eds. *Murray Springs: A Clovis Site with Multiple Activity Areas in the San Pedro Valley, Arizona*. Anthropological Papers. Tucson: University of Arizona Press, 2007.

Heidinger, Lisa Schnebly. *Arizona: 100 Years Grand*. Phoenix: Arizona Historical Advisory Commission, 2011.

Hensel, Suzanne. *Look to the Mountains*. Mount Lemmon, AZ: Mt. Lemmon Women's Club, 2006.

Jackson, Marie D. *Stone Landmarks: Flagstaff's Geology and Historic Building Stones*. Flagstaff: Piedra Azul Press, 1999.

Kollenborn, Tom, and James Swanson. *Superstition Mountain: A Ride Through Time*. San Francisco: Bookpeople, 1981.

Kristofic, Jim. *Navajos Wear Nikes: A Reservation Life*. Albuquerque: University of New Mexico Press, 2011.

Larson, Peggy P., and William Ascarza. *Arizona-Sonora Desert Museum*. Images of America Series. Charleston, SC: Arcadia Publishing, 2010.

Leopold, Aldo. *A Sand County Almanac, and Sketches Here and There*. New York: Oxford University Press, 1987.

Levy, David H. *Clyde Tombaugh: Discoverer of Planet Pluto*. Sky & Telescope Observer's Guides. Cambridge, MA: Sky Publishing Corporation, 2006.

Lowell, Percival Lawrence. *Mars: Is There Life on Mars?* 1895. London: Forgotten Books, 2008.

McGinty, Brian. *The Oatman Massacre: A Tale of Desert Captivity and Survival*. Norman: University of Oklahoma Press, 2005.

Melikian, Robert A. *Hotel San Carlos*. Images of America Series. Charleston, SC: Arcadia Publishing, 2009.

Murray, Vincent. *Gila Bend*. Images of America Series. Charleston, SC: Arcadia Publishing, 2012.

Nabhan, Gary Paul. *Arab/American: Landscape, Culture, and Cuisine in Two Great Deserts*. Tucson: University of Arizona Press, 2008.

Pry, Mark E., and Fred Andersen. *Arizona Journeys: How Transportation Shaped the Grand Canyon State*. Phoenix: Arizona Department of Transportation, 2012.

Ranney, Wayne. *Carving Grand Canyon: Evidence, Theories, and Mystery*. 2nd ed. Grand Canyon Village, AZ: Grand Canyon Association, 2012.

Ring, Bob, Al Ring, and Tallia Pfrimmer Cahoon. *Ruby, Arizona: Mining, Mayhem, and Murder*. Tucson: U.S. Press and Graphics, 2005.

Sevigny, Melissa L. *Mythical River: Encounters with Water in the American Southwest*. Iowa City: University of Iowa Press, forthcoming.

Sheridan, Thomas E. *Arizona: A History*. Rev. ed. Tucson: University of Arizona Press, 2012.

Sherman, James E., and Barbara H. *Ghost Towns of Arizona*. Norman: University of Oklahoma Press, 1969.

Thayer, Dave. *An Introduction to Grand Canyon Fossils*. Grand Canyon Village, AZ: Grand Canyon Association, 2009.

Trimble, Marshall. *Roadside History of Arizona*. Missoula, MT: Mountain Press Publishing Company, 1986.

Wildfang, Frederic B. *Prescott*. Images of America Series. Charleston, SC: Arcadia Publishing, 2006.

Wulf, Andrea. *Chasing Venus: The Race to Measure the Heavens*. New York: Alfred A. Knopf, 2012.

Index

About the Author

Ken Lamberton is the author of *Wilderness and Razor Wire: A Naturalist's Observations from Prison* (Mercury House, 2000), which won the 2002 John Burroughs Medal for outstanding nature writing. He has published five books and hundreds of articles and essays in places like the *Los Angeles Times*, *Orion*, *Arizona Highways*, the *Gettysburg Review*, and *The Best American Science and Nature Writing 2000*. In 2007, he won a Soros Justice Fellowship for his fourth book, *Time of Grace: Thoughts on Nature, Family, and the Politics of Crime and Punishment* (University of Arizona Press, 2007). His fifth book, *Dry River: Stories of Life, Death, and Redemption on the Santa Cruz* (University of Arizona Press, 2011) was a Southwest Book of the Year.

Lamberton holds degrees in biology and creative writing from the University of Arizona and lives with his wife in an 1890s stone cottage near Bisbee. Visit the author's website at www.kenlamberton.com.

Photo by Walker Thomas.